THE
GRAND WHIGGERY

By
MARJORIE (Howard) VILLIERS

LONDON
JOHN MURRAY, ALBEMARLE STREET, W.

First Edition   .   .   .   September 1939
Reprinted   .   .   .   November 1939
Reprinted   .   .   .   February 1946

TO MY HUSBAND

GEORGE VILLIERS

PRINTED IN GREAT BRITAIN BY
LOWE AND BRYDONE PRINTERS LIMITED, LONDON, N.W.10

LIST OF ILLUSTRATIONS

The Duchess of Devonshire and Viscountess Duncannon

PREFACE

TO write the chronicle of a set of people, bound together
by the diverse ties of blood, friendship, and common
enthusiasms is to lay oneself open to almost every criticism
that can be brought against an author. The " set " is not a
circumscribed entity, it is continually changing in dimensions
and in importance. Even the pivot can hardly be said to be
enduring, since at one moment a strong personality may pre-
dominate and later sink into insignificance in the face of a still
more robust leader. In addition, it is no easy matter to ascribe
a definite date to the birth or the death of a " set."

Yet in the history of England many sets have played their
part. Perhaps none has been more brilliant or more distinguished than that which formed itself round the personality
of Georgiana Duchess of Devonshire, in the late eighteenth
and early nineteenth century. Succeeding to a conventional
and circumscribed generation, whose greatest ambition had
been to leave things as they found them, these young people
stood for innovation and experiment. Endowed, in many
instances, with great vitality, warm hearts and fearless minds,
they championed ideas of personal and social freedom and of
a wide toleration that were startling. Much that they stood
for was not accomplished in their time : much is, even now,
unrealised. Yet they brought to birth, or rather to re-birth,
ideas which still fill the minds of their descendants to the fifth
and sixth generation. How far these ideas and ideals have
been, or will be, for good or evil is an open question. But
one thing is certain : we are still under their influence. It
must, therefore, be of interest to discover who were these people
who have kept the world arguing for more than a hundred and
fifty years ? What were their lives, their thoughts, their
actions ? What world did they live in, and what background
did they start from ?

Little things may exert a preponderating influence, and,

because of this fact, it is sometimes as important to know what was the price of coal and capons, as to know the number of men killed in a great battle. The critic may carp that proportion is lost ; and the author must submit that a chronicle of lives lacks many qualities essential to most works of art. Perhaps, indeed, the author would be wiser to claim no literary value for his chronicle ; yet life, even in the multiplicity of its details and the apparent disproportion of its values, evinces a subtle pattern. And so it may be hoped that this book, taken as a whole, will not be found entirely formless.

Not, at least, psychologically formless. There is a progression and an inevitable evolution of views and character. Reverse the relationships of the personalities and the evolution becomes at once apparent. Could Lady Granville have been the mother of the Duchess of Devonshire ? Could Lady Caroline Lamb have been the mother of Lady Bessborough ? Is it possible to conceive of Byron's personality existing in the eighteenth century ? Or of Fox and Sheridan living in a Victorian era ?

The Devonshire House set was no fortuitous congregation of people unrelated to the procession of generations. It was born of its age and gave birth to the next age. Nor can we minimise its importance.

When Fox declared that he hated war, when Sheridan proclaimed the right of America to self-determination, when Grey demanded universal franchise, when Pitt upheld religious toleration, these ideas came with the shock of novelty to their hearers. These were points of view which were new and suspect to the Englishmen of the eighteenth century—to-day they are commonplaces.

The matter of the chronicle is drawn from a number of memoirs, novels, pamphlets, and newspapers of the period, together with data from certain unpublished letters in the collection of the author's husband. It is to be hoped that it will send such readers who are not already familiar with them to the Memoirs of the period, in whose delightful pages the characters speak in the first person.

What personalities they were ! And of many it could be said (as it was said of the Duchess of Devonshire) that they appeared to be " over life-size." Perhaps this noble stature was due to the fact that they were the best examples of well united idealism and realism. Their forebears had been realists and materialists, who cared little for ideas or ideals; their children became so saturated with ideas that they lost all touch with reality and lived in a world of false values and of false theories. And now the descendants of these children are living in a world of crass materialism and realism.

But the circle at Devonshire House had the virtues of both schools of thought. With their heads full of theories and ideals they were no doctrinaires (that was to come later with Holland House); they knew that what they desired had to be worked out by men and women of flesh and blood, and not by columns of representative statistics. Their human relationships were governed by the same twin forces. They loved and hated violently, as no Victorian could have loved or hated; but they knew right from wrong; they had principles to judge life by; and, despite their passions and their *affaires*, they looked up to a higher standard of virtue than that to which they themselves attained. They set these standards before their children and they sacrificed much to keep up the recognition of the decencies of life, much more than post-Victorians, now leading the lives they led, would trouble to sacrifice The age was not an age of saints: individuals, it may be supposed, were no better and no worse morally than they are to-day. But where they broke the moral laws the generation of Devonshire House admitted that they had done so. They accepted the consequences, whether these consisted in the bailiffs or a nursery of illegitimate children.

They may have been weak, but they made no attempt to exculpate themselves, or to formulate a philosophy which should justify them. They did not tamper with the absolute values of right and wrong; and if they often gave evidence of weakness, they also often gave voice to the Christian virtue of humility. Essentially they were full-blooded men and women, and few can get to know them through their writings and remain unmoved by their charm. Indeed, most will surely leave them with a sense of respect and admiration.

ACKNOWLEDGMENTS

THE Author wishes to express her gratitude to all those who have so kindly given her permission to quote extracts from their works or from letters of which they hold the copyright.

To

Mabell Countess of Airlie for permission to quote from *In Whig Society* and *Lady Palmerston and her Times.*

To

The Marquess of Bristol for permission to quote from the letters of the Earl Bishop of Derry, contained in the *Life of the Earl Bishop of Derry*, by W. Childe Pemberton.

To

Sir George Granville Leveson-Gower for permission to quote from *The Letters of Harriet Countess Granville*, edited by the Hon. F. Leveson-Gower.

To

General Sir John Ponsonby for permission to quote from *The Ponsonby Family.*

To

The Hon. Mrs. Grosvenor for permission to quote from *The Letters of the First Lady Wharncliffe.*

To

The Earl of Ilchester for permission to quote from *The Journal of Lady Holland*, *The Spanish Journal of Lady Holland*, and *The Letters of Lady Sarah Lennox.*

To

The Hon. Mrs. Wyndham for permission to quote from *The Letter Bag of Lady Sarah Spencer.*

To

Mrs. Seth Smith for permission to quote from *George IV and Mrs. Fitzherbert*, by Wilkins.

ACKNOWLEDGMENTS

To

Miss Elizabeth Jenkins for permission to quote from *The Life of Lady Caroline Lamb*.

To

Miss Yvonne ffrench for permission to quote from *News from the Past*.

To

Mr. Christopher Hobhouse for permission to quote from *Life of C. J. Fox*.

To

Mr. Beresford for permission to quote from *Life in Regency and Early Victorian Times*.

Her thanks are equally due to
Messrs. Macmillan for permission to quote from
The Memoirs of Lady Charlotte Bury,
A Lady of the Last Century, by Doran,
Memoirs of the Earl of Malmesbury,
The Jerningham Papers,
The Life of Sheridan, by Rae,
The Book of the Boudoir, by Lady Morgan,
Wraxall's *Memoirs*,
Memoirs of Lady Hester Stanhope, by Dr. Meryon.

To

Messrs. Gollancz for permission to quote from
News from the Past, by Yvonne ffrench
Lady Caroline Lamb by E. Jenkins.

To

Messrs. Blackie for permission to quote from
The Two Duchesses, by Vere Foster.

To

Messrs. Longman for permission to quote from
The Greville Diaries,
The Journal and Correspondence of Miss Berry Leven,
Letters of Harriet Countess Granville,
The Journal of Elizabeth Vassall, Lady Holland,
The Spanish Journal of Elizabeth Vassall, Lady Holland.
Raikes' *Journal*,
George IV and Mrs. Fitzherbert, by Wilkins.

To

Messrs. Hodder & Stoughton for permission to quote from
Lady Palmerston and her Times
In Whig Society.

To

Messrs. Batsford for permission to quote from
Life in Regency and Early Victorian Times.

To

Messrs. Hutchinson for permission to quote from
The Diary of Dr. Robert Lee,
Courts and Cabinets, by Buckingham.

To

Messrs. Hurst & Blackett for permission to quote from
The Life of the Earl Bishop of Derry, by W. Childe
Pemberton.

To

Messrs. Constable for permission to quote from
The Life of C. J. Fox, by Hobhouse.

To

Messrs. Heinemann for permission to quote from
The Letters of the First Lady Wharncliffe.

To

Messrs. Murray for permission to quote from
Lord Byron's Correspondence,
Lord Byron's Letters and Journals,
Lord Broughton, *Recollections of a Long Life,*
De Ros, Georgiana Lady, *Memoirs,*
Holland, Lord, *Further Memoirs of the Whig Party,*
Shelley, Frances Lady, *Diary.*

Finally, no one can write of the Great Whig Ladies without
being deeply indebted for their facts to the Earl of Bess-
borough, the copyright holder of the letters of Harriet
Countess of Bessborough, which were so ably edited by
Castalia Countess Granville in her book *The Private
Correspondence of Lord Granville Leveson-Gower.*

"GOOD *night*, my friend."—" Good *morning*, sir." [1]   The
Duke passed quickly across Berkeley Square, and the
cobbler began his day's work, reflecting that, if gossip were
correct, there would soon be a Duchess of Devonshire, the first
in the twenty years since His Grace's mother had died.

It was three o'clock of a " Lunnon " morning of the year
1774, when gentlemen still wore swords and carried their hats
under their arms, when ladies wore powder and a little hoop,[2]
and fashionable heads might burn for an hour before reaching
the scalp ; when footpads attacked the macaronis who braved
the dangers of Hay Hill, and when St. James's Street was
crowded with the carriages of the fine folk walking in the Mall.
Mid-eighteenth century, when Archibald Hamilton advertised for a hermit as an ornament to his pleasure grounds,[3] and
when the last heads at Temple Bar had but recently rolled away.
A curiously vivid, self-conscious pause between two ages :
an epoch of anomalies, where in Florence the Chevalier, now
an enfeebled, paralytic figure, rather absurd in his velvet
greatcoat, his garter and his cocked hat, still paused at the
sight of a British uniform, recalling that England, " dependent
on the sun and the rain, the sail and the seasons," [4] whose
throne had been his father's birthright and his own, but a
birthright which was now fast passing into history, and whose
successor depended " not on sun and soil, but on engineers and
machinery ; not on tides and seasons, but on canals and Acts
of Parliament."

The generation that was coming to maturity in this year had
its roots in a robust past, when ladies rode on horseback and
not in carriages : when the frank words " breeding," " bowels,"

[1] *Table Talk of Samuel Rogers.*   [2] *A Lady of the Last Century.*
[3] *Table Talk of Samuel Rogers.*
[4] *England under the Hanoverians.*   Robertson.

I

and " kept mistress" expressed with simplicity the facts later inferred in the euphemisms, " confinement," " stomach," and " interesting connexion " ; [1] when the noun " boar " was a delightful novelty and retained its original spelling, and when the Hanoverian dynasty was little more than a convenience for the greater continuity of Government by a Whig oligarchy.

Any child out of the schoolroom might remember George II, " that neat little old man, honest, upright, and well-meaning," who passed " his time between his kingdom and his electorate : a troublesome half year in England, the other tranquilly and much more to his mind in Hanover."

And they might, without exaggeration, hope to live on into the forties of the next century. What changes would they see if this came to pass ? What changes indeed ? 1755–1845 ! Can any ninety years show changes so overwhelming ? It is no easy thing to have lived in a world that contained Horace Walpole at one end and Mr. Gladstone at the other.

The rhythm of life works implacably through, and not by individuals. The youth of 1774 could not see their part in the procession of development ; but because this development was going on at a heightened and remorseless speed, carrying them in its advance, they were conscious of isolation, of an essential difference between themselves and their parents, and later they were to be conscious of a still more intrinsic difference between themselves and their children. The change was continuous. Never were they able to stand aside from it and take its measure. Their parents had accepted the first Lord Holland, their children accepted Lord Shaftesbury. What wonder if they were bewildered !

In 1774 one of those personalities who was to be, in some sense, the sun of the system had, as yet, no presentiment of her destiny ; she was hunting butterflies in the fields of Wimbledon. The housekeeper called to her to come back to the villa. She objected. The old retainer broke a lath over her head : Lady Georgiana Spencer submitted to *force majeure*. She went in to see her father, Lord Spencer,[2] and he informed her that, as she was now seventeen, it was high time she married, and

---

[1] Appendix to *The Life and Letters of Lady Sarah Lennox.*

[2] Lord Spencer's father was the reprobate Jack Spencer, the adored and distracting grandson of Sarah Jennings.

that indeed he had arranged for her to marry her cousin, the Duke of Devonshire. Georgiana acquiesced. It seemed a natural plan, and conveyed little to her. Such, at least, is the legend, and the cobbler's gossip had been well informed.

Actually Lady Spencer's devoted affection for her children, her high principles, and her own love match, are guarantees that the marriage was not arranged so casually. She had made her husband an admirable wife, caring little for society, yet loved and respected by all the fashionable world. She had borne him three children, Georgiana, who was seventeen; a son, George John, who was sixteen; and a second daughter, Henrietta Frances, usually called Harriet, who was still in the schoolroom. Her husband had, between 1761 and 1765, risen from a commoner to a Barony, from a Barony to a Viscountcy, from a Viscountcy to an Earldom.

Life had been kind to the Spencers, perhaps because they cared for what was best in life. The children had been brought up very simply, but they had been accustomed to meet everyone who was worth knowing in every sphere. Garrick paid his annual visit to Althorp and entertained the company by reading out scenes from Shakespeare. The improbable Bishop of Derry came to pay his respects to the Countess and to discuss the merits of stucco and white brick, of Raphaels and Giottos; and at Mrs. Montagu's parties Georgiana had sat next to Doctor Johnson and the company had observed marked symptoms of softening on the angry old mask.[1] But if Georgiana was erudite, she was also entirely unsophisticated and very beautiful. Tall, with reddish-brown hair, dark blue eyes, a brilliant complexion, and a magnificent figure, she seemed to have been especially designed by Providence to fill a representative rôle. Her abounding vitality, her quick response to life, her complete spontaneity, these would need to be given form by the outlines of self-restraint and dignity, and then she would make a perfect duchess, a fit châtelaine for Devonshire House and Chatsworth.

As to their future son-in-law, the Spencers were wholly satisfied. William was twenty-four, he was grave and rather phlegmatic, he took his position as head of one of the leading Whig Houses seriously, but he was devoid of all ambition, and

[1] Wraxall's *Memoirs*.

3

also of any taint of that rapacity which was a characteristic of certain other ducal houses. Lady Spencer liked him for being a little old fashioned, very simple, not to say awkward, in his person, very formal and courteous in his manners. Lord Spencer recognised him for an honest man, with immense possessions ; and Georgiana herself had exuberant affections enough to spare for her quiet, undemonstrative cousin.

As for the Duke, he had lost his mother when he was four, his father when he was fourteen. Shouldering a heavy burden of responsibility at an early age, he had taught himself to be reserved, cautious, isolated. He had made for himself a meticulous code of life—though still young. His habits were already set ; he had his regular hours of work and his regular hours for his one pleasure—gambling. He had won much respect if little affection. He had few intimate friends but hundreds of acquaintances ; indeed, he was essentially a " club " man.

In the programme which he had made out for himself his marriage was a first principle. He chose circumspectly amongst the Whig cousinhood. What he desired from his wife was that she should be a great hostess and a prolific mother. He wanted to have children who would bear his name, unlike one he had already had by a certain pretty milliner and towards whom he felt a responsibility without the concomitant of pride.

The general opinion was that Georgiana would humanise her staid husband, and that he in his turn would teach her to restrain her natural impulsiveness. The two widely divergent characters, reacting upon each other to their mutual benefit, might be expected to present a happily balanced marriage to the world. Unfortunately for these pleasant prognostications Georgiana and William were not destined to mould each other, but to grow further and further apart, each developing their idiosyncrasies to the detriment of their union.

However, when on June 6th, 1774, the marriage was solemnised, no one could look into the future. Everyone was happy at the event—everyone excepting Harriet, who suffered acutely at the separation from her adored elder sister.

For a month the miracle happened and William was in love, and Georgiana was supremely happy. At the end of four weeks the Duke returned to his usual way of life and began to criticise his wife for having shown him some demonstration of affection

4

in front of Lady Spencer. From one day to another Georgiana found herself in splendid isolation. Life, at the age of seventeen, to make her own, life with nothing more than the distant friendship and careful advice of her husband to guide her.

The Spencers as a family had been very united, and very intimate with each other. She was unused to privacy and abhorred it. Harriet, with deeper emotions and a far greater capacity for self-analysis and self-control, might have realised the situation in all its implications and taken hold of it to some purpose; but Georgiana was quite incapable of such an action. She did not realise what had happened. She only knew that she was lonely and that the whole of London society was filled with men and women who were only too ready to become her intimates. With complete liberty and boundless means she plunged delightedly into the gay world. William accompanied her when convention demanded it, on all other occasions he went to his club. He made no demands on her, and provided she behaved with discretion he did not much care to hear of her adventures.

The Duchess had no need to take a look at London society before she plunged into it. She had known it from childhood, for her father's duties had required protracted residence in the capital, which were always periods of distress to her country-loving mother. But to follow her through her life, which was the centre of so many other lives, it is essential that the London of 1774 should be as vivid to us as it was to her.

The life-blood of the society in which she moved flowed from the heart of politics. The political situation in the early years of George III's reign is hard for us to grasp at a period when so much that was essential to it has passed away. The present had its roots fifty years into the past or, as some would have it, more than eighty years back. It derived from the fact that the House of Hanover had been called to govern England by a clique of powerful families headed by the Cavendishes and the Russells, who stood out against a return to the Stuart's autocratic principles and adherence to the Roman Catholic religion. They were supported by the great families enriched by the House of Orange : the Bentincks and the Keppels.

The Hanoverians had come over with some trepidation. They found that though their honours sat heavily upon them, they were apt to prove rather insubstantial. They were unused to the scale of English society and English ideas. These haughty noblemen who had nominated them were apt also to patronise them. The very reason for their coming prohibited them from calling upon anything of " divine right " to support them against their ministers. They had no appeal beyond these great Whig families and their partisans, for the remaining great families were Tories, and liable to swear allegiance to the Stuarts at any moment.

Unable even to communicate with their subjects in English, they were obliged to submit to their tyranny, and to escape occasionally to the freedom of petty kingship in Hanover. That the Whigs managed to impose this form of oligarchy, with a foreign puppet at its head, is a witness to their power ; and also to their innovation, " the standing army."

The Tory nobility had always had its strength in the yeomanry, which was a feudal survival dependent on personal ties, and no instrument of the body politic ; but against a standing army it could not be used as a threat. It will thus be seen that up till the times we are writing about, the divergence between Whig and Tory bears no resemblance whatsoever to the Liberal and Conservative as we know them.

The Whigs stood fundamentally *not* for civic liberty or reform, but for a strong government by oligarchy, with a monarchy that existed in name, and for the purpose of being the head of the English Church. The Established Church was their great weapon. The Tories stood for the old liberties of the English gentry, for greater religious freedom, for less centralisation of government. They believed rather in kings than in cabinets, and they were, in general, realists and had no patience with theories. As Mr. Hobhouse tells us so vividly in his life of Fox, this situation was modified by two facts, one of which was the deplorable character of the Young Chevalier ; and the other, the longing of George III to escape from his Whig masters.

George III was more English than German in his outlook, and he aspired to being more than a puppet, so he looked to the party who still held kings in respect and who were for the moment deprived of a deserving recipient for their loyalty. He asked the Tories to transfer their adherence to his person, and with such as did so he formed a Court party, the backbone of which was Scottish.

The Whigs, thus deprived of their own creature, began to quarrel amongst themselves. Some stood for the *status quo* and the maintaining of their vast profits at all cost—these were the Bedfords and the Grenvilles. Another powerful party, under Lord Rockingham and comprising the Dukes of Portland and Richmond, stood for the constitution of 1688 and all that was traditional in Whiggism ; whilst a third party, under the veteran Chatham and his able disciple Lord Shelburne, recognising that Whiggery needed new blood if it were to survive, proclaimed the first statements of reform. If the Tories had captured the king and intended to invest him with power, these acute Whigs would capture the people, and by legislation they would make *them* into a power.

Such were the political antecedents of the situation of 1774. It is necessary next to consider the topical questions and the actors involved in the drama. Only one subject filled the minds of all Englishmen—this was the American question. In the previous year certain indirect taxes had been levied in America by the authority of the British Government. The whole of the money raised by these taxes was to be spent in America itself, but the Colonists resented the principle of the imposition of the taxation without representation. They had given vent to their indignation by every form of remonstrance. Finally they had boarded a ship laden with tea on which the execrated duty was to be levied, and thrown the cargo into Boston Harbour. At this distance of time it seems difficult to understand why the principle of taxation (since the money was to be used for the benefit not of the Mother Country but of the colony) should have been considered so abhorrent. But abhorrent it was to all Americans, and indeed to most Englishmen. Unfortunately, to the king the question appeared in quite another light. If the American Colonists resisted the edicts of the King of England, they were disloyal subjects who must be brought back to obedience by whichever measures of reason or force became necessary.

George III saw in the resistance to the duties the thin edge of a wedge which should one day produce cleavage if it were not withdrawn. In this it may be assumed that he saw far

7

beyond the vision of the American rebels. They hated the imposition of taxes, but they had no question as to their English parentage and their English loyalties. It was a matter for delicate negotiation, but the King did not desire to negotiate. What he wanted was a trial of strength, and by dint of his extraordinary pertinacity he was eventually to have his way.

This then was the fevered question of the hour, the repeal of the duties, or war with America. Here were the human factors who handled the situation; and it was amongst them that Georgiana was to find her friends.

There was, in the first place, the Prime Minister, Lord North, a King's man, bearing indeed so strong a resemblance to George III that his paternity was sometimes called into question. He was honest and good-natured: the King loved him, and depended on him; and he had good reason to cling to him, for the first article of Lord North's code of honour was obedience to his master. Frequently their views diverged, and North would state his objections frankly and offer to resign; but always when the King urged him to remain in office and serve him, the unhappy North consented to become the instrument of legislation of which he frankly disapproved. His opponents bore him no grudge, they knew that he had no love of office, but that he was at all times a slave to his loyalty to the King.

In opposition to North was Lord Rockingham, a shadowy figure supported by the Duke of Richmond, who had never forgiven George III for flirting with his lovely sister, Lady Sarah Lennox, and then marrying a frowsy German princess. And in this party too was Burke, the noblest mind then engaged in the political world; Burke in whom love of tradition and love of liberty were blent in one, in whose well-balanced brain the idealist and the realist fused. Yet despite the amazing gift of oratory and self-expression which he possessed, despite a candid sincerity and a complete disinterestedness, this great man failed to achieve the high position for which he seemed destined. Was it due to his middle-class origin? Was it due to the very violence of his passion for great causes, a violence which led him sometimes to be rough with those who opposed him? What was it that caused him to be cold-shouldered even by those of his own party?

If we read his magnificent speeches it is hard to recall the

fact that at the time he made them he was known as the
" dinner-gong," because his rising to speak was often a signal
for the clearing of the House. But this must be borne in
mind if we are to understand how small a part he played in
the social world and how little impression he probably made
on Georgiana when she first began to enter society as a young
married woman.

The Duke of Bedford had died three years before, leaving
only a grandchild of six to succeed to the title, and no one to
lead his section of the Party. The only other strong Whig
element was that led by Chatham. His was a name to con-
jure with, as the King had found to his cost when he had,
early in his reign, dismissed him and replaced him by the
hated Lord Bute, thereby effectively losing all his popularity
and very nearly the Crown itself. Lord Chatham had steered
the country through the Seven Years War, and he was the idol
of the nation. But he was old now and gouty, and had frequently to absent himself from Westminster, leaving his party
to the leadership of that mysterious man, Lord Shelburne.
With the passing of more than a century, Lord Shelburne
appears to us a brilliant and hard-working politician of markedly
disinterested character and cultivated tastes. But to his contemporaries, for some cause, perhaps of manner or speech (the
Prince of Wales describes him advancing to receive his Garter
" bowing on every side, smiling and fawning like a courtier "),[1]
he was looked upon as the very embodiment of all that was
shady and untrustworthy in the field of politics. He was, in
fact, detested, both as a private and as a public character. This
personal animosity went far to wreck Whig hopes in depriving
them of one of their ablest supporters.

In 1774, however, the Whigs had gained a convert, who
compensated them for all Lord Shelburne's unpopularity, in
the person of Charles James Fox. Fox was the son of the
first Lord Holland, a Tory minister whose hatred of Lord
Shelburne was one of his chief characteristics. This dislike
might have derived from a jealousy as to which was the ablest
or the most hated man in England. At least, in the case of
Lord Holland, the public knew what they disliked in him—it
was his rapacity. The fabulous fortune which the Paymaster

[1] Wraxall's *Memoirs*.

9

of the Army frankly admitted that he had made during the Seven Years War disgusted the nation. When he bought a house opposite the Goodwin Sands, a popular ballad celebrated the event :

Old and abandoned by each venal friend,
Here Holland framed the pious resolution
To smuggle a few years, and strive to mend
A broken character and constitution.

On this congenial spot he fixed his choice ;
Earl Goodwin trembled for his neighbouring sand.
Here seagulls scream and cormorants rejoice,
And mariners, tho' shipwrecked, fear to land. [1]

But Lord Holland was more than a good business man ; he was a devoted husband and father. His marriage had been romantic, for he had run away with a daughter of the Duke of Richmond, and perhaps it had been the scorn which the Lennoxes poured on the match which spurred him on to becoming the richest man in England. His theories as to the upbringing of children were precursors of Rousseau's. Neither Stephen nor Charles Fox had ever been refused anything. Lord Holland's theory was that a boy should be advised but not commanded. If he persisted in disregarding advice he would then have to pay for his knowledge by experience.

What use Stephen made of his liberty we do not know, but it is evident that Charles exerted his will to the full. We hear of him deciding which school to attend, and how long he should remain there. We hear of him throwing an official despatch into the fire and stamping on a gold watch. [2] " Let nothing be done to break his spirit," commented Lord Holland ; " the world will effect that business soon enough."

We hear how his father, having promised that he should see a wall being dynamited at Holland House, and having forgotten the promise and put the work through whilst Charles was at school, felt obliged to have the wall built up again so that Charles might have the pleasure of seeing it destroyed.

Of Lady Holland we know little, except a certain plaintively envious remark to the effect that Lord Chatham's little boy

[1] Wraxall's *Memoirs*.　　　[2] *Table Talk of Samuel Rogers.*

Charles James Fox

was so much better brought up than her sons were ; and that she was much afraid that William Pitt would in years to come prove a thorn in Charles's side. A prophetic utterance if ever there were one. Strangely enough, this lack of discipline did not conduce to idleness in Charles Fox. He left a record for work and application at Eton—even though his studies had been interrupted by his father, who had taken him at the age of fourteen to Spa for six months to initiate him into the pleasures of gambling. At Oxford he worked so hard that he actually received a letter from his tutor, imploring him to moderate his passion for study as it was likely to be injurious to his health.

Armed with this certificate of merit the boy had gone on the grand tour, during which period he seems to have given rein to all his varied propensities. He gambled with a recklessness which caused even the most hardened to exclaim. He drank with a capacity to be envied by four-bottle men ; he travelled from Paris to Lyons to buy a waistcoat, talking of nothing but waistcoats all the while. He was acquiring knowledge : meeting the best brains in every place which he visited : reading everything he could lay his hands on, from the latest lampoon to the most enduring classic.

During his absence his father had had him elected for Parliament. He was not of age, but this disqualification was winked at. It was in 1768, six years before Georgiana's marriage, that Fox had returned to London. A curious figure he must have presented, for he was very ugly; fat and swarthy, with bushy black eyebrows, and a blue chin ' like a crescent moon,' and ' withal, very foppish,' for he had adopted the French custom of wearing red heels, a large buttonhole, and extravagantly long lace cuffs. The man and the dress were oddly at variance ; but Charles was not a Stuart, on his mother's side, for nothing. He had all the charm and all the faults of that unhappy family, and he had in the highest degree their capacity for attaching people to himself.

Wrong-headed, unreliable, extravagant, yet such was his charm and his persuasiveness that to the end of his life and through all his changes of view his friends stuck to him. Not only they stuck to him, but they believed in him as one of the best and most single-hearted men of the age. During the six years which had intervened since his return from the continent, he had held a minor post in the Government under North, but had proved so insufferable that he had been summarily dismissed at the King's personal request. His own reaction to this astonishing event was characteristic : he was convinced that it was merely a practical joke, and it was some time before he could be persuaded of the disconcerting truth. Out of office, he plunged more wildly than before into orgies of dissipation. It was said that he and Fitzpatrick played cards from ten o'clock at night till near six o'clock the next afternoon, a waiter standing by to tell them whose deal it was, since they were too sleepy to know. His father had paid up £140,000 for him without a word of comment. Now, however, his father was dead, and his elder brother Stephen was dead. But in dying Stephen had left a son, born, as Charles remarked, " for the destruction of the Jews," since the existence of the infant Lord Holland cut Charles off from the vast wealth, his inheritance to which had seemed certain to his Jewish money-lenders.

Brought up to be a Tory, Charles was by temperament a Whig, and now that he had been cast aside by the King's party he began to drift into the circle of influence of Lord Rockingham and Burke. It is easy to see why, amongst the various political figures, this " sublime profligate " was to be the one to whom Georgiana was to be attracted. He was just twenty-five, his life was already legendary, he had a vitality and an appetite for life that matched her own, and to his charm she succumbed immediately. Their friendship was to have the greatest influence in her life because it set the course of her mental development ; because she admired Charles Fox, she became in many ways like him.

She developed the same political enthusiasm, the same liberal views, the same passion for gambling, the same appreciation of literature, the same insatiable curiosity, the same generous, open-hearted friendships, the same contempt for conventions; and, above all, his friends became her friends ; as they came into her life in an unending series, Fitzpatrick, Sheridan, the Prince of Wales, Grey, we seem to see each one introduced by the prodigious and saturnine Fox.

She was very young when she had first to make her life in London. Had she fallen under another strong influence she

might never have been the joyous, robust, over life-sized
personality which has become a legend. And if we thus owe
the famous Duchess to Fox, it is a strong claim to gratitude.
There is no doubt that Georgiana and the Devonshire House
set, which was her creation, were to effect a complete alteration
in certain aspects of London life. It is, therefore, essential to
realise what were the customs and the usages in 1774.

Parliament met early, and the House usually rose before four
o'clock, which was the universal dinner-hour. But the young
Duchess was not inclined to early rising. Indeed, four o'clock
was the exact time at which she preferred to rise, and since
three o'clock in the morning became her customary hour for
retiring to rest, it cannot be considered unreasonable.

As the years go by we can observe a gradual alteration in this
respect. The theatre and the opera began later and later, the
dinner-hour was put forward, and eventually Parliament only
met at 4 p.m. Had all England submitted to the Duchess's
habits ? In 1774 assemblies were great affairs : the ladies who
gave them were few in number : the passion for entertaining was
not yet manifest. People were unaccustomed to living in herds.
But Georgiana was lonely, she needed to surround herself with
friends. Night after night she gave parties at Devonshire
House. Week-end after week-end she had thirty or forty people
to her villa at Chiswick. When she died, entertaining had
become the fashion.

In this year of her marriage, the Court was still a feature in
London social life. The King might be pig-headed ; the
Queen might be stuffy ; the royal children might be bullied
and repressed, yet the Court was still the centre of society.
Drawing-rooms were frequent, often weekly affairs.

Those who bore great titles or held high offices were accustomed to attend ; and no one else attended. They were small
affairs, at once dignified and intimate. The King would tell
his peers of his domestic war, how his cooks refused to wear
wigs, how wicked it was that any servant having once registered
at a foreign embassy should be for ever outside the law, how
he was trying to forbid the footmen to crowd the upper gallery
of the theatre, shouting and booing whilst the play was in
progress. Or his voice would rise querulously as he argued
on the subject of " vails," emphasising how astonished

foreigners were that no Englishman could dine with his father or brother without paying for his dinner. He would quote the Duke of Norfolk and Mr. Spencer with approval, telling how they had raised their servants' wages and abolished the custom. Or he would laugh at Lord Taafe who would accompany his guests to the door, and whilst they fumbled, remark, " If you *do* give, give it to me, for it is I that did buy the dinner."

Thus the afternoon would pass pleasantly, with no mention of the American colony or of taxes and duties, until the time came for the gentlemen, in their velvet and laces, with their hair *à la Grecque*, or three or four curls high, and the ladies in their French dress, with their heads bigger than their bodies, to call for their sedan-chairs and return home to play cards.

The span of Georgiana's existence saw all this altered. She and Fox, and later the Prince of Wales, formed a society which not only did not take its lead from the Court, but was in direct opposition to it, and George III's illness contributing to the same effect, the next two decades saw society entirely divorced from Buckingham House. Country life was obscure, and for those of the Duchess's set, infrequent. When they tired of London they went to Bath—where, as Horace Walpole said, " they went there well and came back cured," having immersed themselves in the famous Cross Bath, surrounded by floating japanned bowls containing essences and perfumes from whence they were carried in chairs lined with blankets to their rooms, and afterwards took a stroll to the booksellers' shops, which were a kind of club, or else forgathered in one of the numerous coffee-houses.

Amongst the circle of great ladies who were living this life at the time of Georgiana's marriage, Lady Melbourne was the one destined to have the greatest influence upon the Duchess. In 1774 she had been married for five years to Peniston Lamb, Viscount Melbourne. Herself the daughter of Sir Ralph Milbanke, the marriage had brought her wealth rather than position. Her father-in-law had been agent to Lord Salisbury and to Lord Egremont, and it was rumoured that the antecedents of the Lamb fortune were not very creditable. However that may have been, it is apparent that the Wyndhams bore them no grudge, for Lady Melbourne's devoted admirer was no other than the young Lord Egremont.

Society looked askance at this friendship, but perhaps gossip was wrong. Elizabeth Melbourne was a handsome, redoubtable woman, with a man's brain and capacities. Her large blue eyes and brown unpowdered hair brought her many admirers, and her quick, incisive wit kept them at her feet. She was worldly, ambitious and unscrupulous.

Realising that her marriage had made her entrée into Whig society a little difficult, she set to work to conquer London by strategy. In the first place she determined to create a background worthy of her achievements. Melbourne House, Piccadilly (now the site of the Albany), had belonged to Lady Holland. It was adapted by Payne, the decorations were carried out by Wheatley and Mrs. Damer,[1] the ceilings were painted by Mortimer and Cipriani, panel screens were worked by Elizabeth herself, the gardens were laid out by Lord Egremont.

In this work half her energies were absorbed when Georgiana first met her. She had already one son, Peniston, to whom her husband was devotedly attached. Like so many of the husbands of the famous women of that period, Lord Melbourne appears to us as a ghost. We catch a glimpse of him escaping from his wife's brilliant parties to the nursery, where an old Jersey nurse watched over Peniston, and then he is dismissed with some slighting remark.

Tradition has it that he was a quiet, unostentatious man, a martyr to his wife's ambition. Lady Melbourne was no good influence for Georgiana, but it is a very easy matter to see how naturally their friendship evolved. The young Duchess had a brain and she used it. The vapourings of her newly married contemporaries bored her; in the older woman she met with a robust, active intelligence. Then again Georgiana had a real appreciation of art, and Lady Melbourne, if she had not this gift, had something that simulated it, for she knew what was what, and had a very precise instinct as to what was going

---

[1] Mrs. Damer, daughter of General The Rt. Hon. Henry Seymour Conway, was a great friend of Horace Walpole. She married John Damer, son of Lord Dorchester; left a widow she took up sculpture and sculpted the heads of Thames and Isis on Henley Bridge. She was a great friend of Lady Melbourne as also of Angelica Kaufmann and Maria Cosway. Walpole left Strawberry Hill to her.

to be what. And in addition, to the young woman who was finding life and marriage so different from what she had expected and so difficult, the spectacle of Elizabeth Melbourne's expert handling of an even more difficult situation was in itself a matter for admiration.

But above and beyond all this, there was the political tie, and the strong link of Charles Fox's Friendship. That Georgiana to the day of her death liked and admired Lady Melbourne there cannot be doubt. Looking back to the friendship with the perspective of a hundred and sixty years, it may seem to us curious that the Duchess never realised that nearly all the qualities she liked in her friend were sham. The artistic enthusiasm, the political enthusiasm, the apparently generous friendships, were they not all created and sustained to serve one end —the social advancement of the Lamb family ? This may seem evident to us ; it seemed evident to Georgiana's younger sister as soon as she grew up and came out in the world ; but to Georgiana it would have appeared the greatest heresy.

If then we have analysed the motives of friendship from the Duchess's point of view, from the point of view of Lady Melbourne the case was one of extreme simplicity. She was cold-shouldered by the Whig hostesses, she felt an acute resentment, and seeing Georgiana, potentially the greatest power in society, as yet unattached to any clique, she determined to constitute herself her cicerone.

Georgiana made many friends, but only with Lady Melbourne was she intimate. Nor did she in her new surroundings abandon her mother's old friends. There was Susannah of Tory principles, the third wife of old Lord Stafford, whose little boy Granville had been born the year before ; there was poor Lady Hervey of the same persuasion, with her pretty daughters and that impossible prelate, her husband ; there was Mrs. Montagu herself and many another dim figure silhouetted against the candlelight of Devonshire House in this Georgiana's first season. Quiet, old-fashioned figures which were soon to be jostled into shadowy corners by the gay exuberant troupe led by Charles Fox and Elizabeth Melbourne.

1775

THUS Georgiana began her second year of married life with two intimate friends (Charles Fox and Elizabeth Melbourne), but before the year was out she was to add a third person to the number of her intimates.

The manner of their meeting was romantic : the whole story of their friendship was romantic. One day Georgiana was invited to the house of a certain Mr. Coote, where Sir Joshua Reynolds was at work upon a portrait. On her arrival she found that she was not the only guest. Watching Sir Joshua with great attention were a young couple of " interesting appearance," whom Mr. Coote introduced as Mr. and Mrs. Sheridan. The young man was handsome, in a boisterous, rather florid manner, with blue eyes and chestnut hair. But the young woman's beauty was of an extraordinarily spiritual character and of a rare degree of perfection. The name Sheridan recalled a fantastic tale to the Duchess's mind.

During the previous year the papers had been full of the exploits of a certain Richard Brinsley Sheridan, the son of a dour actor-manager, and the grandson of a feckless Irish Professor, who had been a friend of Dr. Swift.

This youth had fallen in love with a certain Miss Linley, a young singer. She belonged to a well-known family of artists who lived in Bath. The course of true love had certainly not run along smooth channels. Sheridan *père* had disapproved of the idea of marriage of his penniless younger son, whilst Linley *père* had been horrified at a plan which would remove his daughter from the stage and put an end to the large income which her voice provided. Finally, a rich, elderly and villainous admirer of the young lady, named Captain Mathews, had voiced his indignation till Sheridan had felt compelled to take matters into his own hands. He had conveyed Miss

Linley to France, and placed her in a convent whilst the storm broke over his own head. Returning to England, he had fought a duel with the wicked Captain. A few weeks later Mr. Linley fetched his daughter back to Bath and installed her there with strict injunctions to see no more of Master Sheridan.

This ban had been enforced more or less successfully until the day when Miss Linley was informed that Richard Sheridan was at the point of death, having been left pinned to the turf of Claverton Downs by the ferocious Mathews. This shock was too much for Miss Linley. In a panic she announced that before placing her in the French convent Sheridan had taken the precaution of marrying her at Calais. She was Sheridan's wife and she meant to see him. For a while both families tried to discount the ceremony, but when Dick recovered, a second ceremony reinforced the first one, and shortly afterwards the young couple had set up in a small cottage near London—a gig and £1,000 representing their entire fortune.

Such was the story which the Duchess remembered, and there was so much in it that was romantic and so much that was unworldly that she was deeply interested and determined to take the first possible occasion to invite the Sheridans to Devonshire House.

Her husband might not care to have his wife entertain a player's family, though the Spencers·had been friends of Garrick, but the situation was a little out of the ordinary. Sheridan came of a respectable family, and his determination not to allow his wife to sing would appeal to William as it had appealed to Doctor Johnson. Someone had questioned the old moralist as to his opinions of Sheridan's decision. Was Dick a fool or a hero?

Johnson had had no doubts. " He resolved wisely and nobly to be sure. He is a brave man. Would not a gentleman be disgraced by having his wife sing publicly for him? No, sir, there can be no doubt here. I know not if I should not prepare myself for a public singer as readily as let my wife be one." This view would exactly coincide with the Duke's.

It was another delightful coincidence to find that Sheridan was already known to Fox, who appreciated him vastly. So now, when the great Whig cousinhood came to Devonshire

House, they grew accustomed to the unexpected sight of Mr. and Mrs. Sheridan. To Dick's highly romantic and imaginative mind the new vistas that opened before him seemed like an enchanted land : to Elizabeth Sheridan they looked suspiciously like Circe's islands. But no one could resist Georgiana's candid ingenuousness, and Mrs. Sheridan had to admit that despite her husband's new and fascinating friends he was working harder than ever on the play which he was preparing for production. For Sheridan the entrée to Devonshire House meant the possibility of a new orientation to his life; but he was of all men the most proud and the least worldly. If they wanted his friendship they might have it, as equal to equal, but in no other guise.

Through the first half of 1775, Lord Chatham made conciliatory speeches to sympathetic ears, whilst the King fulminated against his rebellious subjects ; and in America an invasion of Canada was being prepared. To the Duchess and her friends Chatham appeared adequate, North contemptible, and the King, a monster. But, though they were loud in their defence of the rights of the Colonists, and though they predicted disaster, not one among them but believed that the situation might still be saved and, indeed, in their heart of hearts they thought that, somehow, it would be saved.

When they met to play Macao and Loo, they talked of the American situation, but it was not as yet their only subject of conversation. They discussed the new plays which Garrick was putting on at Drury Lane, the correct height of heads and widths of hoops, the advantages derived from drinking seawater, and other topics of interest. But, as the summer advanced, the situation became more tense. Hostilities broke out in America : there was bloodshed : the battle of Bunker's Hill was fought. So their prophecies, exaggerated as they had seemed to themselves, were to prove true. The King and his Tories were to succeed in losing America. All possibility of talking America into reason was now lost, and to reduce her to obedience by arms would be no easy matter.

During these anxious days Sheridan's first play made its début at Drury Lane. It was called " The Rivals," and its first performance was a failure ; but, undeterred, Dick rewrote it, and at its second performance its success was instant and immense. London recognised a great playwright. Garrick was generous and enthusiastic in his acclamation. From one week to another Sheridan had become famous. Elizabeth Sheridan was wild with joy; she had always believed that "Chéri," as she called her husband, was destined for some great career. To the Duchess and her friends the success of their protégé was equally welcome. Only the month before it had seemed a little eccentric to entertain an unknown player. Now it was a matter of congratulation to have welcomed the literary lion whilst still an undistinguished cub.

Only to Sheridan himself was there a tinge of bitterness in all the shouting. That night at the theatre, when everyone had applauded, he had seen his father and sisters sitting disapprovingly in the stalls. They had not clapped. To Dick's impulsive nature this cold, calculating hatred was inexplicable. He felt convinced that it could not last, and he had had some hopes that the first night of his play might have been marked by a reconciliation. No advantage from Devonshire House could compensate him for the estrangement from his family.

When the excitement over the play had died down, there remained nothing to talk about but the despatch of drafts to America. Feeling as they did about the war, the Duchess and her friends found the autumn drab and dreary in the extreme, and when the winter came without any promise of a settlement it only added to the dejection of their spirits. Sheridan's play, they claimed, had been the one good thing that had come out of the year.

1776

THE spring of the new year passed quietly, but the summer was to bring a crop of events. In the first place the thirteen United Colonies adopted the Declaration of Independence and threw off their British allegiance. This brought the war to a new phase. Many who had hesitated to enforce the right to levy taxes by arms had no hesitation in obtaining obedience to the Crown by the same means. The King's party gained some ground. But Fox's eloquence in what he termed the cause of liberty remained white hot. "I hope," he wrote, "that it will be a point of honour among us all to support the American pretensions in adversity as much as we did in their prosperity, and that we shall never desert those who have acted *unsuccessfully on Whig principles.*"

Brave words, whatever their implication, which went straight to Georgiana's heart. "Would that I were a man," she exclaimed, "to unite my talents, my hopes, my fortune with Charles's; to make common cause, and fall or rule with him." If this represented the enthusiasm of youth, even older Whigs took the war badly. Fox's aunt, whom the King had jilted, expressed herself forcibly: "I am sure I can thank God very sincerely I am not Queen, for in the first place I should have quarrelled with His Majesty long before this, and my head would have been off, probably. But if I had loved and liked him, and not had interest enough to prevent this war, I should certainly go mad, to think a person I loved was the cause of such a shameful war."

Much sympathy was felt for the British troops who were involved in the war, for they were believed to detest it as much as did most of the civilian population. Yet, under Lord Howe, they won the battle of Brooklyn and captured New York; and even amongst the Whigs the news was received with a secret satisfaction. They held the war to be a bad war, which should be put a stop to as soon as possible by negotiation ; but so long as it continued, well, it was to be hoped that the British troops would be victorious.

But war or no war, the public had to be amused, and the house at Drury Lane was filled to overflowing. It seemed indeed as though the troubles and anxieties caused by the hostilities drove more people each month to find distraction at the play. This was very satisfactory from the point of view of Garrick's purse, but the great actor was getting old. The management of London's leading theatre was a heavy tax on his energies. A plan suggested itself to his mind : he had always liked Richard Sheridan, and he had always believed in his capacities. He considered him not only the best living playwright, but he believed that he might become a brilliant producer. Sheridan had youth, talent, energy and influence. Who could make a better successor to himself at Drury Lane ? The plan was broached, and Richard and Elizabeth were enthusiastic, so were the Sheridans' friends at Devonshire House.

Many difficulties had to be surmounted, for a very considerable sum of money was involved, no less than £60,000. The Sheridans had no capital and little credit, yet, before their confidence, all the barriers of possibility collapsed. Mr. Linley was suddenly and mysteriously possessed of £20,000. A Mr. Lacey came forward with a similar sum and, finally, Richard himself produced the equivalent.

Drury Lane was bought by the syndicate, and on the 10th of June Garrick acted for the last time to a packed house. He took the rôle of Don Felix in " The Wonder," and the receipts went to a stage charity. The audience were much moved, and Garrick himself was in tears. From the pit rose a voice : " In you, sir, we have lost the Atlas of the stage."—" Well, sir, but I have left you a young Hercules to supply my place," came the reply.

Amongst other results the purchase of Drury Lane had the effect of reconciling Mr. Thomas Sheridan to his son. This unattractive old gentleman who had sat through the great night of " The Rivals " without manifesting the smallest desire to congratulate its author, had no sooner heard that Dick had become possessed of the best theatre in London than he became more amenable, and before the year was out we find him filling an important rôle in the management of the theatre with, it is to be feared, disastrous results.

But Dick, generous in his affections, was anxious that since, as an early biographer writes, " The noble house of Cavendish had patented the blood of the Sheridans and the patent had obtained a general assent by the hitherto exclusive and ancient peerage," all his family should share in the good things which life had brought him, both financial and social.

The end of the year saw a gap in the friendly circle of Devonshire House, for Charles Fox, to the King's great relief and delight, spent the winter in France, where his enemies trusted that he might drink himself to death or gamble his way into prison. But his friends knew better. Fox was feeling the pulse of politics very carefully, and it was not long before the Duchess and Lady Melbourne were to be observed shaking their heads and whispering into astonished ears that the French would soon make cause with the Colonists, " and serve us right for abusing them." One night they added a point to their story by telling " how the Marquis de La Fayette had been seen " in the pit at the opera, here in London, " having stopped to see what sort of people we were, and to get what intelligence he could to use against us " when he reached America.

But few people listened to Georgiana's political rigmaroles. What did women know of politics ? And anyway this constant association with politicians was getting her talked about ; worse still, written about. Her older friends were indignant. " The scribblers weekly let fly their pop-guns at the Duchess of Devonshire's feathers. Her Grace is innocent, good-humoured and beautiful ; but these adders are blind and deaf and cannot be charmed." [1]

Nor were her feathers the only source of criticism, for she was roundly upbraided for the custom of wearing " figaries " in her dress ; and even for the hours she kept and customs of her life. " She dines at 7, summer as well as winter, goes to bed at 3 and lies in bed till 4 ; she has hysteric fits in a morning and dances in the evening : she bathes, rides, dances for ten days, and lies in bed the next ten ; indeed I can't forgive her, or rather her husband, the fault of ruining her health." [2]

[1] *A Lady of the Last Century.*
[2] *The Life and Letters of Lady Sarah Lennox.*

Lady Melbourne might have been thought to come in for an equal share of opprobrium, but she was older and far more discreet, and her activities met with nothing but praise in the letters of the period. " I hear much of Lady Melbourne . . . I find she is liked by everybody, high and low, and of all denominations, which I don't wonder at, for she is pleasing, sensible and desirous of pleasing, which must secure admiration." It did, and from Lord Egremont it was said to have obtained more than admiration.

1777

IN the early part of 1777 Sheridan had his revenge upon what Mrs. Montagu had called " the pop-guns of the scribblers," for he produced his great play " The School for Scandal " which had an instantaneous success. Mrs. Montagu wrote approvingly to a friend who had admired it, " everyone agrees with you to recommend it. Of all vices of the human disposition, a love of scandal is the most contemptible. It is now got from the gossips' tea-table to the press," and she was extremely pleased to note that Sheridan was pouring the full blast of his satire upon it. The Duchess too was glad of his chivalrous defence ; and the Sheridans became indispensable at her routs.

Dick joined in the cotillion, whilst his beautiful wife sang, and the celebrated Madame Krampoltz improvised on the harp. Pleasant parties at which Fox was regretted, and of which he received many accounts from Georgiana's pen. She told him also such political gossip as might be expected to amuse him. How at the Newcastle election Lady Strathmore had invented a new form of bribing. She had sat, so it was said, all day at the window of a public house, letting jewels and trinkets fall from her lap, and giving large rewards to the voters who restored them to her. It was a device of an ingenuity to delight Fox's sense of humour.

During the course of the summer Fox returned. His arrival partook of the nature of a thunderbolt. He denounced the war and prophesied calamity with a vehemence which was frightening, especially in view of Washington's victory at Princetown. Opinion was divided and discussions, even in society, became acrimonious. The King's decision to send out German mercenaries aroused general disgust, though the rumours that the Americans were employing Red Indians seemed to take away some of the reproach.

Through the autumn a ding-dong of victory and defeat continued. Then, just before Christmas, news of a decisive action came to hand. General Burgoyne, a personal friend of Fox, had been forced to surrender at the head of his troops. And now the Government were to learn that Fox could be as embarrassing in attacking the conduct of the war as in attacking its necessity. Certain that Burgoyne had been let down by the Home authorities, and equally certain that he would be made the scapegoat for their deficiencies, Fox fell upon the Secretary of War, Lord George Germaine. His attack was merciless, and it was most unfortunate for Lord George that his past held a skeleton.

Years earlier, after the Battle of Minden, he had been tried for cowardice—a regrettable incident in the life of a Secretary at War. Charles had no scruple in using any instrument for the destruction of one whom he believed to be conducting a bad war inefficiently. He made the most of the court-martial episode. But, for the moment, the Government were too strong for him, and though his reputation was impaired for life Germaine survived the attack.

1778

1778 earned an evil reputation, for early in the year the French recognised American independence and came into open alliance against England. The country now embarked upon a double war. On Fox fell the mantle of the prophet. Had he not foretold what had come to pass? Georgiana was proud of her friend. But, although personally he gained in reputation, his cause suffered a severe blow when the French declared war upon England.

The war with America had been hated far beyond the precincts of Devonshire House. But war, as war, was held in no very bad repute save by the Foxites; and war with France was a fact to which the older generation was accustomed. France was *l'ennemi héréditaire*, and it had become quite a habit to fight her. The King was soon aware that public opinion had veered towards his policy, but the satisfaction he felt was mitigated by anxiety.

In the past England had always required the concentration of all her energies to defeat France, and now she had an American war to cope with, disaffection in Ireland, and the Pretender dying, but not yet dead. The situation presented a disagreeable appearance, and George III realised that the country needed a figure whom they respected at the helm of the Ship of State. Such a figure existed in the person of Lord Chatham. It was unfortunate that the King had consistently slighted him; it was also unfortunate that Lord Chatham had always disapproved of the King's American policy. But such a time of need called for magnanimity. The Monarch approached Lord Chatham: "Would he save the country?" The venerable statesman replied that he would. Not only the King, but the whole country was grateful to him. Even Devonshire House thought that the choice might have been worse. But soon it was to appear as though Fate were leagued

with the King's enemies. One spring morning as " his Lordship rose up to speak again, the genius and spirit of Britain
seemed to heave in his bosom and he sank down speech-
less. He continued half an hour in a fit . . . (his sons) in the
greatest agony as to ye doubtful issue." [1] Their uncertainty
was not of long duration, for on May 11th Lord Chatham
died.

Lord North broke out into a cold sweat. It seemed
as though even Providence were against the authors of
the war. Nor was the administration left time in which to
recover from this shock before another blow was dealt
it. And this time the Whigs joined with enthusiasm in the
fray.

So far the trouble had arisen from criticism of the administration of the military side of the war. Now the Naval Depart-
ment was to prove an even more painful thorn. Lord Sandwich, an incompetent Tory peer, presided over the Admiralty,
assisted by his mistress, Miss Ray. He held optimistic views
with regard to the weakness and inefficiency of the French
Fleet, which had its headquarters at Brest, and he urged
Admiral Keppel to go out and meet the puny force, which he
estimated at seventeen sail of the line. Keppel set out, to
discover that the First Lord's estimate had been wrong by
about half, and wisely returned to port to collect reinforcements.

When the two fleets ultimately met and engaged off Ushant,
the result was indecisive, largely owing to the fact that Sir
Hugh Palliser, commanding the rear of the English fleet, failed
to obey his orders, and did not pursue the retreating French
vessels. That Palliser should have been court-martialled
might have seemed a natural sequence of events, but in fact
it was Keppel who had to stand his trial at the instigation of his
subordinate officer.

Why Lord Sandwich should have sanctioned such a proceeding is not to be understood. Keppel was one of the most
popular commanders that the Navy had ever known. He was,
in addition, a man universally respected and belonging by birth
to the powerful Whig connection. At once it became evident
that it would be almost impossible to find officers willing to sit

[1] *A Lady of the Last Century.*

in judgment upon him, whilst Dukes rushed to Portsmouth to his support.

Sir Hugh Palliser was a conservative M.P. and the case became not only one of common justice, but also a political ramp. The rights and wrongs were not doubted. Old Lady Albemarle, Keppel's mother, was the subject of much commiseration. " Your anxiety about Poor Lady Albemarle is very kind and just, for she has indeed suffered a great deal, not from fear of her son's *demerit*, but from fear of ' villainy.' However, she now begins to recover her spirits which were terribly hurt and now she will, I hope, fill up all the *chinks* of fear with anger, a much better companion for the dear old soul " [1] . . . wrote Fox's aunt.

The result of the court-martial was of course an acquittal of the Admiral, with a rider to the effect that the charge had been malicious and unfounded.

Fox and his friends celebrated the Whig victory in an uproarious manner, and ended the evening by storming Lord Sandwich and Miss Ray out of the Admiralty to the sound of breaking glass and shivering doors. This expression of personal feeling was later translated into more sober indignation by a personal vote of censure in the House.

Here, however, Fate stepped in on Lord Sandwich's behalf. The night before the motion, on the steps of a theatre, Miss Ray was shot dead by a crazy clergyman. Lord Sandwich became an object of sympathy, and Fox's motion was a failure.

But it must not be supposed that the whole of the year 1778 was dominated by affairs of political significance. The ladies of Devonshire House danced and gamed and, besides the card-table, they indulged in a new form of gambling, for they became deeply concerned with the dealings of the Stock Exchange. Horace Walpole gives a little vignette of Lady Melbourne, in the summer of 1778, standing before the fire and adjusting her feathers in the glass. Says she, " Lord, they say the stocks will blow up ; that will be very comical."

Towards the autumn, exhausted by so many excitements, society betook itself to its beloved Bath to gather up energy for another season of " raking." In the country etiquette was, to a certain extent, relaxed ; circles impinged which were wide

[1] *The Life and Letters of Lady Sarah Lennox.*

apart in the metropolis. To Georgiana the added freedom was a joy ; but it had its critics. Mrs. Montagu wrote captiously, "I love London extremely, where one has the choice of society, but I hate ye higgledy-piggledy of the watering places." [1]

[1] *A Lady of the Last Century.*

1779

THE new year was to be one of note in the annals of Devonshire House, for during its course two of the most important members of the circle made their first appearance. One was Georgiana's younger sister, Henrietta Frances, and the other was the Prince of Wales. The Duchess's younger sister in no way resembled Georgiana. She was quiet, reserved and very critical; and though the strong temperament which dissipated itself with Georgiana in a hundred loves and a thousand enthusiasms was present equally in Harriet, it was as yet under an implacable control.

She had no looks to compare with those of her elder sister, but her conversation was brilliant and incisive. She was religious but, at the same time, violent. The conflict of principle and emotion had already created a personality. She was nineteen and had, from the age of fifteen, been the recipient of many offers of marriage, to all of which she had turned a deaf ear. She was not and never would be the universal favourite which the Duchess had become. She was not to everybody's taste; but those who loved her were extravagant in their devotion and, whether favoured or rejected, it is to be doubted whether they were ever at a later period in their lives quite free from the effects of her influence. With judgment and heart always at war, with a nature which led her to violent partisanship, and a fearlessly analytical brain, which saw and weighed the most minute faults; life could be neither easy, nor painless. Yet, from the paradox could rise comprehension and a wide humanity.

To Lady Spencer's sensible and orderly mind, her younger daughter's refusal to marry was distressing, whilst to Georgiana's easy-going mentality it was inexplicable. They tried what the influence of the jolly parties at Devonshire House would do. Harriet's critical mind made an immediate analysis of what she found. To begin with, she saw straight through Lady Melbourne: saw her for what she was, a worldly, artful woman, a dangerous woman, yet Georgiana's greatest friend, and for this reason to be tolerated, placated even, but never to be trusted. Next she saw Charles Fox, stripped of his glamour, a kind-hearted, weak, unworldly fellow, devoid of any standards, but so well supplied with instinct that the deficiency would only be noticeable on rare occasions.

But what concerned her most of all was her sister's position. With bitterness she resented the Duke's indifference. What other man in the world would have treated Georgiana as he did ? Yet, as against this emotional reaction, she made allowance for William's temperament, for his upbringing, for those things which did not depend upon his will. She could champion Georgiana's extravagances in face of the world, but she could not bring herself to hate her brother-in-law.

Simultaneously with her own introduction to the Whig world, George, Prince of Wales, made his bow.

The boy was only seventeen, but his father had already been jealous of him for ten years. His mother was indifferent to him, and always ready to take her husband's part against him. He fully realised, if indeed he did not exaggerate, the dislike which his parents felt towards him. He had been repressed and bullied through a drab education with the assurance that he would be kept from any part in the Government and, if possible, from any contact with the people until his father's death.

The more unpopular George III became, the more irritation he felt against his eldest son. The boy himself was naturally affectionate. He loved his brothers and sisters ; he had talents and perceptions in advance of his intelligence. When Peniston had been at Eton Lady Melbourne had been careful always to ask the Prince to dine with them. To the Whigs, an alliance with the heir to the throne would be a triumph. They had hopes. The Prince and the Duke of York had been brave enough to speak to Mr. Fox and to confess their admiration for him. It was said that the King had flogged them. Instantly they became the heroes of the hour. The Prince of Wales, reacting from all that was snuffy and bigoted in his home, inclined to everything of which his father disapproved.

Mrs. Robinson, " Perdita," became his mistress when he was 16 ; in the following year he entered the circle of Devonshire House. As to the impression which he made upon one member of the circle we have first-hand evidence. The romantic Sheridan was dazzled and overwhelmed. Years afterwards he recalled the Prince's appearance in glowing terms for his son's edification. " It was at Devonshire House that I first met with the Prince of Wales, then in the seventeenth year of his age, in the splendour of his youth and the manliness of his beauty. His was a noble presence, Tom, and as the eye rested on his form it was struck with wonder and admiration. He was, indeed, every inch a prince, a prince among his nobles in majesty and beauty. . . . He was the very personification of all that imagination could conceive, or a Phydias portray of beauty of form and gracefulness of deportment. There was a something about him in his early address and gaiety of manners that won you to his side, and impressed you with the warmest sentiments in his favour. . . . In the course of the evening Fox introduced me to him. He was accompanied by the Duchess, who was leaning on his arm and who claimed the privilege of introducing your mother. Fox left early for Brooks's and the Duke of Devonshire merely paid to us a passing visit. He left to attend his club, from which he rarely absented himself." [1]

Admiration and flattery were new and very pleasant to the heir-apparent. He hardly knew to which he was more devoted, to Lady Melbourne or to the Duchess. We are told that the former used to dance with him " rather in a cow style," but to his infinite satisfaction. Between Fox and Sheridan there was, luckily, no need to discriminate ; both could share his exuberant friendship. One of the Prince's most engaging characteristics was his complete lack of " calcul " or self-interest. He chose his friends and his opinions with an entire absence of precaution. This trait, admirable in a private individual, might have caused serious trouble when associated with a Prince of Wales ; but, in this case, it proved fortunate for the nation. For, at a time when the popularity of the

[1] Sheridan's *Life and Times of an Octogenarian*.

Hanoverian dynasty was at a low ebb and the monarchy itself in peril, the fact that the very people who disapproved of the King had no greater favourite than his eldest son, made inevitably for the security of the Crown.

Fox and Sheridan were a liberal education to the son of George III, and if they taught him many deplorable habits, they did initiate him into the lives of his subjects of all classes and categories, and they effectively widened his sympathies. It was not very edifying to know that the Prince of Wales, with Fox and Sheridan, disguised in the poorest clothes and masquerading under the names of Slimstock, Blackstock and Greystock, had been seen to frequent an ill-famed tavern in the lowest part of the town. It was not very creditable to know that they had been arrested by the much-abused " Charleys " and brought into dock.

But, out of these wild adventures, the Prince gained much useful knowledge which he later put to use, when he gave orders for the rebuilding of the worst quarter of the town, the unhappy district of Birdcage Walk, the rubbish-heaps and cesspools of St. James's Park, and the great, newly developing areas of Regent's Park and its environs.

Meanwhile, the year 1779 ran its course. In America the war seemed to turn in favour of the English ; there were successes at Strong Point and in Savannah. As against this, Spain had been drawn by France to intervene on the side of the Colonists. The number of Britain's enemies was growing. And the danger of invasion became a very real one. Sixty-six sail of line appeared off Plymouth, and a vast French army was said to be ready for embarkation. The country grew alarmed and angry. No one but the King had wanted this war with America, and now, see what it had led to ? The cost of living was greatly increased, discontent was general.

In this unhappy state of affairs the Whigs saw an opportunity of coming into office. They exploited the public grievances and they demanded a wiser expenditure of public money and an electoral reform. They held meetings all over the country, and it was evident that they had the people behind them. But, agreed in principle, they disagreed amongst themselves as to the means of reform. Fox made impassioned speeches, but he could not bring himself to make common cause with

Shelburne. So, though the reformers obtained a small majority on the motion that " the influence of the Crown has increased, is increasing, and ought to diminish,"· the whole movement guttered out without results.

In the midst of these stirring events, Georgiana found time to write a two-volume novel entitled *The Sylph*. It was published anonymously and thought by the uninitiated to be the work of Fanny Burney. Indeed, to such an extent did this view prevail, that the more celebrated authoress was obliged to write to her publisher on the subject. Those who were the Duchess's intimates were silent about the book. Those on the fringes of her circle were full of its inner meaning. The story, which is told in the form of a series of letters to a younger sister, is in the conventional mould of an earlier age. An unsophisticated young woman marries a villainous gentleman who, after a few weeks, is more than willing that she should oblige a friend of his and relieve him from a debt. She is given worldly advice by an older woman and sent a series of admonitions by an anonymous writer who signs himself " The Sylph." Eventually her husband comes to a " dreadful end," and on her return to her father's home the Sylph discovers himself and proves to be an eligible young man whom she marries.

In the tale Georgiana's acquaintances were anxious to find a *cri de cœur*. Had she not been quite unsophisticated when she had married the Duke, and with him was she not unhappy, and did she not correspond with her sister, and was she not advised by Lady Melbourne ? And what reason was there for disbelieving in the existence of a " Sylph " ? So they argued, but there seems little reason to be impressed by their arguments. The Duke was no villain, and had he been one, his wife would have been the last person to advertise the fact. In absence of all evidence it is dangerous to suppose that any characters were drawn from life ; but certain descriptions of the habits and customs of the day are a sufficient warrant for reading the little volumes, which are usually described as " tedious " by modern critics.

About this time Sheridan suffered a severe loss in the death of Garrick, his old friend and wise adviser. The public was much moved by the death of their old favourite.

Garrick was buried in Westminster Abbey. The Duke of Devonshire, Lord Spencer and Lord Camden were amongst his pall-bearers. Sheridan wrote a monody upon his passing, and Drury Lane was closed. That autumn saw the Spencers entertaining Bishop and Mrs. Hervey; their two elder daughters were now married to Lord Erne and Mr. Foster respectively. After a long absence abroad this gay prelate was about to return to his Irish diocese loaded with the spoils of Italy. The pen-portraits of Lady Spencer by both the bishop and his lady are worth quoting. The weak and cautious Mrs. Hervey wrote critically : " She (Lady Spencer) is my point of perfection for *these times*, and has I believe as few failings as are possible in her peculiar situation." [1] The Lord Bishop expressed himself with characteristic vehemence.

" Lady Spencer, you know, is my model of woman, and having seen her in retirement and in all her domestic employ-ments my admiration and respect of her increases. She has so decided a character that nothing can warp it, and then such a simplicity of manners one would think she had never lived out of the country, with such elegance 'tis as if she had never lived in it—her charitable institutions are worthy of her, both for their object and their direction. She has reclaimed the manners of a most vicious Parish merely by her charitable institutions in it, and is so bent upon having the Parishioners neat, as well as religious and virtuous, that she is paving every path through, and not ostentatiously, but single flag stones, just to give the inhabitants a taste for cleanliness. The old ones who die with a fair character have a gravestone, at her expense, and sometimes the Duchess of Devonshire has wrote the epitaph, which I promise you is not spelt by an unlettered muse. Nothing could tempt Lady Spencer to London but the restlessness of her poor husband." [2]

The Bishop, whose religious convictions were of the most nebulous description, if indeed they existed at all, might, had he not strayed into the church, have made a brilliant politician or a fine administrator. He was at that moment engaged upon an extensive canvass in favour of rescinding the Penal Laws against the Roman Catholics of England and Ireland.

Soon after he left the Spencers he was to succeed to the title

---

[1] *The Life of the Earl Bishop of Derry.*   [2] Ibid.

of Lord Bristol and the estates of Ickworth, through the death of his elder brother.

Our account of the year ends with a scolding letter from Mrs. Montagu, complaining of the wickedness of the times.

December 29th, 1779.

" Never till now did one hear of all these divorces going forward in one session, in which the ladies of the most illustrious rank and families in Great Britain were concerned." [1]

---

[1] *A Lady of the Last Century.*

1780

THE new year found the Duchess and all her friends canvassing enthusiastically for a Bill which Charles Fox
had much at heart. It was an Act which was to rescind some
of the old Penal Laws against Roman Catholics. The severity
and injustice of these laws was manifest, and for some time it
had been apparent to all parties that laws which deprived a
considerable part of the population from all civic rights were
an anachronism. The Roman Catholic families had always
been devoted to their country, but for many years their loyalty
to the Stuarts had remained unshaken. Not a few were large
landowners, Tory in politics; and now that the Stuart cause
was virtually dead it seemed just that they should be rehabili-
tated with the rest of the Tory party.

Unable to attend a public school or a university, debarred
from entering the Army or the Navy, living under antiquated
laws which made their tenure of land doubtful, and their right
of succession questionable; deprived of their chapels and
religious establishments, they were obliged to be educated
abroad, and for the most part their numerous younger sons
were forced to take service in the armies of the Empire, which
was largely officered by Jerninghams, Dillons, Howards and
Petres, and other names well known in pre-Reformation England. Having no representatives in the Houses of Parliament,
Burke and Fox took on the office of knights-errant. The
Bill was to be introduced by Sir George Savile, a Whig, but
it was no party affair; it had the support of Lord North, of
the Tories and, it was said, of the King himself. It seemed,
therefore, to be assured of a smooth passage.

But the will of one individual withstood the united determination of the House: Lord George Gordon opposed the Bill
with fanaticism; and when he saw himself left without a
following in Parliament he sought allies elsewhere.

38

One June morning Count Maltzahn, the Prussian minister, demanded an interview with Lord North, and announced to the astonished Prime Minister that London was on the verge of a revolution, and that the mob had a plan to attack the Bank. Lord North refused to be impressed, but he was not above taking some precautionary measures. Meanwhile, Lord George Gordon had retired to the poorest quarter of the town, where he was inciting the most violent elements of the mob to riot. With the cry of " No Popery," and the assurance that Burke was a Jesuit, he soon raised a crowd of drunken desperadoes.

The afternoon following Maltzahn's warning, this angry crowd rolled from the East End of London into Bloomsbury, Mayfair and Westminster. From the first it was evident that their numbers were considerable, and that their intention was one of destruction and pillage. They began by sacking the chapels of the Foreign Ambassadors, which were destroyed, and the priests only rescued by the courage of certain members of the Catholic aristocracy who went to their assistance.

Next the mob turned its attention to the houses of the Catholic laity and continued with the destruction of those of the great Whig families who were known to be in sympathy with the Act. Bedford House was sacked, Lord Mansfield's magnificent library burnt, Sir G. Savile's house plundered, Devonshire House itself in such danger that Georgiana left after dusk by a back door and fled to Berkeley Square, to Lord Clermont's house, where a tent bed was made up for her in the drawing-room, whilst Fox and Fitzpatrick, musket in hand, prepared to defend Lord Rockingham's house. And now the crowd, impartial in its attentions, prepared to attack the Houses of Parliament. Newgate was said to be already in flames, the prisoners liberated and the Bank in danger. Lord North, who had troops concealed in Downing Street, warned the crowd to this effect, so that it stood outside, grim and menacing, but unwilling to risk forcing an entry.

The Prime Minister climbed on to the roof with his secretary, Mr. Brummel,[1] and beheld the magnificent but disquieting sight of the capital in flames.

[1] Father of Beau Brummel.

In the crisis one man knew his mind and his course of action, as fully as the crowd knew theirs, and this was the King. From the first, he recognised the gravity of the situation, and knew that only the action of the military could save the day. The troops must be used : but never should it be said that they had been employed by him in an unconstitutional manner. He consulted his legal advisers : " Under circumstances such as these could the troops fire before the third reading of the Riot Act ? " Wedderburn, after consideration, decided that they could. Immediately orders were sent to the Guards to defend the Bank and the bridges, by firing if necessary, and to dig trenches in Hyde Park.

All night the King walked backwards and forwards from Buckingham House to the Royal Mews, receiving news of the latest developments. His personal courage was unquestionable, and his absolute conviction of the justice of his will unshakable. With such confidence James II might have kept his throne.

An account of the night's work by Wraxall brings the scene vividly to mind. He had gone up to Bloomsbury to see what was doing. All down Hart Street and Great Russell Street huge fires were burning, in the broken windows of the magistrates' houses wild black figures were seen silhouetted against the flames, actively engaged in throwing furniture, pictures and books from the rooms into the fires below. The gutter was running with liquor. A silent, frightened crowd watched the proceedings, but seemed to take no part in them. Wraxall passed on and saw Mr. Langdale's House in Holborn burning, and noted that the spire of St. Andrew's church made a pretty silhouette against the blaze. As he stood fascinated, a decrepit watchman with his lanthorn passed calmly by calling " Two o'clock and a fine night—all's well."

From a farther point he saw Fleet Street Prison on fire and the King's Bench in ruins. Then he noted the arrival of the troops to protect the Mansion House and the Bank. Finally the sound of firing from Blackfriars Bridge impelled him to go home. In the early hours of the morning a fierce battle raged. By the next day the town was quiet. But estimates of the losses proved alarming. Some said that two hundred had been killed, and that for the most part their bodies had been thrown into the river. What was certain was that there were about three hundred wounded.

Lord North was appalled. He had a clandestine meeting with Fox behind the Opera House in the Haymarket to learn what ideas the Opposition had with regard to the situation. Perhaps of Fox's hatred of Shelburne was born the abominable rumour that this respectable politician had abetted the rioters in order to discomfort the Government. No greater libel could have been invented. The real cause of all the trouble, Lord George, was arraigned before the House. But no sentence was passed upon him when it was proved that, having started the riots, he had at a later stage done his best to stop them. And so he lived to become a Jew, to submit to even the more painful rites of initiation, and to die in Newgate Prison where he had been confined for some years on account of a libel he had published against Marie Antoinette.

The only person who came really creditably out of the affair was the King. Everyone agreed to praise his courage, both moral and physical. And now, with a perseverance equal to that which he had displayed with regard to his quarrel with his American subjects, he continued to demand the passage of the Relief Act. But the results of the shaking which the Government had received were not easily repaired, and the country made ready for a General Election.

Devonshire House was in a flutter, for many of its favourites were involved. Admiral Keppel was standing for Windsor, and though ostracised by the King it was said that the Royal Princes had condoled with him on the conduct of his enemies and offered him their support. Fox was standing for Westminster, and here again the King's opposition had to be faced. It was said that George III had laid out £8,000 to insure Charles's defeat.

Of even greater interest were the contests of two candidates new to the field of politics ! One evening, at Devonshire House, Lady Cork had asked Sheridan why he did not stand at the next election. And Dick himself wondered why he should not ? He talked the matter over with the Duchess and with Fox, both of whom were delighted with the plan. With his eloquence and command of language he should make a fine figure in the House, and they knew him to be soundly Whig in principle.

Georgiana wrote letters to her parents recommending Sheridan to their interest. He stood for Stafford, where the Spencer influence was an important factor. His methods of canvassing were new. He never asked for a vote, but in speaking to his rural opponents " invariably regretted that so *honest* a man should, without due consideration of the great question of popular rights, differ with him in the means by which these rights might be secured." [1] The specious appeal proved irresistible. The other novice was Billy Pitt, who offered himself as representative of the University of Cambridge.

When the results were known the situation seemed to have changed very little, though some Whig losses were noticeable. Burke lost Bristol, but was given a pocket borough ; Pitt failed to get in for Cambridge, but was provided for by the Lowthers. At Westminster, Fox had been elected, and at Stafford Sheridan had been returned. He became about the same time a member of Brooks's Club ; and it seemed as though his every ambition had been gratified. Only his wife looked anxious. Her Chéri had not too good a head, and she knew it. The younger son of a poor but respectable actor, now the friend of princes and duchesses, the owner of the best theatre in London, a member of the most select club, society's favourite playwright, and bidding fair to become one of its most famous politicians—and all this before he was thirty. Was it not too much ? Sometimes Elizabeth wished for the hard days that had succeeded their marriage—a time of privation, but one of privacy.

Excitement trod upon the heels of excitement. One day when some of the men who formed part of the Duchess's circle were dining at Almon's, a messenger entered with the terrifying rumour that Fox had been shot in a duel. Amongst the diners was one of Charles's cousins, who tells the tale to his wife. " I was quite overpowered with it (the news), and ran away to him and found him lying on a couch surrounded by stars and Dukes, the room as full as it could stick ; he shook me very heartily by the hand, and told me he was very well and only

[1] Hammond's *Life of Fox.*

there to be quiet." [1] A shiver went down the spine of Devonshire House, their idol had been in danger ; and the more they came to consider the situation the more like a planned murder and the less like a duel did the affair appear. The quarrel had arisen when a certain Mr. Adams had accused Fox of being the author of a libellous paragraph concerning him, and had refused to accept Fox's verbal denial of the authorship. The result had been a challenge which Fox, though much bored by the incident, had accepted. Adams chose pistols, in which arm he was very proficient. He fired first, at Fox's request, and wounded him ; Charles then fired and missed. The seconds and Fox himself considered the matter ended, but the persistent Mr. Adams chose to fire again at the wounded man. Luckily his careful aim was not true. As for Charles, he fired his pistol in the air, and was carried from the field with a slight wound in his side.

The affair created a scandal. The Whigs declared loudly that " it is by everybody, and ought to be, considered as a determined plan of assassination to get rid of an adversary they cannot answer and whom they look on as their perdition." [2] It was very evident who the " they " referred to, and it had an ugly sound.

In the late autumn an event occurred which was a cause of great rejoicing to Georgiana : her sister began to show a definite predilection for one of her numerous admirers. The favoured youth was Lord Duncannon, only son of the Earl of Bessborough, and first cousin to the Duke of Devonshire. Born after his parents had been married nearly twenty years, he was a quiet, gentle young man, whose interests were those of a collector and a dilettante. Politics he abhorred but, like all eldest sons, having completed his education at Oxford, he had been presented with a seat in the lower House. He was the representative of Knaresborough, but was so entirely devoid of ambition that, later, when offices were to be suggested to him, he would turn the offers aside with the remark, " however convenient a place may be, independence is much pleasanter." [3]

Harriet may have found his easy-going nature a restful foil to her own violence. She admired him for his contempt of

[1] *The Life and Letters of Lady Sarah Lennox.*   [2] Ibid.
[3] *The Ponsonby Family.*

43

ambition and advancement, and the unselfish and humble qualities of his devotion touched her more than all Fitzpatrick's violence or Sheridan's protestations, or the Prince of Wales's flattery. So, in November, the wedding took place. Already she knew the Bessborough family almost as well as her own. Her father-in-law was seventy-six and redoubtable. Decades ago he had left politics in a huff at the treatment meted out to his brother-in-law, the Duke of Devonshire, and had since devoted his life to collecting pictures and *objets de vertu* for his house in Pall Mall.

His wife had been dead twenty years, and rumour had it that George II's daughter, the gruff and formidable Princess Amelia, had consoled him. Some even said that he had married her. Certain it was that he was an *habitué* of her house in Cavendish Square. But both were now so old as to still the voice of scandal. Lady Bessborough, besides Duncannon, had borne her husband two daughters, the elder of whom, Catharine, was unmarried, whilst the younger had married Lord Fitzwilliam ten years previously. Lord Bessborough who seems to have been very little associated with the Irish estate in County Waterford, from which he derived his title, gave to his only son his property at Roehampton. Originally nothing but a farm, a pleasant palladian villa had been built upon its site. From its windows a magnificent view of rolling hillocks and great oak trees spread out in a vast panorama. Nearer to the house [1] much-admired cedars had been planted and were doing well.

The early married life of the Duncannons was idyllic. In the morning Frederick would go out to shoot snipe and woodcock, whilst his wife planned out the gardens or visited the village, endeavouring to reconstruct it on the lines which her mother had adopted in her own home. In the afternoon Harriet and Frederick would ride together, and in the evenings they would drive up to London to see a play or attend a rout ; or, if nothing enticed them from home, they would sit together playing cribbage and chess till the small hours of the morning. When the House of Commons was in session their visits to London became daily affairs.

The whole picture is one of subdued peace and comfort well

[1] This house is now the Jesuit Seminary " Manresa."

suited to Duncannon's quiet ways, but entirely foreign to his wife's remarkable personality. She appreciated their ordered existence, and often she was to look back to these days with pleasure and regret ; but a character of such vitality was incapable of remaining deliberately undefined and obscure, and, against her conscious desire, her temperament was to lead her back into the turmoil and battle of society. Georgiana's need of her became the cause of her return ; but the instrument was fortuitous, the return certain.

1781

THE year 1781 was happily devoid of untoward incidents. In the spring society saw the revival of the game of Pharo. Fox, Fitzpatrick and Lord Robert Spencer opened a bank at Brooks's Club. Angry old women wrote to each other that in their young days when they had seen the game played abroad, the banker had always worn a mask, so disgraceful was his office considered. But Fox needed money too badly to have time to give to such nice consideration. Already his library had been sold, and now his furniture was being auctioned by his creditors ; and this time there was no indulgent father to produce the immense sum which would free him from embarrassment.

At first the venture was a success. Charles began to pay off his creditors and to entertain his friends. Lord Robert Spencer bought an estate, and Fitzpatrick became a man of fortune. It was all very delightful, and consequently very contagious. Soon Fox's was not the only table in town, and as time went on the ladies joined in the game, and foremost amongst them was the Duchess of Devonshire. The recreation grew into a business, the business into a passion, stakes grew higher and higher, private arrangements subsisted by which the face value of bets was tripled between players to avoid the unwanted cautions of kind friends. Parks, houses, staircases, jewels and, it was even said, wives were, metaphorically, thrown on to the table, when money failed.

If Ste's son had been born " for the destruction of the Jews," the offspring of Charles's imagination—the Pharo Bank —was created for their rehabilitation. The highest in the land of both sexes were in its toils. Fox even put up Pitt for Brooks's, but the young man was no great gambler.

Burke introduced a Bill for the revision of the Civil List. Fox first supported it, and then the House waited breathlessly for the maiden speech of Chatham's son. It was more than what they had hoped for. Sheridan also spoke brilliantly. Burke, Fox, Pitt, Sheridan in concert, how long could the polite and ineffectual North withstand a party headed by such remarkable young leaders ? Surely the Whigs must soon be in power, surely the days of the Court party were numbered ? So thought the Devonshire House set. And when, in October, Lord Cornwallis surrendered a British Army to Washington at York Town, they felt that no government could survive such a disgraceful disaster.

It was useless for the King to go on talking of the necessity for " distressing America," peace must be made, and unless Lord North were wholly shameless it could not be made by him. A party of young men full of ideas and ideals were waiting, straining at the barriers for the signal to rush forward and take possession of ground. They were sure of their ability to rule, they had a thousand plans, they would reform the Penal Laws, the Electoral Franchise ; they would alter the foreign policy and the colonial system ; on every question they had their views and their schemes of improvement, and they believed that now the time was at hand which would give them the power to put their theories into practice. But the inevitable did not happen, and the future held bitter disillusionment for most of them. Before a Whig Prime Minister should sit firmly in the saddle of office, Fox would be dead, and Sheridan and Burke and Pitt and their admirers, Lady Melbourne, Lady Duncannon and the Duchess. In 1781, Lord Grey was only seventeen. How fortunate for them was the existence of the wall that hides the future !

For Harriet, the year passed tranquilly. Towards its close she gave birth to a son. Despite her condition, she had come up more frequently to London as the year wore on. Sometimes she had made the excuse of indisposition to pass the night at Devonshire House. Her anxieties as to Georgiana's growing extravagance had given her conscience its absolution. She owed much to Frederick, but she owed much to her sister too ; and Georgiana, unhappy and nervous, was indiscreet and incapable of looking after herself, whilst dear Dunncannon was exactly the reverse. The scales quivered, and fell to the side of Devonshire House.

47

1782

THE Devonshires and the Duncannons, Fox and the Sheridans, heard the church bells ring in the New Year with feelings of eager anticipation, the King with foreboding, and Lord North, with a concealed hope of release.

By February, the Whig attack was launched. General Conway brought forward a motion, imploring the King to abandon the war—it was only defeated by one vote. But George III was no cowardly opponent; he was always ready to take the attack into his enemies' country, and, as for draggling his coat-tails, that was the breath of life to him. His response to General Conway's attack was to make Lord George Germaine, that scarecrow of the Whigs, a peer, under the title of Lord Sackville.

The Upper House was outraged, Lord Carmarthen brought a motion to the effect that it was derogatory to the House of Lords to number amongst their members a gentleman under heavy sentence of court-martial; but the King was obdurate, and to the House of Lords George Germaine went. It was evident to all that the King was making the most of the last hours of office of his pliable minister. But in March even Lord North's infinite patience and devotion were exhausted. He resigned, and the Monarch sent for Lord Rockingham as the least personally distasteful of his adversaries.

For twelve years the King had governed England in a manner that was in direct opposition to the loudly expressed wishes of his people. Now the hour of liberation had come. Hopes ran very high. But, unfortunately, they ran high not only amongst the public with regard to legislature, but equally high as regards place amongst the protagonists. The whole Whig party was in a ferment, everyone thought he had a right to office, and almost everyone had at some period been promised office by someone! Now came the awful hour for re-

48

deeming those promises. Poor Lord Rockingham was distracted, and Lord North beheld his rival's unhappy situation with a wry smile of irony.

When the nominations were known discussions raged furiously. Shelburne and Fox were joint Secretaries of State, both had perhaps earned the office, but the pairing of lifelong enemies gave rise to doubts. Keppel at the Admiralty and Conway at the Horseguards seemed decided warnings to the King perhaps; Thurlow, the only Tory, was evidently thrown in as a sop.

The Duke of Richmond and Sheridan were provided for, and so was Burke (after a fashion ; but he was only to have the Paymastership). The fact that he, to whom the Whigs owed so much, was not raised to Cabinet rank touched a sense of injustice. The Devonshire House set were keeping all the plums of office for themselves. Pitt had demanded Cabinet rank and had been refused. It was a surprising piece of impertinence from a mere boy, but the refusal was to prove a cardinal error. There was so much on the agenda that it seemed difficult to know on what to begin.

A bid for Electoral Reform proved disastrous, the Government was not agreed, and evidences of severe cracking became visible. A Bill brought in by Burke to abolish many sinecures was successful. The good days when a gentleman might receive a comfortable income for life for the nominal service of supplying sealing-wax to Government offices were drawing to a close.

Devonshire House saw the blow dealt to what they considered " pure graft " with joy. But the matter was in reality not quite so simple. All governments have need at times to reward the men who have done them a service ; whilst the system of sinecures existed it supplied this need. Once abolished, succeeding governments had nothing left to offer save peerages. As years passed the Upper House became cluttered up with descendants of worthy gentlemen who had deserved reward, but whose reward would have ceased with their lives had sinecures been still the fashion. Thus, the House of Lords ceased, in part, to represent the sober views of the great landowners, and, at the same time, the country rendered the payment of its debts hereditary.

In another matter, too, the early days of the Government were unlucky. Lord Rockingham had received an unfavourable report on the conduct of Admiral Rodney (*a Tory*) and sent him letters of recall. Hardly had the ship bearing the unpleasant missive and also Rodney's successor set sail, than news came that the Admiral had won a great victory over the French fleet in the West Indies. The Whigs had not the generosity to own their mistake. Rodney was relieved of his command according to plan and subsequently made a peer. The proceedings gave an unattractive impression of weakness and suggested a mean revenge for the Tory treatment of Admiral Keppel two years before.

But the great, the imminent, question before the country was that of concluding peace, and Fox and Shelburne were ill fitted to work harmoniously to this end. The peace had two aspects—a treaty with America and one with France. The only hope would have been for Shelburne to take charge of the former negotiations and Fox of the latter. With regard to America Fox was committed to the recognition of Independence and to every concession, whereas Shelburne was a dark horse. With regard to France, on the other hand, Fox was likely to uphold the interests of his country. As has been said, he looked upon France as England's natural enemy, and he was always ready to support a war against the Bourbons. A division of labour might have saved the situation, but no such division was contemplated.

Both Secretaries of State sent their envoys to America : Shelburne, a crafty Scottish merchant ; Fox, a young coxcomb. The envoys were destined to quarrel as much as did their principals. Older people had laughed when they saw the idle rakes of Brooks's in office. On Sheridan's door had been found a card bearing the following inscription : " No application to be received here on Sundays, nor any business done during the remainder of the week." The joke misfired. The lounging, dissipated young men proved to be ogres where work was concerned, and also, alas, displayed all the cunning, the jealousies and the qualities of intrigue associated with the names of older politicians ! In particular, Fox was fretting against the curb. He was the first to admit it. His aunt writes : " I saw Charles in the House yesterday ; he told me he feared my brother (the Duke of Richmond) and he must *quarrel* and he shewed a violence that provoked me."

In the summer the occasion for the quarrel occurred. Fox's American agent, Tom Grenville, learnt that Franklin had made a suggestion to Shelburne's agent for a peace based ᴜᴀ the cession of Canada to America by the British Government. Of this suggestion Shelburne had made no mention, probably for the excellent reason that he considered it too absurd to be worthy of discussion. But, with this weapon in his hands, Fox determined to convert Shelburne into a " bogyman," a traitor who was preparing the downfall of English colonial supremacy.

Nothing could have been more foolish, but at this point, as at many others, Fox's invincible charm was a very bad friend to him—he was so brilliant, he was so plausible, he was so surrounded by friends. Had anyone remained with a clear head they could have told him that he was actuated solely by personal spite and ambition ; but the Prince of Wales, Sheridan, Georgiana and Lady Melbourne saw in him only the patriot he believed himself to be. They urged him on. " His resignation would be such an embarrassment to the Government that they would prefer to lose Shelburne." Tempted, he sent it in.

For the second time in his life Fate played him a nasty trick. The morning after he had sent in his resignation he learnt that Rockingham had died. The King sent for Lord Shelburne. Devonshire House was aghast. To co-operate or to fight, that was the question. But Fox *had* to fight, and so they followed him into the arena. All, save a few. The Duke of Richmond refused to be bullied out of his own good sense. As his sister, who was the intermediary between uncle and nephew, wrote plaintively : " Lord Shelburne may be false, ambitious and cunning ; well, but what then ? He finds it his interest to carry good measures into execution, and shall my Brother thwart him in that, on account of dislike of the man ? . . . He has talked (To Charles) and been patient, and tried all sorts of persuasions to inspire them with a *true love of their country*, but poor dear Charles is so surrounded with flatterers that tempt him to think he *alone* can overset the whole fabric, that it's in vain to talk. . . ." [1]

Sheridan, Burke, Lord Robert Spencer and Georgiana's

[1] *Life and Letters of Lady Sarah Lennox.*

brother, Lord Althorp, with some others, followed Fox into
the outer darkness ; but it was not the following he had hoped
to carry with him.   In particular, they needed a sober figure-
head, and now that Richmond had failed them they had to be
content with the Duke of Portland, an amiable and, at the
moment, absent, nonentity.   It was all very disappointing, a
rocket that had not gone off, a damp squib.   Meanwhile the
King was not ill-satisfied with Lord Shelburne.   He had no
high opinion of his Prime Minister, but even this had its
uses.

" He possessed," said the King, " one art beyond any man
he had ever known, for that by the familiarity of his inter-
course he obtained your confidence, procured from you your
opinion of different public characters, and then availed himself
of this knowledge to sow dissensions " [1]   And where dissensions existed the pertinacious monarch saw a hope that the
less clever but more consistent and persevering combatant
might eventually impose his will.

Shelburne made one appointment which was more pregnant
of events than he could anticipate : he gave William Pitt that
seat in the Cabinet which Rockingham had refused him.

Charles Fox, out of office, felt little anxiety for the future.
He was confident of an early return to power, and in the
meantime a return to idleness was very pleasant, and in any
case he had a new interest to which allusion is found in many
letters.   " I hear Charles saunters about the streets and brags
that he has not taken a pen in hand since he was out of
place.   *Pour se désennuyer* he lives with Mrs. Robinson, goes
to Sadlers Wells with her, and is all day figuring away with
her." [2]

For the last three years Perdita had lived in Berkeley Square
in a magnificent house presented to her by the Prince of
Wales, but so great had been the extravagance of the lady that
even the heir-apparent grew alarmed and was much relieved
when his friend Fox undertook the expense of the establishment.   Such, at least, was the Prince's story, but there were
those who whispered that *not* economy but a new passion
swayed the young man's affections.

[1] *Courts and Cabinets.* Buckingham.
[2] *The Life and Letters of Lady Sarah Lennox.*

Some said that Lady Melbourne had supplanted the actress, and others that it was Georgiana who filled her place. The Duchess was now seen more and more at the gambling-table and but rarely in the houses of her mother's serious friends. Old Mrs. Montagu in her new house in Portman Square, where she remarked " that she could see nothing belonging to her that was not pretty, save when she beheld herself in the glass " [1] and where, dressed in a frock on which were embroidered the ruins of Palmyra, she moved from one group of guests to another, " making mathematicians quote Pindar, persuading Masters in Chancery to write novels, and Birmingham men to stamp rhymes as fast as buttons," [2] often waited in vain for her footman to announce the eagerly expected guest. Not that Georgiana was unkind to her old acquaintances. She would still sometimes find a moment to come and admire the great room whose walls were being covered with feathers, or to listen to the accounts of Mr. " Capability " Brown's efforts to convert Mrs. Montagu's country estate at Sandleford into " a lovely pastoral and sweet Arcadian scene " ; but she had no time for this newfangled fashion of tea-drinking, brought to England from France by the Duke of Dorset.

In France where people dined early it had its uses, but here where one was compelled to eat again within two hours of a heavy meal it was absurd. She advanced her own dinner-hour by two hours and thereby finally ostracised the custom.

As the summer wore on, and as all the political excitements abated, the Duchess took herself off to Bath, followed by a numerous train of admirers. In the watering town she could be as gay as she was in London, but in all places one thing irked her. As yet she had borne no children. She had been married eight years and had reached the age of twenty-five. She was devoted to children and her husband's daughter, nicknamed Louchee, was a constant source of amusement to her.

Louchee presented a problem. Georgiana had no prejudice with regard to her husband's illegitimate progeny, and she felt very strongly that the child should be given a fair start in life and placed in some position midway between the situation of her respective parents. The Duke, though apathetic, still

---

[1] *A Lady of the Last Century.*　　　　[2] Cumberland.

felt in a certain degree his responsibility. From his great wealth he was very willing to lay out £400 or £500 a year for the child's education and establishment. But who was to undertake the task ? The money he did not grudge, but he had no time to give to the matter. Since Georgiana was kind enough to be interested in Louchee could she not suggest some lady suitable as a chaperone or governess ? The Duchess thought a moment, and then mentioned the name of Lady Elizabeth Foster. The hesitation had been deliberate, for from the first moment that Louchee's education had been in question Georgiana had desired the post for Lady Elizabeth.

Since they had been at Bath she had seen quite a lot of Lady Elizabeth and of her sister Lady Erne. She had been moved by the younger sister's romantic history. She knew of her financial difficulties and she had heard that her straitened circumstances were about to compel her to take up residence with her aunt, Lady Mary Fitzgerald, who lived in a Methodist community. The idea of Lady Elizabeth being forced into close proximity, even dependence, upon the members of Lady Huntingdon's connexion appealed both to Georgiana's pity and to her sense of humour. And she had forthwith determined to come to her rescue should any opportunity present itself.

The Duke made no answer, and Georgiana, fearing that he might be questioning the wisdom of confiding any young lady to a member of the Hervey family, went on to say that " Bess was a poor little soul and the quietest thing in the world." What picture presented itself to the Duke's mind as he sat there considering the question ? What associations did the name of Elizabeth Hervey bring in its train ? Herveys were not quite like anyone else. Had it not been said " That in England there are men, women and Herveys " ?

And certainly Lady Elizabeth's father was unique and impossible of classification. Descended from Pope's " Lord Fanny " and the famous Molly Lepel, Frederick Hervey had discovered whilst still at the University " that his parts were too lively for the Law " (to which he was destined), and had, somewhat surprisingly, chosen to enter the Church instead. Already in those early days his love of pictures and of works of art was manifesting itself by a series of boyish letters to his grandfather, Lord Bristol, imploring him to buy in a pseudo

Van Dyck which was said to represent a member of the Hervey family, and which had recently come into the market. Whilst still quite young he had made a love match with the daughter of Sir Jermyn Davers—a marriage displeasing to his family owing to the fact that Lady Davers had been somewhat dilatory on the subject of marriage, so that although Mary was certainly well on the safe side of the register, a large, but ill-defined, number of her brothers and sisters were *not*. Time, however, and the birth of two sons and three daughters had softened the Herveys' resentment, and by his eldest brother's interest Frederick had received the Bishopric of Cloyne.

Despite his apparent irresponsibility the young man took his pastoral duties seriously . . . in the debt of privilege for his own advancement he saw to it that none but Irishmen of irreproachable credentials were given preferment in his diocese. He cared for the material wants of his parishioners, and being something of an engineer, he ordered the draining of bogs, the building of roads and bridges with enthusiasm. Yet his duties did not subdue his freakish vein.

One day, as he was engaged in a jumping contest with his curates, a messenger brought him a note. He read it, and then turned to his companions remarking, " I will jump with you no more. I have beaten you all, for I have jumped from Cloyne to Derry." Shortly afterwards, taking himself off to the richer diocese, he began anew his plans for the material improvement of the country. Another matter which he had much at heart was the amelioration of the conditions under which the Roman Catholic clergy were then living.

He offered money for the building of shelters where Mass could be said and he struggled to get Parliament to consider the formulation of an oath of loyalty to the King which should eliminate the supremacy clause and thereby become acceptable to Catholics.

Yet for all these grave matters, the Bishop could instruct the fattest of his curates to race for the fattest of his livings . . . and lest the reader should be appalled at this method of selection, it must be added that since the race was run over quicksands, no competitor reached the goal.

In another light-hearted mood the Bishop begged the neighbouring parishes to build spires to their churches " that his view might be improved." He had a passion for bricks and mortar and his palace at Downderry became a palace indeed.

Ultimately, bored with the restricted life of an Irish bishopric, Frederick Hervey began to make incursions on to the Continent, supposedly for the purpose of educating his children and furnishing his house. These journeys were a misery to his wife and daughters. Poor, plaintive Mrs. Hervey, who complained in speaking of the Alps " that the weakness of my frame does not support objects of terror," was of a very different mettle from her husband to whom a riot, a scandal, or merely an eruption of Vesuvius was an irresistible temptation to hurry to the scene of action.

On his return from one of these expeditions his reverence had succeeded to his brother in the Earldom of Bristol, the possession of Ickworth and of a vast fortune that went with the title.

Soon afterwards he had married his two elder daughters : Mary to Lord Erne, and Elizabeth to an Irish squire, Mr. Foster. On his return from his next voyage, he had been exceedingly displeased to find both marriages going badly. Mary and her little daughter had left Lord Erne, and Elizabeth, who had one son, and who was about to have another child, was determined to leave Mr. Foster.

Public opinion was on the side of the ladies, but the Bishop was adamant. Mary came to an amicable arrangement with her husband, and secured a little estate and enough to live on, but Elizabeth had no provision made for her and her father did not seem in the least inclined to supply the deficiency.

Lady Bristol, who pleaded her cause, met with no success. " If Bess had not enough to live on, she must go back to her husband, and a very good thing too."

Lord Bristol's sister, the methodistical Lady Mary Fitzgerald, was kinder—hence the impending arrangement of residence within the precincts of Lady Huntingdon's connexion, from which the Duchess of Devonshire desired to rescue her friend.

Such then was the general outline of the associations which the name of Elizabeth Hervey brought to the mind of the Duke of Devonshire when Georgiana suggested her as companion to Louchee. He assented. "Lady Elizabeth would do exactly for the part," he could think of no better person. He had met her and thought her pretty and intelligent. Georgiana should make the arrangements forthwith for securing her services.

The Duchess was overjoyed. It was not often that the Duke entered so wholeheartedly into her plans, nor was it often that he would unbend and become as human and gracious as he now became in the company of Lady Elizabeth. When they moved back to London, " Bess " (for there were already too many Elizabeths in the set) came with them to Devonshire House in order to make the acquaintance of her charge and to prepare for the great trip abroad which was to start with a stay at Nice and end in a journey to Naples.

But hardly was she installed amongst her kind friends when a fresh misfortune befell the Hervey family. Really, it seemed as though matrimonial quarrels were epidemic. The latest victims of the contagion were none other than Bess's parents. The whole affair was wrapt in mystery : one day the Bishop and his wife had gone out driving together. During that drive something was said between them—something passed between them—and they came home and never spoke to each other again. Very shortly afterwards the Bishop left Ickworth for Derry and, as it proved, he was never to see his wife again. No one knew the cause of the quarrel, the Bishop never alluded to the incident, and Lady Bristol's allusions were of a cryptic nature.

So now they were all separated from their husbands, the mother and the two daughters. The Spencers were shocked, Georgiana distressed, Bess curious. From her mother she received querulous comments of the Bishop's curious behaviour. " I have great account from time to time of his great spirits and happiness in everything that is going on in Ireland, and he seems quite unconcerned at having placed me here without a plan, view, object or improvement of any sort to occupy a mind so harassed." This was bitter, but it was coupled to another statement. " I now am only intent on drawing all the good possible out of this evil in favour of Louisa " (the youngest child) . . . " and to acquire in solid advantages to her mind and character what she loses in accomplishments."

57

If we have gone in some detail into an account of the Hervey family, it is because from the year 1782 onwards Lady Elizabeth was· to be continuously associated with Georgiana and with the Devonshire House set, until, and even after, its creator should be dead. And when she made a friend, the Duchess extended her affectionate interest to every family concern and connexion of that person, so that in the person of Bess, the Herveys became permanently identified with Devonshire House.

Gay messages came to her from the errant prelate, sad letters from his wife. Mary Erne's affairs formed a matter for her anxious concern ; but a quotation from one of the Bishop's letters to his favourite daughter reassured her. " I am *au désespoir* about your health. What can I do to relieve it ? Surely you want a carriage ? Draw on me for the amount of it, £100 a year will easily keep it. . . . You will want, too, for the little elegancies of life which render it cheerful, even if you go abroad . . . don't stint yourself, but if £100 is not enough, I can bleed more freely." [1]

The charm which caused Lord Bristol to ·be forgiven many aberrations is always evident in his correspondence.

So the year which was to have seen the triumph and establishment of the political creed of Charles Fox ended, not with the apotheosis of Devonshire House politics, but with the addition to their social circle of a personage who was to prove an important acquisition.

[1] *The Life of the Earl Bishop of Derry.*

1783

IN the first month of 1783 Shelburne began to realise
that the very existence of Fox made government almost
impossible. Uncomfortable as he was as a colleague, in
opposition he was more to be dreaded ; and, in this instance,
the hated " Malagrida " (Shelburne's nickname amongst the
Foxites) gave proof of a lack of resentment which went far to
contradict his evil reputation. He sent Pitt to Fox with an
invitation to join the Government. Better advised, Fox
would have consented to serve the interests of his country,
regardless of personal ambition, but the chorus of his admirers proved a fatal incentive to believe himself alone capable
of forming an administration.

Sheridan and Fitzpatrick and all the ladies of Devonshire
House urged him to hold aloof, assuring him that by this
action he would himself be called upon to succeed Lord Shelburne. So that when Billy Pitt came on his errand he was
met with the cynical enquiry : " Is it intended that Lord
Shelburne should remain first Lord of the Treasury ? " Pitt
replied with hauteur that he had come as Lord Shelburne's
emissary, and that his loyalty to his chief was unquestionable.
Fox bowed, and signified that in that case the interview was at
an end. Once again Fox had bluffed, and once again it had
not come off.

As the weeks wore on it became evident that though the
present government might be embarrassed, no one would
contemplate calling on Fox when it should fall. With the
public, his few months of office the previous year had destroyed
all his popularity ; to the King he was anathema ; and all the
admiration of his devoted friends would not compensate him
for his fall. He began to look about for an ally, and his fancy
lit upon the most improbable person—no other than Lord
North, whom he had abused so consistently ever since he had

entered Parliament. Did the late Prime Minister, escaped from the King's clutches, after so many years of painful servitude, feel a grim delight in allying himself to his old master's worst enemy ? Did he feel that he could now accomplish a long-delayed vengeance ? Devonshire House, which had been so proud of Fox's independent attitude a month earlier, were now busily engaged in justifying the new coalition. And such was Charles's charm and plausibility that all of them, the Prince, and Sheridan, Fitzpatrick, Georgiana and Lady Melbourne, no collection of fools, ended by convincing themselves that in entering this queer quadrille their idol was actuated by the most noble motives. With North to give him countenance and to add the prestige of disinterestedness to the attack, Fox proceeded to bludgeon the Ministry on the subject of the peace with America.

By the month of March chaos reigned supreme. Lord Shelburne felt unable to continue in office, and the King unable to part with him. But George III was not to find another North in his present Prime Minister. Lord Shelburne was obdurate. He could not carry on the Government. The seat of the First Lord of the Treasury went a-begging. The Monarch offered it to any of his statesmen, save the two who were determined to obtain it. He even offered it to young Pitt, now twenty-three ; but the perspicacious boy refused the honour. Everyone felt that before any stable government could take charge, the ridiculous North-Fox combination must be allowed to come to grief, openly and without extenuation. After a failure of such magnitude as theirs was likely to be, their successors would be able to govern without interference.

This calculating plan was at last unfolded to the King by the agency of Lord Temple. Meanwhile Devonshire House waited events in trepidation. To some it meant political advancement, to most the justification of their hero, to the Prince of Wales it meant a personal gain, for Fox had pledged himself to obtain £100,000 a year for the heir-apparent if he should be in office when the young man came of age. The Prince was, for a number of reasons, more and more deeply involved in the Whig connexion. "The Prince of Wales is desperately in love with Lady Melbourne," wrote Lady C.

Napier, " and when she don't sit next to him at supper he is not commonly civil to his neighbours."

The other great event of the circle was that the Duchess was expecting a child. She was in the tenth year of her marriage and her excitement knew no bounds. " The Duchess of Devonshire is taken up with nothing so much as the prospect of nursing her child herself, which she talks of with so much eagerness as if her whole happiness depended upon succeeding." [1] The prospect was the more gratifying because Harriet was also " expecting." When the child was born it proved to be a girl and was christened Georgiana.

By the month of April the King's resistance had been worn down, and he sent sulkily for the Duke of Portland, the puppet of Fox and North. George III made no attempt to swallow his medicine with a good grace ; and stated freely that " A Ministry which I have avowedly attempted to avoid by calling on every description of men cannot be supposed to have either my favour or confidence, and as such I shall most certainly refuse any honours they may ask for. I trust the eyes of the nation will soon be opened, as my sorrow may prove fatal to my health if I remain long in this thraldom." [2] For once in his life the King had the country behind him. The masses who had once trusted Fox now held him in execration, considering his alliance with North nothing short of treason. The Tories who had supported North could no longer believe in him when they saw him coupled with " the Man of the People." The Shelburne party held that the Whig cause had been " let down " by the personal ambition of a few young men ; and the Duke of Portland had no supporters at all. It was an unpromising birth.

However, Fox and North were temperamentally well fitted to act together as Secretaries of State, and Sheridan and Fitzpatrick were able assistants. Only Burke became a problem. " Too fond of the right to pursue the expedient " he was again omitted from the Cabinet. It was another flagrant piece of injustice.

In June the Prince of Wales came of age, and that unfortu-

[1] Letter of Lady Bristol quoted in *The Life of the Earl Bishop of Derry*.
[2] *Courts and Cabinets*. Buckingham.

nate promise of £100,000 needed to be redeemed. The King, whose hatred of his eldest son was now verging on mania, fought the grant tooth and nail, and considered the very mention of it another evidence that the Prince was trying to wrest the Government from his father's hands through the medium of Fox. The motion was also badly received in the Commons, and in the end Charles was obliged to go to the Prince and beg to be forgiven his failure.

In July Harriet's child was born, a second son. In October Lord Spencer died. His loss was deeply felt by his children. They had always been a devoted family. Georgiana and Harriet suffered, besides their father's death, the estrangement of their only brother. With the slick, fickle Lavinia reigning at Spencer House and Althorp, life would have lost some of its charm. But old Lady Spencer did not see through her daughter-in-law's ingratiating façade ; and, perhaps, that was a mercy. Their period of mourning coincided, we read, with the fashion for back ribbons . . . one lady was told " to sew some black fancy ribbon upon every ribbon and gown you have of whatever colour, and say it is à la Malbrook. . . . The reason ? Why, the Dauphin's nurse sang a Flemish song of the death of the D. of M., and in it, his page announces it to ye Duchess *tout en noir*." But Georgiana and Harriet wore their black for the great Duke's *grandson*. (The Duchess and Lady Duncannon were great-grandchildren of Marlborough.)

Lady Bristol mentions Georgiana in a letter to Bess who was still abroad. The Duchess " is comforting her poor mother at St. Albans, and I am happy to find so well recovered herself as to be able to go on with her nursing, and to succeed extremely in it." With Lady Bristol's arrival came news of the travellers ; news, however, which had to be severely censored before it was fit for the ears of the Duchess. In reality Lady Bristol was very anxious for two causes. The first was that Louchee was not proving a pleasant companion. In the letters between mother and daughter such comments as " I shall be happy to hear that Louchee improves upon you, for a disagreeable object so repeatedly present is horrid . . . I hope Miss W. will answer to all your care and their hopes, and then it will be a pleasant circumstance between you, but I am sorry she requires strictness . . ." and finally, " What a good thing it would be if Louchee were to draw a veil over her ugly face," were of ill augury ; and in the second place, Lady Bristol was anxious about the levity of her daughter's conduct. Cryptic allusions to the necessity for more circumspection and greater decorum bestrew Lady Bristol's epistles : but to the Duchess, she simply stated that Louchee and her governess were delighting in their visit to Nice and contemplating a further voyage to Naples.

Meanwhile Georgiana helped to console Lady Bristol for the loss of her husband, whose activities in his diocese were beginning to assume a character which seemed likely to embarrass the Government.

Ireland had from the beginning proved a thorn in the side of the Ministry. Apparently no one was willing to go there in the capacity of Viceroy. Althorp had been pressed, and even the Duke of Devonshire, and other Whig nobles ; but eventually no one better than the weak Lord Northington could be prevailed upon to cross the Irish sea. During the war with France, Ireland had been a heel of Achilles to England. It had seemed certain that the French would land troops on the southern coast ; and then what would their reception prove to be ? Would the country rise in favour of their co-religionists and the Stuart cause, albeit that cause was to be led by foreigners, or would the peasants remain loyal to that other foreigner, the King of England and Hanover, who proscribed their religion ? On the face of it, there had seemed good reason to suppose that the Irish would take part against the English ; yet those who knew most about the situation did not consider such a culmination inevitable. Lord Charlemont, a patriotic bigot with weak nerves, determined to unite the Irish loyalists into a corps of volunteers, who should be ready to resist the French ; and the Bishop of Derry, returning to his diocese in 1782, when the danger of an invasion was nearly over, saw, in the existence of the volunteer corps, a means of obtaining Catholic emancipation for the country. He took a prominent part in the movement ; and in November 1783 he called a great convocation at Dublin to demand justice for the Irish people With Fox in office the plea should not fall on deaf ears.

Strange rumours filtered into Devonshire House. The Bishop had arrived in Dublin wearing episcopal purple, white gloves (with gold fringes round the wrist, and golden tassels dangling from them), diamond buckles on his knees and shoes ; he had been drawn through the streets in an open landau by six horses caparisoned with purple ribbons. On either side of the carriage had ridden his own servants in " gorgeous liveries " ; and in front his nephew, Fitzgerald, at the head of a squadron of dragoons in gold and scarlet. A similar squadron had closed the rear of the procession. Trumpets, it was said, had heralded his approach and cries of " Long live the Bishop," had resounded. Some said he had marched thus up to the Houses of Parliament where his trumpets had blown a warning blast.

It was rumoured that he intended to start a revolution. It was whispered that he had gone over to Rome and would be made a Cardinal, or alternatively, that he expected to become Viceroy. Poor Lady Bristol poured out her woes to Georgiana. Her husband was really impossible ; he was lodged with his nephew, " Fighting Fitzgerald," son to the methodistical Lady Mary, but what a son ! A young man who had abducted his youngest brother, who was reputed to have shut his father up in a cave with a muzzled bear. The Duchess did what she could to quiet the incensed lady. She herself was only anxious for the trouble which might be brought on the Government by the unruly prelate. But at least he had not been chosen President of the Assembly, despite all his display. Lord Charlemont was safely installed in the chair, and whilst he sat there, and whilst Lady Charlemont wrote that, " If they [the Roman Catholics] were all Deists and Atheists (like my old friends the French) our lives and properties had been safe ; but with the Catechism of this dreadful school nothing is sacred but Rome," no revolutionary measure of reform need be feared.

Meanwhile everyone concerned was having an unpleasant time, and the Duchess congratulated herself on her husband's refusal of the Viceroyalty. Poor Lord Northington wrote piteous letters complaining of a " bustled head " and begging to be recalled, whilst the Bishop played havoc with Lord Charlemont's nerves. He would visit the anxious nobleman daily and, rubbing his hands, declare " Things are going well, my Lord ; we shall have blood, my Lord, we shall have blood," till the unhappy Chairman was ready to accuse his tormentor of high treason. But in the end it all came to nothing ; opposition, procrastination and apathy defeated the Bishop's enthusiasm. Charlemont dissolved the Assembly, and Lord Bristol took his way back to his diocese, accompanied by his glittering bodyguard and shadowed by two spies set on him by the British Government at the instance of his late colleagues.

The death-blow to the Whig Ministry was to come from another quarter, and Fox was to fall in a nobler cause than the oppression of Ireland. For some time Burke had been concerned with an examination of the affairs of the East India Company. His labours led him to make two discoveries : that the Company, in many instances, abused the natives shamefully ; and that the Government of a great country ought not to be entrusted to a private company. The scheme of Reform which he proposed to Fox consisted in the transference of the administrative powers from the private company to a set of commissioners appointed by Parliament. On the face of it, it did not seem a bad plan, but it had had to encounter bitter opposition from two quarters : from the vast numbers of people who enjoyed or purveyed, the patronage of the British East India Company, and from the King, who was determined that if the Company did come to an end the Crown should be the residuary legatee of its powerful interests. The Bill was opposed from its initiation, but when the names of the proposed commissioners were published and were seen to represent, with one exception, devotees of Fox and North, then the storm burst. The King went so far as to threaten any of the Lords who should vote in favour of the measure with his personal wrath.

The Government were defeated by a small vote, and George III immediately dismissed the Duke of Portland. Early the next morning he sent a messenger to collect the seals of office from Fox and North. He added a message to the effect that he did not wish to behold his late Secretaries of State, and begged that they would not render up the seals in person. The Foxite defeat was overwhelming, but when Devonshire House learnt that Master Pitt had been named First Lord of the

Treasury they failed to measure the full extent of the disaster. They were contemptuous of his youth and inexperience. When they saw that he had refused a cabinet seat to Lord Shelburne they felt reassured. Of the great Whigs, only the Duke of Richmond supported him. Surely it was not possible under these circumstances that he should prove a formidable adversary? Little did they realise that Fox had begun a sojourn in the desert of opposition which should last for twenty-three years.

But in the hour of defeat Fox seemed always to gather new friends, and this time he was to make a connexion which was to last him his life.

Mrs. Armistead,[1] in a period of courtesans, held the palm amongst such ladies. She was beautiful, she was intelligent, she was discreet, she had quiet and cultivated tastes, she appeared to possess a considerable fortune, her influence upon her admirers was said to be beneficent. In the moment of his failure she took charge of Fox. She carried him away from Brooks's to a small country estate at St. Anne's Hill, where the pleasure of introducing her to Homer compensated him for the absence of the Pharo table and the reduction in the number of his bottles of port.

The ladies of Devonshire House looked on a little askance at the liaison. They had been able to ignore his previous *affaires*, but when Mrs. Armistead removed their idol from London it was impossible to forget her existence. However, they had known other members of their circle to sit at that amiable lady's feet, the Prince of Wales included, and each had subsequently returned to the fellowship. But with Fox the case wore a slightly different aspect. He seemed at this moment to desire domesticity and not passion and, curiously enough, Mrs. Armistead seemed to be capable of giving him what he needed. Deprived of Fox's company the Duchess gambled even more recklessly. Horace Walpole wrote sententiously that her passion for gaming was so great that he feared she would soon forget about her good resolution with regard to nursing her child, " and stuff the poor babe into a knotting bag " whilst she continued her game.

[1] Elizabeth Bridget Cane, said to have been waiting woman to Frances Abington, the actress.

1784

THE early weeks of Pitt's Ministry were hampered by Fox to the greatest extent that lay in his power. As he himself said, there was no Bill that Pitt could bring in which he would support. In certain instances this attitude necessarily made him appear in a very unattractive light. When his own India Bill was brought forward, shorn only of the regulations which transferred the patronage from the Company to the Government, Fox opposed it. The action won him no laurels.

From Pitt's point of view Fox's behaviour was all that could be desired, and when he realised that his adversary was afraid of a dissolution, afraid to go to the country, the Prime Minister felt reassured. If Fox were afraid, then *he* had no cause to fear, and when matters became complicated he could always play the trump card of a General Election.

Meanwhile, London began to fill up for the season, and Devonshire House saw a new guest who was to play an important part in its history, in the person of Mrs. Fitzherbert. The lady was twenty-seven, she was the grand-daughter of a certain baronet, Sir John Smythe, who belonged to an old Roman Catholic family of Jacobite sympathies. Her father, a younger son, had been obliged to take service in the Army of the Empire, being unable to find any employment in England. Maria had been educated at the convent of the " Blew Nuns " in Paris, together with her contemporary Petres, Stourtons, Howards and Jerninghams. On her return to England she had married, at the age of eighteen, Mr. Weld of Lulworth Castle, who was twenty-six years her senior. He had died within a year ; and, after three years of widowhood, Maria had married Thomas Fitzherbert. During the night of the Gordon Riots Fitzherbert had taken a leading part in rescuing Catholic priests from the violence of the mob, a chill had been the result, then he had developed pneumonia which had turned to a pulmonary complaint, and within the year he had died at Nice.

So now, for the second time, Maria was a widow; but this time she was a widow with a respectable fortune and a nice house in Mayfair: perhaps it was Lady Jerningham who first introduced Mrs. Fitzherbert to the circle at Devonshire House; but early in the year she was an *habituée*, and it soon became apparent that her remarkable looks had made an impression upon the susceptible heart of the Prince of Wales, who had met her for the first time at the Opera. He saw less of the Duchess, he quitted Devonshire House for the Duchess of Gordon's, Lady Salisbury's, or Lady Cowper's, if Mrs. Fitzherbert were to be present at these ladies' assemblies. But he received no encouragement; perhaps this novelty added to his interest. Mrs. Fitzherbert, after two marriages, was enjoying her liberty.

She was a good woman of high principles, and the last thing she contemplated was an *affaire* with the heir-apparent. In March something happened which took all attention from private concerns and focussed it once more upon politics. On the 25th of the month Pitt dissolved Parliament. The feverish work of a General Election began. After some weeks of routine excitement Devonshire House began to realise that all was not well with the Foxite party. It looked as though in the country Whigs would support Pitt to a man. Charles himself was standing for Westminster; against him were Admiral Hood (who was certain to be elected) and Sir Cecil Wray. Both these gentlemen were upholders of the Government. By the end of the month of April Fox's full count was behind Wray's, and it looked as though he would fail to retain his seat.

That Fox should fail to be returned for Westminster was known to be Pitt's dearest wish. To Devonshire House it was unthinkable. The devoted band of Fox's admirers consulted together as to how they could save him. It was Georgiana and Harriet who conceived the daring plan. Westminster covered a large area, the people in the outlying villages and suburbs had not yet voted. Polling was no easy matter to them. They had difficulty in getting up to the polling-booths in Covent Garden. The Spencer sisters determined that they would fetch them : Fox should supply a list of voters, and then the two women would call at each house and entreating votes would carry the labourers in their carriage to the polling-both and back. Female canvassing and free transport were unheard-of innovations. Fox was overjoyed. Devonshire and Bessborough looked a little askance at the enthusiasm of their wives, but, eventually, they gave their consent to this unconventional manner of assisting a good cause.

Georgiana was the leading spirit—she had energy and determination enough to encompass any labour. And first she thought out costumes suitable for herself and her sister. They should wear blue and buff (the colours of Washington's regiments), and their hats should be decorated with fox-brushes. Every morning the carriage came round at an early hour and did not return till evening. On no single day did she remit her labours. The life of Devonshire House was turned upside down, no more lying in bed until four in the afternoon, no more hysteric fits of a morning. Astonished labourers, sweeps and mechanics were torn from their work by the intrepid ladies and rushed up to the hustings. Georgiana's enthusiasm knew few limits : prayer, entreaties, kisses, all were employed in the service of Charles Fox. Her charm met with few rebuffs.

" If I were God, I'd make her Queen of Heaven," remarked an Irish peasant. " Her eyes were so bright they could light my pipe," said a navvy. Pitt might mock at the episode and say that " Westminster goes on well, in spite of the Duchess of Devonshire, and the other women of the people." He knew that the statement was a lie and that Fox was gaining votes daily. Had he not been told that even Horace Walpole, whose age and infirmities had precluded his leaving his house for many months, " had submitted to being carried in his chair from his house in Berkeley Square to the hustings at Covent Garden." [1] From contempt Pitt passed to imitation. He impressed Lady Salisbury into the defence of his candidates, but Lady Salisbury was no rival to Georgiana. She appeared by comparison old and proud. The Duchess sought to touch the hearts of the poor, and they caught fire from her own

[1] Wraxall's *Memoirs.*

blazing enthusiasm. The Countess only unbent sufficiently to advise and instruct. " The one was unconscious of her rank, the other was conscious of it . . . and sought to compel others to recollect it." There was no question as to who would succeed best in the affray.

At last came the day of the declaration of the poll. The results were Hood, 6,694, Fox 6,234, Wray 5,998. Fox had secured the second seat. A triumphal procession was formed. In front came a horseman with a banner inscribed " Sacred to Female Patriotism," then followed Fox's coach wreathed in laurel, decorated with the Prince of Wales's feathers, on the box sat George North and Adams (the duellist), behind followed the Duchess of Devonshire's carriage and that of the Duchess of Portland, each drawn by six pairs of horses. Harriet Duncannon sat by her sister. The rear of the procession was made up of a vast crowd of Fox's supporters. Slowly the procession moved from Covent Garden to Devonshire House, where the Prince of Wales waited on a platform to receive his friends. Speeches were made and then the party went into the house, to be called upon again to appear on the balcony

Fox, the Prince of Wales, Devonshire, Portland, Fitzpatrick, Sheridan, Georgiana, Harriet, the Duchess of Portland, Mrs. Crewe—the Foxite family united and victorious. 1782 had been the moment of their apotheosis as a party, 1784 was the moment of their personal triumph. The crowd were delighted and went off to break the windows of Lord Temple's house. That evening Mrs. Crewe, of whom (in 1791, when she had a son of twenty-one) Miss Burney would write that she was so beautiful " that she uglified everyone near her," gave a dinner-party at her house in Lower Grosvenor Street. Not only the ladies, but also the men, wore blue and buff. " True blue and Mrs. Crewe," toasted the Prince. " Buff and blue and all of you," replied his hostess. The Whigs were in a merry mood.

The next day the celebrations continued. When the King passed Carlton House on his way to open Parliament he heard the jovial laughter of a gay assembly and, looking through the colonnade, he beheld his son and his son's friends, apparently garbed in Washington's uniform, themselves serving

*Frances Greville, wife of John Crewe,
afterwards Lord Crewe*

an elegant collation to their female guests, who naturally included the ladies of Devonshire House. The Monarch felt that provocation could go no further. He and his Prime Minister were equally angry. In his rage Pitt gave his consent to a mean trick. Wray had demanded a scrutiny of votes, and he was granted his request. The impossible labour began. It cost the country several thousand pounds, and all the while Fox was attending Parliament as the representative of the Shetland Isles (his second seat). Finally it proved impossible of accomplishment, the matter was dropped, and Fox got his rights.

The King was in a bad temper and complained " that Devonshire House in Piccadilly seemed to look down on the Queen's house across Green Park." But though he might grumble, he had cause also for satisfaction. Fox's party had lost 160 seats in the election, and Pitt was safely in the saddle and destined to remain there for many years.

The summer saw the return of Lady Elizabeth Foster. She returned alone. Louchee, if she had not drawn a veil over her face, had at least had the admirable tact to agree to be deposited in Naples to finish her education under the patronage of the Queen of Naples, with a promise that she should later join her household.[1] The Devonshires were delighted with the arrangement, and Georgiana begged Lady Elizabeth to make her home with them until her affairs should be settled. The Duke enjoyed her company, and Georgiana wanted him to be kept amused. She was herself in difficulties. To the Jews she owed about £20,000 and, generous as well as extravagant, she could not bear to forgo the pleasure of helping her mother and Harriet, both of whom were pressed for money and, ignorant of Georgiana's troubles, believed her wealth to be limitless.

Bess brought strange tales of her father. It was said that the Viceroy had demanded the Bishop's arrest, and that the King was in favour of it, and that only Pitt stood between Lord Bristol and the charge of High Treason.

Lord Charlemont was still busy endeavouring to weaken the volunteer movement by antagonising Protestants and Catholics, and the Bishop was denouncing him in round

---

[1] This is an assumption, see *The Two Duchesses*.

71

terms. It was all very worrying, and even " the mild wonder of the new shell-work grottoes " which Georgiana and her friends were constructing in their pleasure-grounds failed to distract Lady Elizabeth. Her situation was very painful. Her mother was desolate and complaining at Ickworth ; her sister was equally desolate and equally complaining at Christchurch ; her father seemed to be exuberantly approaching a scaffold ; her husband was going from bad to worse ; and the husband of her best friend, to whom she owed everything, was rapidly falling in love with her. Much as she enjoyed exercises of mental agility, this situation seemed almost too involved for solution.

Meanwhile another situation strewn with an equal share of difficulties had been developing to crisis pitch. The Prince of Wales's passion for Mrs. Fitzherbert had grown to dangerous violence. Mrs. Fitzherbert had kept her own counsel, but the heir-apparent went about bemoaning his fate. He swore that he was ready to marry her, ready to give up the Crown, ready to fly with her to America ; but still she remained obdurate. He had never met with treatment of the kind, and he was at a loss to know how to cope with it.

One November morning loud rapping at the door of Maria's house in Park Street heralded anxious visitors ; a few moments later Mrs. Fitzherbert's servant announced Lord Southampton, Lord Onslow, Mr. Edward Bouverie and Mr. Keith, the Prince's physician. The gentlemen appeared pale and agitated. They announced that the Prince had endeavoured to take his own life, that he had fallen upon his sword, that he was severely wounded, that nothing but Mrs. Fitzherbert's presence could ensure his recovery. The poor lady was much alarmed, she had not been adored for six months by so charming a young man without conceiving some affection for him. She was sincerely concerned to hear of his condition ; she was horrified at the cause, and she dreaded the scandal. But she had not the impulsive rashness of her friend the Duchess ; the situation was extremely serious, she was a well-known and respected Catholic at a time when Catholic claims were for the first time receiving sympathetic hearing in some quarters. She must do nothing which could be turned against her co-religionists. Cause for scandal she knew she would not give, but an appearance of scandal could also do much harm and must be avoided.

After a few moments' reflection she replied to her visitors that she would pay a visit to Carlton House on one condition only, that she should be accompanied by the Duchess of Devonshire. The chaperone was well chosen, for besides being far the most important lady in London, Georgiana, who had been the object of the Prince's avowed attentions for several years, was not likely to be considered privy to any of his amours. The deputation were thankful to receive a favourable answer and were glad enough to accept any conditions. Mrs. Fitzherbert's carriage was called and she drove to Devonshire House. Georgiana was fortunately at home. She entered sympathetically into the scheme, and half an hour later the two friends drove on together to Carlton House.

The Duchess knew the magnificent building well. She had helped the Prince to furnish it, and he had taken her advice on many points of decoration. To Mrs. Fitzherbert it was a new and exciting experience, but all pleasure was marred by the knowledge of what lay before her. How much might depend upon the interview which was to take place : his happiness, her reputation, their country, their religions, all were involved. Yet, when she saw the Prince, all the difficulties departed, for she had to deal not with a man in distress, but with a boy in hysterics. No reasonable conversation was possible. The Prince lost his self-control, he was rolling about apparently in an agony, besprinkled with blood, hitting his head against the wall, foaming at the mouth. If this frenzy had been assumed in the beginning, it was now quite evidently genuine.

No question of ethics arose, but a medical question : how to restore the patient to his right mind. The Prince repeated over and over again that if he could not marry Mrs. Fitzherbert he should kill himself. He must marry her, immediately, here and now. The two ladies tried to soothe and divert him, but their efforts only brought on fresh paroxysms of despair. The physician looked significantly at Mrs. Fitzherbert. At length she understood that he really feared for the Prince's life. Then she turned to the Duchess of Devonshire and asked her to lend them a ring. At the mention of this word the patient seemed to recover a part of his wits. He took the ring and solemnly presented it to Mrs. Fitzherbert as a symbol of his determination to marry her, and Maria accepted it. When this ceremony was over, the Prince allowed the ladies to retire.

They drove away thoughtfully, the Duchess amused to think that in Scotland the betrothal would count as a legal marriage, Mrs. Fitzherbert reassuring herself by reflecting that a " lie is an untruth told to deceive a rational person." The Prince had not been rational—had she not acceded to his request he might have taken his life—and of course the rite had no legal significance, no canonical significance. Yet the more she thought over the scene the less she liked it. When she got back to her own house she ordered her servants to pack up her trunks and in the early hours of the morning she was on her way to Dover. No one should say that she had helped to embroil the succession to the Crown in a controversial issue, no one should say that she had ruined the heir-apparent. When the Prince received her note of farewell he was overwhelmed with rage and despair. In his distress he rushed to Fox, who was mightily relieved at the outcome of the affair, but who had too kind a heart not to respond to such genuine grief.

1785

THE beginning of the new year gave no evidence of a cooling of the Prince's emotions or, consequently, of any possibility of Mrs. Fitzherbert's return. " Prinny " was distracted. He petitioned his father for permission to leave the country. He declared to his friends that his financial concerns were in so bad a condition that retrenchment and life abroad had become a necessity. His pleas fell upon deaf ears. The King and Queen naturally approved Mrs. Fitzherbert's conduct, and even Fox and Sheridan, though they outwardly professed to sympathise with their friend, were inwardly delighted that he should have been saved from a very serious complication.

When male support was lacking the Prince turned to Georgiana. She at least, who had seen him on the day on which he had stabbed himself at Carlton House, must recognise the depth of his feelings. Day after day he came to pour out his woes at Devonshire House. Georgiana and her sister were seen about less this year, for both were " expecting." As the spring advanced the Duchess went to stay with her brother at Wimbledon ; but even here the Prince pursued her. Probably it was Lavinia who first commented on these visits, for she never seems to have lost any occasion of mischief-making. At all events, we are told of the Duchess that His Royal Highness's visits to Wimbledon were so frequent " as to give umbrage to her brother, Lord Spencer, and even it was supposed, to excite some emotion in the phlegmatic bosom of the Duke, her husband." Later Georgiana was to give her husband good cause for jealousy, but in this instance the charge was unfounded ; and if there was cause of complaint it was rather in the Duke's avowed admiration of Lady Elizabeth Foster. But the Duchess was not open to any such reaction. It was not in her nature to be jealous even

75

where she loved, and though she respected her husband she assuredly did not love him. And besides, Bess was her friend, and so amusing. The tales she told of her father's escapades were so entertaining to the two sisters that they felt they could forgive her much. . . .

Really, when people regaled one with such delightful stories it was difficult to dispense with their company, and the Duchess pressed Lady Elizabeth to stay on at Devonshire House. No wonder that she conduced to the Duke's amusement. Later in the year both sisters gave birth to daughters. Georgiana's child was called Harriet after her aunt (and was something of a disappointment), Lady Duncannon's was called Caroline; having already borne several sons a daughter was welcome.

In Parliament the Foxites, though weakened and depleted, were not idle. Whilst preparing his Bill concerning the East India Company, Burke had come across what looked like incidents of shameless oppression attributable to one, Warren Hastings, the Company's Governor-General of Bengal. Moved by a genuine sense of injustice he demanded an impeachment. Fox and Sheridan supported the demand. Pitt vacillated, he had neither knowledge nor interest in the case, and can have had little conception that it was to last for ten years and to call forth some of the best examples of English oratory.

In other respects the year seemed to be passing away peacefully, with no greater scandal than that of the Queen of France's diamond necklace. Then, early in December, the unexpected happened. Rumours were abroad that Mrs. Fitzherbert was in London. What could this signify? That Maria was tired of her self-imposed banishment, that she considered that the Prince's passion had spent itself, or that she had subdued her conscience and was ready to listen to his entreaties?

Fox was extremely anxious. He wrote immediately to his friend: " Dec. 10th . . . I was told just before I left town yesterday that Mrs. Fitzherbert was arrived, and if I had heard only of this I should have felt most unfeigned joy at an event which I know would contribute so much to your Royal Highness's satisfaction; but I was told at the same time that, from a variety of circumstances which had been observed and put together, there was reason to suppose that you were going to take the very desperate step (pardon the expression) of marrying her at this moment. . . ." [1]

The letter continued with a comprehensive list of the reasons against such a course, and it must be said that, unless the Prince was ready to renounce his succession to the throne, they appeared conclusive.

On the following day the Prince replied to Fox in a letter which was to be pregnant with important consequences. It began as follows : " Dec. 11th, 1785. My dear Charles, Your letter of last night afforded me more satisfaction than I can find words to express (which, I assure you, I did not want) of your having that true regard and affection for me which it is not only the wish, but the ambition of my life to merit. Make yourself easy, my dear friend. Believe me, the world will soon be convinced that there not only is, but never was any ground for these reports which, of late, have been so malevolently circulated. . . ." [2]

With this in his hands, Fox may be pardoned for having felt entirely reassured on the subject of the marriage. Apologists of the Prince have made an effort to prove that his letter denied only unspecified reports, and that he had never referred to the question of his marriage. But no one can doubt that the intention of the letter was solely to convince Fox that no marriage had taken place or would take place.

Yet, on the 15th of December, exactly four days after the Prince had written to Fox, a young curate, the Rev. Robert Burt, made his way to Mrs. Fitzherbert's house in Park Street, Park Lane, and there for the sum of £500 he married the Prince of Wales to Maria Fitzherbert, according to the rites of the Church of England. Henry Errington gave his niece away, Jack Smythe was witness to his sister, and Orlando Bridgeman was present in waiting upon the Prince. So, after a year's resistance, Mrs. Fitzherbert had surrendered upon her own terms. She had not acted without due consideration, and it is, therefore, of interest to determine in what light she considered the marriage. How did the marriage stand (1) in regard to the Roman Catholic religon, (2) in regard to the Protestant religion, (3) in regard to the law of the land ?

[1] Quoted in *George IV and Mrs. Fitzherbert*.   [2] Ibid.

In the eyes of Roman Catholics there was no doubt that the couple were properly married, for marriage, according to this faith, is a sacrament which is administered by the two participants to each other, and in which the priest takes the part of a witness only, and though it is essential that a priest should take this part in countries where the Council of Trent has been promulgated, England was, in 1785, *in partibus infidelium*. The Council of Trent had not been promulgated, and the presence of a priest was, therefore, not required for canonical validity. And since the law of the land required that for a marriage to be legally binding, a clergyman should be the officiant, this was permitted by the Roman Catholic Church (though, in the eyes of that Church, the clergyman could add nothing to the validity of the marriage, which was assured by the vows of the two participants, and filled no role but that of a witness). Thus, in the marriage of the Prince and Mrs. Fitzherbert, all that was necessary and essential had been done, and in the eyes of Rome they were well and truly married.

The view of the Protestant church could only be identical. The Protestant service had been used in its ordinary form, and there were no canonical impediments. In the eyes of the law, however, the position was reversed. There were two laws which had been infringed. A law of the time of the Revolution which forbade the marriage of the heir to the throne to a Roman Catholic, and the Royal Marriage Act of 1772, by which no member of the Royal family could marry a subject without the consent of the King.[1] George III had put forward this Act on account of the morganatic marriages of his two brothers, the Dukes of Cumberland and Gloucester. The Act declared any clergyman celebrating such a marriage to be liable to the penalties of *præmunire*, and further stated that such a marriage was null and void in the eyes of the law. It had been one of the King's most daring efforts to enhance the Royal prerogative, and the Act had not been passed without

---

[1] This applied to all descendants of George II other than the issue of princesses who had married into foreign families. But there was a proviso that any descendant of George II could, by signifying his intention to the Privy Council, and being over twenty-five years of age, marry lawfully—if within twelve months both Houses had not objected to the marriage.

a tussle. But it was law now, and there was no doubt that it formed part of the Constitution and that the Prince of Wales, Mrs. Fitzherbert, and the Reverend Robert Burt were guilty of breaking the law of the land.

When all the subsequent consequences of this marriage are considered, two people may be said to have behaved with remarkable self-restraint : Mrs. Fitzherbert's, who kept her marriage certificate to the day of her death, yet never claimed her rights as the Prince of Wales's morganatic wife, and, despite unthinkable provocation and insult, never showed to anyone the document which proved her position (indeed, she went further and herself cut out the names of the two witnesses lest trouble should befall them), and the Duke of York, who kept silence although he came next in the succession, and was mildly ambitious and would undoubtedly have liked to sit upon the throne. He knew of the marriage and always treated Mrs. Fitzherbert with the greatest friendliness, notwithstanding his wife's dislike of her ; and yet, even when the Prince of Wales's popularity was at the lowest ebb, it never occurred to him that he had it in his power to prove that his brother had forfeited his own succession to the Crown and that he himself was the rightful Prince of Wales.

After the marriage was celebrated, Mrs. Fitzherbert began to make her appearance at Carlton House. A good many people were scandalised, but the rumour soon got about that appearances were deceptive. Orlando Bridgeman and Jack Smythe were not entirely discreet, and it was not long before Lady Jerningham was writing from Cossey :

" Mrs. Fitzherbert has, I believe, been married to the Prince. But it is a very hazardous undertaking, as there are two Acts of Parliament against the validity of such an alliance : concerning her being a subject and her being Catholick. God knows how it will turn out. It may be to the glory of our Belief or it may be to the great dismay and destruction of it ! " [1]

The Duchess of Devonshire and Lady Duncannon were, of course, amongst the first to guess the truth ; but Fox, when he heard their astonished whispers, looked at them quizzically. Had he not got the Prince of Wales's letter with the positive

[1] *The Jerningham Papers.*

assurance that all was well ? But he was too discreet to show his hand. One day, he reflected, that letter would be his trump card. In the meanwhile the Prince never alluded to the subject which, Fox reflected, was natural enough.

1786

THE year following Mrs. Fitzherbert's marriage passed away peacefully. There was a definite improvement in the tone of the Prince's establishment : he drank less, he gambled less, it seemed even as though he had some thoughts of trying to meet his liabilities. Catholics were reassured when they saw that Mrs. Fitzerherbert continued to practise her religion, attending the Bavarian Chapel in Warwick Street. Under these circumstances it was hardly possible that she was living in sin. It was said that the Prince, when questioned on the subject, grew extremely violent, but was never known to have made a categoric denial of his marriage.

The papers were full of veiled innuendos. Gilray's cartoons were exhibited at Humphrey's shop at 29 St. James's Street. They depicted various views of the wedding. One of the most famous was entitled " Wife or no wife, or a Trip to the Continent " ; it collected a curious crowd. In the spring of the year the Duke and Duchess of Cumberland returned after a long visit to France and set up house in London. The Duke was the King's youngest brother, and his marriage to Anne Luttrell, widow of Andrew Horton, had given great offence to George III, who now declared that anyone who should attend the Duchess's routs would incur the Royal displeasure. The Duchess of Cumberland did not, however, find any difficulty in recruiting her guests, and amongst her most frequent visitors was Mrs. Fitzherbert. The Cumberlands treated her as though she were the acknowledged wife of the Prince of Wales, and this, of course, gave further annoyance to the Court.

In this year Devonshire House saw a new addition to its circle in the person of Charles Grey, son of the first Earl Grey, who had just become a member of the House of Commons and who became immediately a devoted follower of Charles

Fox, and an equally devoted admirer of Georgiana. His was a difficult, exigeant nature, and he was apt to make scenes and demands. For the first time the Duchess found that she had an adorer who was not at her feet, who wrote angry letters to Lady Melbourne when Georgiana had failed to keep him informed of her plans ; and also, for the first time, the phlegmatic Duke showed symptoms of definite jealousy. It was bad enough that his wife should be extravagant and unconventional, but now if she were going to have an open flirtation with that young puppy Grey, it would be insufferable.

Seriously alarmed at the prospect of a rupture, Sheridan and Lady Elizabeth Foster rushed to the rescue. They besought the Duchess to be prudent, they implored the Duke to think of his own conduct to his wife, and eventually the breach was mended and some arrangement arrived at whereby the Duke and Duchess ceased to complain of each other's conduct. The situation was saved at the expense of the relationship. As always, in time of trouble, the Duchess paid her mother a visit.

Out at ten o'clock in the morning, made to take their turn at teaching in the village school ; no wonder that the complete change of outlook and occupation served as a sedative to both Georgiana and Harriet, when London life grew too complicated. In the evenings, when Burke and Fox were thundering against Warren Hastings, they would enjoy a little music provided by the country neighbours, or they would sit discussing with their mother the new cure for cancer, which consisted in the juice of crow's stomach, and which was said never to have failed in violent humours.[1] Should the lodge-keeper's wife be provided with it or was it wiser to trust to the efficacy of hemlock ? Questions of life and death—and was Hastings's trial a matter of greater or of lesser importance ?

In August came the news of an attempt on the King's life. As he was arriving at St. James's Palace to hold a levee, a woman named Margaret Nicholson had rushed forward and endeavoured to stab him.[2] Her knife had broken against the Royal waistcoat, which gave food for reflection on the nature of waistcoats. The King appeared unperturbed, and held his levee as usual. The Prince of Wales had come up from

[1] *The Life of Lady Sarah Lennox.*   [2] Wraxall's *Memoirs.*

Brighton to congratulate his father on his escape, but he had been denied access to the Royal presence. The papers were full of the Monarch's placid courage. And a faint wave of popularity was discernible for the first time in many years.

Thus with few untoward incidents 1786 drew to a close, and a period of rest had prepared the Devonshire House set for the stirring events of 1787.

1787

DESPITE the economies of the previous year, despite the fact that he had sold his horses and carriages by public auction at Tattersalls, despite the fact that he had stopped all work on Carlton House and quitted it for his "little Pavilion" at Brighton, still the Prince began the year 1787 with debts to the amount of over £200,000.

The King was presented with an account, and he was furious when he saw an item of £54,000 for setting up Mrs. Fitzherbert ; he himself only incurred debts in respect of the vast bribes he offered to politicians to support the Court party. He absolutely refused to help his son, and therefore the young man felt obliged to put his case before Parliament. His spokesman was Alderman Newnham who, on April 29th, brought forward a motion imploring Parliament to extricate the Prince from his embarrassed position. Pitt's response held a veiled threat. He alluded to the necessity for enquiring into the circumstance which had given rise to the situation. On April 27th Mr. Rolle, a Devonshire member, first began to spar with the gloves off. He had heard that the Prince was married to Mrs. Fitzherbert, he had heard it on unimpeachable authority, he believed it absolutely, and his horror at the thought that the Prince of Wales was married to a Catholic and a subject was unmitigated.[1] He intended to force an admission of the facts by the Prince, or at least by his spokesmen, Fox, Sheridan, or young Grey. His blunt questions embarrassed the Whigs, and his evident intentions were a cause of great alarm to them. In the first skirmish he had made it evident that he intended the next time Newnham spoke to press the question home : " Was the Prince married or was he not ? "

As for the Prince, he was distracted, he was still violently in love with Mrs. Fitzherbert, he had no desire to injure her,

[1] *George IV and Mrs. Fitzherbert.*

84

nor was he entirely dead to a sense of honour. On the other hand, to renounce the throne, weighed down as he was with debt, was not a course on which to embark lightly. All his friends who looked to his reign to make their political fortune would be " let down " and ruined. In his dilemma he did nothing, and said nothing. Mr. Rolle could hardly come and ask him personally if he were married or not, and why should he be responsible for his friends' defence of him ? They, who only guessed at the truth, who had never had a word from him on the subject, would defend him far better than he could defend himself.

Meanwhile, Fox, Sheridan and Grey were in conclave. All three were agreed that it was essential that the marriage should be concealed, denied if necessary. Of the three only Fox, armed with the Prince's letter of Dec. 11th, 1785, believed it possible that no wedding had taken place. To the other two it was sufficient that, since it was against the law, they could justify themselves in saying that it *could not* have taken place. This was as far as they were prepared to go ; they hoped it mighty satisfy Mr. Rolle.

Whilst all the schemes were going forward Mrs. Fitzherbert herself was unaware of the dangers which threatened her reputation. She was used to cartoons and pamphlets, and paid no attention to them, though of late some had even been of a favourable nature. Mr. Horne Tooke's pamphlet on " The reported marriage of the Prince of Wales " had had allusions to " a justly valued female character whom I conclude to be in all respects both *legally*, really, worthily *and happily for this country* her Royal Highness the Princess of Wales." It was nonsense, but flattering nonsense. If she allowed herself to put any value on to it, it reassured her. Even Mr. Rolle's questions reassured her, for now, perhaps, she would be recognised and justified and cease to be a reproach to her co-religionists.

A visit from Sheridan upset her. Of the four men involved in the affair he was the only one to think of the person who would be most affected by it. He had a good heart, and he did not want Mrs. Fitzherbert to suffer an undue shock when the question was handled in the House. Had Maria been alive to the situation he would have done his task admirably, but she was so totally unaware of the gravity of her position that he felt himself unable to open her eyes. Good-natured, pliant and sensitive, he was too weak to inflict pain even where this was urgently necessary. So his visit only served to make Mrs. Fitzherbert vaguely uncomfortable and formed no preparation for what was to come.

On April 30th Newnham brought forward his motion that Parliament should vote a sum of money for the settlement of the Prince's debts. At the end of his speech he stated that Mr. Fox would reassure the House concerning a question relating to the Prince of Wales which seemed to be on the minds of a certain number of its members.

When Newnham sat down Fox rose and made a fiery oration, denying the " miserable calumny and low malicious falsehood " which had been circulated. He emphasised the fact that what Mr. Rolle *feared* might have happened *could* not have happened." So far, the defence had taken the line previously agreed upon, but the Foxites had been optimistic if they had believed that such abstract statements would satisfy their opponents. Rolle wanted facts, he did not wish to be told what *could* or *could not* happen, he wanted to know what *had* happened.

Therefore, Fox made a categoric denial : " The fact not only never could have happened legally, but never did happen in any way whatsoever." The Foxites looked sheepishly at each other, but Charles, with the Prince's letter in mind, felt justified. Yet even now the pertinacious Mr. Rolle remained unsatisfied. Did Mr. Fox speak with authority, or was he merely advancing his personal opinion ? Fox replied " that he spoke with authority."

It was perfectly plain that Rolle continued unconvinced, but short of calling Fox a liar he had nothing left to say. Grey and Sheridan spoke in support of Fox. At Carlton House the Prince walked up and down in an hysterical condition. Notes came to him every half-hour from the House to acquaint him with the state of the debate. When it was all over Fox drove to Brooks's feeling well satisfied with himself, for he believed that he had saved his friend and his party from disaster. In the card-room of the Club he met Orlando Bridgeman who addressed him in these words : " Mr. Fox, I hear you have

denied in the House the Prince's marriage to Mrs. Fitzherbert.
You have been misinformed, I was present at the marriage."
Fox bowed, and no doubt congratulated himself on having
met Mr. Bridgeman only after the debate had taken place.

Whilst this untoward incident was taking place in St. James's
Street, Sheridan and Grey were closeted with the Prince at
Carlton House. They found him in a frenzy. It was all very
well to have denied the legality of the marriage, but to have
denied the fact of it was frightful. Sheridan tried to calm him
and to reassure him by suggesting that since he himself had
kept silence he could not be considered to have forsworn
himself. They stayed long into the night, and very early the
next morning the Prince ordered his carriage and drove round
to Mrs. Butler's house where Mrs. Fitzherbert was staying.
He must see her before news of the debate reached her.

He saw her alone and taking both her hands exclaimed :
" Only conceive, Maria, what Fox did yesterday. He went to
the House and denied that you and I were man and wife !
Did you ever hear of such a thing ! " It was well, he felt, to
take it lightly. Perhaps Mrs. Fitzherbert would not realise
the full implications of the denial ? But she *did* realise them
instantly and fully, and she told the Prince that she could
never live with him again, or forgive him, unless this wrong
were righted. The Prince was beside himself. He swore that
Fox had acted on his own initiative. This Maria could well
believe, for she had always dreaded Fox, believing him to be
her husband's evil genius and her own enemy. But though
this induced her to forgive the Prince, nothing would induce
her to give rise to the scandal which must be created if she
were again to live as his wife.

The Prince left in despair, and sending for Grey, implored
him to go to the House and give the lie to Fox. Grey refused
to do so, he was devoted to Fox heart and soul. " Well," said
the Prince, " if no one will do it Sheridan must," and a
messenger was despatched to the obliging Dick. Nearer to
the Prince in temperament than were Fox or Grey, he felt for
him and promised to do his best. To say anything more about
the Prince would, he felt, be impossible ; but there was no
reason why he should not take up the cudgels for Mrs. Fitzherbert, and he did so. " There was," he said, " another

person entitled in every honourable and delicate mind to the same attention, on whose conduct truth could fix no just reproach and whose character claimed and was entitled to the truest and most general respect." The House was perplexed. What did Sheridan mean ? Fox had promised them that the Prince was not married, Sheridan had assured them that Mrs. Fitzherbert was not his mistress, it all sounded rather too charming to be true. Rolle and others took it as a confirmation of their belief that Fox had lied ; but most members believed that it was simply a pretty compliment to Mrs. Fitzherbert, and meant nothing. But, confused though they were, they voted the Prince £161,000 to pay his debts, £60,000 with which to complete Carlton House, and raised his income by £10,000 a year. It was a successful way out of his financial troubles, but it did little to compensate him for the loss of Maria's company.

The Devonshire House circle had been in a turmoil during these anxious days, the affair involved so many members of the set. When the outcome was reached it produced a cleavage in the usually solid ranks of the Foxites. All the women stood for Mrs. Fitzherbert, all the men for Fox ; only Sheridan remained undecided and on friendly terms with both parties.

It must have been a source of great satisfaction to Mrs. Fitzherbert that at the time of her trial, so far from being deserted by her friends, she had added to their number. Georgiana and Harriet stood by her despite their devotion to the Prince, to Fox and to Grey ; the Duchess of Cumberland took peculiar pains to be civil to her ; and the Duchesses of Portland and Gordon, who had never received her, now sent her invitations. The Archbishop of Canterbury complained that " it was very odd," and the Prince of Wales fell seriously ill. Illness was always his trump card and now, as before, it took the trick. Soon Maria was informed by the doctor that he could not be responsible for the Prince's life if she would not return to him.

She felt now that her position had been recognised by all the important and impeccable ladies of London society ; (and since, after all, the Prince was her husband, whatever he might say), it was perhaps her duty to humble her pride and to go back to him. Eventually Sir Sampson and Lady Gideon

gave a party which became known as " The Feast of Reconciliation," and at which Maria and the Prince sat together at the
head of the table. Soon afterward, the pair went down to
Brighton, where the Prince bathed and played cricket and led
a healthy life, and where Mrs. Fitzherbert began to believe that
she had acted rightly in returning to him.

Whilst the Prince's affairs were thrust into such prominence
the indictment of Warren Hastings continued and Burke, Fox
and Sheridan laboured together to obtain a trial. Early in the
year Sheridan, now at the zenith of his powers, made what his
contemporaries were always to quote as his greatest speech.
The subject was the despoilment, by Hastings, of the Begums
of Oude. Sheridan spoke for six hours. Not only the Foxites,
but the whole House was proud of his oratory, and the speech
rallied many waverers to the cause of the prosecutors.

During 1787 Lady Elizabeth Foster continued to live at
Devonshire House. She was now accepted not only by
Georgiana, but also by society, as one of the Cavendish family.
Only her father, with more worldly sense for his daughters
than he had ever evinced in his own interests, disapproved.
He had returned to his diocese and wrote testily to his daughter
Lady Erne to complain of the extravagance of one of her sisters
and the avarice of the other " . . . Elizabeth has wrote to me
for £50 to pay *two* pictures of Mr. Day's. How can two minia-
tures come to £50 ? Louisa has *sold* the beautiful gown I gave
her, because the shape was not *fashionable*, and I have redeemed
it and paid her the price. I think you would not have sold my
present at any era of your life for ten times its value—' *Mais je
me suis fait à tout.*' " [1]

[1] *The Life of the Earl Bishop of Derry.*

1788

THE spring saw the height of Mrs. Fitzherbert's influence over her husband. He felt that he owed her every possible reparation for her ill-treatment at the hands of Fox. She was living in a fine house in Pall Mall, not far from Carlton House, and in order to make her position less invidious she had to live with her a certain Miss Pigot, who was a lady of the most unimpeachable character. The craze that season was for " animal magnetism " as exhibited by one, Doctor Marmaduke, and all the Devonshire House circle attended his séances with various effects : Georgiana went into hysterics, the Prince of Wales into a faint, whilst Lady Salisbury slept soundly, and even Lady Palmerston and Mrs. Crewe responded to the effects of his hypnotism.

Entertaining went on furiously and some of the older generation complained with Hannah More that " the little old parties are not to be had in the usual style of comfort. Everything is great and vast and late and magnificent and dull." In France the eve of the revolution was manifesting itself in an even greater magnificence. From Chantilly, Bess's father, once more on his travels, describes a meet of the hounds :

" I returned here from Paris . . . to see the Prince of Condé's hunt on the great festival of St. Hubert, but like most other things it did not answer. He and his family dressed like so many drummers and trumpeters in a peach coloured cloth, coat, waistcoat and breeches laced down the seams with silver, their hair as completely dressed as if going to a ball, and their jack boots the only emblem of hunting ; except indeed a large French horn, slung round the shoulder of each of them, which the Prince and his grandson the Duc d'Enghien, a youth of sixteen, sounded from time to time." [1]

The scene annoyed the irritable prelate :

[1] *The Life of the Earl Bishop of Derry.*

" This frippery country is still the same, a skipping, dancing tribe, fit only for themselves, and when the circling glass goes round they talk of beauties which they never saw, and fancy raptures which they never felt." [1]

February saw the outcome of Burke's industry, and the eloquence of Fox and Sheridan, when Hastings was brought to his trial in Westminster.

August found Georgiana in action again on Fox's behalf, another election was in progress, but this time Charles's danger was not sufficient to warrant personal canvassing.

When the polls were declared everyone left London ; the Prince for Brighton and Fox for Italy, whilst the Devonshires and Lady Elizabeth went down to Chatsworth. Mrs. Fitzherbert and the Prince were still at Brighton in November when a messenger arrived from Windsor with the terrifying news that the King had gone mad. The implications of such an event were almost incalculable. Without an instant's delay the Prince started for London, where he met the Duke of York, and the two young men proceeded to Windsor. In the Castle they found a scene of distraction. The King was sullen, the Queen terrified, the princesses in hysterics. When he saw his two sons before him George III became violent. His intense dislike of the Prince of Wales, uncontrolled by reason, induced him to attack the Prince, and attendants had to intervene to save the young man from his father's frenzy.

After making suitable arrangements for keeping the King under restraint, the princes returned to London, where they found Mrs. Fitzherbert unpacking her house in Pall Mall to which she had invited Richard Sheridan and his wife. Maria did not forget kindness easily. She knew that at the time of Rolle's inquisition Sheridan had been her only champion, and she was glad to be of service to him. In addition, she vastly preferred his influence over her husband to that of Fox. And it was a source of great satisfaction to her that in this moment of crisis " the black animal " was sunning itself in Italy, all unconscious of the momentous events that were taking place in London.

Meanwhile, from the country the Whigs poured back into London. At first the general belief was that the King would

[1] *The Life of the Earl Bishop of Derry.*

occurred would she care for £20,000 a year, would she like to be made a duchess ? Only a very trivial condition was attached to the offer—she must live abroad. Maria replied that she should detest to be made a duchess, the creation of such a title having precedents of an equivocal nature ; and that as for the money, her rights as a wife were not for sale. Fox was baulked ; with Mrs. Fitzherbert in the country he felt himself unable to face the questions with which Mr. Rolle was sure to besiege him when the debate on the Regency should reach its climax. He was ill from his exhausting journey home, bitterly disappointed at its results so he took himself to Bath, refusing to be drawn up to Westminster on any pretext.

The Devonshire House circle was solidly behind Fox's unconstitutional assertion that the Regency was already vested in the Prince, and they made it quite clear that when the new era began they anticipated that the Prince would call on Fox to form a government. In their minds there was never any doubt as to the relative precedence of Fox and Sheridan ; only on the matter of Mrs. Fitzherbert had they ever disagreed with their idol ; and loyalty to Fox was a far greater tenet in their creed than loyalty to the Prince of Wales.

1789

EARLY in the New Year it became evident that the Regency Bill would pass with the restrictions which Pitt had brought forward. " Prinny " let it be understood that as soon as he came to power he should make Fox First Lord of the Treasury, Sheridan Treasurer of the Navy, the Duke of York Commander-in-Chief, and then there was to be a garter for " Uncle Cumberland." The influence of Devonshire House had predominated, and once again the Foxites were a united family. But Fox still remained at Bath, whilst Burke led the party on to victory.

The canvassing of doubtful members went on furiously. Georgiana gave great parties at which all the ladies wore Regency caps, and Mrs. Fitzherbert was equally active. There was a most indecorous air of triumph and festivity amongst the Whigs, and evident satisfaction at the bad news which reached them from Windsor. In the other camp the Duchess of Richmond led the attack valiantly. She gave rival parties at which all the ladies wore garter blue and sported ribbons inscribed with " God save the King " in their hair. The whole performance was most unseemly. Whilst Georgiana had youth and charm on her side, and as her contemporaries wrote, " feminine graces, accomplishments of mind and elegance of manners," the Duchess of Richmond was a redoubtable adversary. She was noted for a horse common sense and for a " pertinacity which no obstacle could shake, masculine importunity, emancipation from ordinary forms, propelled by hope of place and by views of interest." [1]

Mr. Rolle was, as usual, to the fore. He desired that a clause should be added to the Regency Bill to the effect that the Regency should lapse, not only if the Prince of Wales were to marry a Roman Catholic, but also if he " shall at any time be

[1] Wraxall's *Memoirs.*

95

proved *to be* married, in fact or in law to a Papist." The clause was a direct challenge to Fox's veracity; but Charles was not to be drawn. He swallowed the insult and went on sulking in the country.

Pitt, either because he was now convinced that no marriage ever had taken place, or because he thought it as well not to aggravate the rising sun, gave it as his opinion that the clause was redundant, and that the uniformity clause was in itself sufficient for the circumstances. Grey then took it upon himself to improve upon what Fox had stated two years before. He alluded to the rumours of the marriage " as false, libellous and calumniatory." [1]

Mrs. Fitzherbert resented his conduct bitterly; but this time Georgiana could not bring herself to sympathise with her, for her own feelings were too intimately involved in all that concerned Charles Grey.

On February 19th the excitement was at its height, and the Bill under discussion in the House. Late in the morning Pitt rose to speak; his face was curiously sardonic : " Gentlemen, His Majesty the King's condition is much improved. . . ." The House was petrified. Was it a ruse, or was it the truth ? Was the King really going to recover ? The Prince behaved with decency; but the majority of the Foxites were plainly in despair. It seemed as though they were dogged by bad luck.

On the 27th an Irish Deputation came to offer the Prince the unrestricted Regency of Ireland. He thanked them and offered them a banquet to celebrate the King's recovery. The Prince of Wales and the Duke of York went down to Windsor to congratulate their father on his recovery. He received them civilly. The Duke of York was his favourite son, and he bore him no grudge for having tried to secure the post of Commander-in-Chief during his father's illness. The Queen, on the other hand, refused to speak to her sons; and shortly afterwards displayed great courtesy to Colonel Lennox who recently fought a duel with the Duke of York, having challenged the Prince on inadequate and insulting grounds.

So much has been written concerning the supposedly heartless conduct of the princes during their father's illness that it is

[1] *George IV and Mrs. Fitzherbert.*

interesting to note that upon the King's recovery it was the Queen and her circle who ostracised the Foxites and that, as far as George III was concerned, the position did not seem to have been further embittered. Perhaps this may have been due to an incapacity on the King's part to realise the events which had taken place during his illness ; but it may also have been occasioned by a recognition of the fact that the Queen had been outrageous in her demands and violent in her endeavours to obtain power for herself. At a fête which she gave to celebrate her husband's recovery and at which the ladies wore their garter blue, the princes were treated with marked incivility and, indeed broad hints had been given them that their presence was not desired. The young men had, however, had the good sense to attend a reunion where their absence would have been noted as most unseemly, though they withdrew when ordered to dance in a quadrille with Colonel Lennox.

If the princes were in any way embarrassed at the turn of fortune, the rank and file of the Foxites were in despair. They saw all their hopes of office and emoluments lost, perhaps for many years, and they knew that many of them had been guilty of considerable indiscretions which were likely to percolate in time to the Royal ears. Many went into the country ; but Fox, on the contrary, came up to town. The " Black Animal " laughed ; for once a mistake of his was turning out well. He, the most hated of the King's opposition, had been denied the opportunity of aggravating his situation by engaging in any but the early debates on the condition of the Royal patient. He had had no occasion to say the things which Sheridan and Burke had said of the King, and he wondered if some reaction in his favour might not set in in the depths of the Monarch's mind.

Meanwhile the news from France was bad, the whole country seemed to be in a political turmoil. It was all very well for Lady Elizabeth Foster to receive reassuring letters from her father. " All is now commotion and all soon will be sing-song, in the meantime the hotheads let one another's blood, the clergy rise against the Bishops, and the laity against the nobles. . . ." [1]

Of quite another mind was Burke, who, studying the situation

[1] *The Life of the Earl Bishop of Derry.*

with a fascinated horror, made London's blood run cold with his prophecies.

In July the revolution broke out, and the Bastille fell. "How much the greatest event that ever happened in the world! And how much the best!" cried Fox. His hatred of the Bourbons was invincible; perhaps it was a stronger motive power than his love of liberty. Burke shuddered. He hated all tyranny; but most of all he hated "the multiple tyranny of the masses." He hated lawlessness and brutality, and he saw, incipient in the French Revolution, a revolt not only from the laws of an absolute monarchy but also rebellion against all the laws of religion and morality.

Georgiana followed Fox in his light-hearted enthusiasm. Harriet and Lady Elizabeth Foster sided with Burke. The division cleft the Devonshire House set from its apex to the base; but as yet the crack was hardly visible, and no one, except Burke, had any conception of the tremendous consequences which were likely to ensue from the destruction of a State prison.

In the autumn an unexpected anxiety arose. Harriet Duncannon became very gravely ill as a consequence of what was believed to be a stroke. As she was only thirty at the time and as during the remainder of her life she seems to have suffered intermittently from a series of these attacks and to have made rapid recoveries on each occasion, it seems unlikely that the diagnosis was correct. When she was convalescent, after this first serious attack, she went to pay a long visit to her mother, and it was on this occasion that old Lady Spencer suggested that she should have her little grand-daughter Caroline to live with her whilst Harriet recovered her health. Caroline, therefore, at the age of four, left her mother's villa at Roehampton and took up residence with her grandmother at St. Albans, in whose care she remained for several years. An old maid, "Fanny," went with the child. But it was not long before Lady Spencer grew anxious about Caroline. The little girl was terribly highly strung and frighteningly precocious, and, moreover, she seemed to be entirely lacking in self-control.

Eventually Lady Spencer became extremely concerned about these violent paroxysms of temper, which verged on hysterics, and, with an understanding rare in that generation, she had

Lady Spencer and Child (afterwards Georgiana Duchess of Devonshire)

recourse not to punishments, but to a doctor. The physician reassured her. Caroline was, he said, quite normal, but she was exceptionally nervous. She must be kept as quiet as possible and on no account must her brain be forced. The priory at St. Albans, with its quiet, well-regulated life, was a far better background for her than the gay, exciting life at Roehampton, where she was either spoilt by the guests or, in her mother's frequent absences in town, left to the care of the servants.

1790

DURING the eighties of the century the Duchess of Devonshire had been the cause of all the heart-burnings and jealousies that centred in Devonshire House. Fox and Sheridan had sat at her feet, the Prince of Wales and Charles Grey had been her adorers. Harriet Duncannon had been in the background. She too had had her admirers, but they had been kept out of the public eye. No one had told tales of her affairs, or noticed her growing attractions. But now, in the year 1790, she was at the height of her charm ; shy at first and reserved, ten years of marriage had taught her to be easy and witty in society, without breaking down one particle of her privacy. So it became gradually apparent to certain frequenters of Devonshire House that Lady Duncannon had far more wit and brilliance, far more depth and character than her charming sister, and therefore, by the turn of the decade, certain of Georgiana's swains changed their allegiance. Sheridan was amongst the first to do so. He fell violently and irretrievably in love with Harriet. Elizabeth Sheridan, used to minor infidelities, was at once aware that, in this instance, something of real importance had befallen her husband. She suffered cruelly, and Fox became her confidant. What made the situation, if not more dangerous, at least more humiliating was Harriet's complete indifference to Sheridan's devotion— a coldness which stimulated him and aggravated his wife.

Yet, superficially, they were all on excellent terms. No shadow of love or anger showed across their conversation or their letters. Sheridan wrote flippantly to Harriet on the subject of her conquests.

" Yours is the sweet untroubled sleep of purity . . . and yet, and yet beware ! Milton will tell you that even in Paradise serpents found their way to the ear of slumbering innocence. Then, to be sure, poor Eve had no watchful guardian to pace up and down her windows, or clear-sighted friends to warn her of the stealthy approaches of T(ownshend)s and F(itzpatrick)s, and others and a long list of wicked letters—and Adam, I suppose was . . . . at Brooks's. Fye, fye Mr. S(heridan.")

" I answer ' Fye, Fye, Fye, Lord D(uncannon). Tell her to come with you and forbid her coming to a house so inhabited.' Now don't look grave. Remember it is your office to speak the truth.

" I shall be gone before your hazel eyes are open to-morrow, but (pray) for the sake of Lord D(uncannon) that you will not suffer me to return. Do not listen to Jack's elegies, or smile at F's epigrams, or tremble at C. W.'s powers, but put on that look of gentle firmness of proud humility, and pass on in maiden meditation fancy free.—Now draw the curtain, Sally." (Sally was her maid.) [1]

From the tone of the letter it is evident that Sheridan was already devoted to Lady Duncannon, but that his sharp wits had told him to walk warily ; knowing that his advances would meet with a rebuff, he had adopted the character of the Sylph in Georgiana's novel. He was to be the Wise Counsellor, the friend who paid no compliments and always told the truth. Harriet was not deceived. But she felt sorry for poor Dick, who was apparently not accountable for his fancies and who was evidently trying so hard to present his devotion in a form which would not be hateful to her. She laughed at the very idea of Sheridan's guardianship. Had she not, when she was still in the nursery, a clearer vision of men and of values than he would attain to at the end of his life ? Still, it was all very touching and quite unlike the violent demands made to her by other men. She was grateful to him, and consequently she was kind.

From the first the relationship was a false one, and in its fulfilment it was to drive Sheridan to the verge of madness ; but in this, its first year, it seemed to both actors to give a fair promise for the future : Harriet thought she had found a friend ; and Sheridan was confident that he had found a mistress. It was an age-old mistake, fruitful of unhappiness and misunderstanding.

In the spring another election occupied Fox's friends, and

[1] *Life of Sheridan*—Walter Sichel (quoted without names).

once again they had the satisfaction of seeing him at the top of the Poll at Westminster. In foreign politics a situation arose which bore some parallel to the one which arose sixty-four years later and led up to the Crimean War. Pitt was ready to defend the Turks at all costs, whilst Fox absolutely refused to embroil England in the affairs of the Porte. For once Fox had the country behind him, and for the first time in eight years the Foxites were popular, so popular indeed that Pitt had to draw in his horns.

It was a short-lived triumph, they were divided amongst themselves on the subject of France. Burke still exclaims: " I hate tyranny, at least I think so ; but I hate it most of all when most are concerned in it . . .",[1] whilst Fox and Sheridan applauded every success of the *Tiers état*. But so little did even those in Paris realise the situation that they complained of the boredom of a state of affairs where everyone was turned theorist and pacifist and where no one had the courage to fight for his convictions or his interests.

This spring the Duchess and Lady Elizabeth Foster were spending some time in Paris. The reason for their absence from England was variously explained. One May night when Lady Elizabeth was at the Opera a messenger came to her with an urgent note. It was from Harriet Duncannon to announce the birth of a son to Georgiana. After eighteen years of marriage she had given an heir to the dukedom. The Duchess was then in the thirty-sixth year of her age. For some time she had grown rather stout, and on this occasion her condition had not been apparent to the less intimate members of her circle. The child's birth came, therefore, as a surprise to them ; and knowing, or suspecting that Lady Elizabeth Foster had been on very intimate terms with the Duke for some years and had already had a son by him, they shamelessly asserted that the new baby was no child of Georgiana's, but that it had been born to Lady Elizabeth in Paris, and that Richard Croft the physician had had it conveyed secretly from Lady Elizabeth's bed to that of the Duchess. Twenty-seven years afterwards, an echo of the old tale was made to cause considerable pain to the boy whom it slandered ; by this time the story was much improved. The Duchess had given birth to a daughter,

[1] Burke's *Thoughts on the French Revolution*.

Lady Elizabeth to a boy—the two had been exchanged. Hartington was said to have a knowledge of the proceedings, and
to have entered into a compact with his uncle, Lord George
Cavendish, never to marry.

Soon afterwards Bess met her father who was returning to
England from Italy where his liberality had " reanimated the
fainting body of art in Rome," and together they journeyed to
London, where Lady Elizabeth took up her old quarters at
Devonshire House. London seemed " very much itself " to
her, the Prince and Sheridan still roystered at the Salutation
Tavern and attended the bear-baiting, the bull-fights and the
dog-fights of Tothill Fields. Burke still denounced the events
in Paris in the voice of a prophet. He had written a book
named *Reflections on the French Revolution*, which was to sell
32,000 copies in a year. As a result of its publication, he and
Fox were scarcely on speaking terms. And poor Mrs. Fitzherbert was so deeply in debt that when she was served a writ
for £1,835 returnable the next day, the bailiffs, who were
already in possession of the house, would let nothing go out
of it—and the Prince was obliged to pawn his jewels—London
had not changed much in the months she had been absent.

1791

IN the early months of 1791 Burke and Fox came into open
conflict in the House of Commons on the subject of the
French Revolution. Burke accused Fox of having become a
Jacobin, and Fox abused Burke for having gone back on his
Whig principles. High words passed between them and ended
in Fox, with tears pouring down his face, declaring that their
long partnership and real friendship had come to an end. This
time the breach was final. They never met in friendship again.

The death of Mirabeau on April 2nd quickened the pace
of events in Paris. With him the Court party lost its last hope.
Late in June England was shocked to hear of the flight to
Varennes and its disastrous conclusion. More than twenty
years before old Lord Spencer had taken Georgiana and Harriet,
then children, to the Court of Versailles and they had retained
vivid memories of their visit. Now they heard that the King
had been suspended from his office.

In England Paine had just published a book called *The Rights
of Man*. It was revolutionary in tone and proved a formidable
rival as a best seller to Burke's *Thoughts on the French
Revolution*. Amongst the Nonconformists and the lower
middle classes a wave of republicanism was manifesting itself.
The members of this party were unwisely enough anxious for
notoriety ; but the moment that their activities became known
three-quarters of the nation began to agitate against them.

The Duchess of Devonshire and Mr. Fox might play their
Pharo unperturbed by the thought that in Manchester and
Birmingham there were people foolish enough to accost each
other as " Citizen Brown " and " Citizen Robinson." But, to
honest Mr. Smith, taking his pint of beer in Edgware, or little
Puddleton, the story was one to " give him the horrors." And
it was not long before anti-Jacobin riots became epidemic. A
very severe fracas took place in Birmingham which had as its

motive a detestation of Dr. Priestley and his principles. In September came news that the National Assembly had been dissolved, and in October that the Legislative Assembly had met. All the watching world held its breath ; but the outcome was long delayed.

Meanwhile Charles Grey's devotion to Georgiana was becoming an embarrassment. Scenes grew more frequent and more violent, and even Lady Melbourne reproved him for his want of discretion. He wrote back penitently . . . " indeed I never meant to plague her, but I believe I am born to be a plague to everybody." It seemed as though he were right. Relationships had grown terribly strained at Devonshire House, and eventually the ladies decided to take their revenge and go off in a body to the Continent, leaving the Prince and Charles Grey and Sheridan to work off their jealousies upon each other. London regretted them and found the season dull without them.

A quotation from a letter of Lady Bristol's describes the state of the ladies' nerves on the eve of their departure as being far from good.

" . . . her (Elizabeth's) fright was owing to the horses having kicked and run away with a carriage downhill in which was the Duchess and Lady Duncannon, herself and two children. It was not overturned, but Lady Duncannon was almost in fits with fear, and had so bad a return of her spasms that she could not be carried home, and though the Duchess showed great courage, yet the whole scene was so affecting that her nerves were seized in such a manner that Tissot sat with her all night. It was a great while before she could be brought to cry. She was relieved by it. But the Prince of Wales followed with excessive violence ; in fact she was very ill with it, which is no wonder." [1]

[1] *The Life of the Earl Bishop of Derry.*

1792

THE early months of 1792 saw a flood of refugees surging from France to England, and the Bishop of Derry, who was at Plymouth, preparing for another trip abroad, showed himself particularly kind to the dignitaries of the Roman Catholic Church who were in difficulties. Writing to his daughter, Lady Erne, he asks her assistance :

" I am now buoy, who would think it ? In procuring lodgings, diet and accommodation for two miserable French exiles whom I met at St. Austell's in Cornwall. One is certainly a Bishop, the other, I conclude, his Grand Vicaire. When you are quite at leisure I wish you would send for Chevalier and ask him if he could not procure for these two exiles one room with two beds up two pairs of stairs in the neighbourhood of some good cook-shops where a man can fill his belly without much emptying his purse. I daresay General Hervey, who rambles everywhere and knows everything, could lead my two friends, French ecclesiastics to some of these cook-shops in the alleys near St. Martin's Lane, where a man fills his belly for 4d. or 6d., and with two pence more dilutes the whole with good beer. Dear Mary ! if you are your father's own daughter, and I doubt it not, help me to extricate these poor exiles, all French as they are, from their present distress. . . ." [1]

Whilst Lord Bristol was thus occupied in charitable design, Bess, Harriet and Georgiana were enjoying the sunshine of Nice and making new friends amongst the English visitors ; and since one of these friendships was to be of life-long duration and of considerable importance, it is necessary to go with some detail into the description of the person concerned, who was young Lady Webster.

Elizabeth Vassall was a rich American heiress, perhaps one of the first to marry into the English aristocracy ; and, if this

[1] *The Life of the Earl Bishop of Derry.*

be the case, she has also other claims to be considered their patroness, for she was the perfect specimen of a now familiar phenomenon. Elizabeth Vassall had a vitality which would be envied even by her twentieth-century imitators. She had an abhorrence of all convention ; as to religion, she was sceptical, except in moments of great emotion. She had, on the other hand, a strong moral sense which never left her in peace when she deviated from its dictates ; she had great loyalty of heart joined to a complete cynicism of intellect, and a preference for the under-dog. She was rude, crude, domineering ; she pushed and elbowed her way into society ; but she was a good judge of a man, and a good judge of a garden.

Her forbears had lived in America. Her father had made his fortune in Jamaica and retired to live at Bristol, where he had perpetrated practical jokes. When he had died, his American widow had married Sir Gilbert Affleck. Elizabeth Vassall was, as has been said, extremely rich. She was married at fifteen to Sir Godfrey Webster, who was forty-eight. At the time, she had been contented with the arrangement, but, as she grew up, the honest, coarse, county gentleman, who was totally devoid of ambition, bored her to distraction. He was to inherit Battle Abbey. But, for the moment, his aunt, old ' Widow Whistle Webster,' inhabited the great house, and the newly married couple had to be content with the Dower House. This situation irked Elizabeth, and she cannot have added to the peace and quiet of family life, for she was reputed to have sent round messengers to the Abbey at frequent intervals to enquire " If the old hag were not dead yet ?." On another occasion she staged a pretended French invasion, and on yet another an army of pseudo ghosts were introduced into the venerable pile, in the hope of expediting the old lady to another world. But " Widow Whistle Webster " was by no means dead yet. She quietly withdrew from the house, taking all her servants with her and locking all the doors, so that her uninvited guests were made to feel exceedingly foolish ; and what was more were exceedingly hungry by the time she decided to return and release them ! Outgrowing these childish pranks, Elizabeth next demanded to be taken abroad ; and the harassed Sir Godfrey, hoping to placade his young termagant, had consented to take her to Nice for the winter of 1792. So here it was that she fell in with the family of old Lady Spencer, a meeting which opened her eyes to fresh and wonderful fields for her ambitions. Lady Webster, despite six years of marriage, was still only twenty-one. She was ready for any adventure, and she appealed especially to Georgiana who, though she was now thirty-seven, was equally ready for fun and frolic. Soon it was decided that the Websters should join the party and travel on with them to the south. The association was a loose one ; and often they separated for a week or two, to meet again at a point farther along their route.

On one of these expeditions the Websters met Lady Stafford's son, young Granville Leveson-Gower ; but he himself was bound for Russia, and it thus happened that, on this occasion, by a narrow margin, he failed to meet the Duchess and Lady Duncannon who were to play so great a part in his life.

Lady Stafford, who dreaded the example of the Devonshire House set upon her sedate son, was delighted to think of him safely removed from the sphere of their influence. She adored her son, and she desired that he should become a credit to his family. She was strict with him, and ambitious for him. In his extraordinarily good looks and indolent disposition she foresaw dangers which she tried to prevent. But despite many admonitory passages, her letters are always simple and affectionate.

Whilst things went on, as the Duchess said, " thus jollily " with the travellers, and Lady Webster was indulging in a wild flirtation with Lord Spencer, to the great annoyance of her husband, more than one of their friends at home was in trouble. Poor Sheridan had begun that hospitality to bailiffs which was to be a recurrent incident in his later life. His burden of debt was crushing, and it seemed beyond the limits of expectation to hope for any solution. Elizabeth Sheridan, exhausted with financial worry, anxious about the fate of her children, was already showing symptoms of consumption. She worked on bravely to keep things together, entertaining for her husband in the face of ruin, and getting what amusement she could by making the bailiffs hand round the ices at her parties. How long ago seemed the days of their romantic courtship, and indeed twenty years was a long time !

Dick was one of the leading members of the Whig party.

He was the friend of the future king, the friend of dukes and duchesses, and a still greater distinction, the friend of Mr. Fox. His eloquence was recognised, he was admired and petted by the great. But he wrote no more plays. His management of Drury Lane had led to financial disaster, he made debts, he drank, he neglected his wife and was unfaithful to her. And in her heart Elizabeth knew that he had sold his birthright, not for fame, but for a mess of pottage. For a few years she too had felt the glamour of society, but now, tired and ill as she was, she knew beyond argument that Dick had missed his life. The tradition of the stage and of letters were his by birth. He could have been the greatest actor-manager, and one of the greatest playwrights of the English stage, but as a politician he would never be outstanding, and well she knew that his dear and illustrious friends would never consider his occupying the seat of the First Lord of the Treasury, whatever turn the wheel of fortune might take. It would be the story of Burke over again. Yet, in her distress, she was just; his friends had done him an injury, but it was an involuntary blow. Their friendship for him was sincere, but it had its limits, and that was what he had been and always would be blind to.

She wrote often to the Duchess, and gave her news of events in London.

August was heavy with the shocking tale of the sack of the Tuileries, the slaughter of the Swiss Guards, the deposition of the King and the imprisonment of the Royal Family. Even now Fox defended the rebels, and Sheridan followed him loyally. And Burke congratulated himself that he had made his position perfectly clear a year earlier.

The Gowers were recalled from Paris, to Fox's wrath, but Chauvelin remained on in London. All England was shocked and horrified at the events. It was reported that twelve thousand people had been killed by the mob and that Mr. Linley, who had been dining with the Duc d'Orléans on the day of the massacre of the prisoners, had been horrified by his host's callousness, who, in answer to a question as to the cause of the commotion in the streets, had received the reply, " *Ah, ce n'est rien, c'est la tête de Madame de Lamballe qu'on promène.*"

The Spencer party was in Rome when an account of these tragedies reached them. France in revolution made a return to England difficult, but when, in October, the news of the death of Lord Duncannon's father came to them, they determined to attempt a circuitous route home. Accompanied by Lady Elizabeth Foster and one, Mr. Pelham, whom they had constituted their guide and cicerone, they started back. When they reached England they found it in a sorry state. The harvest had failed and there was distress and discontent everywhere. The French revolutionaries had lately proclaimed their intention of helping revolutionaries in other countries. Fox laughed at the threat as vain words, but Parliament was anxious and called out the Militia. Fox fought the Militia Bill. He found himself alone. Even the Dukes of Portland and Devonshire, even Lords FitzWilliam, Carlisle and Grenville supported the measure. It cost them much to vote against their leader, and Lord FitzWilliam is described by Mr. Hobhouse as having " left London from distress of mind concerning Mr. Fox."

Only Georgiana consoled and supported him. Lady Bessborough was well again now and everyone was glad, even the Bishop of Derry, though he said that he had thought Lord Bessborough might have married Lady Erne had he become a widower. What was to have been the fate of Lord Erne we are not told ; but in any case Harriet was recovered, and Sheridan was running down to Roehampton to plague her.

A quotation from a letter of Lady Sarah Napier expressed his views exactly.

" . . . The Government does very foolishly in trying to raise up quarrels between the Catholics and the Protestants, for the purpose of an *excuse* for an Union, which will ruin Ireland, for the nasty Presbyterians will run away with the bone." [1]

France given over to the mob, England held down by the Militia, Ireland on the verge of revolt, people awaited the New Year fearfully.

[1] *The Life and Letters of Lady Sarah Lennox.*

1793

ON January 21st, 1793, Louis XVI was executed. From that moment war with France became a certainty.. To realise the deep impression which the King's death made upon the minds of most Englishmen it is essential to recollect that the 30th of January, 1649, when Charles I had gone to the block at Whitehall, was only 144 years distant from the Englishmen of whom we are writing. In 1939 we are 146 years distant from the events of 1793, yet we do not feel so very far removed from that generation. One hundred and forty-six years is not an arc of time which effaces memories. Tales of the horror of the Civil War were still vivid, and the revolution in France gave rise to genuine terror in England. Even Fox's most ardent disciple, Charles Grey, on hearing of the King's death remarked . . . " bad as I am thought, I cannot express the horror I feel at the atrocity, and," he added, " . . . war is certain. God grant we may not all lament the consequence of it."

But Fox himself was obdurate. He continued, it may be assumed from obstinacy, to declare his delight in the French Revolution, and he also continued, from sincere conviction, to preach pacifism. He now saw himself abandoned by all his old friends. Sheridan hedged, though officially he was supposed to support Fox. Yet such was Charles's extraordinary charm that even in these trying circumstances he managed to attach a new disciple to himself in the person of the twenty-eight-year-old Duke of Bedford. This young man had become a constant *habitué* of Devonshire House ; he had great charm and good looks, and a sincerity which earned him not only the affections but also the admiration of Georgiana, Harriet and Lady Melbourne. Their own contemporaries, Fox and Sheridan, Fitzpatrick and FitzWilliam, were getting on in years. It had been a pleasure to add Charles Grey to the circle; and now Francis Bedford, or "Loo," as he was affectionately called, seemed an unexpected bonus from fate. The ladies were all quite silly about him. It is a wonderful testimony to their lack of jealousy that he seems to have been considered as their joint property. They were willing to share his admiration amongst themselves, but woe betide any outsider who should cast eyes on "Loo."

With this young man and Georgiana's admiration for support, Fox waged war against the Government. Those of his friends who had been forced by their conscience to differ from him solaced their distress by paying all his debts and assuring to him £3,000 a year for his life. Thus, for the first time since he had come of age, Fox was on his feet financially; and, with the wise assistance of Mrs. Armistead, he managed for the future to live within his income.

Meanwhile Pitt, faced with the certainty of war, was distracted. His mind was an admirable, a brilliant administrative organ, but unfitted to cope with foreign policy and strategy. He wavered, for the first time since he had been in office; he did not know what to do; he had no views of his own. On the one side he heard Burke preaching the war as a crusade against the heathen; on the other he heard Fox declaiming upon the beauties of peace. For himself he vastly preferred peace to war, for any ideal; only in times of peace could he put through his legislation; only in times of peace could he function and come into his own. Yet, in February, war came to him, and England found herself pledged to fight in the company of Spain, Holland, Austria and Prussia, against France.

Pitt gave important commands in the Army and Navy to the Duke of York and to Chatham respectively. Neither choice showed much perspicacity.

The flood of refugees continued to flow towards England and Devonshire House, for all the republican sentiments of its mistress, became a haven of safety to many French aristocrats and their families. Indeed the nurseries of Devonshire House at this period were full to overflowing. There were in the first place the Duchess's two daughters, Georgiana and Harriet, and the baby Hartington. Then in the holidays there were often the Bessborough's three boys and little Caroline

who was still so wild and strange. In the holidays too came
Bess's two Foster boys, and there were, besides these, Clifford
and Caroline and Eliza, whose parentage was not mentioned,
though the two eldest bore a strange resemblance to Bess.
Starting with a round dozen there was little ·inconvenience
in adding a few French brats. Of the many who received
this hospitality one child eventually married an English peer
and remained for life closely identified with Devonshire House ;
this was Corisande de Gramont who, with her brother
the Duc de Guiche and her sister, came to reside at Devonshire
House about this period. The Regent later gave the boy a
Commission in the 10th Light Dragoons in which he served
in the Peninsular War, returning to France in 1814 and following Charles X into exile at the time of the *coup d'état*, whilst
the other sister married first General Davidoff and then the
Corsican General Sebastiani.

Corisande married Lord Ossulston, afterwards Lord Tanker-
ville, and continued throughout her life to see the Cavendishes.

A picture of the nursery life at Devonshire House had been
left us by Caroline Ponsonby. They were, she says, " served
on silver in the morning and carried their own plates down at
night and believed the world to be divided between Dukes and
beggars." . . . " We had no idea that bread and butter was
made, how it came, we did not pause to think ; but had no
doubt that fine horses must be fed on beef. My kind Aunt
Devonshire had taken me when my mother's ill-health
prevented my being at home. . . ." [1]

The children were confided to the care of one, Miss Trimmer
—a pleasing, not pretty young lady with great serenity of
manner. She was the daughter of the celebrated Mrs.
Trimmer who wrote stories for children. She remained on in
the family till her death.

It was indeed disappointing to all concerned that the improvement in Lady Bessborough's health, which had been the
result of her time abroad, had not been maintained on her
return to England, and in consequence the spring of 1793 saw
Lady Bessborough and the Duchess of Devonshire travelling
once more towards Italy, accompanied of course by Lady
Elizabeth Foster. This time the journey was lengthy and

[1] Raikes' *Memoirs*.

precarious. But May found them once more in Naples, where they met with Lady Webster, who was delighted to see them again, but complained much that . . . "the late hours of Devonshire House are transferred to Chiaia . . ." and grumbled that as they would never start out on an expedition until six, it was usually dark by the time they arrived at their destination.

In June the Reign of Terror began and even Fox had difficulty in finding anything amiable to say about the Revolutionaries. Late in the summer, Lady Elizabeth and the Duchess decided to come home, leaving Harriet to derive what benefit she could from the southern sun. For once in their lives a cavalier was not to hand, and Lady Webster notes with some acrimony, "Lady Elizabeth wishes Mr. Pelham to escort her and the Duchess home. I think it is a bad thing for him, as he imputes his late very long illness entirely to the worry he suffered from both of them in conducting them from Lausanne to Florence." However, with or without the assistance of poor, broken-down Mr. Pelham, the ladies reached England in August.

Soon after they had arrived we hear of an "explosion" at Devonshire House. As to its nature we are left in the dark, but since the Duchess and Lady Elizabeth remained on the best of terms the injured party must have been the Duke. For a short time Bess left the Cavendish household, and her mother remarked, " . . . Bess's coming here will be some (expense). But I think it essential to her. All is to pieces at D.H. and no plan settled. I expect her to-morrow and to stay a month. I think she looks well tho' she is very thin indeed."

But by October she was taken in favour again and attended the gay parties of which Lady Webster, also home from Italy, gives us an account :

" . . . our parties at Devonshire House were delightfully pleasant. Lady Melbourne is uncommonly sensible and amusing. . . . The Duke of Bedford is attached to her ; he is quite brutal in the *brusquerie* of his manner. . . . Mr. Grey is the *bien aimé* of the Duchess, he is a fractious and exigeant lover." [1]

This autumn the hours of the ladies were altered, for the Duchess and Lady Webster developed an unexpected passion

[1] *The Journal of Elizabeth Vassall, Lady Holland.*

for chemistry and set the fashion of rising early to attend Dr. Higgins's lectures.

In this month too came the shocking news of Marie Antoinette's execution. She was well known to Georgiana and Harriet and to many members of English society. Many of her husband's nearest relations were living in London, and a black pall seemed to overshadow society.

In the middle of these distresses Sheridan suffered a heavy blow. His wife died of consumption contracted while nursing a sister who had died of the same disease. During the last months of her life Sheridan had been untiring in his devotion to her. He forgot the House of Commons and Drury Lane, he forgot all his smart friends, and he nursed her untiringly, only occasionally snatching a few minutes to write the latest news to the Duchess whom he knew to be sincerely attached to Elizabeth, or to pour out some part of his self-reproaches. He took her to Bath ; they passed the spot where he had fought his duel with Mathews, and the poignancy of the situation drew an agonised scrawl from his pen. He recalled how Miss Linley had nearly died during their flight by boat to Belgium, and how he had determined to drown himself in the event of her death. Always introspective and highly emotional he was as much engaged in mourning for his own lost youth as for his wife's danger. Yet, easily buoyant, on the slightest sign of improvement in the patient, he would scribble a note to say that Elizabeth was recovering. Actually life was retreating very gently from Mrs. Sheridan's exhausted frame. She seemed to have lost all hold upon the world and all attachment to it. Their lives, hers and Dick's, had worked themselves out so differently from what they had once hoped and planned ; fulfilment of their early ambitions was now impossible, nothing could set back the hands of the clock, they had lost too much time, followed too many gaudy, insubstantial fantasies, and now half in one world and half in another she saw this clearly. It would be too hard to come back to life with such clear sight as she now possessed. She was content to die and only sorry for poor Dick, who would be lost without her for a while.

When she died he was petrified ; emotion he understood, but not the stark reality of grief. Her funeral remained a nightmare that haunted him all his life. Miss Linley had once been a public character, the glory of Bath, and Bath had not forgotten her. Hundreds of people lined the roads, and the church was full to overflowing. The visitors to the watering town came from curiosity, the inhabitants for old time's sake, and all the Linleys who had not died of consumption were surrounding him.

When Sheridan came back to London he seemed to be a broken man ; but, as no one had known better than his wife, the fibres of his heart were resilient, and it was not so very long before he began to take up his old life again.

1794

IN January 1794, rumours were current of an untoward event in the Royal Family. It was whispered that Augustus, Duke of Sussex, had been privately married in Rome to Lady Dunmore's daughter, Lady Augusta Murray. Here was another flagrant breach of the Royal Marriage Act. The Duchess of Cumberland and Mrs. Fitzherbert prepared to receive their new sister-in-law with enthusiasm. Devonshire House laughed, but the Court party were furious, and old friends of the King like Lady Stafford were genuinely distressed; the more so when they learnt that the ceremony in Rome had been reinforced by another at St. George's, Hanover Square.

Soon after the first rumours were circulated Lady Augusta was reported to be very dangerously ill, and later it was learnt that she had given birth to a son. In February Granville went to Naples in the company of Charles Fox's nephew, Lord Holland, and a Mr. Topham Beauclerc. What could be more natural than that they should frequent the company of their compatriots, Lady Webster and Lady Bessborough. To the exiled ladies their arrival was a matter of great rejoicing, and Lady Webster writes on February 3rd:

"Lord Leveson-Gower and Lord Holland came here the day before yesterday. The first I knew at Dresden. He is remarkably handsome and winning; a year or two ago he created a great sensation in Paris when Lady Sutherland introduced him as her *beau beau-frère*; she also initiated him in the orgies of gambling, an acquisition he has maintained." [1]

On Lord Holland she made no comment. How little did either lady dream that the arrival of these young men in Naples was to be the most important event in their lives.

Superficially matters went on very normally. Lady Web-

[1] *The Journal of Elizabeth Vassall, Lady Holland.*

ster was expecting a baby, and she could not make the more strenuous expeditions. What more natural than that the quiet, gentle Lord Holland, who was himself incapacitated from all exercise by a lameness from which he had suffered since childhood, should sit at her side, and listen to her complaints of her husband who cared for nothing but horses and dogs and who would not remain with her in Italy. On the picnics Topham Beauclerc would flirt with Lady Bessborough with whom he believed himself to be in love, and Harriet, laughing at his extremity with Granville, would find young Leveson-Gower a delightful companion. He was so serious, so sensible, so self-assured, so much less of a cub than the other young men. And Granville, flattered at her confidence, delighted in a flirtation in which no mention of love was made. They all moved to Rome.

Lady Webster chronicled a picnic at Tivoli at which " Lord Bessborough grew very cross and from a fit of jealousy about Mr. Beauclerc compelled us all to return to Rome and disquieted our mirth." From Rome they went on to Florence, still in a band, and there, on the 12th of June, Lady Webster gave birth to a daughter. The child was christened at Mr. Wyndham's house, Mr. Pearce officiating. It was given the names of Harriet Frances, in compliment to its godmother Lady Bessborough.

Granville used often to come and sit with Lady Webster, but her attention was now fixed on Lord Holland. She wrote in her journal that he was " *quite* delightful. He is eager without rashness, well bred without ceremony. . . . His bosom friend, Mr. Beauclerc is far from resembling him in any one amiable point of view. . . . He is deeply in love with Lady B. and abhors Lord Granville who is his rival."

Lady Webster pitied Lord Holland for his infirmity, and Lord Holland pitied Lady Webster for her miserable marriage ; their sentiments were not long to remain static. Their life was particularly delightful : " gambling and gallantry filled up the evenings and the mornings." And as the days passed four people's hearts became involved beyond what they desired. Granville's devotion to Lady Bessborough was no longer concealed, and travellers brought back news of it to his mother. The young man had always been gay, but from the first Lady

	Granville Leveson-Gower		
Georgiana	Susan	Charlotte	Anne
=	=	=	=
2nd Earl of	1st Earl of	6th Duke of	Edward
St. Germans	Harrowby	Beaufort	Vernon Harcourt
			Archbishop of York

*The Children of Earl Gower (afterwards Marquess of Stafford),
with whom " The Grand Whiggery " was so much associated*

Stafford realised that this affair was no passing fancy. She wrote constantly to her son, imploring him to be careful. She made no allusions to any person by name, but she warned him against the dissipations and difficulties which might arise from an association with people of the gay world of Devonshire House, whom she genuinely believed to be heartless as well as wicked.

If Lady Stafford believed that Harriet's love for Granville was assumed, she was in error. So far from pretending to love the boy and caring nothing for him, Lady Bessborough's trouble was that she was pretending *not* to love him. She was a very religious woman and devoted to her family. Had she for one moment admitted to herself that she really loved Granville she would have taken measures drastic and immediate to save herself from future complications; but this was her first experience of a real passion, and she found every possible reason for failing to recognise it for what it was. In the first place Granville was about twelve years younger than herself. She refused to believe in the possibility of real attachment, she pretended to imagine that she was touched by his youth and intended to put her worldly wisdom at his disposal. Their conversations were extremely elevating. She warned him against gambling and other dissolute habits, but always with a genuine humility which made her advice acceptable. Unconsciously a desire for sympathy seized her. It brought a most dangerous inflexion to their relationship, adding just what was necessary to hold Granville. She hinted that in interesting herself in the lives of others she was only trying to escape from the troubles of her own existence. Granville returned to England, and absence set its seal on their affections.

Lady Bessborough wrote regularly. She told him the news of the gay circle he had left behind, and then she asked him of his life in England. She said that Lady Webster was in good looks and admired by all, and Granville, used to the jealousies of female relatives, admired her generosity and felt more than ever convinced that there was no one like her.

Danton's head fell in Paris, the British armies were driven out of Holland, in the Channel Lord Howe defeated a French fleet, and at Plymouth Granville drilled his militia men. He annoyed his mother by certain foppish affectations, and she reproached him with never having recovered from his tour abroad. She besought Mr. Pitt to give her son some appointment, but for the moment nothing presented itself. Meanwhile Lady Bessborough was in Venice, which she loved and from which she wrote letters which she convinced herself must make Granville understand the futility of his devotion whilst, at the same time, retaining his sympathy.

The execution of Robespierre in July brought the Reign of Terror to an end, but not before the nerves of the English public had been badly shaken. Pitt demanded a temporary suspension of the Habeas Corpus Act and though many Foxites opposed the measure, it was passed by a highly excitable House.

In the autumn, Lady Bessborough returned to England. She was overjoyed to see her sister again; there was much, very much, which she had to tell her, and something too which she hesitated to talk of, her growing and all-absorbing interest in Granville.

From Holywell she went on to see the Duke of Bedford at Woburn. For Loo she had a deep respect, though he was younger than she, he did not hesitate to give her good advice and now he talked to her very seriously and begged her both to give up her gambling and also to be very careful in regard to Granville Leveson-Gower. He besought her not to make a fool of herself. She agreed in her heart with every word he said, and congratulated herself that she had as yet received no letter from Granville during her visit to the Duke. But the good resolutions did not last long.

The winter began drearily, it was cold and wet, and news came that the Duke of York's army was in retreat. Lady Bessborough's cough and her heart attacks began again. She went to Teignmouth. Lord Bessborough remained in London and spoke in the House of Lords, a rare occurrence, and one which filled his wife with anxiety, the more so as his moderate views were not those of the Foxites. Granville paid her a visit at Teignmouth and assured her that he vastly preferred its amenities to those of London.

In true eighteenth-century tradition he begged for a lock of her hair. She replied that she should send one in the spring if he would promise her that he would not gamble during the winter. It was all very charming and extremely dangerous. Meanwhile at Devonshire House little Caroline Ponsonby " toasted muffins for the Duke, learnt the Foxite creed, and drank damnation to the Tories in glasses of milk."

1795

IN January Granville, falling in with his mother's wishes, stood for Lichfield and was elected. Not since 1784 had the ladies of Devonshire House felt so keen an interest in any poll. But it was an irony of fate that Granville should be an admirer of Mr. Pitt and a friend of that clever young man, Mr. Canning. Neither the Duchess nor Lady Bessborough could help in canvassing for him, and their assistance was limited to the offer of some lip salve and a little sticking plaster to repair the damage wrought by voters. Admiration for Mr. Pitt they could condone—they were used to it, almost it was an hereditary feature of English political life—but admiration for quiet, calculating Mr. Canning with his " scornful lips, blue chin, slightly freckled face," and " hair which before he wore powder a raven might have envied " was inexplicable to them. Canning indeed, except to his intimates, was as unpopular a personality as Lord Shelburne. When the result of the election was known it was found that Granville's beauty had stood him in good stead. Flushed with success he was more than ever devoted to Lady Bessborough.

She extolled the charms of friendship, rather unconvincingly, and suggested that he should look upon her as a sister, fully aware that their respective ages hardly warranted the suggestion.

Late in January she came up to London, and her family fell upon her. She had been used to being teased about Topham Beauclerc and the Duke of Bedford, about young Robinson, and the harmless and good-natured chaff had flattered and amused her. But now, the position was entirely different. Georgiana, Lady Melbourne and the Duke of Bedford each and severally talked to her seriously on the subject of Granville. This she could not bear, the more so that what they said was unanswerable. She was making a fool of herself with a boy, and a boy out of the Opposition camp. She replied that there was no harm in their relationship, that as for her conduct it had never been discreet, why should they choose to criticise her in this particular case rather than in any other ? But she knew quite well that there was a difference. . . . Worse still, on the other side, Granville was getting overwrought and making scenes. She implored him to go about and to see if he did not find other women to admire. She confessed that the news of his marriage would come as a shock to her, but she insisted that if she were to be the first to be informed of it, her unselfish joy in the result would outweigh any pain she might feel on her own account. Thus she tried to reconcile conscience and inclination with rather disappointing results. Nor was Granville without his critics ; his mother was distracted at his behaviour and implored him not to ruin his career, his health and his looks in the dissipations of Devonshire House.

Back at Teignmouth, Lady Bessborough went on writing good advice in letters that defeated their object. She blamed him for choosing Lady Melbourne and her friends as his companions. She warned him that he had made an image of her vastly differing from the reality and that one day, when his illusions were threadbare, he would dislike her in proportion to his present love.

But it was a year of romances and theirs were not the only hearts involved ; indeed three of the most important members of the Devonshire House set were to be married within its course—one, it is true, bigamously, one secretly, and the third, the greatest surprise of all.

For some time the Prince of Wales had neglected Mrs. Fitzherbert in favour of Lady Jersey, and for some time his debts had become once more unmanageable. Once before, they had been discharged against his denial of his marriage to Mrs. Fitzherbert ; this time the conditions were harder, he must marry someone who could take her position as Princess of Wales and provide an heir to the Crown. Indeed, the choice had already been made for him. Princess Caroline of Brunswick was destined to be his consort. She was his cousin, she came from a coarse and immoral court, she was fat and plain and vulgar ; but as the Prince had no intention of being faithful to her, he seems to have been entirely uninterested. If he could bring himself to commit bigamy, the choice of the lady seemed a very secondary matter.

Eventually he took the decision. Years afterwards some correspondence was published which was supposed to have passed between the Prince and Princess before their marriage. There is a letter from the Prince stating that he is compelled to marry against his will, that he does not even consider himself free to do so, but that giving way to *force majeure* he will go through the ceremony and live with the lady until an heir is born, after which event he intends that they should have different establishments. If, on these conditions, Caroline cares to become Princess of Wales, she will only have herself to thank for the consequences.

And there is a reply from Caroline, stating that she is glad to know the situation, but that on the advice of the King she intends to accept her position and hopes eventually to obtain her husband's affections. Though the book in which these letters appear bore the name of Lady Anne Hamilton, there seems little doubt that both the work and the attribution of the authorship were fictitious.

Undoubtedly Caroline knew all about the Prince's life except the actual marriage with Mrs. Fitzherbert; she was not expecting to find a model husband, but she thought that her exalted position would far outweigh the disadvantages which she knew she must accept. What she did *not* expect was the deadly enmity of her husband. Yet when Lady Jersey was chosen to meet her on her arrival in England she had some misgivings. An account of the wedding comes in Lady Jerningham's letters. . . .

" The Prince was serious more than can be told; indeed, one of his equerries told me to-night that he was *très morne*, did not speak enough to his wife, and twice spoke crossly; he was so agitated during the ceremony that it was expected he would burst out into tears. H.R.H. behaved gravely and decently during the ceremony, as I was told, but was in the greatest hurry possible going to the Chapel, and did nothing but chatter with the Duke of Clarence while she was waiting with him at the altar for the arrival of the Prince."

Afterwards the King held a drawing-room at which, we are told, " the Prince looked like death and full of confusion, as if he wished to hide himself from the looks of the whole world. I think he is much to be pitied. The bride, on the contrary, appeared in the highest spirits when she passed us, smiling and nodding to everyone."

And finally we have it on the Princess of Wales' not very reliable authority, that when they retired the Prince " consoled himself with a bottle of whiskey and spent his night with his head in the grate." [1]

A happier event was the marriage of Fox to Mrs. Armistead. To her he owed in a great measure his moral and financial rehabilitation. She had broken him of his habit of heavy drinking and since the handing over of the fund raised by his friends to keep him from bankruptcy, she had helped him to keep away from Newmarket and from the gaming tables. He was anxious to make her what return he could by offering her marriage. At the same time he had no desire that the people who had cut his mistress should visit his wife, and he took a cynical pleasure in keeping his marriage a secret. Mrs. Armistead consented a little ruefully to this arrangement. She loved Charles and was ready to sacrifice herself to his every whim. It was an event supremely happy in its consequences to both parties ; no couple were ever more devoted and to the last she remained his wisest counsellor and most loyal friend.

The third marriage of which we have made mention had a comic element in its origin. Sheridan's eldest son, Tom, was now a young man about town, and he knew that it was his father's wish that he should marry. This belief was confirmed when he received a letter begging him to meet his father at a certain inn, " as he wished to introduce Tom to a very charming young lady." [2] When the boy arrived he found his father wreathed in smiles, and what was his astonishment when he was introduced to the daughter of the Dean of Winchester, not as his bride but as his future stepmother ! So Sheridan had recovered from the loss of his first wife in the short space of two years. The lady whom he now married and whom he introduced to the Devonshire House friends as Hecca, was not to be compared to Elizabeth Linley. She was

---

[1] *Diary of Lady Charlotte Bury.*
[2] *Sheridan and his Time.*

a commonplace, rather jealous woman, with a quick temper, who soon grew to have a contempt for her erratic husband.[1] With Elizabeth he had been "*Chéri*." With Hecca he soon became "Poor Sherry." They quarrelled and made it up and quarrelled again; sometimes Mrs. Sheridan was frightened of her husband, and sometimes she was furiously jealous of him; but never was she conscious of all the romantic idealism which Miss Linley had loved in Sheridan. Perhaps these qualities were not so evident in the fat roystering fellow in the forties as they had been in the gallant young man of more than twenty years ago.

From the time of his second marriage Sheridan's private life presents the spectacle of disintegration. He drinks more, he gives up all hope of extracting himself from his financial difficulties, and a certain sordidness seems to pursue his later career.

The acquittal of Warren Hastings in June was a blow to the Whigs, and in particular to Burke, Fox and Sheridan, who had denounced him so eloquently.

In the autumn the Duchess of Devonshire's health gave rise to anxiety, she was said to be in great danger of losing her sight. Her mother and Lady Bessborough were constantly at her bedside, and the doctors resorted to the most terrifying remedies. They saved her eyes by almost strangling her with a handkerchief and forcing all the blood up into her head, and then bleeding her with leeches.

Apparently, the astonishing treatment was successful, but the convalescence was lengthy. Lady Elizabeth Foster, always in residence, amused her with stories of Lord Bristol. The mercurial Bishop had made great friends with Emma Hamilton at Naples. Indeed, his open admiration of her caused some tittle-tattle, but the Bishop it seemed still drew the lines at some things. The story went that one day when he was visiting Emma, a certain notorious lady was announced. The Bishop rose and prepared to depart, whereupon Lady Hamilton remarked petulantly, "Why, my Lord, you are not going, are you? Our company is not, I hope, disagreeable?"[2] To which Lord Bristol had responded curtly, "It is permitted to

---

[1] Sheridan's *Life and Times*.
[2] *The Life of the Earl Bishop of Derry*.

a bishop to visit one sinner, but quite unfitting that he should be seen in a brothel."

The early winter saw increased signs of discontent in the great towns, and a crop of repressive legislation was the result. The Treasonable Practices Act was a measure which the Foxites fought against unavailingly. It forbade public meeting, and it made writing, printing, preaching, or speaking against the Crown punishable. Much of the anti-revolutionary reaction was due to alarm at the activities of a Jacobinical Society known as the "Friends of the People" with which Mr. Grey was associated. Its aims were definitely anti-constitutional, and though Fox never belonged to it many of his followers were numbered amongst its members.

With the suspension of the Habeas Corpus Act and the passing of the Treasonable Practices Act, the Whigs had some right to complain that they were being ruled by a despotic government. Before the end of the year the name of Napoleon Bonaparte had come into prominence. He had put down an insurrection in Paris, and the Republic had ceased to be and a Directory had come to birth.

1 7 9 6

A YEAR of French victories set in. Under Napoleon the French armies were as ubiquitous as they were victorious. When Bonaparte crossed the Alps, news of the English in Italy was anxiously sought by their friends at Devonshire House.

In April, Lady Webster wrote to tell her husband of the death of the child Harriet Frances, to whom Lady Bessborough had stood sponsor in Florence. She described her as having "taken the measles at Modena, and died of convulsions consequent upon the disease." Sir Godfrey was not likely to be severely affected by the news of the death of an infant which he had scarcely, if ever, seen ; but what would have been his surprise had he known that at the moment in which he received the letter an old nurse, Sarah Brown, was travelling back to England with a healthy child, and that the Burial Service of the Church of England had been read over a young goat.

In May Charles Fox expected his nephew Lord Holland to return to England, and when he did return his arrival was shortly followed by that of Lady Webster. Before long scandal associated their names. Lord Granville received a bundle of correspondence on the subject. Lady Stafford was horrified. Perhaps she saw a parallel in the story, and feared that Granville might be encouraged by such a precedent.

It is curious to realise how entirely she had misjudged her son if she really believed that there was any fear of his eloping with Lady Bessborough. Apart from his moral principles, which were sound, Granville had far too much " calcul " and worldly wisdom to accept the consequences of an action so universally reprobated. But Lady Stafford's fear started from two fundamental errors. She believed that Lady Bessborough was Granville's mistress, and also she believed her to be wholly a-moral. Neither fact was true. She could not, however, leave the matter alone, and she covered pages with entreaties to her son to mend his evil ways. There was not a little irony in the situation, for the wretched Granville's conduct had actually been kept by Lady Bessborough within the strictest bonds of morality. Granville's answer to these exhortations was awaited with the keenest anxiety. When it arrived it gave the greatest delight to Lord Stafford, for the comments on the incident seemed to correspond identically with his own views. He was delighted at his son's good principles. Lady Stafford, though relieved, remained unconvinced. She upbraided him with his astuteness in simulating sentiments which she did not believe to be genuine. She warned him gravely that if he were not careful she might have to send him abroad at whatever sacrifice to herself. Impressed with all these warnings, Granville had no thought but to caution Lady Bessborough from holding any communication with Lady Webster. The warning was useless. She had known of the affair from the beginning, and so far from avoiding Lady Webster, she had on the contrary seen as much of her as possible in an endeavour to restrain her from any desperate measure.

Indeed, she had almost succeeded in arranging an amicable separation between Sir Godfrey and his wife, when Lady Webster had suddenly acted upon impulse and without forethought. Whilst Harriet reprobated the action heartily, she begged Lady Webster's detractors to recollect that the subject of their reproof had been married at fifteen to a man nearly three times older than herself and entirely distasteful to her. Extenuating circumstances did not make *wrong right*, but it might be hoped that they would restrain harsh criticism from those who had fortunately not found themselves in similar circumstances.

It is probable that Granville was slightly shocked at the tone of Lady Bessborough's letter, for, despite Lady Stafford's fears, neither had his morals loosened, nor his mind appreciably broadened from his contact with the wicked world of Devonshire House.

Meanwhile at Carlton House matters had gone from bad to worse. In January the birth of a daughter, who had been christened Charlotte, after her grandmother the Queen, had proved a disappointment to the Prince of Wales. But though a girl, the Princess Charlotte could inherit the throne. The Prince felt that he had done his duty in providing an heir, and he adhered firmly to his resolution of leaving his wife immediately upon the birth of the child. He now lived openly with Lady Jersey.

The King was horrified, and in June he set about trying to achieve a reconciliation. He wrote a kind letter to his daughter-in-law and begged her to write to the Prince. Caroline obeyed and wrote what Lady Stafford termed " the prettiest letter you ever saw." The reply she received was " formal, cold and stupid " by comparison. On the Monday after the receipt of this letter the Prince came to dine at Carlton House, but left for Lady Jersey's immediately after dinner. His conduct to his wife was observed to be frigidly correct. Lady Jersey's behaviour can hardly share in even that scanty meed of praise. She was insufferably insolent, and was known to ride even through " the courts of Carlton House attended by a servant in the Prince's livery." [1]

The Princess of Wales' coarse nature had made a bad impression upon London society, which considered the Prince, in the matter of his marriage, to be a victim of unjust coercion ; but his later treatment of her brought her the few friends she was ever to possess.

Yet whilst public opinion questioned. the heir-apparent's relations with Lady Jersey, that young man was making a will which would have astonished them. This document, dated 1796 and quoted by Sarjeant by kind permission of His Majesty, contains the following phrases :

" I now therefore George, Augustus, Frederick, Prince of Wales etc. do by this my last will and testament leave, will and bequeath after my death, all my estates, all my property, all my personalties of whatever kind or sort to *my Maria Fitzherbert, who is my wife in the eyes of God, and ever will be such in mine.*"

In July the eye affection from which the Duchess of Devonshire had suffered during the previous year returned with renewed violence. At first it was thought that there was no hope of saving her sight. Lady Bessborough was in her room

[1] *The Jerningham Papers.*

night and day, and witnessed the terrible operations which had to be performed without any alleviations. Yet, despite the tortures they inflicted, the surgeons refused to give a favourable verdict. But Georgiana, suffering agonies and entirely blind, had at least no conception of their unfavourable views. It became Lady Bessborough's duty to hear the latest reports and then to go to her sister and keep up her spirits with hopes which she herself believed to be fictitious.

There came one dreadful night when the doctors despaired not only of the Duchess's sight but also of her life. Lady Bessborough's heart attacks returned with renewed violence. It seemed almost as though she would soon be in as grave danger as was her sister. When the surgeons came out of the Duchess's room the next morning she was obliged to drink some brandy before she could bring herself to hear their verdict. When she heard the news it proved unexpectedly to be good. The crisis was over; if nothing further occurred, the Duchess might not go quite blind. Lady Bessborough hardly dared to hope again after the crisis of the last days.

Yet Mr. Phipps, the oculist, was proved right. Very gradually the Duchess gained strength and began to throw off the effects of the infection. Granville hoped to come and visit Lady Bessborough, but this time a change in his own plans made it impossible. She wrote to him that she was glad of it. She could not have seen him. When she left her sister's room it was only to go into the garden of Devonshire House and take a breath of air. She apologised for the shortness of her letters, but explained that she was overwhelmed by all the numerous duties of a good nurse. Lady Elizabeth Foster was equally devoted and attentive, but she had less talent for nursing and did her share rather in looking after the household and the children, and also, it may be mentioned, the Duke.

In October Pitt began peace parleys with France and, remembering Lady Stafford's solicitations, he appointed Granville Leveson-Gower to accompany Lord Malmesbury to Paris on the mission. Lady Bessborough well knew for what reason he had been sent abroad, and she warned him rather satirically against the dangers of Paris and told him that she had no interest in exquisites, and that if he were to become addicted by the vices of Paris she for one would cut him. After all, there was no reason why Lady Stafford should have the sole right to lecture Granville ?

But soon the Duchess was ill again, and Lady Bessborough had no thought but for her sister. Another operation was performed ; Georgiana bore it with great courage, but it was frightful to witness. Granville wrote gravely that Paris was indeed the worst town he had ever visited, but that fortified by Lady Bessborough's sentiments he had upheld religion and morality.

He added that he had taken to wearing a wig, a practice which he was to adhere to for the rest of his life. Lady Bessborough's interest was aroused, she had just cut her own hair short and she implored Granville to send her a wig by the bag. The young man was delighted and wrote enquiring whether he should not send some rouge too, if she would inform him of the price and the shade. But Lady Bessborough waited for the wig in vain and complained that Mr. Canning must have taken it out of the bag and be wearing it.

Once again the Duchess took a turn for the better, and Harriet's spirits rose.

It became apparent that Lord Malmesbury's mission would be a failure and that the Directory desired war, and before the end of the year hostilities had begun.

In Ireland rebellion was imminent. The Government, ordering the raising of a body of Yeomanry, Lord Carhampton and Lord Camden desired that the Loyal Irish Catholics should be eligible for service ; but the Chancellor turned down the suggestion. His action forced the Catholics into enmity to England. Lady Sarah Napier wrote bitterly :

" . . . I could not imagine upon *what grounds* to form the *reasoning* that actuates the Government *to urge on a civil war with all their power* ! But since from some unknown cause *it is* their plan, I will do them the justice to say they have acted uniformly well in it, and have nearly succeeded.

" . . . By this means the power of the Republican party grows. . . . This I *assert* because I *know* it, for, alas, we are but too well *au fait* of the whole of the secrets on both sides. Within this month *our* footmen and twelve Castletown servants and workmen have been taken up as housebreakers and United

Irishmen. . . . We are bound to see that he has a fair tryal, which, alas, is the fate of *few* in these terrible times." [1]

In December, General Hoche landed in Bantry Bay with a small force, but was repulsed. In Wales a few convicts were disembarked and, terrified by the distant sight of red coats which they took for reinforcements, they surrendered. Actually the red coats belonging to some old women on Lord Cawdor's estate, and the strategem was said to be the Earl's ingenious invention. During the course of this year Mr. Foster, the husband of Lady Elizabeth, died. The event was of importance, for the Duke of Richmond was said to be in love with Bess.

[1] *The Letters of Lady Sarah Lennox.*

1797

ENGLAND had now to face a seemingly endless war. Early in the year the Bank ceased gold payments, and Charles Fox, disgusted by what he considered the folly and incompetence of the Government, seceded from Parliament. This decision, which came as a shock to his followers, came also as an embarrassment to Pitt. The Prime Minister required the criticisms of his great adversary in order to gauge the temper of the country. But neither friends nor foes could induce " the Black Animal " to change its mind, so Fox went down to St. Anne's and devoted himself to the study of the classics.

If the finances of the country were in a sad way, those of the Duchess of Devonshire and Lady Bessborough were equally involved. Despite the assistance of the kind Duke of Bedford, Georgiana was obliged to borrow from her oculist, Mr. Phipps, and to endeavour to obtain £200 from Lord Holland ; and Harriet was actually arrested at Lady Buckingham's house and fined for gaming.[1] It was all very humiliating. The two ladies owed some £23,000 to the Jews, and they could scarcely alight from their carriage to enter a friend's house without being pursued by duns or bailiffs. The good resolutions Lady Bessborough had made in Naples three years previously had not borne fruit, and though her liabilities were as nothing compared to those of her sister, her husband's estates were unfortunately similarly unequal to bear the strain.

Lady Bessborough, exhausted by financial worries, spent much of the spring with her mother at Holywell, near St. Albans. The sharp contrast with the hours of London life came as a welcome relief. At eight o'clock in the morning there were family prayers : at eight-fifteen breakfast. All through the morning Lady Bessborough gave lessons either in

[1] *Diary of Lady Charlotte Bury* (probably untrue).

the village school or to her daughter Caroline, who was, at twelve years old, nearly as illiterate as any of the village children. At three o'clock the family met for lunch. During the afternoon they drove out ; at six they met again for tea, followed by a little music ; then at nine prayers, followed by supper and bed at ten.

Granville's letters and those received by Lady Bessborough's maid, Sally, from her sweetheart, were the only excitements in the well-ordered life of Holywell. How eagerly these letters were awaited ! Harriet and her maid, Sally, sat up at the window waiting for them after the rest of the household had gone to bed, and when they heard the postman's approach let down a string to which the letters were attached in order that they might be drawn up to the bedroom by the expectant women.

Lady Bessborough was high in the thirties : half London had made love to her without any encouragement ; no wonder if young Granville, at the age of twenty-four, felt a little elated.

Early in the year, whilst Napoleon was gaining fresh victories over the troops of the Empire, one consoling piece of news came to comfort the nation. The British fleet, under Jervis, had won a great victory over the French fleet at Cape St. Vincent. This did much to restore the confidence and the self-respect of the country, which had suffered severely during the previous year. But this satisfaction was short-lived, for, towards the end of the month of May, the Fleet at the Nore began to give trouble. The men had a considerable number of grievances to which the Admiralty had turned a deaf ear. The result of this attitude was a mutiny on a large scale. All the ships of Admiral Duncan's fleet, with the exception of the Flagship and Admiral Onslow's frigate, hoisted the red flag. Lord Spencer, the brother of Georgiana and Harriet, was at the time First Lord of the Admiralty. During the small hours of the morning he went to consult Mr. Pitt as to the proper course of action to pursue. He found the Prime Minister asleep ; being very much alarmed at the gravity of the situation, he insisted that Pitt should be roused. Pitt listened courteously to Spencer's report and gave some advice, after which the First Lord retired ; but two minutes after he had left the room Spencer recollected an important detail which he had forgotten to communicate to Pitt. He, therefore, ran back into the bedroom, only to find the Prime Minister asleep. Whether such indifference was reassuring or alarming, Spencer could not decide.

The mutineers addressed a very impertinent letter to the King which began with the words " Health and Fraternity," and ended by announcing that, if George III would not consent to change his Ministers within twenty-four hours, they, the mutineers, " would do something to astonish the world." All the while Sheerness was in a state of siege ; an attack by the mutineers was expected at any moment, and the guns of the forts were ready for action ; indeed, the two loyal ships, the *Repulse* and the *Leopard*, were fired upon. But now, dissensions broke out amongst the mutineers : parleys ensued ; the Government weakly offered concessions, which, if just, should have been granted to representation, and not to rebellion. Finally, the mutineers agreed to give up their ringleader, named Parker, and a few other notable rebels.

On June 10th the red flag was lowered, and the fleet sailed in, having made an unconditional surrender. A few days later Parker and his companions were hanged from the yardarm. Thus ended the discreditable affair.

In the same month, negotiations for peace with France began again, and once more Lord Malmesbury, accompanied by Granville, sailed for France. The young man noted with interest how few remains of republicanism were now visible in that country. Soldiers saluted, the peasants were polite, the dress of all classes had become gayer and richer.

It was not to be supposed that Lady Bessborough would take kindly to Granville's departure. Sheridan, who had loved her for many years, and since he was married to Hecca, loved her more than ever, was amongst the first to realise that her heart was at last seriously engaged. When she left Roehampton and came up to London in July she found him on the doorstep of the house in Cavendish Square, come to see in what state she might be. He teased her unmercifully. The purpose of Lady Bessborough's visit to London was to attend the marriage of her friend, Lady Webster, to Lord Holland.

" On July 4th," Lady Holland writes, " my wretched

marriage was annulled by Parliament. On the fifth I signed a deed by which I made over my whole fortune to Sir G. W. for our joint lives, for the insignificant sum of 800*l.* I was married at Rickmansworth Church by Rev. Mr. Morris to Lord Holland, on July 6th." [1]

Her stepfather, Sir Gilbert Affleck, gave her away. She was twenty-six and Holland was twenty-three, and she commented on " the horrid disparity."

Thus began Lady Holland's great reign at Holland House. But most ladies were less broad-minded than Lady Bessborough and the Duchess of Devonshire ; and the Hollands, at their receptions, had to content themselves for the most part with male society. The deprivation of female friends was not felt severely by Elizabeth, for she made it her business to collect all the best male brains of the day, and over their debates she presided as a Queen. Her other source of interest was her garden, into which she introduced many flowers until then unknown in England, including the dahlia.

In this month of July 1797 Burke died. Deserted by all his friends, his closing years had been passed in political and social isolation. The most disinterested of men he had never resented the manner in which he had been cold-shouldered by the Whigs ; but when the same treatment was meted out to his son he suddenly became bitter. And the irony of it was that, whereas the slights heaped on Burke had no justification, the scant notice taken of his son seemed to be forgivable, since the young man had little but a devotion to his father to recommend him. [2] A short time before his death Burke sent a message to Fox, begging him " to forgive any harshness and warm temper " he might have shown against him, and " assuring him of his dying esteem." Fox, always generous, was ready to rush at once to his friend's bedside, but Burke stoically refused to see him. [3] Such a meeting might, he thought, seem to imply that, at the last, he had come round to Fox's point of view.

Burke's funeral was attended by men of all parties ; yet few had any realisation of the greatness of the man whom they honoured. Lady Bessborough makes scarcely an allusion to

[1] *The Journal of Elizabeth Vassall, Lady Holland.*
[2] *Life of Fox*—Hobhouse.   [3] *Life of Fox*—Hammond.

his death in her frequent letters to Granville. Rather she was concerned with the distressing fact that Granville's friend, Charles Ellis, had, it would seem, somewhat peremptorily announced that, unless Granville broke with Lady Bessborough, their friendship must come to an end.

Harriet was made miserable by a knowledge of the incident. The more so that, having Granville's welfare genuinely at heart, she felt a sincere affection towards all those with whom he was connected but who, alas, did not reciprocate the sentiment.

These excellent feelings bound Granville closer to her. Towards the end of September he was sent home with despatches. It was evident that the negotiations were going to break down, and that Lord Malmesbury would soon be home again. There were Royalist riots in France and these inspired Lord Bristol with a wonderful plan, of which he wrote post-haste to Bess, begging her to bring it to the notice of the Government, or at least to beg the Duke of Devonshire to promote it : by the agency of England and Prussia, France was to be partitioned : north of the Loire there was to be a Republic ; south there was to be a kingdom under Louis XVIII, having its capital at Toulon.[1] The net result would be a France too weak to cause any further trouble in Europe.

Already, he said, he had interested the King of Prussia in the scheme by representing to him how much worse a neighbour a republic would be than a kingdom. Over this plan the Bishop was as excited as he had been over the marriage of Frederick Hervey and the Countess de La Marche. But it is to be feared that Lady Elizabeth saw in her father's inspirations matter only for the entertainment of her friends at Devonshire House, and that she did little to forward his schemes.

In October Admiral Duncan's fleet wiped out the memory of the May mutiny by winning a victory over the Dutch fleet at the Battle of Camperdown ; and, in the same month, Napoleon, who had annihilated the Austrian Army, and entered Vienna, made peace with the Empire at Campo Formio. Milan and Belgium were ceded to France ; and the rest of Europe trembled. Lord Malmesbury left Paris.

Meanwhile, Granville's return to England was not proving

[1] *The Life of the Earl Bishop of Derry.*

as delightful to Lady Bessborough as she had hoped. He spent the autumn staying with Pitt and Canning ; both of whom disapproved of Devonshire House in general, and of Lady Bessborough in particular. Moreover, he was surrounded by his mother's friends, and Harriet sensed danger ; nor was she mistaken. Through Lady Stafford's influence, a mission to Berlin to congratulate Frederick William on his accession was offered to the young man of twenty-four. Granville had no desire to leave England ; he was in some doubt as to his capacity for so great an undertaking, and he decided at first to refuse. Lady Bessborough was perplexed. She had every reason for desiring that he should remain in England, yet she knew that it would be wise for him to accept the mission.

Under the circumstances she was careful not to give advice of any sort, and when she heard of his decision she hardly knew her mind. Lady Stafford was in no doubt as to *her* view of the situation ; she warned her son that he would get a good scolding from his father, who had no doubt but that the refusal derived from a desire not to stir from London on account of " an attachment."

Eventually the Staffords, as usual, had their way ; and Granville withdrew his refusal. Lord Stafford was overjoyed.

Curiously enough, Harriet felt almost relieved at the release from responsibility for his rejection of the offer, and in December Granville prepared to sail.

1798

IN January the King's illness delayed the departure of the mission, and Lady Bessborough thankfully enjoyed the reprieve. The expense of the war was beginning to fall heavily upon the general public, and the letters of the period are full of allusions to taxation. A tax was levied on powdered heads, and Government spies were set to see whether ladies who had failed to pay for licences were wearing powder or not. One of the first victims was Lady Bessborough. She had given the money for the payment of the tax to their steward Easton, but the latter had forgotten to obtain the licence, and one day Harriet was summoned to appear before the Justice at Westminster.

The informer kindly offered to perjure himself for a large bribe, but this Harriet refused to allow. So she went down to the Court where she was bullied for three hours and fined £60. A punishment she might have avoided had she availed herself of some of the witnesses' kind offers of perjury.

Another reference to taxation comes in a letter to Lady Jerningham, which shows how willingly the burden was shouldered, and how real was the fear of invasion.

" . . . I am sensible the taxes must bear hard on you . . . (But) if the pigtail messrs. should come, they will make us smart more severely, and leave us, at best, to live without a shift. *Ainsi*, we may be glad to do what we can to serve the nation. . . . If you and the Cossey family hire a convoi and a man of war to go over to America (will you) take us with you to found a convent . . . but I confide we shall never be obliged to leave good old England, which I love with all my heart nonesuch." [1]

Another topic of conversation was the Prince's rupture with Lady Jersey. "Who is now in the transit of Venus," says

[1] *The Jerningham Papers.*

Lady Jerningham. The situation was made more difficult by the fact that the lady herself absolutely refused to recognise her fallen estate. She pursued the Prince everywhere, it was said, purely for the pleasure of " plagueing him." The Prince's position was extremely difficult. He desired to let Lady Jersey down gently, and he wished to resume his life with Mrs. Fitzherbert ; yet neither lady would fall in with his plans.

And still Granville's departure hung fire. Both he and Harriet had worked themselves up to a high pitch of emotion over the parting and, now that it was delayed, they suffered from nerves. Granville accused her of being insufferably capricious and unbalanced ; at one moment, he said, she would see him, and at another refuse him admittance ; in one day she would run the gamut of all the moods. To which she replied vigorously that she was ill and worried and that, in addition, her love for him could not make her forget what she owed to her other friends and to her family. If she had refused to see him it was because she had had to visit some old friends who required her assistance.

In February, little Caroline caught chicken-pox, and Harriet was entirely withdrawn from social life. Luckily the attack was a slight one and no marks were to remain. The child, who admired Granville, but did not like him, told her mother that she feared that Lord Granville would never look at her again if she were to become pock-marked.

When Caroline was well again Granville was gone. With his departure Sheridan took the field again and succeeded in making Lady Bessborough's life exceedingly difficult for her. As soon as she came to Cavendish Square he called, expressed astonishment that Lord Granville had allowed her to come to town during his absence, and announced that he should stay and dine alone with her. Harriet was annoyed and surprised, but she could only acquiesce in the arrangement, and Sheridan took pains to make himself agreeable, but his stay was of prodigious duration.

At length, fearing that he meant to spend the night, Lady Bessborough ordered her chair and went out to pay some calls ; but Sheridan was up to the ruse, he followed her everywhere, and as she found all her friends out he eventually followed her home. But fortunately her chairman had outstripped his, so that she was able to reach her house in time to order the porter to close the door and refuse all admittance. Finally Sheridan was left expostulating in the street.

It made a good story to write to Granville, and she felt it might be well for him to know that she had had three violent declarations of love in the last weeks. It was just as well, she thought, that he should not think himself too secure.

Startling news came from Italy in March. The whole of Lord Bristol's property and effects in Rome, to the amount of £20,000, had been sequestrated. Instantly, the undefeated prelate wrote to beg Elizabeth to intervene on his behalf, by inducing Pitt to send him as Minister " to congratulate the Roman people on their emancipation." [1] " Now," he wrote, " if either your friend Lord Spencer, or, above all, your greater friend, the Duke of Devonshire, or the Duchess, would effectually join in this lottery, you see, dearest Elizabeth, I should literally get the £20,000 prize." The plan was ingenious, but unfortunately it did not commend itself to those in authority. The Bishop's life was supposed to be most immoral, he was accused of acts of the most sacrilegious nature, and was considered no fit representative of Great Britain.

In addition to the confiscation of his goods in Rome, he had other troubles. Certain of his effects had been carried to Naples by sea, in an effort to save them from the invaders, and Messrs. Panton had charged the exorbitant sum of £1,800 for their conveyance. The Bishop was furious, the more so, he protested, that they only consisted of " busts, some carrara statues and other marbles to the amount of £750, more or less, and the pictures are chiefly Cimabue, Giotto, Guido da Siena, Marco di Siena, and all that old pedantry of painting. . . ."

But worse still was to befall. For a month after the seizure of his goods, Lord Bristol was taken prisoner by the French and detained at Milan for nine months. Then, letters fly all over Europe, imploring the great and powerful to exert themselves on his behalf. But not all sympathised with the adventurous prelate, and Lady Holland comments acidly enough on his attempted escape :

" That abominable, wicked old fellow, Lord Bristol, is still kept prisoner at Milan. I believe, even in his confinement,

[1] *The Life of the Earl Bishop of Derry.*

1799

THE early months of 1799 saw Napoleon's invasion of Syria and the gallant resistance of Sir Sidney Smith at Acre. They saw also the release of the Bishop of Derry from his captivity. He immediately indicted a characteristic letter to Lady Hamilton, rejoicing over an Austrian victory and his own liberation :

" Hip ! Hip ! Hip ! Huzza ! Huzza ! Huzza ! for dearest Emma ! Those doubly damned miscreants, first as French, secondly as Repts, have thrown doublets and within these few days been beat—nay, completely beaten twice." [1]

Soon he was up to his usual tricks, busily writing home to his daughter, begging them to draw Mr. Pitt's attention to the advantages of a Wine Monopoly, which would not only put a stop to smuggling, but would also put two or three millions in the Government's empty pockets. Alas, like all his schemes, it was destined to oblivion. Bess had other interests. It was thought that the Duke of Richmond was about to ask for her hand. Lady Holland commented on the affair :

" His conduct to Lady Eliz Foster is very unaccountable. He is always talking and writing as if he intended to marry her, and yet the marriage is not more advanced than it was two years ago. She came here the other morning. As soon as ye Dss of L(einster) heard she was here, she immediately begged to see her in her room, and this very much flattered Lady E. and added to her hopes." [2]

But whatever the Duchess of Leinster may have said concerning her brother, nothing came of the interview. Perhaps Bess felt that the situation would be too difficult. There were not only the two Foster children to be considered, there were also those two unexplained infants Caroline St. Jules and

[1] *The Life of the Earl Bishop of Derry.*
[2] *The Journal of Elizabeth Vassall, Lady Holland.*

Clifford, whose education was the concern of the Duke of Devonshire.

Lady Bessborough spent the spring in nursing her husband through a bad attack of gout, and was half consoled and half distressed by his statement that her attentions to him more than compensated him for the pain he suffered. She felt remorse, but it did not go very deep, for she wrote an account of her sentiments to Granville. His elder brother had been raised to the Upper House and Granville stood, therefore, for the vacant county seat.

Despite their differences in political opinion, Georgiana and Harriet did all that they could for him, and even wrote imploring Sheridan to secure him some votes. But the days of their canvassing were over. Alas, it was even doubtful if, since the Duchess's illness, she would have had the same powers of persuasion. Lady Holland wrote sadly :

" The change in form is painful to see ; scarcely has she a vestige of those charms that once attracted all hearts. Her figure is corpulent, her complexion coarse, one eye gone, and her neck immense. How frail is the tenure of beauty ! Alas ! too true, too trite a saying." [1]

It was fifteen years now since the Westminster Election of 1784. Then Granville had thought it very shocking that the ladies of Devonshire House should canvass for Fox. But now he himself was being assisted by many fair canvassers.

Life was curing Granville of much of his priggishness. Having won his seat he went to stay with his parents, and, though he was anxious to come and see Lady Bessborough in London, she restrained him. Her boys were back from school and she did not wish to have him about the place whilst they were at home. She also urged upon him the claim which his elderly parents had on his time.

In May (?) a story was current which caused a great deal of chatter : it was said that Lady Holland had restored a child of six years of age to Sir G. Webster. Lady Bristol comments with astonishment on the subject. (Lady Holland) " lay in of it in Italy. When she was coming home, conscious that she was to be parted from Sir Godfrey, and being doatingly fond of this child, she continued to have it pass for dead,

[1] *The Journal of Elizabeth Vassall, Lady Holland.*

and had it brought to England under a feigned name, and has constantly seen it ; but at last, convinced she was acting in a most unjustifiable manner, both to Sir Godfrey and the child, she owned the whole thing." [1]

The story was substantially correct. What Lady Bristol did not know was that Sir Godfrey, having heard rumours that the child was alive, had just given orders for the exhumation of the body at Sienna, and that it was the knowledge of this plan which induced Lady Holland to disclose her deception, rather than any pangs of conscience. Some sympathy may be felt for her. All her Webster children had been taken away from her, and years later, when her second son, by Lord Holland, was a grown man, he was to meet his stepsister, then married, and not even know who she was, so complete had been the separation between the two families. [2]

In the summer came the interesting news of Mrs. Fitzherbert's reconciliation with the Prince of Wales. The matter was one of great difficulty. Mrs. Fitzherbert was very loath to swallow her pride and live with the Prince unless her marriage were recognised. But she had no desire to ruin her husband and the witnesses to her marriage, nor to place the Princess of Wales and Princess Charlotte in an extremely disagreeable position. It may be noted, however, that the Princess of Wales and Mrs. Fitzherbert were always subjects of sympathetic interest to each other. Caroline was said to have remarked that " she hoped her husband would not feel her any impediment to the reconciliation he was so desirous for." And later she remarked to Lady Charlotte Bury, in a conversation regarding Mrs. Fitzherbert, " that is the Prince's true wife, she is an excellent woman, it is a great pity for him he ever broke with her. Do you know de man who was present at his marriage, the late Lord B(radford). He declared to a friend of mine that when he went to inform Mrs. Fitzherbert that the Prince had married me, she would not believe it, for she knew herself to be married to him." [3]

If Caroline was generous, Maria was scrupulous ; but, after receiving from the hands of the Duke of Cumberland, a letter

---

[1] *The Two Duchesses.*
[2] *Memoirs of the Fourth Lord Holland.*
[3] *Diary of Lady Charlotte Bury.*

full of entreaties and reproaches she consented to meet her husband in the presence of Sir Henry Rycroft at Kempshott. As a result of this interview Mrs. Fitzherbert decided to send Father William Nassau, one of the priests from the Warwick Street Chapel, where she went to Mass when in London, to Rome in order to obtain the Pope's judgment on the case.[1] Maria told the Prince that if her marriage were recognised as canonically valid she would return to him ; if not, she should live abroad. That the validity of the marriage would be upheld (as it was) was almost a foregone conclusion (*vide* evidence examined in an earlier chapter). Yet, till the answer came, Mrs. Fitzherbert was obdurate. But the knowledge that the reconciliation was impending brought other reconciliations in its train. Georgiana had loved the Prince too well to remain entirely estranged from him since his denial of his marriage. Yet she had seen less of him, and Harriet had not seen him at all. Now all was to be made up, and Lady Bessborough had a reconciliation with the Prince—a matter which gave great pleasure to her sister. Harriet herself was not attracted to the idea, but the Prince was in so gay a mood that, despite her abhorrence of his conduct during the past years, Harriet ended by giving way to his charm and good humour.

Mid-summer was darkened by disasters to the arms of the Allies. In July Napoleon won a great victory over the Turks at Aboukir, and in August the Dutch expedition failed ignominiously. Yet these disasters were not without their personal compensations in some quarters, and on October 19th Lady Holland wrote :

. . . " The whole Dutch expedition has failed . . . out of evil, there is good. Lords Morpeth and G. Leveson had offered their services and were upon the point of going. Lord G. is raising a regiment and is appointed Lt. Col." [2]

. Lady Bessborough, who had gone to the sea for her health, witnessed the departure of the troopships with an inner thankfulness that those other ships, in which Granville and his friends would have embarked, were not to sail.

Meanwhile, in London the Duchess was bringing out her eldest daughter Georgiana. Horace Walpole's friend, Miss

[1] *George IV and Mrs. Fitzherbert.*
[2] *The Journal of Elizabeth Vassall, Lady Holland.*

Berry, who had recently made acquaintance with the Duchess, describes the child as a " natural, unaffected girl of sixteen, with a warm heart and good understanding," whom, however, she fears " will never . . . be handsome to compare with her mother, but has much of her captivating manner." [1]

One November evening they made up a party for the play, collecting " the few men that remained in London to their box," and it was during this performance that news came of the " marvellous revolution in France," whereby Napoleon became First Consul and the Directory ceased to be. Miss Berry remarks sagaciously, " For my part, I think it will be better dealing with one, or even with three rogues, than five hundred ; but it will, in all probability, shortly end in Bonaparte's assassination."

Shortly after this event Napoleon made proposals for peace to the English Government. For the first time in many months Fox left St. Anne's Hill and came to the House to support the Peace Party ; but his effort was vain. Pitt turned down the proposals (as the Foxites thought, very rudely), and the war continued.

In America, Washington died at the close of the year. His death caused some interest amongst the Devonshire House circle who had stood his friends in the past ; but Lady Holland's obituary notice of him is hardly flattering : " His name will stand high in the page of history, and posterity will be apt to outstep truth to bestow enthusiastic eulogy upon him, who has been great from his mediocrity." [2]

[1] *Journal and Correspondence of Miss Berry.*
[2] *The Journal of Elizabeth Vassall, Lady Holland.*

1 8 0 0

AN expensive year began with the turn of the century.
Bread cost 1s. 5d. the quartern loaf, coal was priced at
six guineas the caldron, turkeys cost 16s. and capons 8s. 6d.,
and all meat was at a price that was prohibitive to the lower
classes. And amongst the more wealthy many who had been
supporting French refugees for several years began to feel the
added expense irksome. Moreover, in this year and the preceding one, a new wave of emigrants had reached the hospitable
English shores. These were, for the most part, members of
the monastic orders who had manged to stay on in France
during the first years of the revolution, but who now found it
impossible to continue to subsist in their native land.

In March we hear of the Duchess, Lady Bessborough and
Lady Georgiana making a visit to the house of " The Blew
Nuns " at Bodney with a view to placing a young relative of
Lord Bessborough under their care.[1] These were the nuns,
nearly all English by birth, whose convent in Paris had been
the school to which most of the Catholic aristocracy had sent
its daughters for the last fifty years. The nuns had been
carried to England through the kindness of Lady Jerningham,
an old scholar, and for many months they had been housed at
Cossey.

The number of religious bodies now sheltering in England
had been sufficient to cause alarm to the opponents of Roman
Catholicism, and Sir H. Mildmay brought forward a Bill " to
check the increase of Catholicism by preventing the nuns at
Winchester from giving the veil," and to cause the making of
a proselyte to become a penal offence. But the Duchess of
Devonshire and Lady Bessborough were no bigots ; and they
were delighted with what they saw at Bodney and invited Lady
Jerningham's daughter-in-law to a great fête at Devonshire

[1] *The Jerningham Papers.*

152

House, of which Lady Jerningham gives an amusing description :

"We got there a little after three and were told that the Duchess was in the Pleasure Ground. We accordingly found her sitting with Mrs. Fitzherbert by an urn. Several Bands of Musick were very well placed in the garden, so that as soon as you were out of the hearing of one Band, you began to catch the notes of another ; thus harmony always met your ears. This sort of continued concert has always a most pleasant effect upon my nerves. There is a Temple which was destined to the Prince's entertainment and was very prettily decorated with flowers. There were about twenty covers, and when we understood that the Duchess and all these fine people were in their temple, we took possession of the house, where we found in every room a table spread, with cold meat, fruit, ice and all sorts of wine. It is a fine house, and there are the most delightful pictures in it. After the eating and quaffing was over, the young ladies danced on the green. Lady Georgiana Cavendish (a tall, gawky, fair girl, with her head poked out, and her mouth open) dances however very well, she has learned of Hillisbury. Lord Hartington (like the Duke) danced best. There were several other young girls, so that I never knew which was Lady Harriet or *Caroline*. There were a great many French, both men and women. . . . The Prince was *en Polisson*, a brown dress, round hat and a brown wig. He stood almost the whole time by his band, with Dr. Burney, ordering different pieces of musick. Lady Jersey was coasting round the spot where he stood. . . . The Prince was quite annoyed with her and eyed her askance. . . ."[1]

A fine Ball to celebrate Georgiana's presentation at Court was also given. Comments on the scale of the entertainment are amusing. . . . "About 800 were invited, a great many French and it will cost, it is said, near £1,000. It was computed at that if the garden was illuminated, but I am not sure it was so."[1]

Caroline Ponsonby was already a general favourite. She still spent most of her time at Devonshire House, and her cousin Hartington was devoted to her. Writing later of these days she says :

[1] *The Jerningham Papers.*

" My cousin Hartington loved me better than himself ; and everyone paid me compliments shown to children likely to die. I wrote not, spelt not, but I made verses which they all thought beautiful. For myself, I preferred washing the dog or polishing a piece of Derbyshire spar." [1]

About this time, Mrs. Fitzherbert adopted the daughter of Lord Hugh and Lady Horatia Seymour. The Prince of Wales was devoted to the child, Minnie, and a good deal of gossip centred around her parentage. The fact that Maria was now openly living with the Prince of Wales caused much distress to her Catholic friends, who knew only rumours about her marriage, and nothing of her appeal to Rome. Lady Jerningham wrote disconsolately in the month of March : " I comprehend it no longer, for I had always thought Mrs. Fitzherbert a woman of principle. . . ." " The *affaire* of Mrs. Fitzherbert and the Prince becomes very incomprehensible, it is a fact that he meets her whenever he can, and a conversation ensues that takes them both out of company." [2]

To a person of Mrs. Fitzherbert's temperament it was no small sacrifice she made to her husband in allowing him to conceal all the facts that made for her justification, and to endure criticism and reproach from valued friends, without any attempt to defend herself. The queston of Minnie Seymour's parentage is no longer a matter of doubt. If any proof were required other than was produced in the Seymour case it is, as Mr. Shane Leslie writes, to be found in the fact that Mrs. Fitzherbert consented to have the child brought up as a Protestant, which she would never have permitted had the child been her own. [3]

As to whether she ever did have any children by the Prince, though it is a fact that several pages were torn out of the baptismal register of Brighton Church (pages which cover the first years of the nineteenth century), this in itself seems hardly sufficient evidence to lead anyone to the assumption that Mrs. Fitzherbert bore a child or children during this period. [4] She had had no children by either of her previous husbands ; she

---

[1] *Passages in my Autobiography*—Lady Morgan.
[2] *The Jerningham Papers.*
[3] *The End of a Chapter*—Shane Leslie.
[4] *Brighton*—Osbert Sitwell.

had no children during the first period of her life with the Prince of Wales. There seems, therefore, no adequate reason to suppose that she bore a child when considerably older, and at the very time at which she decided to adopt Minnie Seymour. Nor is it likely that, had she had a child which lived, she would have completely ignored its existence in her will.

The year passed on quietly until May, when London was startled by an attempt on the King's life. One evening George III had just entered the Royal Box at Drury Lane when a man named Hadfield raised a pistol and fired point-blank at the King. The bullet missed him by an inch. George III was perfectly cool as he had been on all occasions of danger. Indeed, he remained in the front of the box, bowing to the excited audience. Sheridan, who had been in the box with him, ran out into the corridor to meet the Queen, who was just arriving. He assured her that the noise which had alarmed her was nothing but a squib. Until she had seen her husband safe and sound Sheridan did not allow her to know that an attempt had been made on the King's life. And George III, persevering in his gratitude, as well as in his enmity, never forgot this small act of courteous presence of mind, and was from that day onwards kinder to Sheridan than to any other member of Fox's party.

Meanwhile, the audience was wild with enthusiasm,[1] and it was not long before the versatile manager of Drury Lane was leading community singing in a new verse which he added to the National Anthem, and which ran as follows:

> From every latent foe,
> From the assassin's blow
> God save the King.
> O'er him thine arm extend,
> For Britain's sake defend
> Our Father, Prince and Friend.
> God save the King.

Simultaneously in the wings of the theatre the would-be assassin was being questioned by various gentlemen, who came to the conclusion that the man was mad. On this report being

---

[1] *The Journal of Elizabeth Vassall, Lady Holland.*

brought to the King, he replied with some point that only a lunatic could wish to kill him.

Whilst all this was passing at Drury Lane, the Prince of Wales was dining peacefully with Lady Melbourne. Suddenly an excited footman came to inform her Ladyship of the murderous attempt on the King's life.[1] Without an instant's delay Lady Melbourne bundled the heir-apparent, a little reluctantly, into his coach, and ordered him to go at once to the theatre and offer his congratulations to his parent.

The next morning the Prince learnt that all London was talking of his generous alacrity in rushing to pay his respects to the King. Acts such as these were Lady Melbourne's one redeeming virtue. She *did* know how people should behave under given circumstances, and though often she derived this knowledge from worldly sources, it was none the less valuable. She was thereby often able to impose a wise line of conduct upon the young men who sat at her feet, and they remained grateful to her for her advice long after they had ceased to recollect the charms of greater beauties.

The following month (June) saw Napoleon's crushing victory at *Marengo*. For the second time all Italy lay at his feet. During the same month, and in the same country, we learn of a marriage which is of no little interest. The bride was Miss Elizabeth Ashburne, who was in attendance on one of the Queen of Naples' daughters, and the bridegroom was one Signor Perconte. Present at the wedding were Sir William Hamilton and Emma, his wife, together with all the Neapolitan Royalties. Now Miss Eliza Ashburne was no other than the unfortunate " Louchee," the child of the Duke of Devonshire,[2] by a milliner, Miss Spencer, whom Lady Elizabeth Foster had been charged to conduct to Italy when she first came into the circle of Devonshire House seventeen years previously, and whose disappearance had roused so much curiosity (this is an assumption made also in *The Two Duchesses*—for more evidence see that work).

Evidently Bess had kept in touch with Louchee, for the latter writes affectionately to her : " My own dear Mamma, my kind, my generous benefactress. I should have unspeakable satisfaction if my reverent Lord Bristol had also come to my

[1] *In Whig Society*—Lady Airlie.   [2] *The Two Duchesses*.

wedding, but he has remained in Naples. . . ." And it is to be supposed that on Lady Elizabeth's later and frequent visits to Italy she must have seen the young woman whom she had been instrumental in conveying into surroundings so widely different from that in which Louchee had passed her early childhood.

Still in the same month an event of importance befell another member of the Devonshire House set.

" Early on Wednesday morning last, ye 4th of June," writes Lady Holland, " we were roused by a loud rapping at the bedroom door opening into the drawing-room. My mother cried out that she had brought great news, that Sir Godfrey Webster was dead. . . . I could not hear of his death without emotion, and was for some time considerably agitated. But, my God ! how was I overcome when Drew showed me a hasty note written by Hodges to apprise me of the manner of his death. He shot himself, he added, in consequence of heavy losses at play. With him dies all my resentment. . . . Peace be to his soul, and may he find that mercy I would bestow." [1]

Sir Godfrey's death regularised the Hollands' marriage in the eyes of the strictest. Women, except for the Duchess and Lady Bessborough, had not been in the habit of going much to Holland House ; and now, fear of Lady Holland's sharp tongue kept them away, so that the salon of clever men continued to be little adulterated by female wit.

During all this time, occupied as he was with war on the continent and finance at home, Pitt still worked to achieve the union of the English and Irish Parliaments. The state of that unhappy country at the turn of the century is well described by Lady Sarah Napier in a letter discussing the chances of a French invasion of Ireland :

" . . . If it is the politics of the French to give up good troops, money, time and attention to the conquest of Ireland, I fancy they will succeed ; but if they mean it only as a desultry war, just to keep England in hot water about Ireland, we people of the first rank won't suffer ; the second rank will, in the mercantile way, and the farmers will be undone, for this is their situation : robbers come to them under the name of ' United Gentlemen,' ask for food, drink and horses, and leave word that

[1] *The Journal of Elizabeth Vassall, Lady Holland.*

if he don't send the army after them, he shall never be touched ; if he *does* give information his hay, corn, and cattle, etc., are destroyed. . . . Then comes the furious loyalist, who puts the poor farmer in jail because he was robbed.

" . . . Thus he unwillingly turns rebel, who could have been a faithful subject, had government protected him well." [1]

The state described is not unfamiliar to modern readers. It was under these distracting conditions that the Act of Union was passed in July of the year 1800. Catholic support had been obtained by Castlereagh's promises of Catholic emancipation. The pledge was to be redeemed only twenty-eight years later ; but, as in 1780, it is to be supposed that the principals were in good faith when they made their promises. Pitt intended to pass the Act of Emancipation ; Fox and his party supported it. Yet one man stood now where Lord George Gordon had stood in 1780, the implacable enemy of any form of emancipation, and this man was the King.

In December came the news of Moreau's great victory at Hohenlinden. Vienna was at Bonaparte's feet, and it looked as though the second coalition were to be no more successful than the first Coalition had been.

In the same month Lady Bristol died. The Bishop appeared little touched at the event, except that he was moved to anger by the fact that his wife had disposed in her will of certain property which he declared it was not in her power to leave away from him.

About the same time Lady Holland lost her son, Stephen Fox ; and Lady Bessborough, who had gone down to Chatsworth for Christmas, lent her house in Cavendish Square to the Hollands, in the hope that a change of scene might raise their spirits.

[1] *The Life and Letters of Lady Sarah Lennox.*

Devonshire House

1801

ON the 22nd of January, 1801, the first Parliament of Great Britain and Ireland met. And Pitt, like an honest man, prepared to draw up his Emancipation Bill. News of his activities was brought to the ears of the King by the Prime Minister's personal enemy, Lord Loughborough. The Monarch let it be known that he should refuse emphatically to give his consent to emancipation in any form ; indeed, he declared that he believed it to be against his Coronation Oath to countenance such a measure. Since 1780, his mind had weakened and he had come under the influence of those who felt that the Roman Catholic element in England provided a real danger to throne and state.

Pitt took the measure of the situation. His personal honour was involved in the question ; but, on the other hand, if the Government were to resign in a body, Fox must come in, and Pitt genuinely believed that a Foxite Ministry would lead to the destruction of England. He, therefore, decided to steer a middle course. He offered his personal resignation in favour of his dull friend " Doctor " Addington. The King, on hearing of the arrangement, went mad.

For a month all decisions were suspended, then on March 4th the King was considered sufficiently recovered to bear the shock of Mr. Pitt's resignation. Pitt's action called a curious situation into being. The Foxites were bitterly disappointed that they were not to be his heirs, yet, on the question of emancipation, it would have been impossible for them to differ from him. But if their position was anomalous, that of Pitt's friends was even more so. Their leader had resigned, yet in resigning he had asked them to support his successor. This attitude might have the support of expediency ; it could not have that of logic.

After much heart-burning, Granville and his brother, Lord

Gower, Lord Spencer, Lord Grenville, Canning, and some others seceded. As Granville wrote to his horrified parents : " The dregs of Pitt's Ministry " were hardly likely to make a success of Government where the great man himself had failed. Granville had no personal views upon emancipation, but he felt that he could not be wrong in subscribing to the views of Pitt and of Canning, whose judgment he respected.

For once, Lady Bessborough and the Duchess were delighted to be able to approve his political activities. More than ever he became " part of the family," and for the first time he grew well acquainted with old Lady Spencer, and found her delightful company. She seemed to bridge the difference in outlook and upbringing between his own home and Devonshire House. Lady Stafford heartily approved the friendship. She had much the same opinion of Lady Spencer as the Bishop of Derry held, and she believed that her influence would only be for good.

Two defeats of the French forces by the British, one at Alexandria by Abercrombie and one off Copenhagen by Nelson, led to *pourparlers* in the autumn. And, to the astonishment of all parties, it soon became apparent that to the despised " Doctor " would fall the honour of bringing the country to peace again. Pitt supported the negotiations, so did Fox, in a manner that did more credit to his goodness of heart than to his intellect. To give a helping hand to the Government who had no *raison d'être* but to keep him out of office, was magnanimous ; but openly to proclaim his admiration for Bonaparte was hardly consistent with either his love of liberty, peace or patriotism, and did much to shake any lingering faith in his political ethics.

To people of the old school, like Lady Stafford, any peace with a country holding the views and principles of Napoleon was a doubtful business, and Granville did not remain untouched by his mother's sentiments. He criticised many points of the peace terms, but ended by voting with the Government. His conduct was open to criticism, but now he found a strange defender in Fox, with whom he had taken special pains not to get acquainted at Devonshire House.

Lady Melbourne was nonplussed by the occurrence. " What makes Mr. Fox take up ' Beamer ' so ? Is it his natural liberality and candour or has he any particular acquaintance with him ? I did not know he knew him." [1] Lady Bessborough was overjoyed at Fox's conduct. She still loved and admired him, and she felt that his influence might broaden Granville's outlook upon life and politics.

Whilst the *pourparlers* of peace were going forward Lord Holland, despite the refusal of the Duke of Portland to grant him a passport, slipped over to France. On his return he was the object of much curiosity. He reported that the French were most anxious for peace ; that all the churches were rebuilding, Mass said almost everywhere, general toleration encouraged, a good harvest, and every prospect of prosperity.

All through the summer " the Doctor " ruled not through any merit of his own, but simply because he, and he only, stood between the country and Fox. The year is poor in accounts of the personal vicissitudes of the members of the Devonshire House set. During the summer the Prince of Wales and Mrs. Fitzherbert set about the building of the new and startling pavilion at Brighton, of which Sidney Smith said it looked as though " The Dome of St. Paul's had gone to the sea and pupped." [2] And at about the same time the Bishop of Derry was writing and imploring Lord Liverpool to appoint him Minister to the Vatican.

" I have wondered," he wrote, " my dear Lord, considering the extension and important connexion we have with the Court of Rome, on account of our millions of R. Catholik subjects in Ireland—all acknowledging hitherto ' Imperium in Imperio ' that the King has no Plenipotentiary here, especially since the Pope has solemnly acknowledged the Protestant family on the Throne, and that all our property as well as our persons here, for want of such an asylum as an Ambassador's House is totally unprotected ; and I often wished for many reasons that I myself was that representative. . . ." [3]

It was a last gallant and unsuccessful effort to save his effects from the sequestration which had been placed upon them. Like most of his schemes it was fated to be sterile.

[1] *The Journal of Elizabeth Vassall, Lady Holland.*
[2] *Brighton*—Osbert Sitwell.
[3] *The Life of the Earl Bishop of Derry.*

1802

NEW YEAR'S DAY, 1802, saw Harriet and Georgiana at Chatsworth, surrounded by their families. Both the Duke of Devonshire and Lord Bessborough were ill with the gout, and consequently morose, but a tribe of children and a large house party kept the festivity. Yet Lady Bessborough could not shake off the depression which Granville's departure had caused her. Amongst the guests was Granville's friend, Lord Morpeth, whose decided preference for Georgiana Cavendish was soon to end in an engagement. She would be the first of the second generation to marry, and her departure from the family circle would be as hard a blow to the second Harriet as the marriage of the first Georgiana had been to Lady Bessborough.

Christmas trees were still unknown at Chatsworth, but on New Year's Day they had the " Drawing at King and Queen," which made a very delightful form of distribution of presents. Once New Year's Day was over, Lady Bessborough felt anxious to return to London, where she might have an occasion of seeing Granville ; but the Duchess's health made it impossible. She felt ill, and she begged the Bessboroughs not to desert her ; and in addition, she wanted their help for the composition of a tragedy which she hoped that the two families might together perform in the spring. The plot was taken from the table of *Siegendorf*, and later, when Lord Byron was to publish *Werner*, there were those who declared that he had never written the work, and that it was simply the Duchess of Devonshire's *Siegendorf*, bearing a new title.

Untoward incidents of various kinds lent excitement to the winter at Chatsworth. First there was a hurricane which not only blew down trees in the Park, but also blew in doors and windows.

The next day the storm was succeeded by a fire. Lady

Bessborough was the first to hear of it. With great calmness she gave orders that all the windows should be closed, and she forbade any shouting or alarm which might have upset the Duchess in her delicate state of health. As it was, a part of the staircase was destroyed, and we hear of the party dining in the music-room because the dining-room was full of water and of smoke.

The following day the fire broke out again, and this was almost more than the most hardened nerves could stand. But at last, with the removal of a smouldering beam, all was returned to quiet. And Lady Bessborough had no worse anxieties than those which the reports of Granville's flirtations with Lady Sarah Villiers and Lady Asgill were to cause her.

At last she came back to town, and there she was to find Sheridan on the doorstep full of lurid accounts of Granville's infidelities. He had a real respect for Lady Bessborough and, jealousy apart, he actually suffered when he saw her apparently hypnotised by this unstable boy. But his admonitions reached deaf ears.

February brought a crop of engagements. Little Georgiana was now definitely to marry Morpeth, and the wedding was fixed for the 21st of March. It was an altogether satisfactory business. But a second engagement came as a terrible blow to the circle of Devonshire House ; it was no other than that of Francis Bedford, their beloved " Loo," to a daughter of the eccentric Tory Duchess of Gordon. To Lady Melbourne and the two Spencer sisters, the event was little short of a tragedy. Georgiana wrote angrily :

" . . . What a futurity for Loo to be surrounded with plotting, shabby Scotsmen ! The very *amabilité* that some-times arises from the grotesque originality of Scotch people is in a line very different from what one should have thought would be Loo's election for the mistress of Woborn. . . . No possible event could have so thoroughly overthrown the habits of our society as this. . . ." [1]

But, alas, they had no need to worry about " Loo's futurity." Within a month he had ruptured himself playing tennis and, in spite of a fearful operation, he died. Many people, including Lord Holland, were staying in the house at the time. But the

[1] *In Whig Society*—Lady Airlie.

Duke saw only his two brothers and his surgeon, Mr. Kerr, who remarked that he had never seen such courage as that evinced by the Duke, " who in the agonies of pain and death, could have governed the world." [1] Before he died Loo asked his brother to take out a lock of his hair to Lady Georgiana Gordon, who was in Paris.

The office of comforter was well performed, for after wearing mourning for Francis, to the anger of the ladies of Devonshire House, Lady Georgiana married Lord John, who had been the bearer of the memento. So that there was little need for the sympathy of Lady Jerningham, who wrote, on hearing of the Duke's death. " The Duke of Bedford was positively engaged to Lady Georgiana Gordon, she is to wear mourning for him ; and indeed it must be a dreadful disappointment." [2]

The death of the Duke of Bedford was to be regretted in many ways. An honest politician and a good friend, he had always been a restraining influence since he came into the lives of Georgiana and Harriet ; and, moreover, time and time again he had helped them in their financial difficulties and placed his limitless credit at their disposal. After his death their creditors became more pressing and their financial position more involved.

The months of March, which had begun with personal sorrow, ended with public rejoicings, for the Peace of Amiens was signed. As Sheridan said, it was " a peace of which every man is glad and no man proud." England made multiple concessions to France, and it was aggravating to hear afterwards that Napoleon had been astonished at the leniency of the terms we had put forward. In May he was made First Consul for life.

As the year went on, some benefits due to the cessation of the war became perceptible : the income tax, which had been brought in in 1798, was abolished ; and conditions all over the country seemed to show signs of improvement. It was good to be at peace again, at least at peace so far as Europe was concerned.

In the East battles were still being fought by British troops ; and from India came news of Arthur Wellesley's capture of

[1] *The Journal of Elizabeth Vassall, Lady Holland.*
[2] *The Jerningham Papers.*

Delhi and Agra ; but such tales travelled slowly over great distances, and were but faint echoes, very unlike the thunder of the guns of Marengo and Hohenlinden, when they reached Lady Bessborough's ears as she played at shilling whist with the Mayor of St. Albans, his son, and a local beau, during her visit to her mother at Holywell—a quiet period punctuated with no greater excitement than a game of bowls with the neighbours, or a game of chess with the children, or perhaps the excitement of reading Calonne's *Life of Bonaparte.*

In August Lady Bessborough passed through London on her way to Ramsgate. Three of her admirers were in town and they were assiduous in their attentions, and Granville had the impertinence to reproach her with their visits and to accuse her of want of firmness in dealing with them. She answered him with some bitterness, saying that if they had really loved her a desire to avoid her anger might indeed have restrained them.

What an irony there was in her life : for three years Granville had adored her extravagantly, and she had been able to treat the affair lightly ; but now, for more than four years, she had worshipped him, and during these years he had been uncertain, imperious, unfaithful to her affection. The less devoted he became the more she held to him, and unwisely she let him know it.

Even Lady Melbourne became an object of envy, and Harriet complained to Granville that though Lady Melbourne was old and fat, yet the number of her admirers had rather increased than diminished—and to one and all she was haughty and distant. But, unfortunately, the affection which Lady Bessborough felt for Granville had little room left for pride. It was useless writing and telling him that she knew that he was peculiarly fitted for marriage, and that she hoped he would soon find a wife. Granville knew only too well that this was the last thing she desired, and it is to be feared that about this time he began to have occasional moments of panic, in which he felt himself tied and trapped by a much older woman. These moments were still followed by a complete revulsion of feeling, and he returned to her after them with greater affection than before ; but they were symptomatic of revulsions from which there should be no return.

In September Fox decided to profit by the peace, and go to Paris to look up some documents for a Life of James II which he was writing.[1]   Mrs. Armistead was, of course, to accompany him, and now, at last, he decided to announce his marriage to his friends.   Was it fair, he asked, to allow his wife to suffer abroad from the seemingly dubious position which she tolerated in England ?   Astonishing to relate, the news of the seven-year-old marriage came as a complete surprise, even to such old and intimate friends as the Duchess of Devonshire and Lady Bessborough.   In the main they were delighted, and much amused at the horror expressed by many ladies in society, who had been quite content that Mr. Fox should have a mistress, but were outraged when they discovered that he had a wife,[2] but those who knew Fox best were not astonished, they had always realised that with him was all kindness and all weakness where women were concerned.

The family party at Ramsgate was very happy.   Harriet Cavendish practising on the harp with Mlle Memel, Corisande de Gramont on the pianoforte, Caroline St. Jules on the guitar, and Caroline Ponsonby upstairs on another pianoforte. The only anxiety was in regard to Duncannon, now a good-looking young man about town, whom the wicked Lady Jersey, the Prince of Wales's mistress, was trying to capture for her daughter Lady Elizabeth Villiers.   The boy was flattered at the attentions which Lady Jersey paid him, the girl was beautiful and charming, and all Lady Melbourne's children were hotly urging him to pay no attention to his mother's dread of the connexion.   At first Lady Bessborough was afraid of making matters worse by interference, but at last she could bear it no longer and spoke to her son on the subject.   She limited her advice to urging him not to continue the flirtation if he did not intend to marry Lady Elizabeth, and her restraint was rewarded.

Duncannon asked her opinion as to the marriage, and on hearing her serious objections, he was low for a day or two and then left Ramsgate, followed by the laughter of the Lambs.   In December the Bessboroughs, taking Mr. Fox's example, set out for France.   It was curious to be in Paris again after so many years, and after such a series of terrible

[1] *Life of Fox*—Trotter.   [2] *Life of Fox*—Hobhouse.

events. Soon Lady Bessborough met a good many of her mother's old friends, but the remains of the guillotine still stood on the Place Vendôme, and she wrote that she could not say how distressing it was to her to see the beautiful houses of her old friends turned into hotels—or completely destroyed. A spirit of fear was still in the air, no one spoke openly, and frequently the door into the antechamber had to be opened and a search made before people would speak at all openly. Yet things were getting slowly back to normal. One day they saw crowds round the churches, and heard that the caps of liberty were being removed and the crucifixes replaced. It was one of many signs. They visited Madame Recamier and found her receiving, undressed in that bed with its curtains of gold and muslin, its sheets trimmed with lace and its incense burners of which they had seen many prints. The effect was not to their taste.

Another night they dined with Talleyrand ; a great dinner of seventy-eight covers, and very little food. At the end of the room a glass swung slowly back and disclosed a band of musicians. Once again there was incense ; perhaps this time it was a reminiscence of Talleyrand's episcopal past. They were not the only English in Paris and Caroline Ponsonby made her début one night at a splendid ball given by the Duchess of Gordon, whose daughter, with brighter hopes for the future, had ceased to mourn for Loo.

1803

INSTEAD of "drawing at King and Queen" the Bess-
borroughs began the New Year of 1803 with an introduction to the ceremony of Étrennes, which filled Harriet with
amusement : such a curious assortment of gifts as they received
from their smart friends, she had never before seen.

The visit to Paris was being a great success, especially now
that Lady Elizabeth Foster and the young Morpeths had come
out to join them. Their life was strenuous with much sight-
seeing and much entertaining. Harriet had friends in both
camps. Moreau took her to see a review at which Napoleon
inspected his army, riding on an old white horse which had
belonged to Louis XVI. Narbonne sat at her feet and told her
how he could have saved the Royal Family had Louis XVI
listened to his advice and been willing to put himself at the
head of the troops. Discussion on the subject of Napoleon's
divorce was already rife. Nearly everyone was against it.
Josephine was liked and pitied. Lady Bessborough felt sorry
that her political convictions prevented her from showing
Madame Bonaparte some civility, and, if she was sorry at first
from compassion, she was sorry later, for a more interested
reason.

Rumours that the Bessboroughs were not only anti-Bona-
partists, but that they had led the other English visitors to
imitate their ostracism of the First Consul, got abroad, and at
one moment it looked as though they might be peremptorily
turned out of the country. Therefore, taking discretion for the
better part of valour, they soon afterwards returned to London.
This was in March. Two months later England was at war
with France. The French refusal to evacuate Malta was the
casus belli.

Fox made what he believed to be the best speech of his life
against the declaration of war. But it carried few votes. Pitt

supported Addington, and the Grenville party were of opinion that not only that war should be declared, but that hostilities should be pursued until the Bourbons were re-established on the throne of France. The funds fell, Fox predicted disaster, and even those who approved of the war were anxious as to its outcome whilst Addington remained Prime Minister ; but the persevering Doctor had his way.

Despite the war, life went on gaily. Georgiana Cavendish was now married, but there were Harriet Cavendish, Caroline St. Jules and Caroline Ponsonby to entertain for ; and Miss Berry gives us an account of some of the festivities that took place during the summer.

" Three or four balls at Devonshire House kept the young people in motion ; there have been, also, several morning dances, followed by a breakfast, by way of practising quadrilles. Lady Elizabeth Foster brought some pretty music from Paris, and some of the young ladies just come forth proved themselves excellent dancers." [1]

Lady Bessborough was glad to see Granville again, but the young man was in no gay mood, for his father was dying. Their flirtation remained in abeyance.

In July came the news of the death of Lady Elizabeth's father, the astonishing Lord Bristol. The poor Bishop had died suddenly, whilst on his way from Albano to Rome, of gout in the stomach, and the letters added that he had expired in the outhouse of a cottage, with no one about him but untrustworthy servants. [2] His funeral in Rome had been attended by eight hundred artists, and his coffin had subsequently been enclosed in a packing-case and sent back to England, labelled, with a certain irony, " antique statue," in order to outwit the prejudice which all sailors felt against carrying a corpse on board.

His affairs had been left in a terrible state of confusion. Cardinal Erskine kindly took charge of his effects in order to avoid pilfering, and later most of his pictures and statues were sold ; and the one ship-load which had been despatched to England disappeared, so that little remained of all his purchases.

No monument was raised to the Bishop by his children,

---

[1] *Journal and Correspondence*—Berry.
[2] *The Life of the Earl Bishop of Derry.*

but two memorials are still extant, an obelisk in the Park at Ickworth, subscribed to by the people of his Diocese of Derry and also by the Roman Catholic Bishop and the Dissenting Minister of the See ; and a great chain of hotels which, stretching through about five countries, still bears witness to his reputation as a connoisseur of taste and comfort.

Now that the nation was again at war, many intrigues were set on foot to wrest the Premiership from Addington, but the little doctor sat firm in his seat : more firmly indeed than when, meeting Lady Bessborough in the avenue at Roehampton, his pony shied at Harriet's umbrella and nearly laid the First Lord of the Treasury prostrate at her feet.

Fox, pacifist though he was, had always held the opinion that " if a nation can't avoid making war, it may as well make an efficient war " ; and for this reason it was not long before parleys began to take place between himself and Pitt. Pitt snatched at the offer of support ; he knew that he could count on Grenville too, and with such followers he believed that he might form a really strong government.[1] However, when he sounded the King on the possibility of dislodging Addington and forming a Coalition Cabinet, which should contain Grenville and Fox, the Monarch replied acidly " rather a civil war than Fox in Office." Yet once again Devonshire House had reason to feel that its hero was being persecuted.

[1] *Courts and Cabinets*—Buckingham.

1 8 0 4

FROM the close of the year 1803, a subtle change is evident in the interests and occupations of the Devonshire House set. With Charles James Fox withdrawn from politics, with the Duchess's failing health, with Lady Bessborough and Lady Melbourne primarily occupied in bringing out the younger generation, parliamentary news becomes scarce, and personalities out-shoulder causes.

The seemingly endless vista of opposition, personified by an eternal Pittite eternally Prime Minister, had cooled the enthusiasm of the most sanguine. The Foxites were discouraged, not one of the measures which they had championed had been passed, and it seemed as though none of their ideals would attain to any realisation. The establishment in life of their children came to fill the gap caused by disillusion.

They were growing old; Lady Bessborough was in the forties, the Duchess was high in the forties, so was Bess, and Lady Melbourne had turned her half-century. Now, if they were to think of achievement it must be in regard to their children, and this thought had its pangs. They believed that their own parts had been played to an empty house. And, looking at their children, it did not seem as though this second generation would pick up their lost cues. The young people were sedate, and for the most part either apathetic or critical.

Georgiana looked at her family: there was her eldest daughter married to Morpeth. She was gentle and charming and very religious; but she would never scour the purlieus of Westminster in an endeavour to obtain votes, not even votes for her conscientious husband.

There was *Harriet*, fat and comfortable, with an active conscience and critical sense of satire at war with each other, and above all, of a laziness that defied all enthusiasm. And then there was *Hartington*, now at Eton, gentle and deaf and whimsical, and most unlikely to take a part in politics.

From her own family the Duchess turned to look at her sister's brood. *Duncannon*, quiet and reserved, might make an efficient administrator but was certainly not cut out for a leader. *Frederick*, who had a more robust nature and a greater force of personality, had not the type of intelligence which could apply itself to politics. Whilst *Willie*, the baby, seemed, so far as could be judged at so early an age, languid and effeminate. *Caroline*, alone, might have some spark of the Foxite flame. Her enthusiasm for Charles James partook of the nature of hero-worship, and since she had been a child she had been interested in ideas and ideals. But her mind had always a freakish twist to it which disconcerted her aunt.

Bess's boys were dear, dull creatures from whose faces no one could augur a flaring future. And Caroline, their sister, had a horror of publicity which, though it was a shield to a highly sensitive intelligence, was to prove a certain guarantee against ambition.

On the whole it seemed more likely that Elizabeth Melbourne's offspring would make their mark in the world rather than the children of Devonshire House. Not, certainly, the eldest boy, Peniston, who was like his father, gentle and retiring ; but the second son, William, who was clever, with a proud, detached, disillusioned brilliance ; and the third son, Frederick, who had a good brain too, with a strength and force derived from a vanity and a selfishness that were to remain intact for many years. And, above all, Emily, the only daughter (since Harriet had died of consumption). Emily who had all her mother's ambition and worldliness joined to greater flexibility and greater charm. Perhaps these would be the residuary legatees of Devonshire House. It was a bitter thought, for they had not the quality of their forebears, nor their disinterestedness, nor their enthusiasm. They were opportunists, but in default of better men, competent opportunists must come to the fore.

Between the generation of Georgiana and that of her children there stood, of course, another vintage. The men who were turning or just turned thirty in this year of 1804.

Charles Grey, Lord Holland, Canning and, above all, Granville Leveson-Gower and Morpeth, on to their shoulders would first fall the burden of Fox and Pitt. But in their hands politics should lose something of their vividness. Charles Grey had, perhaps, a little of Mr. Fox ; but Lord Holland was purely a theorist, he was always remote from life.

And Canning, who should succeed to Pitt's leadership, seemed to be impregnated with a dullness which only his small set of devoted friends could afford to ignore. Granville and Morpeth were able administrators, conscientious and honourable men, but nothing more.

The ageing Foxites looked in vain for a statesman amongst their descendants. And then, failing to discover any sign of incipient greatness, they set politics aside and wondered what were to be the lives of these, their successors. What connexions would they make ? How would they be paired off in the quadrille of life, and would the years bring them happiness or sorrow ?

And amongst those whose anxiety was the keenest was old Lady Stafford. She was not at all happy about Granville. There he was with all his intelligence, beauty, charm and fundamental good sense wasting his youth at the feet of Lady Bessborough. An attachment to any married woman would have been horrid enough, but in this particular instance there were more than ordinary causes for anxiety. His connexion with her admitted him into the stronghold of Fox and Sheridan and the Prince of Wales—he, the pupil of Pitt and the friend of Canning—whose family was wholly devoted to George III and to the Tory cause. And if even his politics were not contaminated, how about his morals ? The Devonshire House set were renowned for drinking, gambling and the loosest living. And though she believed that his principles were excellent, he had gambling in the blood, his father had been a reformed gambler, Lord Gower and his lady were, as yet, un-reformed ! Now that her husband was dead she felt that almost the only *raison d'être* for her existence lay in her capacity for guiding this son away from the dangerous influences by which he was surrounded. She realised at once that she had a choice of two courses to pursue : either he must marry and settle down—or, if this were impossible, then he must go abroad again on some mission. She prayed that the former might be achieved, for she was old, and she wanted to know his wife, and if he went away, she might not live to see his return.

The suggestion that it was his duty to marry, to bring up a family, to achieve political eminence found an echo in his mind. He had never for a second questioned that that was to be his fate, he had no pre-Byronic romanticism—nothing could appeal to him less than the idea of sustaining a hopeless passion. The only difference that arose between mother and son was the question of the exact time at which he should break with Lady Bessborough and settle down to domesticity. Lady Stafford had thought that there should be no further postponements, almost she convinced him that she was right.

He had looked about amongst his flames—Lady Boringdon might have been his choice, but then she had married one of his best friends. Lady Hester Stanhope was too wild, and too old. There was Miss Pole ? But that would not be a very brilliant connexion. There remained Lady Sarah Fane. She was very beautiful, she was exceedingly gay, she sang and danced and chattered from morning till night, but as she grew older she might sober down a little and make an excellent ambassadress. Lady Stafford was enthusiastic. Early in the year Addington's Ministry had fallen and Pitt become once more Prime Minister. It was a good moment for Granville to launch out for himself ; if he married and showed a capacity for work he might get a post, whilst a friendly hand was on the tiller of the state. Granville was assiduous in his attentions to Lady Sarah—he wrote detailed accounts of his activities to Lady Bessborough. She had always proclaimed that she wanted to be his most trusted friend. If these assurances were true she should be glad of his resolution.

Lady Bessborough was torn in two—it was right that Lady Stafford should wish her son to marry, it was right that " dear Granville " should marry, she had been sincere in all that she had said to him. But, was Lady Sarah worthy of him ? Marriage in theory had her blessing, but this particular marriage. . . . She lay under no obligation to give him up to a rattle, a shallow child. She was determined to use her influence entirely in Granville's interests. No one loved him as she did except his poor old mother. She felt an instinct of affection for Lady Stafford, deprived of her husband and so devoted to her son. How sad it was that life must place them in opposite camps. A strange correspondence grew up between them and lasted until 1804.

They wrote much on the subject of his marriage—the necessity for it—the desirability of it. They discussed the various young ladies whom they held to be worthy of such an honour.

Lady Bessborough rather rashly sent various presents to Lady Stafford—whereupon the old lady hastened to despatch gifts of a like nature in return. Yet as the years passed her opinion of Lady Bessborough softened. She recognised that the affection which she bore Granville was of a deep and unselfish character. Even, she felt sorry for her. It was one of those cases where the element of time intervenes with catastrophic effect.

If all this had happened fourteen years earlier—before Lady Bessborough had been associated with her sister's fast friends —before she had married . . . but at that time Granville was only a child. Now there was nothing to be done but to close the mind to these speculations.

Meanwhile it was really admirable, thought Lord Granville, to have so comfortable a situation between his mother and Lady Bessborough. But strangely enough, the latter did not give him good news of his prospects with Lady Sarah, who seemed to speak with equal enthusiasm of Granville and of Lord Villiers, and to enjoy herself with every young man who came within the orbit of her attraction. It was all very provoking and difficult to understand, until, in May, Lady Sally actually married Lord Villiers.

Lady Bessborough sank thankfully back, exhausted with the strain. She had really done her best, she had put no obstacles in the way. She had tried to be absolutely just, and . . . she had been delivered. Lady Stafford reacted in another fashion to the disappointment. Napoleon was declared Emperor of the French, Pitt had formed an alliance against France, Russia was to be a party to it. Someone would have to be sent to St. Petersburg. . . . Someone would be nominated immediately.

The scheme was successful. Granville was offered the appointment. He hesitated, he had no very great desire to be exiled for three or four years, just when life in London had become so exceedingly pleasant. In these circumstances Lady Bessborough was heroic, she had been spared the final cleavage which marriage must have brought to her, in her thankfulness she was disinterested. She made no doubt as to what it would cost her to see him go, but she urged him to accept. If he slighted such a singular compliment, his reputation would never recover. Seeing his mother and Lady Bessborough allied with his own ambition, Granville hesitated no longer. His departure, after many alterations, was fixed for October.

If Lady Sarah's marriage had caused him anything but relief he did not show it. With his future settled and the season of hard work advancing upon him, he made the most of his few months' respite.

As has already been mentioned the very formality of his own mind led him to be attracted by the unconventional and exotic in women. He had been much with Canning, and consequently much with Pitt. At the Prime Minister's house he met the Prime Minister's formidable niece, Lady Hester Stanhope. She was older than he, and plain and *mal soignée*, but she had a vitality and a mordant wit which fascinated him. Though her fantastic Oriental career had not yet begun, she had already effected the escape of her brothers from the house of her fanatical father, and she had sought liberty for herself in the house of her uncle, where she acted as hostess.[1]

Rough, imperious, generous and wilful, something of a visionary and something of a bully, she gave a tang to London society. Lady Bessborough saw the growing intimacy with anxiety. Where Granville enjoyed only a verbal rough and tumble and a sort of school-boy comradeship, she detected more serious symptoms. Lady Hester, for all her contempt of sentiment, was a woman, a very passionate, uncontrolled woman, and Granville, even where his heart was not engaged, had often proved devastating. In July she sent a warning.

Granville must be made to realise that he was playing not just with a conventional little flame but with a volcano. Moreover if Lady Hester really believed that he intended to propose to her, and if she informed Pitt of her hopes, the situation might take a very ugly turn. Granville might even end by finding himself married to Lady Hester, a fate terrible to contemplate.

[1] *Lady Hester Stanhope*—Haslip.

Granville, knowing his own security, and probably considering the possibility of anyone marrying Lady Hester in the
nature of a joke, made light of the whole affair. Lady Bessborough grew more insistent, nor can she in this instance be
accused of acting from motives of jealousy alone. A marriage
between the sedate Granville and the eccentric Lady Hester
could only have ended in disaster, and if this flirtation were not
to end in marriage, it could only lead to scandal and unhappiness.

In the autumn the anxiety of Granville's friends was justified
—the daily press announced Lady Hester's engagement. This
was followed by a certain amount of not unnatural triumph
on the part of those who had warned him so frequently of the
danger in which he stood. But before the talk had assumed
serious proportions Granville's departure for Russia silenced
speculation.

When the moment of going was upon him, he wrote a
generous note of farewell to Lady Bessborough. It had taken
a hard blow to revive his affection for her, but it was still
there, and it was still real.

Perhaps Lady Bessborough felt rewarded for her share in
urging him to undertake the mission. Lady Stafford sent him
some religious books, she was old and ill, wondered if she
should see him again. She met Lady Hester and was out-
spoken in her disappointment.

Perhaps sorrow had helped to make her plain. She alone
had come very poorly out of the whole business. Even Lady
Bessborough looked pale and shrivelled. On Granville's departure Hetty had written him a note, which he forwarded
immediately to Lady Bessborough. Its meaning was obscure
and filled them both with dismay ; it might be considered to
imply an intention of committing suicide—or else of following
the British minister to Russia. Either eventuality was horrid,
and Lady Bessborough determined to see more of Lady Hester
and do what she could to calm her. In some curious way all
those who loved Granville in their diverse ways drew together
at his departure to sustain each other in their common loss.

Poor Hetty came for news—and came to talk of her faithless
lover ; then she would announce that it was for the last time,
and that she intended in future never to mention him, never
to enquire after him, and if possible never to think of him

again. Each time was to be the last time, and then each visit proved to be the penultimate. But the relationship between the two women was too difficult. It had to end in disaster, and it did. Perhaps someone, seeing Lady Bessborough and Lady Hester in conclave, made an allusion to a fellow feeling, and perhaps the remark reached the ears of some member of the Pitt family. The friendship certainly gave rise to surmises and Lady Hester was ordered to break off all acquaintance with Lady Bessborough.

The harm was said to have been done either by the spiteful Queen or the jealous Prince. Hetty saw the truth behind the unkind criticism, she was her uncle's guest and she knew what she owed him—but she was no person to skulk out of any relationship. With perfect courage and complete cruelty she decided to go to Lady Bessborough and explain the matter clearly. When the interview took place she found it unexpectedly distressing. She pointed out with entire frankness that her desertion was not to be due to any change in her feelings. The fact was that Lady Bessborough could not be considered to be a suitable friend for a young lady in her position.

The shock and the pain which this statement caused Lady Bessborough may seem exaggerated. Never for a moment did she deny its justice ; she had never absolved herself, but she had grown familiar with the situation, and in the world it had been accepted without criticism. It was very painful to see other people judging one as one judged oneself.

She recognised that, according to her lights, Hetty had acted bravely in coming to tell her a truth which she would have preferred to forget. With a certain fine humility she advised her to follow the advice of those who loved her and who must therefore be the best judges.

Later she wrote a full account of the affair to Granville. She saw herself judged by the world with the severity with which she always judged herself—the ordeal was a painful one.

The Bessboroughs went to Hastings for the autumn, and here fears of invasion provided a counter-irritant to loneliness. So seriously did the authorities fear a landing that the cannon of the little fort were prepared for action, and horses and waggons were kept in readiness to convey the women and children away from the coast in case of attack.

There was a family counsel as to the propriety of staying on and they agreed to take the risk. On Guy Fawkes' Day they were still there, still awaiting the arrival of Bonaparte's army, and the forbidden bonfires, which were none the less lit, were mistaken for a signal announcing the arrival of the French.

There was little news that autumn and nothing came to fill the aching void made by Granville's departure.

If she felt the separation, so did he. Petersburg was far and cold and strange, and Princess Serge Galitzin, the only woman worth knowing, was unkind. His mission was not to be a very lengthy one and he counted the weeks as they passed and brought him nearer the hours of his return.

The words brought comfort to Lady Bessborough. She repeated them—they echoed eventually in the seclusion to which Lady Stafford had retired. She was extremely displeased. Suppose that Woronzow, the Russian minister, were to hear of them. What would he say of a person accredited to his emperor who wrote back that he was delighted that three months of his exile were over? Granville's sisters contradicted the report. He might well write such falsehoods to pacify a lady, but they could bear no relation to the truth. Lady Stafford wrote a sharp reprimand—he must remember that what was written to one lady at Devonshire House became almost instantly the property of the whole set with all its ramifications. As well give a piece of news to the town crier as to one of their number.

Meanwhile, at Devonshire House, a crisis was impending. During the past thirty years so much had passed within its walls which might have been supposed to result in scenes and drama, yet all these happenings had failed to modify the stately tread of life, so that now, at this late hour, when all its inmates were middle aged, it seemed hardly possible that its peace should be disturbed. Like a calm sea appearances had flooded over reality, presenting a polished mirror to the gaze of the spectator, who might guess at the jagged rocks beneath its surface, but never behold them. But in 1804 the tide had run very low and an outcrop of rock was beginning to make a tiny ripple.

Ever since her marriage Georgiana had gamed. It may be that she had caught the passion from her husband, but at all events she had played recklessly and with little good fortune

for twenty-two years. Her losses did not appear to her friends
to have been enormous for one in her situation—at least not
such as to cause her permanent embarrassment; but appearances were deceptive. When she played faro at Martindale's
table a loss of £500 actually represented a loss of £1,500, for
there was an arrangement between them that doubled or trebled
the face values of the stakes. Over years, the mass of debt
weighed heavily and she was afraid of her husband. She had
tolerated much from him, she had put up with Clifford and
Caroline, she had grown to love Bess, and he had asked no
questions—not even enquired about Eliza Grey.[1] The only
thing that he required of her was propriety in public and silence
in private. Their whole relationship had as its corner stone
complete estrangement.

She had not dared to tell him of her debts—he knew of them,
but he simulated ignorance. For the last five years they had
been very pressing. She had tried to find means of satisfying
her creditors. She, who found it so easy to speak openly,
sincerely to all her friends, she who had wept with Sheridan
over her losses, and accepted with grateful simplicity what the
Duke of Bedford had been happy to contribute could not speak
to " Ca "—he was the only person in the world with whom she
could not be natural and truthful and herself. She who cared
so little for public opinion, or private opinion either, broke
down every time the idea of revealing her situation to her
husband was suggested to her. She was terrified of him—
appalled at the thought of opening a real issue between them.

When it became apparent that disclosure could only be
delayed and not averted, she lost sleep, health and almost
reason. Too much injury lay between them, she was too
simple for pride, she was only grateful that Bess should broach
the subject with the Duke. She did not mind his knowing,
she wanted him to know, she might even have written to him.
The one thing she could not do was to speak to him himself.

Bess was ready enough to do what she could—she wasn't in
the least frightened of the Duke and she knew all about financial
straits. When she opened the subject she found " Ca " very
cross and undecided. He knew that his wife had debts—he
didn't want to hear of them. Bess urged that they must be

[1] *The Two Duchesses.*

settled—to delay was cruelty—already she had been pushed to expedients which would look very queer to society, in order to be able to pay the interest. And this provided the greatest difficulty. Not only must the debts be paid, but the matter must be kept secret. Heaton, the Duke's business man, who had always hated the Duchess must have no knowledge of the transaction. The Duke demurred, it was bad enough to have to raise a large sum, though he was not ungenerous, but he liked his affairs conducted in an orderly manner—why in the world should not Heaton deal with the matter.

There were many reasons why Heaton should not do so. Lady Bessborough urged absolute sincerity. Georgiana must tell the whole truth. Then even " Ca " would realise the necessity for discretion.

At last the Duchess agreed to the confession and the Duke agreed to the payment of the principal, but the sum involved had never been mentioned. Bess thought that he only antici-pated a tenth of the actual debt. Yet eventually it was all settled, thanks to her, and Lady Bessborough was thankful that Georgiana was rescued from anxiety and misery which had preyed on her health.

So ended the year 1804.

1805

THE first month of the new year was overshadowed by a tragic death which proved pregnant with consequences. Peniston Lamb had been ailing for some time and despite every effort on the part of his physicians the cold and damp weather told on his lungs. By Christmas it became evident that he would not live long enough to receive the aid of his old ally the spring. With what feelings could the Lambs see this charming, gentle creature dying discreetly and unostentatiously as he had lived. His brothers and sister adored him. They recollected Harriet's death, now Emily was coughing too—they seem to have experienced a sense of fear and despair, the recollection of which was never lost to William or Frederick.

To Lord Melbourne it was a *coup de grâce* : he was to lose the only member of the family whose retiring nature coincided with his own. He was to lose the one child of whose paternity he had no doubt, and for whose sake he had endured the vagaries of his wife's ambition. As for Lady Melbourne— in retrospect her emotions may have been mixed but at the time there is plenty of evidence to prove her genuine sorrow. If she had a slight contempt for her first-born, she was none the less his mother. If her adored William were now to be heir to a great position—she would all the same have preferred to see her eldest son succeed, about whose birth there were no stories. Lady Bessborough was amongst the first to hear the news—it mattered not that she and Lady Melbourne were unsympathetic to each other—or that this death gave her some private reasons for anxiety. Two years ago the second son, William, had been in love with her, that had been a joke— now Caroline was in love with him, and that was no joke. She was terribly shocked, and she ordered the carriage and drove straight to Whitehall (Melbourne House is now Dover House, the Scottish Office).

In their confusion and sorrow they were all glad to receive her. She stayed with them until Lady Melbourne went to bed, then she drove to see her sister.

Her heart was heavy. Lord Melbourne had looked as though he himself had died, and the mother and daughter were violent in grief as in happiness. It was very sad, and in addition it made her very, very anxious about Caroline. So long as William remained a penniless younger son, without a career, marriage was out of the question and she had been able to take the matter lightly, but with Pen's death everything would be changed. William would be a considerable *parti* —he could marry when he pleased and she feared that his mother would approve of the marriage. Approve was indeed an inadequate verb—actually Lady Melbourne would be overjoyed at such a brilliant connexion. If William and Caroline were agreed, the Melbournes abetting, and her own husband amiably indifferent, what could she hope to do ? Was there indeed any real and sufficient ground for her fears ? Where everyone else foresaw happiness, why should she foresee disaster ? William's brilliant mind was exactly suited to Caroline's sensitive reactions—but his manners were unrefined and she suspected his principles. The Lambs were not of her world—old Melbourne might be quiet and decent, but he was not of their society, and Lady Melbourne she knew for a hard, ambitious, unscrupulous climber.

She and her sister were, alas, no paragons of virtue, but at least they *respected* certain standards even where they did not live up to them. Their failings might be as bad as and worse than those of Lady Melbourne, but they had the humility to recognise them as failings. They were ashamed of their lapses and they had never made a philosophy of them. Their children had been brought up strictly—they were still entirely ignorant of their parents' behaviour.

She could not face the idea of Caroline's reaction to the open cynicism and complete materialism of the Lambs' *milieu*. It may be too that Lady Bessborough shuddered at the thought of Lady Melbourne's handling of her own reputation. In her anxiety it may be that she misjudged William Lamb. It is a tragedy that he and she who were so well fitted to be friends by temperament and conviction never understood each other. When she saw the blatant cynicism of the mother echoed by the son she attributed the same source to the two utterances. Failing wholly to distinguish between the genuine crassness of the one, and the subtle shield of defence over a highly evolved and sensitive nature which gave rise to the other.

As for Caroline, she had never come in contact with cynicism and had no instrument with which to gauge it. In William she saw only " the embodiment of the ideas of liberty represented by Fox," that hero of her childhood.[1] And so inevitably Lamb was misjudged as completely by his future wife as he was by his future mother-in-law. The Duchess and Lady Bessborough had always been open with each other, but on this night, as she came tired and strained to her sister's house, Lady Bessborough could not relieve her mind by unguarded conversation. It had been Georgiana's dream, not only that Duncannon should marry Harriet—and indeed a sort of engagement subsisted between them—but that Hart should marry Caroline. He was younger than she, actually he was still at Eton, but there was no doubt that he adored her, and he was such a delightful fellow, such a good heart, so considerate, so generous, so unselfish. Apart from the happiness of keeping the families together, and from the brilliant situation —where else would Caroline find such devotion and so much character ? Georgiana was determined upon the plan by which she believed that Hart's happiness could be secured. His deafness cut him off from his contemporaries and from any sort of political career—he was not very clever, but he was so reliable, so honourable, so exactly what he should be for the position which he would some day fill. And Caroline's qualities would balance his, she knew Greek, French and Italian ; she had a talent for caricature, she was an excellent musician—yet she was anything but a blue stocking, her conversation was brilliant, she was a fearless rider. Where he was diffident she was quite unself-conscious ; where he was doubtful she had conviction and unbridled impulse.

Between them they would have all the brilliance and all the solid good qualities of English society—and together they

[1] *Passages in my Autobiography*—Lady Morgan.

would carry on, and perhaps even improve upon, the great tradition of Devonshire House.

Poor Lady Bessborough hardly knew what to hope—she loved and trusted Hart, but he was deaf, and slow, and it would take a very great passion to endue her Caroline with patience.

She left Devonshire House for Cavendish Square very sad and anxious. Some symptoms of her old troubles were returning. She hoped she should not be ill at a moment when her family required all her energies.

Granville wrote very seldom and his letters were formal. Lady Stafford's advice had been taken. In her anxiety she felt his absence unbearably. And Sheridan was beginning to give trouble. He had loved Lady Bessborough when they were both young—even when he was married to his first wife —she had consistently repulsed him. Aggravated, but still respectful, he had been willing to allow their relationship to drift into one of good-natured *camaraderie*. With the advent of Granville all this had been spoilt. He was shocked and unhappy at her failure to live up to what he had believed of her ; he was furious and indignant that such a coxcomb should have been successful where he had failed. And the worst of it was that since he had married Hecca he loved Lady Bessborough more than before. He felt that he had been taken in—cheated—and his jokes grew to have a bitter tang to them. Whilst Granville was in England he had had perforce to restrain himself, if for no other reason, because it was so hard ever to see Lady Bessborough alone. But now that he was in Russia Sheridan sought to revenge himself. He was getting on in years, he had always drunk an immense amount, and his wits and his sense of taste were not quite what they had been. His persecution of Lady Bessborough was extravagant.

He did sentinel outside her doorstep—at a Ball when she was sitting out between two very proper old ladies, he pursued her, very drunk, knelt before her and declaring that he had never loved anyone else, implored her to shake hands with him —when these proceedings failed to obtain the desired result he lost his temper and restorted to cruder methods.

Lady Bessborough began to receive a series of scurrilous letters—worse still, they were illustrated.

There were accusations against the Duchess of taking money

from her lovers—worse still against Lady Bessborough. Ultimately they were sent also to Caroline.

Lady Bessborough was beside herself with fury and misery.

It is only fair to say that although the authorship of the
letters was made a matter of the most careful research no
definite attribution was ever made. But in the minds of Lady
Bessborough and her sister no doubt existed that they came
from Sheridan. They believed him to be almost the only
person who would have known all the stories which were
alluded to in the correspondence, and this belief was responsible for Lady Bessborough's subsequent treatment of her old
friend. Wild, irresponsible, impertinent as Sheridan always
had been—drunken and bankrupt as he then was, it ill accords
with his taste and kindness of heart to have perpetrated such
an enormity.

Now that poor Pen was dead it seemed natural to Lady
Melbourne, and probably also to the rest of the family, that
the £5,000 settled on the eldest son should revert to William.
But here for once this imperious woman found her indolent
husband adamant. He had put up with much, he had been
hoisted unresisting up the social ladder, he had been made
to exchange his nice newly decorated house for the Duke of
York's magnificent mansion. When he had wanted William
to go into the Church Lord Egremont had intervened and the
boy had been sent to the bar instead. Whilst Pen was alive
he had borne these things in the hope that he might profit by
them. But allow William to take the place of his eldest son,
he would not. Lady Melbourne, in the rising fifties, but young
as ever " in art and artifice," struggled in vain to change his
determination. William should have £2,000 and not a penny
more. It was a cruel differentiation, implying as it must to
the outside world either a disapproval of William's conduct,
for which there was no ground, or else a confirmation of the
rumour concerning his paternity. It may well be that the
strong vein of irony, the gentle disillusionment that character-
ised him in later years, germinated in this incident. The name
of Lamb—the succession to Pen's inheritance—were the
foundations of his prospects, and what right had he to either
the one or the other ? The right of sufferance—it was all
sham—but toleration permitted it, and toleration became the

first article of his creed, domestic and political. However, two thousand a year and his prospects were a sufficient basis for marriage. He was incapable of passion, but his nature had the possibility of infinite tenderness and devotion. For some time he had been fascinated by Caroline Ponsonby. There was no worldly motive behind his attitude towards her. His detachment was attracted to her impulsive enthusiasm—his indolence to her activity.

She believed in so many things, in liberty and in love, in politics and in the arts, and above all she believed in herself. Nor did the difference between them end in the mental sphere. Where he was gentle she was passionate, where he was sensual she was cold. Moreover, she was sincere, original, contemptuous of convention. He decided to speak to her.

As to Caroline's opinion of William—it may well be said that she had none, because she did not know him—her interest in people lay wholly in her own reaction to them, it was her image of them that counted—she neither knew reality nor wanted to know it.

William was beautiful and brilliant, he had a charming voice, a strange illusive manner, she had decided that he was the embodiment of all that was best in the ideas of Charles James Fox—if a divergence from these tenets was observable it was a mistake—that was his true self, which she knew better than he did himself. Her enormous egoism demanded satisfaction—that William needed her was a *sine qua non*—in reality Lamb was singularly self-sufficient—his need was to give himself—not crudely, implacably, regardless of necessity as she was ready to do—but all the same, little as they suspected it, they shared this trait, different in degree but identical in kind. But where William was over sensitive and discreet, Caroline was a blatant and determined giver. Much unhappiness might have been spared them if amongst so many differences this ultimate differentiation had also been theirs.

When Lamb proposed Caroline was, if not very young, at least extremely young for her age ; in particular, though fully developed physically, that side of life had no echo in her mind. There is no doubt that she was very much in love with Lamb and had been so for some time—but the problem presented itself to her in an intellectual form only. She thought the matter over carefully and came to the conclusion that until she had obtained a more complete mastery over her temper she ought not to marry—more especially not to marry anyone so good as William. Lamb, we conceive, was not unduly upset by this precise pronouncement. He knew that Caroline loved him—loved him even in a way in which he did not love her. He withdrew with perfect courtesy and waited for nature to take her course.

Whether Lady Bessborough ever knew of this proposal or not is a matter of conjecture. The weeks passed slowly for her, filled with hollow amusements. In some salon Lady Hamilton would do her " attitudes," and despite her enormous size give satisfaction in all save the Bacchante scenes, or she would sing at the top of her great " Poll of Plymouth " voice, some laudatory ode, and Nelson would bend over her beating time to his own panegyric and joining in the chorus.[1] On the legitimate stage young Roscius was the rage, and Mrs. Siddons and Kemble had wisely withdrawn from the passage of the meteor. The Royal Dukes rioted and roistered as usual. Clarence abused the King so scurrilously to Lady Bessborough that she felt obliged to reprove him. The Bishops, too, were admonitory—they ordered that the Opera should be closed at twelve on Saturdays, and an infuriated mob smashed up the House.

Lady Bessborough went to her mother at Holywell to try what solitude and regular hours would do for her depression. She was sent upstairs at ten, and lay in her four-post bed with her ancestors gazing at her. They seemed to her to bear a reproach in their expression—and it was wrong, very wrong, that with her large family and all her devoted relations she should care so little for life—but were they themselves, when they were alive, in any position to throw stones, she wondered.

She had an attack probably of angina, and her nerves were in a bad way. The Duchess wrote to Granville—her debts were settled, but people had sharp tongues and had not spared her—she missed his ready defence.

When Lady Bessborough returned to London she thought that Caroline looked ill—and she had little difficulty in divining the cause of her pale cheeks and heavy eyes. It was a strange

[1] *Passages in my Autobiography*—Lady Morgan.

irony indeed to have to pray that William Lamb might ask her daughter to marry him. William, with perfect judgment, saw the exact moment at which his proposal would be successful. He wrote to her again. This time Caroline knew only that she was in love with him and that she could not live without him. If he had to suffer from her temper she couldn't help it. And as it proved, this characteristic of hers was perhaps the one of which he had least occasion to complain. Even Lady Bessborough thought William's letter beautiful. He told her, with great simplicity, how, whilst he was a younger son, and never likely to be in a position to marry her, he had tried every means of overcoming his devotion to her, and how unsuccessful all these efforts had been.

Caroline knew too well how averse her mother had been to the connexion ; but she knew also how to manage her relations. She threw her arms round her neck—swore that she loved William better than anyone except her mother, but that she should give him up if it were asked of her. . . . Who could take such a responsibility ?

Lady Bessborough could only leave the decision to Caroline herself. Lord Bessborough, too, shirked any responsibility. That night the mother and daughter went to the Opera where William was to meet them. Caroline was radiant, Lady Bessborough so nervous that she could scarcely speak. Lamb was waiting for them in the passage. From their faces he knew that he had been accepted. He asked anxiously whether Lord Bessborough had raised any objection. When he was told that all was to be left to Caroline's choice, he flung himself into Lady Bessborough's arms—and two eminent politicians who chanced to enter the passage at that moment left hurriedly, commiserating with the absent Granville. The young couple were oblivious, but Lady Bessborough felt it necessary to see the intruders at the close of the performance and let them into the secret of Caroline's engagement. The necessity for doing this created the necessity for going to Devonshire House immediately. The news would be about the town by morning. Lady Bessborough dreaded the interview ; but Caroline was too happy to have any consideration. They were all there, the Duchess, Bess, the Duke, Hart and Harriet. The news, whatever effect it may have made, was received enthusiastically by Georgiana, and kindly by Harriet and Bess. Only Hart remained silent, his face white. Then when the congratulations had subsided he burst out into a torrent of reproaches. He had always loved Caroline, he had always meant to marry her when he was old enough—she had known this—tacitly it had always been understood that she should be his wife—if he had not declared himself it was only because he had believed it more honourable not to do so until he could marry. Caroline had known this all along. Her infatuation for Lamb would not last. He understood her and could make her happy. How could she associate herself with those worldly, cynical upstarts? Would she not now, before it was too late, change her mind? Caroline was angry, hurt, embarrassed; she loved William—that was an end of it—poor, dear, stupid Hart, she would be sorry for him later, but not now whilst he was making himself so ridiculous. The family rushed to her assistance. Georgiana took Hart into another room, she felt deeply for his disappointment, and for the shame which she knew he would suffer to-morrow. Alone with her, he lost control of himself and was reduced to a violent attack of hysterics. She sent at once for a physician. By degrees the boy recovered his self-possession. Lady Bessborough and Caroline waited for reassuring news of him; then they left for Cavendish Square. Lady Bessborough hoped it was not a bad omen. It was, anyway, a horrid thing to happen on the night of Caroline's engagement. She felt sorry for them all, for Caroline and Hart and Georgiana and for herself, and had the future been visible to her she would perhaps have given more sympathy to William Lamb than to any of the rest of them.

The engagement created a sensation in the circle of Devonshire House, and it is probable that more than a few mothers and daughters breathed a sigh of relief—Caroline had broken more hearts than those of William and Hart, she so far outshone Georgiana and Harriet, Corisande and Caroline St. Jules in charm and wit and beauty that from the point of view of her girl friends, her marriage was little less than a godsend.

There had been a present-giving dinner-party at Devonshire House. Not only had Caroline received gifts but she had also made some: Most of the presents consisted of the fashionable jewellery of the day : an aquamarine clasp from Lord Morpeth, a little pearl and diamond cross from Lady Elizabeth, a set of amethysts from Lord Melbourne, a diamond wreath from Lady Melbourne, a burnt topaz cross from Harriet Cavendish.[1] The Duke of Devonshire gave her her wedding-dress, and the Duchess her veil.

To the outside world Caroline had appeared very happy —to her mother she seemed low and very nervous. It had been settled that the young couple should occupy an apartment in the Melbournes' magnificent mansion—an arrangement which may have seemed a fianancial solution, but which was undoubtedly disastrous to their future happiness. Even at the time people commiserated with poor Lady Bessborough who, in order to visit her daughter, must now enter the house of one who had always been profoundly inimical towards her, and who when she had visited her on the occasion of Caroline's engagement had had the effrontery to express a hope that the daughter be an improvement upon the mother. Lady Bessborough swallowed the insult, only reflecting that Lady Melbourne's worldly wisdom (not her example) might help Caroline to become a good wife to William.

On the 8th of June the marriage took place. Lady Elizabeth wrote that " Caro was dreadfully nervous, his manner to her was beautiful, so tender and considerate." Honeymoon couples were not left in those days to carefully guarded privacy, and it was only because Caroline was ill and refused to see anyone that Lady Bessborough was unable to visit her till three days later. When she did so she was horrified at her daughter's appearance, and wrote resentfully on the favouritism manifested by nature towards the male sex.

Lady Elizabeth Foster wrote to her son Augustus, who had heard with horror of the marriage : " You may retract all your sorrow about Caro Ponsonby's marriage, for she is the same wild, delicate, odd, delightful person as before, unlike everything, witness her dating to Lady Maria Lane, ' from Brocket Hall, Heaven knows what day ! ' "

It was a year of marriages, for hardly had William and Caroline's engagement been announced than that of Emily Lamb's

[1] *The Two Duchesses.*

to Lord Cowper became known. This was a marriage of reason—a good establishment.

Lord Byron was to discover later that " after all, Lady Melbourne is a good woman. There are *some* things she will stop at." She had been reputed to have explained to the young married women of her acquaintance that they had one duty towards their husbands—they must provide them with *one* legitimate male heir. When this had been achieved she for one would not examine the features of the younger children with an unkind or enquiring eye. It may be that Emily was the recipient of such advice. It is certain that mother and daughter had much in common. Both were hard, worldly, brilliant and witty ; both were conventional, un-impulsive, deficient in heart, but saturated with a horse com-mon sense and a highly developed family feeling.

As enemies they were vindictive, unscrupulous and im-placable—as friends they were uncertain, as relations they were wholly admirable. For many years it must have seemed as though Emily were only destined to be a slightly softened sketch of her redoubtable mother, but her old age drew from her one strong, unselfish, devoted affection of which Lady Melbourne would have been wholly incapable. However, in June 1805, she was marrying the rich, respectable and to us shadowy Lord Cowper, who was not, alas, destined to be the recipient of this devotion. Their marriage took place in the drawing-room of Melbourne House—it was smart, crowded, conventional, a symbol of their early married life.

Lady Bessborough, exhausted with her activities, went to Brighthelmstone to recuperate. For the first time she visited the now completed Pavilion. It was indeed a wonder and a portent to the lovers of palladian symmetry.

According to Creevey, Mrs. Fitzherbert's influence was now used to keep the Prince away from Devonshire House, where Mrs. Creevey related that he " now only went from motives of compassion and old friendship " or as the result of " perse-cution." He was living a most domesticated life, and in reply to enquiries regarding the manner in which he had spent his day he remarked :

" I went to Mrs. Fitzherbert's at one o'clock and stayed talking with her till past 6, which was certainly UNFASHION-

ABLE."—" Surely," comments Mrs. Creevey, " he must have been thinking of her as his lawful wife ? "

Sheridan, too, was much at the Pavilion, and Creevey gives us some characteristic vignettes of him. In one, he is disguised as a police officer appearing to take up the Dowager Lady Sefton for playing at an unlawful game. In another he is seen creeping into the kitchen at a late hour, and cajoling the servants into cooking him a dinner, by telling them how much better accommodation he would give them if he were prince.

Finally, and most characteristically, he is meeting Warren Hastings for the first time since his trial and assuring him of his " great personal respect." To which sentiment the maligned administrator replies that " if Mr. Sheridan would make these remarks more public it would be a consolation to him."

Lady Bessborough came back to more worries—Duncannon announced his intention of marrying Lady Maria Fane. This was a complication, because as has been already mentioned there was a tacit understanding that he was to marry his cousin Harriet Cavendish. It had been a dear wish of Georgiana's and Lady Bessborough had echoed it with only a little less warmth. Duncannon was dutiful and sedate and hard-working—Harriet was plain but remarkably intelligent, she was capable of great devotion and had a highly developed sense of duty. In many ways she might have suited Duncannon perfectly—but in his mother's opinion she had one defect—her small clear eyes looked steadily and critically at life, she had in a sense as wide a humanity as that of her aunt, but it was a gentle, sober quality of the mind, not the passionate heartrending impulses which could reconcile Lady Bessborough to her worst enemies in one flash of pity.

And if there was one thing which the tolerant Harriet could not tolerate it was a depth of feeling which surpassed her own ; also this young woman who was to come to maturity in the Victorian age was already imbued with Victorian standards, and already by these standards she judged her aunt and disapproved of her.

In November came the news of Trafalgar—the great pæan of victory was cruelly damped by the account of Nelson's death. Lady Bessborough wrote to Granville in the spirit which echoes through a hundred other letters. Relief, pride, grief, each had their share in the sea of emotion. So universal was the wearing of mourning that it seemed unnecessary to proclaim a national mourning in honour of the event.

On December 1st we hear of " Lord Aberdeen making pendant at the Priory to Caroline and William Lamb, who flirt all day long *e felice adesso*." [1] That day and the next England went quietly about her business unconscious that on the field of Austerlitz Napoleon's arms had gained a victory which went far to neutralise all the advantages of Trafalgar. When the news became known the feeling of fear and depression was intense. For Lady Bessborough the national danger was brought home more clearly by personal anxiety. Granville was believed to be with the Allied Armies—for weeks she lived in an agony of dread. To make matters worse Frederick's regiment was ordered to the front, and Morpeth, who had been on a diplomatic mission, was said to be flying for his life before the advancing troops. The bleak December days dragged out their dismal span until Christmas Day came and with it news of the safety of Granville; that of Frederick and Morpeth had been assured some days previously.

[1] *The Two Duchesses.*

1806

THE spirit of centuries is not so far subject to mathematicians' laws as to die at the precise moment at which two noughts come to replace the double nine on the calendar. The year seventeen hundred and ninety-nine had died away and the year eighteen hundred taken its place without causing any perceptible alteration in the life of England. Mr. Pitt had remained in his accustomed place at the head of the Government, Mr. Fox from his seat of retreat had played his usual disapproving part, the ridottos at Devonshire House had been as brilliant as before, Georgiana had remained the same brilliant, vivid, "more than life-sized hostess," Lady Hamilton had "done her attitudes" with Nelson in attendance, the Royal Dukes had drunk and gambled and the war had dragged on, and the Irish had continued to prepare for rebellion—and it seemed as though one century were very much like another.

Five years passed and still the change was imperceptible ; 1806 followed 1805 and no fearful omen of comet or eclipse came to give warning that the eighteenth century having outlived the allotted span was now to expire. Yet, surrounded by the familiar figures, with only Nelson's gap to remind her of the passing of time, Lady Bessborough felt oppressed with an impending sense of disaster.

The preparations for Nelson's funeral occupied the whole of the first week of the New Year. From Chiswick and Roehampton, from Osterley and Brocket, the Christmas parties returned to their town houses, and made their arrangements for viewing the procession. No bitter feeling of class or party marred the general grief.

Nelson had saved England from a great, though not an imminent danger—he had brought victory to her forces and glory which, for a generation, had been disassociated from her

arms. Yet these facts are insufficient in themselves to explain
the hypnotic influence which his personality exercised over the
minds of his contemporaries. His gallant, slightly melodramatic, figure put a spell over the age of sensibility and
sophistication.

A society, highly conventional despite its raffishness, a
formal, free-thinking, anti-national society, fell prostrate at
the feet of a man who went into action invoking Lady Hamilton
" For Emma and England " ; and died, leaving his mistress
to the nation ! In a word England, the English : each,
severally and as a mass had fallen in love with Nelson.

The 9th of January was fixed for the state funeral. The
body was to arrive by water on the preceding day, and to lie
that night at the Admiralty. Louisa Hawkesbury, the old
Bishop of Derry's youngest daughter, now married to Lord
Hawkesbury, a rising politician of the King's party, who always
evinced a lively curiosity in morbid events, is our authority
for the proceedings of the 8th of January. The day was
brilliant, but as the funeral procession sailed up the river,
there was a sudden change from bright sun to lowering clouds,
followed by a violent hail-storm, and she noted with appreciation " ye awful appearance and the peculiar look of the air
and the water " as the coffin was borne to the Admiralty.
Then a strange fancy took her " to see ye coffin " and she
" asked Sir Evan Nepean to indulge me." [1] The wife of a
Secretary of State was not to be refused, and so she " beheld
ye melancholy chaplain in his mourning cloak at ye head of
the bier and looked at that little coffin and thought of what it
contained."

Lady Bessborough took the funeral more soberly ; she had
known and appreciated Nelson, she had lately visited Lady
Hamilton who had never left her bed since hearing of his death,
she was even sorry for his disagreeable wife. Above all she
was anxious not to bore Granville with an account of what he
would read in the papers. He was becoming no easy corre-
spondent, critical as to the matter and legibility of her letters,
no more could she write freely as she had done in the old days
in Paris, but always in an attempt to please and amuse him.
She was with her sister and Lady Elizabeth Foster in a win-

[1] *The Letters of the First Lady Wharncliffe.*

dow at Charing Cross, and she was moved by the sight of that countless multitude of bowed heads which were uncovered as the coffin passed and at the deep silence of the mob. She was proud too of Fred's perspicacity, who, being on guard, was the first to discover that no places had been allotted to the foreign representatives and avoided what promised to develop into a matter of dispute by detailing his dragoons to escort them, and sending a frantic message to the Duke of York to request that seats be reserved for them in St. Paul's.

That night the scratching of a thousand quill pens sent accounts of the solemn event to the provinces, to Europe, and even to America.

Lady Elizabeth, writing to Augustus Foster in Washington, comments on the stillness of the multitude, broken only by ejaculations as the car passed : " God bless his soul who died for us to protect us, never shall we see his like again." [1] She adds that " the show was altogether magnificent, but the common people, when the Crew of the *Victory* passed, said : ' We had rather see them than all the show.' " Everyone, high and low, wore crape scarves and black cockades with " Nelson " inscribed on them. Lady Hawkesbury, writing to her niece, Caroline, the daughter of Lady Erne, reiterates the general impression " ye moving off the car with ye coffin amidst the immense concourse of mob and military was very grand and very Gub—(' Gub '—adjective used by the Herveys in the sense of ' moving '). The dear 48 *Victory* men and ye 48 pensioners were also Gub to a degree." [2] So ended the first of the great funerals of that year in which it seemed that England was engaged in unceasing obsequies for the dying century.

By the middle of January Lady Bessborough was seriously alarmed about the health of the Prime Minister. Pitt had committed the country to war with France. It had been done in the face of much opposition and he felt the weight of the responsibility—in the autumn he had gone down to the country with " the Austerlitz look on his face " ; indeed, since he had received the news of this defeat he said that he had never been free from a band of pain round his stomach as

[1] *The Two Duchesses.*
[2] *The Letters of the First Lady Wharncliffe.*

though he were being cut in half.   His friends, and Canning in
particular, seem to have been optimistic as to his condition,
but they judged less well than his old opponents at Devonshire
House.   Lady Bessborough had no illusions.   Pitt was dying,
and, astounding to relate, her emotions were those of unmixed
regret.   During nearly all her adult life Pitt had been Prime
Minister, and she and her friends had held views contrary to
those of his party and had used all their wit and charm and
money to defeat his ends ; but he was become so familiar a
figure, so much a part of England, that the thought of his
disappearance filled her with alarm, besides which age had
toned down the asperity and enthusiasm of her views—and
then also, it was too late, the country was definitely embarked
upon Pitt's policy—the hands of the clock could not be put
back, and he was admittedly best fitted to carry this course
through to the end.   And then there was Fox ; Fox was too
old to become Prime Minister for the first time, with twenty-
two years of opposition behind him, years that had been a bad
schooling for the rôle—and (may this not have been the most
cogent reason for sorrow) Pitt was the friend, the hero, of
Granville.   Granville, who was exiled in the Russian winter,
how he would suffer when what was inevitable happened.
Such were Lady Bessborough's feelings and emotions, as she
tried to break the news gently to Granville—it may be that she
took unnecessary trouble, judging his careful emotions by her
own spontaneous reactions.

By the 20th there was no hope, and Lady Hawkesbury
(who besides having Mr. Pitt as her husband's chief and their
country neighbour was personally his devoted admirer) wrote
lugubriously : " There is no hope . . . the interval is terrible, and still more terrible will be ye end." [1]

On January the 23rd he died.

He had been a prodigy of moderation, tenacity and private
and public impeccability.   At the time of his death it might
have seemed that his policy had failed and led only to embarrass-
ments, but his views were long, he regarded the immediate
causes of anxieties as transitory and inevitable and he had no
doubt whatsoever as to the ultimate justification of his political
creed.   After his death certain reports of dramatic death-bed

[1] *The Letters of the First Lady Wharncliffe.*

utterances were circulated. These were untrue. Mr. Pitt, who had detested heroics during his life, was unlikely to have indulged in them on his death-bed. His actual words had been characteristic : " Remember, I die at Peace with all men, public and private. I am sorry to leave the country in such a situation."

Lady Hawkesbury was overcome by the blow. . . . " All is over. We were woke with ye sad tidings. The event took place at half-past four this morning. I can say no more. I not at all well and it is all I can do to keep up ; it is cold and worry joined and as it has fallen on my bowels I dare say it will carry itself off." [1] Devonshire House was generous. Georgiana wrote a note of sympathy to Granville, concluding with the somewhat questionable statement that " Mr. Fox would be well pleased indeed could he recall him to live and place him in his Cabinet."

Fox's own comment was probably a truer version of his views : " Impossible, impossible ; one feels as though there was something missing in the world." Pitt and Fox, the two most brilliant politicians of their generation, always in opposition to each other since the day more than thirty years ago when Fox's mother had written that Lord Chatham's little boy was so well brought up, so differently from their children, and would she believed, in later life, prove that he would be a thorn in little Charles' side. Pitt, the sane, the careful, the prudent, who had always stood with his two feet embedded in the nation's common sense blocking the way to power for the idealists ; Pitt was dead.

Had he never been born Fox would have undoubtedly held office during those twenty-two preceding years.

But now it was too late. The years of frustration followed by years of retirement had taught Fox detachment; all ambition, all desire for office was dead. He remained convinced of his principles—and with this in mind, and making proof of a certain moral courage, he refused to give his assent to the laudatory speeches made in House over the political greatness of his dead opponent. The mass of the people were incensed —one might thwart a man during his life, but once he was dead his opinions should become worthy of respect. Fox had a

[1] *The Letters of the First Lady Wharncliffe.*

belief in the immutability of truth and stood by it. He voted for the payment of £40,000 of debts left by Pitt, but he voted against his burial in Westminster Abbey.

Even in America the death of Pitt seemed to be a reversal of nature. " Pitt has haunted me ever since his death," wrote Augustus Foster, " I think I see his figure every hour, thundering over poor little Addington. At such a distance as this, when one hears of the death of so great a man as he, one really cannot conceive it." [1] It was left to little Mr. Trotter's little mind to pronounce the views of the smaller fry amongst Pitt's enemies :

" The passions of the vulgar made and kept Mr. Pitt a Minister. . . ."

" Mr. Pitt, under the control of an extensive and liberal genius, like Mr. Fox, might have made a useful minister of Finance." [2]

" The dear and valuable King feels it acutely," states Lady Hawkesbury, and this was doubtless true, for the old monarch must have known that whether as Prime Minister or in some lesser office, he should shortly have to come into contact with that champion of his peccant son—that bugbear of the Court— Charles James Fox.[3]

In the crisis the King called upon Lord Grenville to succeed Pitt. Grenville realised that he could not, with the sole support of the bereaved Pittites, hope to form a government strong enough to carry the country through the war and into peace. He offered the Foreign Office to Fox—Canning was not to be given office, Lord Grey went to the Admiralty, despised Mr. Addington was made a peer and Lord Privy Seal to almost everyone's displeasure, and to Lady Hawkesbury's satisfaction her lord was given the Wardenship of the Cinque Ports. Fox's friends for the most part disadvised his taking office—they considered it beneath his dignity to serve under Grenville and believed that he could not, with honour, help to wage a war of which he disapproved.

The fatal blow to Tory ascendancy fell too late for the members of the Devonshire House set. They, who had cared for politics, for the causes of Liberty and Reform, as few men

---

[1] *The Two Duchesses.*   [2] *Life of Fox*—Trotter.
[3] *The Letters of the First Lady Wharncliffe.*

and women have cared for any ideal, were grown old in opposition.

Of all policies, theirs was one which needed the vigour and enthusiasm of youth for its accomplishment, but when the first promise of opportunity broke upon them, the Duchess was nearly blind, Sheridan only continued to exist as an impossible and preposterous ghost of his former self, and upon Charles Fox, who had once been consumed with a fearful fury of righteousness, a sort of divine detachment and sad urbanity had descended. The dawn of power revealed a sadly shabby and exhausted band. For twenty-two years they had strained their weight against Pitt, so that when this barrier fell, they could not recover their balance, but seemed to fall prostrate upon his grave. And their sober children were in no way fitted to carry on the urgency of the old tradition—Duncannon, William Lamb, Lord Holland, Lord John Russell. The emotional vitality and sincerity of Devonshire House was about to be replaced by the cold theorising of " the Mountain."

Fox, faced with the never-solved decision of taking office under a chief of whom he did not approve, or refusing to serve his country at a time when his name might strengthen her prestige, decided to sacrifice his peace of mind and it might be even his reputation. He said good-bye to his dearly loved life at St. Anne's, to his mornings with Homer and his evenings with Mrs. Armistead, and, against the wishes of all his friends, he joined the government, which, according to the faithful Trotter, had carried on war till no object remained, and till peace seemed to be almost as dangerous as the continuation of war ! And besides the criticisms of his friends, Fox had his own doubts as to the fitness of his taking office. He was ill, ought he not to hand over the reins to younger men, to his own nephew ? But this he could not make up his mind to do—life had given him so few years of offices—so few opportunities of working for those things for which he had a heart. He wrote apologetically to Lord Holland : " Don't think me selfish, young one ; the slave trade and peace are two such glorious things, I can't give them up even to you. If I can manage *them*—I will then retire." [1]

[1] *Life of Fox*—Hammond.

A few days later, he was characteristically warning Napoleon of a plot to assassinate him. No wonder that the English, even the Tories, had a weak spot for Charles James despite all his wrong-headedness.

And, as though public misfortunes were not sufficient, private sorrow became allied to it. On the 1st of February Caroline began to be in labour; the child was not due for some weeks. Lady Bessborough hurried to nurse her daughter and send a message to bring back William who was travelling in the north. He returned with all speed, but as he reached the door of Melbourne House he saw a little knot of people about it and a small coffin being borne out. He was extremely agitated, but Caroline was safe. His mother-in-law observed his manner towards his wife and found it perfect ; really, she began to believe that William alone amongst the Lambs had failed to inherit any part of Lady Melbourne's hard, false nature.

Caroline recovered rapidly and the *ménage* seemed to be of the happiest.

But a greater misfortune than any which had already occurred was in store for Lady Bessborough. Indeed, it was a blow from which she was never to recover. On the 22nd of March her sister was taken very ill—on the 23rd she was worse, hope was not yet gone, but the danger had increased. Lady Bessborough never left her.

Bess too kept unceasing vigil. The Duchess was suffering tortures, she wanted them all about her, her husband, Georgiana, Harriet, Hartington, but more especially Lady Bessborough and Lady Elizabeth. The curious relationships that existed between them were sunk in a sea of suffering. She loved them all, and they, how they loved her, she was the pivot of their existence, and they were unable to conceive of any life without her. Several times before, she had been very ill and had said good-bye to them, and then she had recovered. Her vitality was seemingly inexhaustible, surely she would rally once again ? In reading through their anxious notes it is painfully apparent that they could hardly bring themselves to believe in the possibility of her death.

Then on March the 30th the end came, terribly. She had gone, and yet they who had been so far less vital were still alive.

Georgiana Duchess of Devonshire

They were indeed alive, but it seemed to them that they had gone into the tomb with her. During her illness crowds had pressed at the gates of Devonshire House to hear the latest bulletin. Now there was utter solitude and silence. They lived on amongst themselves in that house which she had filled, till they were " in a stupor . . . not awake to the certainty of the horrid event." [1] Lady Elizabeth wrote to Augustus telling him that she had sent for Clifford to comfort Hartington, she echoed Lady Bessborough's words " he (Hart) saw his adored, mother every day, even afterwards, and so did I ! And I am alive to tell it to you." So much was she present in their minds that they caught themselves saying : " I'll tell her this " as though she had been absent on a journey.

She had left all her papers to Bess ; a curious disposition and one that did not satisfy all parties. But she had understood Lady Elizabeth, she knew about her neglected childhood, her miserable marriage, her unhappy abandonment, she knew too that life had been very hard upon her, and realised that she had had to live by her wits and if Georgiana had been wronged by her, she forgave the injury, and perhaps she hoped that this final bequest might serve to protect Bess from the tongues which, during her own life, had been kept silent by her defence of her friend. Lady Bessborough, for one, saw the will in this light and for the rest of her life she protected Bess.

From all parts of the world letters of condolence began to pour in.

Eighteenth century mourned its own death at the grave of the beautiful Duchess. They wept, they offered flowers ; for a moment they felt older, more insecure, more lonely. Then they passed on. The world was less amusing, but still, it was the world, and one must make one's way through it. Even the children would recover from the shock as the weeks passed, the Duke had felt it the least perhaps of all, it had been distressing, horrible, but it was over, and maybe life would be simpler—and Lady Elizabeth ? Well, the Hervey blood was buoyant, they were capable of deep feeling, but their feelings were always well controlled.

[1] *The Two Duchesses.*

Only to Lady Bessborough the sorrow grew and deepened. At first it had been too annihilating for pain. Only as the months went by could she bring herself to speak of it even to Granville. It had shaken her to the depths of her being. It had made her revise all her values and look into herself—the survey alarmed her—how far she had travelled from the ideals which she and her sister once held in common, in the very old days at Althorp. From the time of the Duchess' death it is evident that she made the resolution to break with Granville. And from that day, with many waverings at first, and many backslidings, she did honestly endeavour to induce him to marry. Her unhappiness was far too great for any palliative ; she judged herself, the situation, even her beloved Georgiana, with perfect candour, believing that by her death the Duchess had expiated any sins which she might have committed and holding that her own loneliness might also be turned to a kind of atonement for the past. Would Granville understand this ? He too had suffered cruelly at the hands of death.

If he failed her now it might be that the ultimate surrender would be easier. But alas when she saw him all her judgment of his worth was always to desert her. Even now she quickly reconstructed her image of him. He was to be associated with her, her second self—however little he might seem or endeavour to fill that rôle.

They went to Chiswick. They returned to Town . . . from one set of memories to another.

Meanwhile Fox, old, ailing and saddened by the loss of his friend, made a brave effort to save the life of the " All Talents " Ministry. Sir Francis Vincent, " always in a hurry and ready to wear out a hundred pairs of shoes to oblige the Secretary of State for Foreign Affairs," endeavoured to keep some of the strain off the tired shoulders of his chief ; even the Irish rallied to his side and, rather than embarrass him, decided to postpone pressing their claims until he was well established.

He worked unceasingly to preserve the peace of Amiens, he worked with absolute integrity, taking no sinecure for Lord Holland or any of his relations. By May he broke down and was confined to Holland House. The Prince of Wales called every day to enquire for him. Fitzpatrick, Fitzwilliam, Lord Robert Spencer, were his constant companions—only his colleagues neglected him, " Lord Grey came seldom, Lord Grenville never."

His one desire was to return to St. Anne's. But the journey was considered too long for him to undertake as yet. The Duke of Devonshire suggested Chiswick as a halting-place, and the offer was gratefully accepted. It was hoped that the change of air might do him good. . . . He was drawn round the garden in a chair by the indefatigable Mr. Trotter, who questioned him on botany and natural history. " Palladian Chiswick," where he had spent so many days talking of things far removed from horticulture with Georgiana. No wonder that " a shade of melancholy sometimes stole over his countenance, when objects reminded him of the late Duchess." [1] Once already he had been tapped, again his size " grew inconvenient " and the painful operation had to be repeated. His curious mind, considering his own symptoms, suggested to him that each doctor should place his signed diagnosis in a sealed envelope to be opened at his post-mortem. He had no illusions about his health.

His wife, Lord Holland, Mr. Trotter read aloud to him all through the day and often long into the night—his appetite for literature had become even more voracious, he wished to hear the Aristo once again and Herodotus and Virgil and Shakespeare and many more . . . if there were time. Sometimes his conscience pricked him : " Does this amuse you, Mr. Trotter ? I hope it does ! "

Mr. Trotter, voiceless but devoted, read on until sleep came to relieve him from his post ; his nerves, never very good, were frayed by his ceaseless vigil ; trying to reach the garden one night he blundered into the late Duchess' dressing-room—it was only a few weeks since she had died. The music book was still open, half-opened notes lay scattered about, books were strewn on the table, as though she had left the rooms some seconds before on a temporary absence—poor Mr. Trotter (the only person awake in the silent house at Chiswick) was reduced to a paroxysm of hysteria.

Lady Bessborough came down to visit Fox. Perhaps he had not seen her since her sister's death, for he was so shocked when she took off her veil that he exclaimed in sorrow at her

---

[1] *Life of Fox*—Trotter.

changed appearance. But they had little heart between them
for gaiety. Fox felt the irony of his own position. After
twenty-two years of opposition to die within eight months of
joining the Ministry. It was best to forget the world in a
game of chess. And so they played, as she had played at
Roehampton with Duncannon when first she married, before
she had been caught up in the vortex of Devonshire House ;
as she had played with Fitzpatrick that night when Granville
went to Russia ; as she had played so recently at her sister's
bedside. Life went on remorselessly—one was young and
one became old, one was beautiful and one became plain, one
was happy and one became miserable—but beautiful and happy:
or plain and miserable, always, it seemed, that one was asked
to play chess.

She went sadly back to Cavendish Square. Before so very
long Granville would be back, but even this prospect was
mingled with bitterness. She was no longer the same person.
She was a person different in experience and in values from
the woman who had said good-bye to him. This holocaust
of the Great was a frightening experience. It impressed
even the Tories. Lady Caroline Stuart Wortley voiced it
when she wrote :

" Poor Mr. Fox, I fear there is now no prospect of his life
being prolonged. I am not a Foxite, but I confess I feel quite
a coward at the thought of his dying, because I hear of nobody
to look up to after he is gone." [1]

The vigil at Chiswick was drawing to an end ; urbane,
gentle and considerate as ever, Fox knew that his life's span
was now numbered in days. He mentioned Lady Bessborough
to Mrs. Fox, " She will feel this—and she was low enough
already."

On the 13th of September, between five and six in the
afternoon, whilst the Tower guns were firing for the victory of
Buenos Ayres, he turned to Mrs. Fox : " Keep up—keep up—
I am quite happy, but I pity you," [2] without a sigh he relin-
quished life which he had so much enjoyed. A strange
paradoxical man " whose heart," said Grattan, " was as soft
as that of a woman, his intellect adamant, his weaknesses his

[1] *The Letters of the First Lady Wharncliffe.*
[2] *Life of Fox*—Trotter.

virtues." A great classical scholar, a statesman of complete integrity. "The echoes of his youth clattered at his heels throughout his career, and his conscience and his enemies took care, he should hear of them." [1] His youth, when he had gambled away £140,000 before he was twenty-four, and believed to be engaged in committing suicide had been found reading Herodotus—his youth, when he had travelled all the way from Paris to Lyons with Aristotle in his pocket to buy a waistcoat more gorgeous than any that had been seen in London, his youth ; amply out-weighed by the sober dignity of his manhood.

In a room next door to the bed-chamber a crowd of anxious friends waited—suddenly the door opened and Lady Holland strode through the room, her apron over her head. The friends dispersed. [2]

Contrary to Fox's wishes the Government decided to bury him in Westminster Abbey. For three weeks the coffin lay in his house in " Stable Yard." Outdoing Lady Hawkesbury in morbid enjoyments Mr. Trotter " had a melancholy gratification in having my bed in the adjoining room and eating my meals in it." [3] Of the funeral Cyrus Redding writes in *Fifty Years' Recollections* :

" I saw the obsequies of Fox, a walking funeral from Stable Yard, St. James's, by Pall Mall and Charing Cross, lines of Volunteers *en haye* keeping the ground. I recollect the Whig Club among the followers and a large body of the electors of Westminster, with the Cabinet Council, but no royalty for which some kind of excuse was made. Literally the tears of the crowd incensed the bier of Fox."

Those who had left Enlgand in the previous year would find their return would be marked by such changes as almost to make them dread it. " Good God ! What a change in England since you left it ! It is frightful to think of, and makes me tremble for those precious lives which still must attach me to life," wrote Lady Elizabeth to Augustus. [4]

From the time of Fox's illness the affairs of the country seemed to take a turn for the worse. Napoleon's victories continued, even the South American venture turned out

[1] *Life of Fox*—Hobhouse.   [2] *Table Talk of Samuel Rogers.*
[3] *Life of Fox*—Trotter.   [4] *The Two Duchesses.*

badly and the captors of Buenos Ayres were themselves shortly to become captives. At home the impeachment of Lord Melville, and the delicate enquiry into the Queen's affairs cast a further gloom over society. The Government fell in the late autumn, and by November the country was in the fret and fuss of a General Election. About this time that shadowy person, Lady Bessborough's husband, became ill. A report had been spread that he was dying, and their house was thronged by people who called to enquire for him. Suddenly she realised the esteem which his quiet self-effacement had won. For the moment it seemed as though, haunted by remorse, she might endeavour to bring something real into her relationship with her husband.

But she had ceased so many years ago to regard him as anything but a kind, delightful, inefficient companion, who must be humoured and kept out of mischief. They lived their lives on two such different planes of intensity—she felt that she understood him quickly, easily, and had so much left over beyond this comprehension. And he, he did not understand her, and she had neither the patience nor the love to teach him. After her sister's death she was even kinder to him than before—and he shudderingly buried himself even more deeply in his library, his prints and his *objets de vertu*.

It may be that Granville too felt a certain anxiety lest on his return he should be overwhelmed by her abundant emotions —now deprived of some of their customary outlets. By chance, or by designed cruelty, he alluded to Princess Serge Galitzin more and more frequently. She was a beautiful woman, brilliant and eccentric, whose conversation was said to be the best in Petersburg, and whom eight years later Lady Lyttelton described as "carrying her head and wearing her shawl in a way of her own." [1] She lived a strange life, "going to bed at three in the morning and staying there twelve or thirteen hours." In 1806 she was about twenty-two years old, and lived with a *dame de compagnie*, her husband having left her at the door of the church immediately after their marriage.

Granville had a weakness for eccentric ladies, the first mock-

[1] *The Letters of Sarah Lady Lyttelton.* Sarah Spencer, daughter of Lord Spencer and Lavinia, married Lord Lyttelton. She was consequently niece to Lady Bessborough.

ing allusions to his new interest are soon lost in a series of anxious enquiries—the lady will not see him alone—does Lady Bessborough consider this a good omen or a bad one ? The lady says she hates him and will never see him again—or she changes her mind and permits him to visit her in the presence of the *dame de compagnie*, for a specified time—finally, he is spending every morning with the Princess Serge. . . . He was very much in love—more so than he ever had been before, and with the cruel instinct of self-preservation he took Lady Bessborough for his confidante.

What could she say, poor woman, when she recollected the hundreds of times she had written to him imploring him to regard her only in the light of a friend and counsellor ? With perfect irony Fate was carrying out the resolutions which she had made after Georgiana's death. Yet it was one thing to desire that Granville should marry some English peer's daughter and settle down to an ordered existence, and quite another that he should return from his embassy with a Russian *divorcée*. She tackled the situation with the most delicate skill. Would the poor little Barbarian be happy in England ? she wondered —Granville thought that she would—it may be assumed that he felt tolerably sure that, married to him, any woman might be happy anywhere. For how much of this impression was Lady Bessborough herself responsible ?

After tragedy came worry—which was worse ? Her pain over Georgiana's death, and Fox's, had been the measure of her love for them, and of the happiness they had had together. But now Lady Holland and Bess were on bad terms, and their quarrels gave her pain. And, to add to her discomfort, Emily Cowper was disparaging Harriet and taking every opportunity of showing her to be a fool, which was very unjust. And besides all this there was Princess Serge. . . . The good old care-free days of the eighteenth century, when it had not seemed to matter what anybody did or said, were over. Life was growing less exuberant, small things seemed to matter more. The nineteenth century was beginning to rear its puckered face. Lady Hawkesbury fixed one of its first gestures in a letter to her sister, Lady Erne :

" Tell Caroline I saw a good invention of Morel's at ' Wilderness ' (Lord Camden's house). This is a strip of cloth, wide as you please, in lieu of ribband for the bells. It is attached to the brass ring like ribband, and has a little pattern at ye end. Lady Camden's was Black Cloth, bound with very narrow blue binding, and the pattern just over the long square brass ring, in blue cloth, cut out and fastened in black." [1]

[1] *The Letters of the First Lady Wharncliffe.*

1807

THE new year, which saw the introduction of gas lighting, and the disappearance of candle-light and of the link-boy, gave success to the French arms and brought Granville home from Russia. The victories of Eylau and Friedland prepared the way for the Treaty of Tilsit, and long before the Emperor and the King of Prussia had made peace with Napoleon, the rôle of the British Ambassador in Petersburg had ceased to have any justification. Granville came back on leave in high spirits; these were not to be attributed to his pleasure at seeing Lady Bessborough, but rather to his belief that he had been successful in his attack upon the heart of Princess Serge Galitzin.

He read her letters out to his sister the Duchess of Beaufort, and she was of the same opinion as her brother—it seemed evident to her that if Princess Serge could obtain a divorce, she would marry Granville.

And why should she not obtain a divorce—or even an annulment—her husband had abandoned her since the first days of her marriage. She had lived ever since with perfect propriety, and she had the goodwill of the Emperor to help her cause. Granville was anxious to know what attitude London *société* would adopt towards the *divorcée*.

The Duchess of Beaufort was sanguine. The Court, she felt sure, would welcome her, and she would be received in nearly all circles. Lady Bessborough held other views—she knew that she was not well fitted to judge the case, she begged him to rely not principally on her opinions but rather on the kind interest of his sisters—yet, all the same, would not many people feel that a matter of principle was involved ? She knew that Princess Serge had been more sinned against than sinning, that it was a hard case; but one couldn't alter a principle

¹ *News from the Past.*

because of the individual sufferer. And as for hard cases, was not the whole of English society full of them ?

Once one admitted divorce—where was one to draw the line ?

Granville was not much impressed by these austere views. But for the moment he could do nothing to further his project ; he might therefore enjoy his holiday whole-heartedly, and leave the final attack until his return to Russia in the autumn.

Caroline was again expecting a child. Lady Elizabeth Foster was gloomy in her anticipation. " Her (Caroline's) uncertain health prevents one's knowing what is her state, or almost what to hope." Lady Bessborough stayed on in London to be near her. She went to the opera to distract herself and hear Catalani's *adieu*.[1] It was the first time she had been into her sister's old box—now it was her own box. The Duchess of Devonshire's name had been taken from the door, which bore Lady Bessborough's name in new black letters.

By August 28th Caroline was very unwell. Her mother was at her bedside ; late in the evening a footman brought Lady Bessborough a note. It came from Mrs. Sheridan, and in it she implored Harriet to come to their house—Sheridan was in a desperate condition, he was almost demented, and he must see Lady Bessborough.

It was midnight before she felt that she could leave Caroline for an hour or two. She called for her carriage, and drove round to the Sheridans. She was shown into Hecca's bedroom, where the distracted woman began to give an account of her husband's condition, but after a few moments Sheridan himself came in.

Lady Bessborough saw at once that he was exceedingly drunk. He talked wildly, he begged her pardon, he said that he was a vile wretch, that he had treated her abominably, that he had done her innumerable injuries, that she must forgive him or he would go mad, for that, even at that moment, he loved her more than any woman he had ever met.

The first part of his tirade had had certain effect upon his listeners, but the finale roused Hecca's indignation and Lady Bessborough's laughter. However, Sheridan was not to be

[1] *The Two Duchesses.*

stopped. He continued to pour out his complaints and his professions, brushing aside his wife's astonished reproaches.

Alone in the babel of reproaches, Harriet, the cause of them, sat silent. She was slightly disgusted, slightly amused, but above all things anxious to get back to Caroline. After three hours she effected her escape by locking her host up in his dressing-room.

The next day, August 29th, Caroline gave birth to an enormous child—it was a boy. Everyone was delighted; William, Lady Bessborough, and even Lady Melbourne thought better of her daughter-in-law for producing so substantial an heir. It seemed as though life were taking a turn for the better, when scarcely a fortnight later Lord Castlereagh sent to enquire whether Lady Caroline Lamb could bear the firing of the guns for the victory of Copenhagen.

And finally Lady Bessborough had her own particular piece of good news, when Granville's first letter reached her on his return to Russia. Princess Serge would have none of him. She had one bad husband, and she would not wish to exchange him for any but the most steady and sedate. She had determined that her happiness lay, not only in refusing to marry Lord Granville Leveson-Gower, but likewise in not seeing him and in not thinking of him any more.

Granville took his dismissal cheerfully—after all—suppose that Lady Bessborough had been right . . . suppose that a *divorcée* had not been acceptable to London society—what complications, what unhappiness might there not have been for both of them.

Early in October Caroline's child was christened at St. George's, Hanover Square. It was a double christening, for George Lamb's wife—Caroline St. Jules—had also recently produced a son and heir. The first cousins were christened together, and had a joint godfather in the person of the Prince of Wales. George Frederick Augustus were the chosen names. After the ceremony the party returned to Caroline's apartment, which had been turned into an illuminated temple. The rooms were so large and there was no crowd and no heat, but for all the magnificence there was an unexpected contretemps.

Sheridan had begged for an invitation. Recollecting her recent adventure in Hecca's bedroom, Lady Bessborough had sternly refused to be his advocate—and for once Caroline and Lady Melbourne were of one mind : Sheridan was so disreputable, so excitable, so often drunk, that his presence was too great a risk. Entreaties were of no avail. He was told that only immediate relations were to be present—the refusal was adamant. But Chéri was not in the habit of accepting " no " for an answer, and when the great doors swung open to admit the portly form of the Prince of Wales, they gave way also before his gentleman-in-waiting, Mr. Richard Brinsley Sheridan. It was too good a joke for resentment—the ladies forgave him, as they were always forced to in the end. The party, which began at five o'clock, lasted till two in the morning. The rather dangerous game of mottoes served to keep the guests amused. Sheridan's verses were apt to contain innuendoes of the most devastating character, and his invention was so quick that he found no difficulty in transforming any replies, which it fell to his lot to read, into panegyrics to his own honour.

When the festivities were over, the Lambs went down to Brocket, and Lady Bessborough to Roehampton—alas that the neighbourhood of Chiswick was now only a source of sadness and a growing anxiety to Harriet. There were things going on at Chiswick which gave her a warning pang.

She was worried about her niece Harriet Cavendish, whose position was difficult. The Duke hardly knew her, he never saw her alone, everywhere she went she sailed in the shadow of her governess, Miss Trimmer, and Miss Trimmer did the talking, and Harriet, who was lazy by nature, was content to let it be so—no one got to know her, and this was a matter of particular regret in the case of one whose quiet affections were only given to those whom she knew and trusted. Her aunt felt that if the Duke once got acquainted with his daughter, he might lean less upon Lady Elizabeth Foster's advice. And much as she liked Bess, she had begun to fear her influence.

Then Lord Bessborough had a plan of offering Roehampton to Louis XVIII, who was homeless, and that too needed consideration.

She wrote about all her worries to Granville, she tried not to bore him, she knew that his interest lay rather in the passing of the Slave Trade Act, and the fall of the Government over

1809

CORUNNA gave a sad flavour to 1809. And to Granville's old flame, Lady Hester Stanhope, it brought a more personal sorrow. During Granville's years of exile she had learned to forget him, and a new attachment had bound her to Sir John Moore. Whether he had any more intention of marrying her than Granville had evinced is an open question; but he admired her, and she loved him, and as he lay dying his last words were a message to Lady Hester. His death was an overwhelming blow to her. He had seemed, at least to her, to provide a solution to her life.[1] Now that he was dead, what was to become of her? A few days later came a long-delayed despatch by which she learnt that not only was Sir John dead, but that her favourite brother, Charles, had also been killed in that dreadful engagement.

For a moment public criticism of Moore's capacities roused her to a show of her old spirit—she wrote and told various statesmen, and more particularly Mr. Canning, not only what she thought of this abuse of the dead, but also what Mr. Pitt had thought of Sir John. England seemed a desert to her—perhaps worse than a desert, since it contained Granville, though it is more probable that recent experiences had robbed his presence of any significance to her. Be that as it may, she longed to get away, to go abroad, and so one day she sailed with one of her brothers to Gibraltar—little dreaming that she should never see England again—never again see any of her friends or relations, and yet live on for thirty years, to become a legendary figure—The Queen of the Desert, The Great Sitt, in whose presence Emirs hurriedly promised to release their prisoners, and fugitive Albanians or plague-stricken Armenians begged for succour, and at the sight of whose weighty letters consuls and ambassadors blanched and sweated.

[1] *Lady Hester Stanhope*—Dr. Morgan.

Everyone was sorry for Hetty ; what a good thing it would have been if Sir John Moore had lived to marry her. She had been tiresome sometimes, and absurd, and she had been badly treated by Granville, and now she had been badly treated by Fate—prevented from accomplishing the only sensible plan she had ever made. Everyone approved her going abroad.

She was sure to come back soon enough, and in some ways London was a more peaceful place devoid of her presence.

In July the expeditionary force of forty thousand men sailed for the Walcheren. In three months' time, mismanagement and sickness had so decimated and demoralised one of the finest armies that England had as yet sent to the continent that everyone was sighing for the evacuation, to which the Government had eventually to resort.

This disaster signed the death-warrant of the Duke of Portland's ministry ; and Canning being in no very good repute at the moment, Mr. Perceval took on the somewhat thankless task of Government, little dreaming, poor man, what was to be his fate.

Whilst these great public events were taking place, the lives of Lady Bessborough and her circle ran on smoothly enough. William, Caroline and Augustus, after a gay summer in Town, spent an equally gay August in the Isle of Wight, for dinners, balls, evening parties, and the Duke of Gloucester made of Cowes a very proper counterfeit of London. Then, a little weary, they retired to Ryde, where they found the Spencers, intelligent and sedate.

They laughed with Sarah over her Grandmother Lucan's gloomy forebodings. The old lady wrote frequently to her favourite grandchild, and her letters were filled with prophetic utterances of the most devastating nature. This month " we shall have a revolution, a scarcity, and Siberian frost and snow." [1] A miniature revolution seemed indeed to be taking place when the party, on their way through London, in the month of October, visited the new theatre at Covent Garden —for through the whole performance the audience whistled, roared, hissed, rang great bells, blew French horns, and made cat-calls in protest at the raising of the price of admission. In the same month occurred the Jubilee of George III. Alas

[1] *The Letters of Sarah Lady Lyttelton.*

that we have no account of it from Lady Hawkesbury's pen. But a letter from William Ogilvie to his wife, the Dowager Duchess of Leinster, gives us a picture of the festivities which took place in Dublin where the Duke of Richmond was Lord Lieutenant :

" The illuminations far exceeded anything I ever saw in London or Paris. Nothing ever equalled the Brilliancy of the Illuminations—I do not believe there was a window in this great city that was not illuminated down to a Cobbler's stall, and the variety and fancy of the transparent pencillings was very great—and had a fine effect." [1]

To the Devonshire House set it was a matter of indifference. To the Spencers it was an irritation : Lavinia refused to attend the service on October 25th, " as pray for King George, she cannot and will not." She offered her assistance, however, to Mr. Allen in the choice of a text for his Jubilee oration. Why not she demanded :

" Forty years " (or fifty, if you like) " long we have been grieved with this generation."

The Treaty of Vienna, which was concluded during the month, was not a dignified memorial to the reign.

During the autumn of 1809 Lady Bessborough had little attention to give to such grave matters, for private affairs of devastating importance to herself occupied her whole attention.

It was now twenty-seven years since Georgiana had used her influence over Ca to induce him to entrust Lady Elizabeth Foster with the care of his illegitimate daughter. It was twenty-seven years since Lady Elizabeth, destitute, abandoned by her husband and her father, had accepted to take that grand tour with the unattractive Louchee of whom she so successfully disposed before her return.

All through the succeeding years she had lived almost entirely at Devonshire House and at Chiswick. There, she had brought up her two Foster boys, and there she had brought up Clifford and Caroline St. Jules.

Who shall know now how the rôle she played was made possible ? That she had been devoted to Georgiana and grateful to her was never doubted by those who were nearest to the Duchess. Yet she had lived in the house for twenty-

[1] *Memoirs* of Georgiana Lady de Ros.

seven years, and during the greater part of that time she had been the Duke's mistress.

It would be easy to dismiss her as the common adventuress, rapacious and heartless, yet this was not the impression which she made upon those who knew her best—they saw many good qualities in her. It is probable that the secret of her extraordinary personality lay to a large extent in the circumstances of her upbringing. In her incredible father she saw a complete sceptic, drawing vast revenues from what he believed to be other people's folly—with this money he was (usually) generous, distributing it back to the fools it came from, in a manner which seemed to him suitable. Not only devoid but positively unaware of all spiritual qualities, he was mentally well endowed; and his natural taste and his reasoning both inclined him to recognise that those virtues to which others attached a moral or spiritual significance had for him a rational justification. He was, therefore, capable of advocating a high line of conduct, whilst at the same time allowing himself a perfect liberty to deviate from such a course when it appeared to him that an opposite line of action would succeed better. Elizabeth had inherited from her father a lack of faith—a super-abundant vitality, an insatiable curiosity, an independence that nothing could daunt—and from her mother she had derived a very good heart. When deserted by her husband, she had found herself destitute, she had realised at once that she must live by her wits, and, with them, do the best she could for her boys and herself. She had accepted Georgiana's help without hesitation. It is probable that when she came back from her foreign tour she had at once taken in the significance of the situation at Devonshire House. The Duke, cold, formal and cynical, was not amused by Georgiana's naïveté, he did not appreciate her enthusiasm or even her affection, but he did appreciate the more sophisticated mind of Elizabeth, her disillusionment, her knowledge of the world, her dry humour.

Georgiana was terrified of her husband; she didn't mind his neglect, what she could not bear was his cold disapproving scrutiny. Since they could never understand each other, why shouldn't each live their own life? Not that Georgiana was like Lady Elizabeth, a sceptic or a-moral. If she committed specific errors, they were acts of weakness—she regretted them

and made no excuses for herself. But she was no great philosopher, she probably held that the moral laws were very
different in their application to men and to women—she did
not wish to judge her husband. If he amused himself it was
none of her business. All she asked was that he should not try
and force her into his frigid mould—if he would only leave her
alone and not criticise her perpetually, she would do her best
to satisfy him.

She had liked Lady Elizabeth, because Bess understood her
—understood the situation—and was calm and sincere, almost
brutal in her analysis of it. In a society, feline and emotional,
Lady Elizabeth was at home that strong restful factor, a *realist*.
And probably Bess, judging the situation coldly and without
the smallest moral misgiving, decided, without enthusiasm,
that in becoming the Duke's mistress, she would make an
excellent situation for herself, conduce to Ca's happiness,
and do Georgiana a service rather than an injury, by occupying her husband's attention, and managing him as Georgiana
could never hope to manage him. In some such way it all
happened, and for twenty-seven years it had continued so.

Although outwardly the conventions had been maintained,
no one in society was ignorant of the situation. Lady Elizabeth's position in London was very dubious, but she had much
influence behind her, and where that influence did not extend,
she was far too wise to force herself. This discretion was a
small price to pay for all that she derived from the arrangement.
Ultimately not the situation itself, but its derivatives, had made
Georgiana very unhappy—had actually broken her health and
her reputation, and perhaps accelerated her death. But she
had never seen the real cause of the disasters that befell her in
her later life, and to the end she had counted Bess as her best
friend. After her death it was impossible for the Duke to
break a habit of twenty-seven years' standing. He was old—
and he couldn't get on without Lady Elizabeth—she seemed to
him much more his wife than Georgiana had been. Bess was
in difficulties, and characteristically she faced the situation.
After all that she had received from the Duke she couldn't
abandon him now, old and ill as he was. On the other hand,
with the disappearance of Georgiana, her presence at Devonshire House would have but one implication. . . . She had

never desired notoriety or the outraging of convention, besides which the situation for Hart and for Harriet would be disagreeable in the last degree—and she was sincerely fond of Hart.

There was only one sensible solution as far as she could see —and that was that she should marry the Duke. People would say unpleasant things, but they would say unpleasant things anyway, and with truth. Then it would make her slightly ridiculous and perhaps offend some of Georgiana's relations who had always upheld her. These were nasty considerations, but, on the other hand, she felt convinced that she could not do better for herself and for everyone ; so, early in the autumn, she broached the matter to Lady Bessborough—the latter was for the moment shocked at the unexpectedness of what, on reflection, she found that she had been anticipating all along. Because she was flurried, she did not probe into the matter, but let the subject drop. Afterwards she regretted this, for Bess would not allow the subject to be brought up again, but she had said enough to make Harriet realise that the marriage was decided upon, and would take place soon, and in secret.

The more she thought of it the less Lady Bessborough condemned Lady Elizabeth. She put herself in her position, and she knew that she was taking the best course, but also, the more she thought of it the more certainly she knew that Lord Spencer and Lavinia and Harriet would all be horrified at such an event —and that they might easily persuade her mother also to take up an uncompromising attitude. She wondered if they knew already. She wanted to hear more details herself, but Bess was not easy to draw.

She heard that in October the Duke and Lady Elizabeth were to go to Chatsworth—perhaps the wedding would take place there. . . . If it *did* take place, another event would become imperative : Harriet must marry. Life would become intolerable for her at Devonshire House.

Lady Bessborough talked it over with Granville. . . . Harriet must marry, she must marry at once, she must marry a man of fortune, of situation, of merit, someone not too young, someone with a future, for she was essentially made for the wife of an ambassador or a statesman—and Lady Bessborough paused in horror as she recognised the portrait she had drawn.

Harriet must marry . . . but must marry—who ? . . . nor
was Lady Bessborough alone to recognise the portrait.   Granville was frank in his certitude that he qualified for the part—
he was also expeditious—he asked his sister Beaufort to invite
Harriet to Badminton during his visit there.

What had she done, thought poor Lady Bessborough,
as that absolute certitude, which never errs, came to her
that this was to be Granville's fate—marriage with Harriet
Cavendish.

She had been frightened of Sally Fane, a little disturbed by
Hetty Stanhope, really alarmed by Princess Serge Galitzin . . .
but how different had she felt then, fear, anxiety, doubt—but
now she had no fear, no anxiety, no doubt, nothing but certainty, and despair born of it.   How obvious it was that
Granville would marry Harriet, how could she ever have
conceived that he should do anything else ?

And Harriet had all the qualities of judgment and self-control
that she lacked and that Granville admired.   And Harriet disapproved of her.   And he would live with her through months
and years and decades and learn to disapprove of her too.   He
would not find the lesson difficult.   He had always had a little
tendency to superiority.   But then, she really did love Granville, and with the part of that love which was selfless she
saw clearly how happy they would be, how suited to each other.

People who had nothing to reproach themselves with are
really in a different order of being from those who have.   And
those two had kept their self-respect intact.   If she had one
virtue in an exceptional degree it was humility.

They were so sure, this generation of the nineteenth century,
that all was well with the world and with themselves.

She wrote to Granville to ask about the progress of his suit.
She was sincere about her own feelings, above all things she
wanted Granville to be happy, and she quite honestly desired
Harriet's happiness also.

To her the marriage was already an accepted fact.   She
would have liked at least to aid and abet it—to do that much
for Granville, but now she realised that her love for him had
only one office left—to do nothing.   Her help could only do
him damage.   She must stay out of it all, and give her mind
to Bess's affairs.   Her mother had heard a rumour, she was

coming up to Town to consult her eldest son as to a line of conduct to follow when the marriage should be declared. Old Lady Spencer, left to herself, felt with Lady Bessborough that, much as the marriage might wound them, it would be best to accept it with seeming goodwill.

But Lord Spencer, under the influence of Harriet's sister, Georgiana Morpeth, and of his own wife, was for no compromise. Lady Bessborough was horrified. It was all of a piece with Lavinia's hypocrisy. Whilst Lady Elizabeth's position at Devonshire House was that of mistress, they were all to be on friendly terms, but when she chose to regularise her position, they must ostracise her. It was Fox's story over again.

If necessary, Lady Bessborough would stand alone with the Duke and Bess against all her family, and against Georgiana's children, but it was a bitter decision.

She saw Lady Elizabeth again and she learnt that the latter meant to suggest to Lady Spencer not taking up the title, as a mark of respect to Georgiana's memory. Lady Bessborough thought that anything unusual would only draw attention to the peculiarity of the situation, and, much as she disliked the idea of hearing her sister's title borne by Bess, she still advised it, and in the bottom of her heart she had a real affection and a surprised admiration for Bess.

Granville, at Badminton, watched Harriet's face closely when she received her post, and wondered when she should hear the news. The marriage took place in October.

When it was announced, Sarah Spencer wrote on the subject with a pen dipped in acid:

" A marriage is said to have taken place which shocks her (old Lady Spencer) very much ; it is a dead secret, and only told in whispers by everybody, to everybody as yet. . . . It is not an interesting ' *union de deux jeunes cœurs* ' but rather the crowning of a perseverance in vice and artfulness, which is, I fancy, unheard of. Clifford, of course, knows it, as it is no other than the long-expected wedding of his venerable parents. I can't understand why my grandmother takes it so to heart ; it is mortifying to poor Harriet, to be sure. . . . No ostensible change is said to be intended yet awhile. That is, the lovely bride is not to have ' in soft sound ' your grace salute her ear.

226

How long her humility will dispense with the honour is difficult to calculate. But I daresay before you can answer this letter the Duchess of Devonshire's parties and the Duchess of Devonshire's perfections will be talked of in London." [1]

Lady Bessborough tried to distract herself with the news of the day. Lord Castlereagh's duel with Mr. Canning was a shocking affair. It would upset Granville. But Granville had little time to think of his friends. He was too much concerned with his own affairs.

From Badminton he had followed Harriet to Chiswick. On the evening of November 14th, 1809, he proposed and was accepted.

His first act was to write to Lady Bessborough. He wrote very simply and sincerely, stating the facts as they had occurred —his proposal, his acceptance, his interview with the Duke. It was the model of what a letter under these difficult circumstances should be. A letter which might lay a solid foundation for the future.

The letter told her nothing which she had not anticipated —the blow had in reality fallen months earlier.

She must answer him without delay. And she did so. Her letter was generous, if a little more emotional than his. She desired happiness for both of them, and she prayed that God might bless them.

It was a perfect letter to show to Harriet, if need be. And she felt she had laid a safe relationship for their future—that preposterous future in which they were to fill the rôles of aunt and nephew to each other.

Granville was delighted—as well he might be, and Harriet was completely dazzled by his charm and adored him humbly —but she was no cipher, she had strong principles and she intended, by a judicious mixture of ambition and domestic happiness, to lead him away from the gaming-tables and into more serious paths. He knew that married to her, if at all, he would make a great career, and bring to fruition those talents which his mother had tried so hard to preserve from loss.

Yet, after all, Harriet was a generation younger than he was, and he saw no reason to give up his agreeable correspondence

[1] *The Letters of Sarah Lady Lyttelton.*

with Lady Bessborough. For so long now his feelings towards her had been so entirely platonic that he could not feel that there was anything surprising in such a continuance of his habits. He decided that he must explain the matter to Harriet, indeed, she had already asked him if they might have a talk on the subject. He told her that her aunt was a very wonderful woman, that for years he had consulted her upon every subject and confessed all his follies to her.

Harriet listened intently. It is probable that she knew much, if not all, about her aunt and Granville—and if this was so it is probable that she considered that he had been the victim of a wicked old woman.

She had been very frightened of Lady Bessborough's influence, but since a recent conversation with her she was reassured, for she was convinced that her aunt really meant to relinquish her hold over Granville, and really wished them well—and, after all, she was nearly fifty now.

Harriet was very wise, she listened without comment to Granville's story of how he had described every stage of their courtship to Lady Bessborough, and of how much encouragement he had received. It all sounded reassuring, for, however disagreeable it was to realise that her aunt knew so much about their affairs, it *did* seem to imply that, for one reason or another, she approved of the marriage.

Society was delighted with the engagement—Sarah Spencer wrote enthusiastically to her brother :

" Very good news, which you will be almost as glad of as I am. It is a match, and not to keep you in suspense, it is my best friend, dear Harriet, who is going to be married. Her future is Lord Granville Leveson-Gower. Her situation at home is so extremely unpleasant now that I should be very happy at her marrying anyone, and I am, of course, much the more so, as Lord Granville is very sincerely attached to her, and there is good reason to hope he will make her a good husband. A happy man I am sure he will be with so good a wife." " . . . He is reckoned very handsome, and is extremely gentlemanlike in his manners, besides which, he is very well connected." [1]

Only one person disapproved, only one person thought that

[1] *The Letters of Sarah Lady Lyttelton.*

Granville had behaved shabbily to Lady Bessborough, and that was the Prince of Wales, whose sympathy took a strange form of expression.

He too, like Sheridan, of old had asked that of Lady Bessborough which she refused. Unlike Sherry, Granville's situation had aroused no jealousy in his heart, but Granville's desertion put him into a fury.

He came to visit Lady Bessborough, and began with a vehement tirade against Granville for marrying. This was followed up by a list of all Granville's inconstancies, and culminated in a violent scene in which the heir-apparent flung himself upon his knees and burst into tears and poured forth vows of eternal love intermingled with abuse of Granville. If only she would forget that worthless, that despicable puppy, and console herself with her old friend, she should make her own terms. He would break with Lady Hertford, break with Mrs. Fitzherbert. She should dictate his life and his morals. And Mr. Canning should be made Prime Minister. The incongruity of the scene was such that Lady Bessborough, torn between amusement and disgust, laughed helplessly.

At last she quieted him, and he resigned himself to a return to their old basis of friendship.

On Christmas Eve, Sunday, December 24th, 1809, Granville was married to Harriet Cavendish in one of the rooms of the Duke of Devonshire's villa at Chiswick.

His first letter to Lady Bessborough was a proof of how completely happy their union was to be, and how ideally they were suited to each other.

1810

THE old year had petered out rather miserably with the enquiry into the Walcheren expedition, and for the first time William Lamb had been brought into notice. He was now a Member a Parliament, and he voted, with a small minority, for the cessation of the enquiry—it was virtually a vote of censure. Early in 1810 Granville and his wife were established in London, and Harriet was delightedly presenting him to her friends. Their reception was cordial.

" . . . Dear Harriet was looking uncommonly well, and in manner and kindness and cordiality is exactly what she was —better she cannot be, to my taste.

" As to our new cousin, he is a very tall, large man of thirty-six, and certainly uncommonly handsome, though perhaps, to my aforesaid taste, rather too much of a fair, soft, sweet sort of beauty. His manner is very amiable, and she seems quite as happy as I wish her to be." [1]

They dined often at Devonshire House. The men sat round the table with " their stiff white neck cloths, blue coats and brass buttons, short waisted white waistcoats, and tremendously embroidered shirt fronts," [2] discussing the divorce of Josephine, or the illness of Princess Amelia, or the credibility of the Persian Ambassador, a dark complexion man in a fit of jaundice, in whose reality " many people disbelieve, thinking him to be a witty Jew amusing himself by making fools of all the poor folk." " No beards were to be seen, and only cavalry officers wore moustaches." [2]

Sometimes they went to the play with the Bessboroughs and the Spencers, and saw Mrs. Siddons in *Henry VIII*, or another of her famous rôles. If Hartington were of the party he had to provide himself with a book, for his deafness was now

[1] *The Letters of Sarah Lady Lyttelton.*
[2] *Memoirs of Colonel Gronow.*

so stubborn that it cut him off entirely from general conversation.

A piece of good fortune came the way of the Bessboroughs this season, for an old Mr. Cavendish died leaving £120,000, of which a sum producing £6,000 a year went to Lord Bessborough. They were badly off and it was a considerable help to them.

In the early spring London was treated to the curious spectacle of a respectable gentleman besieged in his house, and for a matter of two days successfully resisting arrest. Mr. Burdett, a liberal politician, had published an article in *Cobbett's Register* declaring the imprisonment of a Radical orator, by order of the House of Commons, to be an illegal act. An indignant House thereupon ordered the arrest of its critic. But Mr. Burdett was a favourite with the mob—they surrounded his house, and, for two days, all the King's horses and all the King's men could not obtain possession of the person of Mr. Burdett.

The Bessboroughs went to Chiswick—it was a curious experience for Harriet to see Bess taking Georgiana's place. She did ample justice to her efforts, the receptions were vast and magnificent. But certain things were not what they used to be—the food was bad, and, judging by Lord John Russell and Tierney's exclamations, the wine was worse! She decided to tell her brother-in-law. The Duke bore the criticism good humouredly, he was happier than he had ever been in his life ; how the Duchess bore it was not told.

A great innovation had been brought back from the continent by Princess Lieven—none other than the waltz. At Chiswick there was " waltzing every night and all night long." And as for Granville's former love, Sally Villiers, she began with a dancing master at six in the morning. Gossip and London tittle-tattle filled the day and told how the Queen took a pound of snuff when she heard of Marie Louise marrying Napoleon.

" Hart " safely despatched to Ireland, Lady Bessborough began to worry about Caroline and William. She didn't like the drift of that establishment. Caroline was becoming extremely erratic and some of her new hobbies were beyond a joke. All London had laughed at her correspondence with the

notorious Lady Oxford on the theme " Does Greek learning
inflame or purify the passions " ! It was tiresome that she
should make a laughing-stock of herself, and Harriet felt that
Lady Melbourne, who was more qualified to discuss the passions than Caroline would ever be, was getting more and more
irritated by her daughter-in-law. As for Lamb, he showed
not the smallest annoyance ; indeed, he appeared to find Caroline's freaks delightfully amusing ; and Caroline, on whom
affection had so much effect and criticism so little, saw no
reason to restrain herself.

On the contrary, from theory it seemed as though she was
going to pass to experiment, for she began to carry on a silly
flirtation with that great dragoon Sir Godfrey Webster. The
affair went on under William's nose: he was perfectly certain
of Caroline—the incongruity of the personalities amused him.
And Caroline herself took the matter very lightly ; it was an
amusing game, it shocked her mother-in-law, it made people
talk about her, and both these circumstances were, unfortunately, extremely pleasant to her. She paraded Sir Godfrey
about much as though he were a dancing bear. Lady Melbourne would have forgiven Caroline a lover—a secret lover
—but she would never forgive her the semblance of an affair—
affected in public and devoid of reality.

For a long time she had criticised Caroline's choice of
friends—she herself had always been so discreet in her selection
—why should she be afflicted with a daughter-in-law who
positively sought out those whom the world despised or
hated ?

To her censure Caroline had been deaf, and, in the face of
William's perfect satisfaction, it had been hard to do much.
But now she felt that she had a far more serious ground of
complaint. She argued with Caroline until she thought she
should have a seizure—she, whose brilliance had subdued all
the fine ladies of her generation, was openly flouted by this
child. In the end she wrote her a letter.

" I see you have no shame or compunction for your past
conduct. I lament it, but, as I can do no good, I shall withdraw myself and suffer no more vexation on your account. . . .
When anyone braves the opinion of the world, sooner or later
they feel the consequences of it, and, although people at first

may have excused your friendships with all those who are censured for their conduct, from your youth and inexperience, yet, when they continue to see you single them out and to overlook all the decencies imposed by society, they will look upon you as belonging to the same class . . . you think you can blind your husband and cajole your friends. . . . I repeat it—let me alone, and do not drive me to explain the motives of the cold civility which will henceforth pass between us." [1]

It was a magnificent document, but it had not the smallest effect upon Caroline.

Fate, however, rescued her from the false position in which her pride might have retained her.

Sir Godfrey had given Caroline a dog——

The dog bit Augustus——

The dog might be mad——

Augustus might die.

And all this horrid succession of events would have had for *cause* her wicked flirtation with Sir Godfrey.

In an agony of remorse Caroline vowed that she should never see Sir Godfrey again—and it is certain that she never saw much of him after that date. Where the question arose of a possible injury to those she loved Caroline knew no doubts. But she was determined that, if by the aid of Providence Lady Melbourne had obtained what she wished, she should at least hear some truths before the subject was closed.

She too wrote a letter, and perhaps it was because of the truth of much that it contained that Lady Melbourne seems from this period onwards to have really hated Caroline with a hatred which had not for object any peculiar defect, but enveloped her whole personality, and could only be satisfied by her destruction.

" God knows I am humiliated enough, and did not expect I should ever act in this manner. Some heads may bear perfect happiness and perfect liberty, mine cannot, and those principles which I came to William with—that horror of vice, of deceit, of anything that was the least improper, that RE-LIGION which I believed in then without a doubt, and with what William was pleased to call my superstitious enthusiasm

[1] *In Whig Society*—Mabell Lady Airlie.

—merited praise, and ought to have been cherished—they were safeguards to a character like mine, and nobody can tell the almost childish innocence and inexperience I had till then preserved. All at once this was thrown off, and William himself (though still unconscious himself of what he had done), William himself, taught me to regard without horror all the forms and restraints I had laid so much stress on. With his excellent head, heart, and superior mind he might, and will, go on safely without them. He is superior to those passions and vanities which mislead weaker characters, and which, however I may be ashamed to own it, are continually misleading me. He called me prudish and said I was strait-laced, amused himself in instructing me in things I need never have heard or known, and the disgust I at first felt to the world's wickedness, I till then had never heard of, in a very short time gave way to a general laxity of principle, which little by little, unperceived by you all, has been the undermining of the few virtues I ever possessed." [1]

In the vehement self-justification there was much truth. It must seem almost incredible that any young lady brought up at Devonshire House should have been " strait-laced "—and yet, what of Georgiana Morpeth and Harriet Granville? There can be no doubt that they were brought up strictly and in complete ignorance of the peculiar morals of their relations —and if they had remained so untouched by the lives lived around them it is probable that Caroline was in the same position. Anyway, having exhausted her eloquence upon her mother-in-law, she wrote quite simply to her husband.

" I think lately, my dearest William, we have been very troublesome to each other, which I take by wholesale to my account, and mean to correct, leaving you in retail a few little sins which I know you will correct."

Between husband and wife the most complete comprehension reigned. And it was to take ten years before the hatred of Lady Melbourne, aided by that of Emily Cowper, was to find a fulfilment.

In the autumn the Princess Amelia, the youngest of the princesses, who had been ill for some years, grew worse— ordered a mourning ring, and, shortly after presenting it to

[1] *In Whig Society*—Mabell Lady Airlie.

234

George III, died. The King, whose favourite child she had been, thereupon relapsed into incurable insanity.

The question of the Regency was raised again, and William Lamb spoke in favour of giving the fullest powers to the Prince of Wales.

Meanwhile Lady Bessborough was trying bravely to build up a new relationship between herself and Granville—but the friendship was not proving a success. He had now the outlet and the audience which his nature required. He was grateful to Lady Bessborough for the past, and he did not neglect her—but she felt acutely and unreasonably the fact that he was satisfied.

What had happened was right, fitting and inevitable—but oh, how disagreeable and how painful.

1811

THE early months of 1811 passed uneventfully. The
Regency of the Prince of Wales, the birth of Napoleon's
son, provided topics of conversation, but nothing happened
which touched Lady Bessborough or her circle—till on July
29th the Duke of Devonshire died. The event was full of
significance and complications for his family, rather than of
grief. To his children he had been almost a stranger. To
Lady Bessborough his loss was principally a death which
revived the memories of Georgiana. Only to Bess it was
" the tearing asunder every tie of long affection." Her whole
appearance bore testimony to her grief—but she was perfectly
composed, anxious to see people—anxious that Hart should
have George Lamb to keep him in spirits—bearing cheerfully
with their youthful gaiety.

For once, Lady Elizabeth's judgment was at fault, she overdid
her consideration (there was no doubt that her life was completely shattered by the blow), but coming from her father's
self-controlled stock, she forgot that amongst the emotional
young Cavendishes and Ponsonbys her forced gaiety was
taken, literally, for heartlessness.

Hartington, whom she really loved, and in whose hands her
future now rested, was shocked. Lady Bessborough saw
the misunderstanding and its cause, and she was sorry for it,
and did what she could to explain each to the other. They
all went down to Chiswick together. She had been so happy
there and so miserable there that she could not visit the spot
without emotion, and now one more link with the past had
been severed. Hart was irritated by his stepmother—Lady
Bessborough asked him to consider how ill she looked, but he
replied coldly that he only perceived that she wore no rouge.
All this was a bad beginning for the very delicate negotiations
as to the will which had to take place. Nothing was clear.

There was a will, a paper, a promise—and all conflicted. There was no doubt that the Duchess believed that her husband had meant to allow her the use of Chiswick for her life— but there was nothing written to prove this.

Both sides came to Lady Bessborough with their complaints ; Bess grumbled that Hart would not discuss the question openly with her. She counselled her to empower her brother, Lord Bristol, to settle the matter up with Heaton and Hart. But Lady Elizabeth demurred, it might give an appearance of *désagrément*, and that she should dislike above all things, besides which she alone knew the promises which had been made her and she was the right person to communicate them to her stepson. Then Hart came to his aunt and asked whether £6,000 a year would not be the right sort of jointure for his stepmother—and would Lady Bessborough please explain to her that she could not have Chiswick, to which he himself was much attached, and to which she had no possible right. Lady Bessborough acquiesced. She, herself, thought £6,000 a year very handsome, but she knew that it fell far short of Bess's ambitions.

She suggested to her nephew that he might add the purchase money of a house to the yearly income.

Eventually they discussed the matter with " Caro " George ; at first Mrs. Lamb considered even £5,000 a year a generous settlement, but later in the day she returned to the subject and said that on further consideration it appeared to her inadequate, the more so that she was sure the Duchess expected more. Lady Bessborough was miserable and feared an open conflict, but Hart was sanguine, he knew his stepmother better than any of them did. She would try and get as much as she could—that was part of her nature and she couldn't help it—but when the ultimate sum was fixed on and the transaction finished she would be delighted with the result, and bear no resentment against those who had failed to fall in with her wishes.

And he proved right ; for whilst Lady Bessborough was arguing with Bess and trying to convince her that Hart's intentions were generous, and meeting with sturdy opposition— at the very same time that she was clamouring for more, and complaining of what she got, to the Cavendishes—Lady

Elizabeth was writing to the world at large and to her own family in particular of Hart's unequalled kindness and generosity. Eventually the financial question was decided. £5,000 a year to the Duchess and £5,000 a year to Caroline (Mrs. George Lamb). That Bess was satisfied is beyond doubt, for in return she expressed a wish to relinquish her right to all the jewels.

When all was concluded the young Duke gave £2,000 to Heaton, the family solicitor. This totally unexpected generosity drew tears from the old man, who had looked after the late Duke's affairs for forty or fifty years, who had been the intimate witness of so many difficulties financial and matrimonial, and who, to the two Spencer sisters, had always been a sour, inimical personage. Yet Lady Bessborough was glad of it. She rejoiced that Hart should behave handsomely.

She and her nephew were devoted to each other and she spent long mornings in Lawrence's studio admiring the portrait which the artist was making of the young man. On the way back Hart told her as a secret the amount of his income— £125,000 a year. There were many debts on the estate . . . but all the same, she was amazed at the figure—and then she thought of Georgiana's terror of her debts. What a small figure they cut against that total ; and how astonished she would have been had she guessed what her husband's fortune amounted to.

In September Frederick Ponsonby was expected back on leave from the Peninsula, and the whole family were waiting at Roehampton in the greatest state of excitement. Then, early one morning at the very end of the month, the groom, Nicholls, came galloping up to say that he had landed at Portsmouth some days ago, and was already on his way to London. Before an hour had passed Lady Bessborough had the carriage at the door and was driving off to meet him.

As she drove through Roehampton every soul was at the gate of their cottage to congratulate her, for Nicholls had shouted out his news as he had come through the village. When she came to Putney the street was lined and the bells were ringing.

The demonstration moved her—still more it moved her, when Frederick had arrived, to see how all the servants and all the poor people came in to congratulate him on his return. Spontaneous, generous, and utterly without hauteur, the whole Bessborough family was loved by its tenants, whether English or Irish, and in addition, Frederick was now a hero, for he was one of the few cavalry officers who had received individual praise from Sir Arthur Wellesley.

When Frederick was rested they went up to London and plunged into a whirl of gaiety. Hart, with his great position and vast fortune, was the quarry of a hundred mothers. Even Madame de Staël had thought it worth while bringing Albertine over to England to join in the fray. She took a house, and taught her daughter English manners—and when all hope was extinct she comforted herself by declaring that the Duke was incurably attached to the Princess Charlotte (the Prince of Wales's daughter) and would never marry.

. The Duchess Elizabeth, with her affairs in order, looked much happier. But she still had some more straightening to accomplish, and one evening Lord and Lady Holland were astonished to hear from George Lamb that his wife now knew that she was the daughter of the late Duke, and still more astonished to hear him say that she had long known who was her mother.[1] It only confirmed what everybody knew, but it seemed a curious tale to tell about the town during the life of the Duchess Elizabeth.

Had they but known it, the tale was told at that Lady's express wish, and shortly afterwards she herself confided in Lady Bessborough. She gave Harriet an exact account of the births of Clifford and Caroline, and explained that she felt her subsequent marriage made it all right, made them, in fact, so nearly legitimate as to render further concealment unnecessary. Lady Bessborough was shocked and distressed— shocked, not at the fact, which she knew, but at the complete shamelessness with which the Duchess admitted them—distressed, when the thought of Georgiana's position was thus thrust upon her.

All the family felt miserable at the prospect of endless rows between the Duchess and Hart, which might perhaps end in the destruction of the real affection which existed between Hart and Clifford. Bess had the folly to ask her stepson to

[1] *Journal of Elizabeth Vassall, Lady Holland.*

grant the Cavendish arms and crest to her children, and when he refused she still more foolishly herself gave them the Hervey crest. A few days later Lady Spencer received a line from her nephew, congratulating himself on having seen his stepmother's departure. With Devonshire House and Chiswick closed to her, Bess travelled to Portsmouth, with Clifford, who was due to sail in a short time.

Lady Bessborough was distressed that she should draw such attention to their relationship. She offered her Roehampton, but she knew that Bess would not accept it. And the worst of it was that Clifford himself was being ruined by the affair —he had begun making himself absurd in the Mess by demanding the precedence of a Duke's son, and in private by rudely pushing past the Lambs. Caroline, luckily, was taking her parentage more calmly. Lady Bessborough went to Althorp and read *Sense and Sensibility* to distract herself. She thought the end stupid, but for the rest the book amused her, and Lavinia and all the Spencers were enthusiastic in its praise.

She was called back to London by a burglary at Cavendish Square. Despite watchmen, bars and bolts, and even alarm-bells attached to the windows, the thieves had forced an entrance and taken everything that lay within their reach. It was a great bore to lose cherished possessions, but this was the least of Lady Bessborough's anxieties—her one dread was lest the thieves should be caught—for in those days a conviction for burglary meant death. This fortunately she was spared, for no trace of the thieves was discovered.

The next journey was to Portsmouth, from which port Frederick was to sail back to the Peninsula. It was a sad business, rendered the more protracted by the fact that the wind was contrary for many days. Frederick, his servant James, his cook and his dragoon waited patiently for orders to embark, and then at last they came and all was hurry and commotion.

And then Lady Bessborough hurried home and made all her arrangements for departing the next morning—but when the next morning broke—what was her surprise to find the ship by the quay, Frederick in the house, and the whole voyage postponed owing to contrary winds. More than once this occurred, but at last there came a morning when no sign of the troopship was visible and Lady Bessborough made her way back to London.

In December Caro-George wrote to her half-brother, Augustus Foster. " I am just come from Brocket. They are all going on very jollily there and Caro is a little less mad than usual." [1]

It was the calm before the storm.

[1] *The Two Duchesses.*

1812

THE beginning of 1812 marks the arrival of a new element
into the circle of Roehampton and Melbourne, in the
person of Sidney Owenson, Lady Morgan. This woman was
the daughter of a Shrewsbury tradesman who had lived in
Dublin for many years—Sidney, whilst still in the teens, had
published a book, *The Wild Irish Girl*, which had had a prodigious success in London. The Duchess of Abercorn had
sought out the young authoress and before very long Sidney
was to find herself married to Sir Charles Morgan, the Duchess's
physician. Under powerful patronage she set out to conquer
society. If her literary efforts have appeared somewhat
second-rate to later generations, her character has seemed
equally uninteresting. She was very common, a snob, and
somewhat of a sycophant, with a good heart, a keen sense of
observation and a strong suit in carefully preserved *naïveté*
and ingenuousness. She amused Lady Bessborough mildly
and Caroline a great deal.

And her importance in their story lies in two points, in the
first place much of our information regarding the life of
Harriet and her daughter during the period 1812 to 1828
comes from her pen—and from this same pen it is easy to
realise what a bad influence she exerted upon Caroline, who
had always a tendency to appreciate the company of flatterers.
She encouraged Caroline in her unfortunate literary ventures,
and what was worse—having found an assured lack of convention spread over a shrewd common sense to have succeeded
very well in her case—she recommended Caroline to flout all
the rules of society—little realising that her friend was utterly
devoid of that core of worldly wisdom that always told Sidney
where to stop being naïve.

Caroline was delighted to find her vagaries praised as acts
of social courage—forgetting that much was forgiven in Lady

Morgan which would not be forgiven in Lady Bessborough's daughter.

About this time Lady Morgan wrote that she had spent an evening . . . " seated on the second flight of stairs between Lady Caroline Lamb and Monk Lewis. The beautiful Lady Oxford sat a few steps above us, the Aspasia of the Pericles who lay at her feet, wooing her in Greek. At two in the morning Lady Caroline Lamb proposed we should go and sup snugly at Melbourne House, and return to waltz, when her Grace's rooms should thin."

And then she went on to describe Caroline as she looked then, tall and slight, with a grave face, large dark eyes that were very bright, a fair complexion, a soft low voice, and great eloquence.

" She was adored but not content. She had a restless craving for excitement. She was not wicked, or even lax, but she was bold and daring in her excursions through the debateable land between friendship and love. If she never fell, she was scarcely ever safe from falling."

Caroline was having a very gay time, and she was enjoying it—she had some foolishness but no serious matter with which to reproach herself, and it is probable that the first months of 1812 were the last months of her life in which she was to be completely carefree and happy. Even Augustus' fits seemed to be yielding to treatment. Lady Bessborough too was having a good time, and if the gaiety rang a little hollow, she none the less enjoyed it and laughed at the world and at herself.

When Caroline herself recollected these times in years to come it was always with a halo of gaiety. . . .

" At that time I was the happiest and gayest of human beings . . . Devonshire House was closed from my Uncle's death for one year—at Melbourne House where I lived the waltzes and quadrilles were being daily practised, Lady Jersey, Lady Cowper, the Duke of Devonshire, Miss Milbanke and a number of foreigners coming there to learn. You may imagine what forty or fifty people dancing from twelve in the morning until near dinner time, all young, gay and noisy, were. In the evenings we had either opposition suppers or went out to balls and routs. . . . Sally Jersey was already the tyrant " who governed Fashion's fools and compelled them to shake their caps and bells as she wills it." [1] She had black hair and beautiful pale complexion and an activity which caused her " eyes, tongue, head and arms " to be perpetually in motion. [2]

Charles Greville has made her portrait for ever.

Emily Cowper was still much as she had been as a girl, pretty in a neat, trim style, animated, witty, devoted to her family, but fundamentally hard and worldly.

And Hart was the same as ever, shy and reserved, because of his deafness, but whimsical and delightful and generous to a fault—escaping with perfect humour from the attacks of the massed army of dowagers—gay and irresponsible, and still devoted to Caroline. The inclusion of Miss Milbanke's name demands an explanation—she was a flame of Augustus Foster, that erstwhile swain of Caroline's. Anna Isabella was twenty, she was the daughter of Sir Ralph Milbanke and Judith Noel, his wife, and consequently she was a niece of Lady Melbourne's and a first cousin of William's.

She had no looks, and her passion for mathematics, theology and Greek did not recommend her to her aunt—even her verse, which many competent authorities considered remarkable, did not impress Lady Melbourne, but there was about her a precision, a formality and a self-assurance which went to the heart of Caroline's mother-in-law, and so curiously enough the ill-assorted pair were frequently found in alliance against the other cliques of their society. The Duchess and Caro-George did all they could to promote the affair for Augustus, he too was pompous and it looked as though the match might have held happiness for both—but alas, in a bad day for herself, " The Medae of Mathematics " would have none of him.

Totally different accounts of Caroline Lamb's meeting with Byron having been given by Caroline, by Byron, by Lady Melbourne, Lady Morgan and Lady Holland, and other pseudo eye-witnesses. I have had to choose what seemed to be the most likely account.

One evening in March Caroline went to a ball at Lady

[1] *The Book of the Boudoir*—Lady Morgan.
[2] Greville's *Diary*.

Jersey's—everyone she knew was there and one person she did not know. Did he appear to her, as he appeared to Sidney Owenson at that same party :

" A strikingly sullen looking handsome creature, whose boyish person was distinguished by an air of singularity which seemed to vibrate between hauteur and shyness. (As) he stood with his arms crossed, and alone, occupying a corner near the door, and though in the brilliant bustling crowd, was not of it." [1]

At all events she recognised him immediately for the young Lord Byron. She had heard of him even before his reputation had preceded him to London, as a ward of her mother's friend, Lord Carlisle.

She knew that he had been a troublesome, dissolute boy, whom his guardian had forgotten to ask to dinner on his twenty-first birthday, and whom no one had noticed when he took his seat in the House of Lords. She knew too that from these unpromising beginnings he had already risen almost to fame, his flamboyant good looks, his impertinent criticisms of modern authors, his vigorous verse, his flagrant disregard of all conventions, social and moral, had brought him to the notice of those who had been prepared to slight him.

He advertised his romantic philosophy of despair—and where until now unhappiness had been used to wear a decent veil, he now displayed her features in triumph. To the English eighteenth-century man or woman, sorrow had seemed a private affair, to be kept within bounds so that it should not infringe on to the happiness of other people. But Lord Byron preached a new doctrine—unhappiness was the lot of chosen spirits—it was interesting—it was absorbing—it was distinguished. To the generation of the Bishop of Derry this theory would have appeared to be raving nonsense, to Lady Bessborough's contemporaries it was exceedingly distasteful—but to Caroline and her friends it came as a revelation. With less vitality and grip on life than their forebears, they were many of them unhappy—and now, how fitting to discover that unhappiness was in reality a sign of grace ! But Caroline was no fool and though later she was to subscribe to so convenient a doctrine, for the moment she rejected it,

[1] *Book of the Boudoir*—Lady Morgan.

and when Lady Westmorland asked if she might introduce her to Lord Byron, she turned away with a refusal, saying " that he was mad, bad and dangerous to know." Perhaps when she had refused to meet him, she was sorry. Perhaps afterwards she saw him standing there amongst all the dancers, and all the smart young men of London society, beside " Teapot " Crawford of the 10th Hussars (who had obtained his name from the small black teapot which he had carried from Eton to his regiment with him), besides that other officer, of the same regiment, Beau Brummel who could throw away a dozen stocks before one was tied to please him, besides " King Allen " whose title was said to be as good as board wages to him, and " Apollo Raikes," that first cit to get into society and who was said to rise in the west and set in the east ; and Edward Montagu, and Lord Worcester and Henry de Ros—perhaps then, when she saw him against that rococo assembly, she wondered whether he were not more " real," more " alive," more " aware," despite all his perverse nonsense, than they were. She looked at his lame foot and little did she realise that it accounted for almost all his tiresome quirks—accounted for his sense of inferiority, with its correlated desire for fame, accounted for his anxiety to obtain " the envy of men rather than the admiration of women "—with its corollary which made him seemingly irresistible to the female sex which he held so fundamentally in contempt.

At all events, the occasion for the introduction was past, and she had no intention of changing her mind.

Two days slid by ; the afternoon of the 22nd of March was cold and wet and windy. Caroline thought she should like some exercise. She ordered her horse and her groom and she set out for Holland House. The country ride through Hyde Park, through the village of Knightsbridge and on to Kensington would do her good. And besides this, she always enjoyed the trepidation of a visit to Holland House—she enjoyed it, from snobbishness—for few young married women cared or dared to go—and she enjoyed also, and sincerely, the good talk and lack of conventionality. The mantle of Fox's greatness and vigour had not fallen upon his nephew, Lord Holland, but all his charm and all his culture seemed to live on again, and those who had loved the uncle stood by the nephew, who, for a while after his runaway marriage, had been cold-shouldered by society.

Many another scandal had been forgotten more rapidly, but Lady Holland, aggressive and assertive, was not easy to forget.

She, who insisted on having Dutch herrings sent over to her in the Foreign Office bag, she who was perhaps the first lady in England to make her garden pay, she who later slowed the Great Western railway train to less than twenty miles an hour for her convenience, she who bullied the end of *Nicholas Nickleby* out of Dickens before that novel was published, who dined at an extraordinarily early hour, *pour gêner tout le monde*, as Talleyrand said, she who despised the Order of the Bath because " it could only be got by deserving it "—she who " took up Napoleon " during the heat of the war and who made herself the arbiter of fashion, tearing a wreath of roses from Mrs. Norton's head with : " There, *now* you look decent ; those roses were quite out of keeping with your style." She, who was *en somme* the ancestress, the patroness of the American in London society—was impossible to forget—and if by any chance she were neglected for a while, she did not submit, but sent round a neatly written notice :

" This is to certify that E. V. Holland is alive and inhabiting the Borough of Kensington though entirely neglected by her friends."

Yet with even these shock tactics there were many women who resisted and Lady Holland consoled herself very satisfactorily by filling her salons with men. No dandies or macaronis were to be seen there, but all the most intelligent and the most brilliant made it their rendezvous. So Caroline must have wondered who she should find, certainly Rogers, the poet, of malicious stories, who defended himself saying " as I have a weak voice if I did not say disagreeable things no one would listen to me," and whose epigrams cost him sleepless nights and a knocker tied up with straw.

He was a cadaverous, ghostlike personage, resembling " some velvety caterpillar which leaves a blister behind." [1]

And certainly Luttrell, the bustling, irritable wit, " the last of the conversationalists," and perhaps Sidney Smith, the chaplain, who, asked to describe heaven to the unbelieving,

[1] *Memoirs of Colonel Gronow.*

defined his conception of it as " eating *foie gras* to the sound of trumpets."

Would Lady Holland be in a good temper ? It was doubtful, she was so seldom in a good temper. Either she was ordering the servants to take away Lord Holland's crutches, or telling them to remove him altogether because he had dared to appear at dinner in a white waistcoat, looking for all the world, as Luttrell thought, " the image of a turbot on its tail," or she was letting her napkin drop till the unfortunate d'Orsay questioned " *ne ferais-je mieux de m'asseoir sous la table pour vous passer la serviette plus rapidement* "—or it was Sidney Smith who was ordered to " poke the fire " or ring the bell—till he answered sweetly, " Shall I also sweep the floor ? "

So, when Caroline arrived at the door she asked the servant what visitors were already arrived. In the string of names one name rang out—" Lord Byron." Well, now they would meet, and it was none of her choosing, she wanted to meet him, she felt that for her there was attractive danger in the meeting— she had done her best to keep out of it and now her conscience was clear.[1] And since she was going to meet him she might as well look her best—she sent a message to ask if she might go up and tidy herself as she was wet and muddy.

Lady Holland passed on the message to Lord Byron with comments—Caroline had never been known to take such trouble before—the young man was flattered.

When they met they talked of literature, all those present talked of literature, but through the brilliant, brittle splintering of views it seemed as though two urgent pulsations of reality were trying to reach each other. Caroline and Byron talked for each other and at the end of the evening George Gordon asked if he might come to Melbourne House on the following day to see Augustus. In this request he had found a way of dispelling the remaining hesitation that stayed in Caroline's mind—" he was not artificial, perverse, complicated, false, as people believed ; on the contrary, he was a real, simple, unhappy person in a world of shams—and if his morals were bad it was the fault of those who should have taught him the beauty and not the severity of morality." Undoubtedly, she felt an affinity with him—perhaps it was an unconscious recognition of

[1] *Book of the Boudoir*—Lady Morgan.

an egoism as great as her own.   They had both of them found life cruel, in that it would not listen to them, they were both impelled by the desire to stamp their personalities on society. So in their common discomfiture they drew together, and in their relationship to each other Byron's greater coarseness predominated and it was Caroline who " was for the moment denuded of her own personality and re-created on the lines of one of Byron's tender subservient heroines, without any sense of humour." [1]

And as for Lord Byron's reactions—who should fathom them—perhaps his curiosity was piqued by Lady Westmorland's story of how Caroline had refused to meet him— perhaps he was flattered by her evident admiration when she did meet him—certainly he was not unmoved by the circles into which her friendship was to lead him.   And, besides all this, she was so elusive, so unlike other people—considered so highbrow and so complicated, that people quoted Pope :

> With pleasures too refined to please,
> With too much spirit to be e'er at ease,
> With too much quickness to be ever taught,
> With too much thinking to have common thought,

but to him she appeared so simple, so impulsive.

He called at Melbourne House and admired the baby, and with a little cynical smile he presented a rose to Caroline " Because I am told that your Ladyship likes all that is new and rare for a moment." [2]

What did he mean by that ?   That he had penetrated the falsity of what the world and her own family believed of her ? Caroline was moved and excited.

As for Byron, he recognised at once that she was in love with him—she who was supposed to be so blue-stocking, who only chose to play at flirtations.   Another thing he saw too, that she was completely unconscious of the fact.   His reactions were infinitely complicated—he had set up a doctrine for himself—women were nothing to him but a physical necessity or a mental stimulus—companionship did not exist.   Women were of two kinds—neither kind satisfied him, they were not

---

[1] *The Life of Lady Caroline Lamb*—Jenkins.
[2] Lord Byron's Correspondence.

to count in his life. Also there was in the bottom of his soul a puritan strain—turned often to vice, but still existent. The combination of opposing emotions made him alternately cynical and sentimental. In three days he got a letter from Caroline. It began well :

" The rose Lord Byron gave Lady Caroline Lamb died in despight of every effort made to save it ; probably from regret at its fallen fortunes."

The tone was good, but alas as the letter lengthened a spring of self-revelation burst forth.

" When Lady Caroline returns from Brocket Hall she will despatch the *Cabinet Maker* to Lord Byron, with the flower she wishes most of all others to ressemble, as, however defficient its beauty and even use, it has a noble and aspiring mind, and, having once beheld in its full lustre the bright and unclouded sun that for one moment condescended to shine upon it, never while it exists could I think any lower object worthy of its worship and admiration. Yet the sunflower was punished for its temerity ; but its fate is more to be envied than that of any less proud flowers. . . ."

And that, even, was only a beginning—the letter went on to ask humbly for criticisms and corrections of conduct and advice.

What had happened to Lady Bessborough when she met Granville had now happened to her daughter. Both women were married to husbands they respected, and, in Caroline's case, actually loved, devotedly, both had already had many slight flirtations, both had an absolute belief in the moral standards of Christianity—and a natural love of their home and of their children : and both fell passionately and irrevocably in love with a good-looking boy, and in each case the passion was to last them their life.

But alas, there was a difference, Caroline was no realist like her mother—she had no idea that she was quite simply and plainly in love with the handsome young poet She believed that her feeling for him was of some celestial quality. She cultivated and admired her own reaction with emotion. She completely misread his character and his feeling for her—she gave him nothing—and yet she created a scandal, the echoes of which are faintly audible over a hundred years later—she wrecked her husband's happiness and she made a ruthless and implacable enemy of Byron.

But in 1812 these dark prospects were hidden and she was delighted with her new friend who came often to Melbourne House. Indeed, he found it contained not one attraction but two : Lady Melbourne was now sixty-two, she had known everyone of note from the time of Garrick and Chatham onwards. Her judgment, her psychology and her wit made her a dreaded figure in London Society—to Byron they were powerful attractions. Where everyone else applauded, she saw through him—where everyone else praised, she laughed . . . she was impressed neither by his speech nor his verse, neither by his notorious wickedness nor by his famous charm. A little acidity where all was too sweet pleased Byron, and to Lady Melbourne it was more than delightful to have the hero of all the young women of London at her feet.

Caroline was so much in love with Byron—so wholly interested in her own reactions that she failed to notice the growing intimacy between her mother-in-law and her admirer.

She was, as the Duchess Elizabeth wrote to Augustus Foster, " doing all sorts of imprudent things for him and with him." [1] She added that he admired Caroline very much, but that it was a nice question as to whether he did not admire their Caroline more ! Imprudence went from bad to worse. William laughed, Lady Bessborough remonstrated, Lady Melbourne raged, but all in vain. One night after a party at Devonshire House to which she had not been invited, Rogers saw her waiting by Byron's coach to catch him as he left. And yet " In spite of all this absurdity," concluded the old cynic, " my firm belief is that there was nothing criminal between them." [2] And he saw the situation more clearly than many contemporary and subsequent critics. When she could not see Byron, she wrote to him—she sent him books including one by Miss Milbanke.

Byron read them with attention. Who could imagine that that " short, round-faced, prudent, amiable icicle " who had refused Augustus Foster's suit because she had decided that she ought to marry a person of good fortune, who could believe that this " Princess of Parallelograms " could produce

[1] *The Two Duchesses.* [2] *Table Talk of Samuel Rogers.*

poems " displaying so much fancy and feeling," verse which
" I have no hesitation in saying, were it proper and requisite
to indulge, would have led to distinction." [1]

But Byron did not consider that it was proper or requisite
for a young lady to publish verse, any more than he considered
it proper or requisite for a young lady to waltz. His admiration,
however, was so emphatic that Caroline suggested a meeting,
but, filled as it were with the same instinct which had warned
Caroline not to meet him, Byron himself refused to meet
Annabella Milbanke. " I have no desire to be better acquainted with Miss Milbanke, she is too good for a fallen
spirit to know, and I should prefer her were she less perfect." [1]

Alas, in both cases the wise resolution was over-ridden, to
the eventual tragedy of the individuals concerned.

On the 11th of May an event occurred which shattered the
brilliant surface of the London season. One afternoon, Mr.
Perceval, the innoxious Prime Minister, was walking up the
steps of the House of Commons when he saw a respectably
dressed middle-aged man approach him. The stranger
addressed him.

" I am John James Billingham, a merchant of Liverpool,"
and he stopped speaking,[2] drew a pistol and shot at point-
blank range. Perceval fell with a cry of " murder." W. Smith
and some others who were present carried him into the " Vote "
office where he died in two minutes.

Billingham was arrested, and what was the horror of Lady
Bessborough and of Harriet when they heard that he had said
he was much disappointed, for he never intended to kill poor
innocent Mr. Perceval—the bullet had been meant for Lord
Granville—against whom he had a grudge regarding some
commercial matter concerning Russia.

For a second the steady pulsation of London's life stopped—
then the balls and parties began again, and with them the
occasions for Byron and Caroline to meet. He was attracted
to her : " I have always thought you the cleverest, most
agreeable, absurd, amiable, perplexing, dangerous, fascinating
little being that lives now, or ought to have lived two thousand
years ago." At first he may have thought that his feeling

[1] Lord Byron's Correspondence.
[2] *Recollections of a Long Life*—Hobhouse.

might have developed into something stronger, but now he knew that whatever she might do, Caroline had no intention of giving him any more than she had already given him. It amused him to see the fury of Lady Bessborough, who evidently took the matter seriously, since she kept on telling him that Caroline's flirtation with him was only in order to arouse William's jealousy. And Lady Melbourne's rage was delightful to witness. But as for getting into a real scrape and having all the most powerful ladies of London against him, he did not even consider such a possibility. And though he drew Caroline on to a certain extent, his letters were full of paternal advice :

" I never knew a woman with greater or more pleasing talents, general, as in a woman they should be, something of everything and too much of nothing. But these are unfortunately coupled with a total want of common conduct. For instance, the note to the page—do you suppose I delivered it ? "

But whilst Byron could take the affair coolly, Caroline was in a frenzy. At times she imagined that Byron loved her, and that she would run away with him—but in the bottom of her heart the images of her mother and of William denied such a possibility.

Then she would find consolation in viewing the tragedy of both their lives—lived out in unrelenting sorrow till they died, but hardly had this picture proved comforting than a letter would come from Lord Byron telling her that he must soon make up his mind to marry, and asking her advice—and she would write back to him :

" Do not marry yet, or if you do, let me know first. I shall not suffer if she you choose is worthy of you, but she will never love you as I did."

How history was repeating itself. Only seventeen years before, her mother had been writing to Granville : that the news of his marriage would come as a shock to her, but that the pleasure would outweigh the pain if she were to be the first to be informed of his choice.

Was it possible, she wondered, that Byron really loved her and that he would marry magnanimously in order to give her peace ? She would have liked to have believed it, but her critical sense forbade such a conclusion. Her mother was really miserable about her behaviour. Lady Melbourne was coldly cutting. Lord Melbourne was frankly furious. Only William—William whose anger would have been a reassurance to her—laughed a little sadly.

On the afternoon of the 12th of August, her nerves and her temper frayed; she was having a discussion with her mother at Melbourne House. Lord Melbourne entered the room. He saw another of the incessant scenes he had lately had to bear in progress, and he lost his temper. Caroline was in no state to stand abuse, and declared roundly that she should go to Lord Byron, to which her father-in-law replied feelingly that she might do as she pleased.

Lady Bessborough had an instinct of real danger. In such a moment she felt that Lady Melbourne's icy sarcasm might bring them both more quickly to their senses than her own distress. She went out of the room to fetch her. When they returned Caroline was not to be seen.

Lord Melbourne said that she had rushed down the stairs. Seriously alarmed, the two ladies went down to enquire of the porter. He said that he had seen Lady Caroline rush out of the house a few moments before.

Lady Bessborough's heart sank. If she had gone to Byron would William ever take her back ?—and if he did, on what terms ?—and if she were not with Byron, what might she not have done to herself ? Lady Melbourne was cool and collected, this was a moment for action—recriminations could come afterwards.

She ordered her carriage, and she and Lady Bessborough drove to the Albany with anxious hearts. They found Byron alone—he was very much astonished to hear their story. Both ladies looked to him as their only hope. He was bored, amused, anxious and he promised to do everything that was possible, and immediately. He begged them to go home quietly, and leave all to him, he would keep them informed.

Lady Bessborough went back to Cavendish Square, and tried to keep calm.

Lady Melbourne went back to Melbourne House—William was out and her husband gone to see the Prince of Wales— she was angrier than she had ever been in her life—to have William made the laughing-stock of London.

Meanwhile Lord Melbourne took his troubles to the Prince

Regent. Caroline, he explained, drove him mad with her infatuation for Byron, and as for his wife and Lady Bessborough, they were almost as bad—as far as he could see Lord Byron had betwitched the lot of them, mothers and daughters and all. And they made such a fool of him—hadn't they insisted on his asking Lord Byron to his house when the affair was as plain as a pike-staff to an ordinary man ? [1] " Prinny " laughed immoderately. " Taking the mother and mother-in-law as confidantes—what would people have said if he had taken Lady Spencer in his confidence in the old days." [1]

Lord Melbourne felt a little comforted—it appeared there was someone left who could still distinguish black from white. And during all this time Byron went on his peculiar errand.

He began his enquiries amongst the coachmen, and after a while they were successful, for he came upon a man who had a note written by Caroline and addressed to her mother. Bribery unloosed the good man's tongue, and he promised to take Lord Byron to the address at which he had deposited his fare. It proved to be a small house belonging to a surgeon. Byron, anxious not to betray Caroline's name, asked if he could see the young woman who had recently arrived. He was met with a peremptory refusal. He sent in another message : he must see her—he was her brother.

Caroline had always been devoted to Willie—she could not resist the appeal. What were her feelings when she was confronted with Byron. Byron deputed by her family to come and fetch her home, and tell her " to be a good girl."

At first she refused to go with him, but at last he persuaded her. They should go together to Melbourne House and face the family. He would stay with her all through the scene which would follow. And if at the end of it she should feel that she could betray her mother and William—well, then he would take her away. But he would never take advantage of her agitation—she should go back and see them all and decide what to do.

As they rumbled back in the carriage together, she told him what she had done, how she had driven to a chemist and raised some money on her ring—how she had taken a seat in

[1] *In Whig Society.*

255

the coach to Portsmouth—how it was her intention to take the first boat sailing anywhere and never to see her family again.

In the drawing-room at Melbourne House everyone was assembled.

Argument rose against argument. First William and the Melbournes were persuaded by Lady Bessborough to take Caroline back—then she turned to Caroline herself—but she was obdurate. Live in Melbourne House again she would not.

They expostulated in vain. Then Byron coaxed her gravely and gently till at last she gave way. After the tempest of contending wills there was a great quiet. Lord Byron, the *Deus ex machina* of the affair took himself off to a ball, Caroline went exhausted to her room, Lady Melbourne reflected on the horrid impression given to the servants at Holland House by the vision of her daughter-in-law flying past them in a hired carriage. Lady Bessborough went back to Cavendish Square—she was as tired as possible and felt ill—suddenly she had a violent hæmorrhage.

The next morning Caroline received several letters. The first one was from old Petersen, the housekeeper at Cavendish Square. It expressed the situation clearly and sincerely in terms of the servants' hall, and ran as follows :

" Cruel and unnatural as you have behaved, you surely do not wish to be the Death of your mother. I am sorry to say you last night nearly succeeded in doing so. She had fallen in a fit at the bottom of her carriage and with the utmost difficulty her footman got her out. Oh Lady Caroline could you have seen her at that moment you surely would have been convinced how wickedly you are going on. She was perfectly senseless and her poor mouth drawn all on one side and cold as marble, we was all distracted, even the footmen cryed out shame on you, for alas you have exposed yourself to all London. You are the talk of every groom and footman about Town. A few months ago it was Sir Godfrey and now another has turned your head and made you forget what a husband you have, what an angel child, besides making you torture all your kind relations and friends in the most cruel manner. Your poor father too was heart-broken at seeing the wretched state you had reduced your mother to. We got Mr. Walker quick as possible and thank God she is better. Lord Bessborough would not let me send for you, he said the sight of you would make her worse. You have for many months taken every means in your power to make your mother miserable and you have perfectly succeeded but do not quite kill her—you will one day fatally feel the wickedness of your present conduct. Oh Lady Caroline pray to God for strength of mind and resolution to behave as you ought for this is dreadful.

2 Cavendish Square, Monday. (J. H. PETERSEN.)

" I feel by sending this I offend you for ever, but I cannot help it." [1]

So that was the end of her great adventure, of all her heroics. To be scolded by the old housekeeper, and told that she was a wicked girl. She bore Petersen no grudge—it was all true—but what an irony.

But beyond all thought of herself came the knowledge of her mother's illness—her mother whom she adored . . . she was distracted and she turned for consolation to another letter. It was from Byron. That young man, half touched at her fantastic devotion, half relieved to feel that after this incident their relationship must alter, and above all really anxious about her condition, wrote the most cruelly kind letter which she was ever to receive from him.

" My dearest Caroline,

" If tears which you saw, and know I am not apt to shed—if the agitation in which I parted from you—agitation which you must have perceived through the whole of this most nervous affair, did not commence until the moment of leaving you approached—if all I have said and done and am still but too ready to say and do, have not sufficiently proved what my real feelings are, and must ever be towards you, my love, I have no other proof to offer.

" God knows I wish you to be happy, and when I quit you, or rather you, from a sense of duty to your husband and mother, quit me, you shall acknowledge the truth of what I again promise and vow, that no other in word or deed, shall ever hold the place in my affections, which is and shall be most sacred to you, till I am nothing. I never knew till that moment

[1] *The Ponsonby Family.*

the madness of my dearest and most beloved friend ; I cannot express myself ; this is no time for words, but I shall have a pride, a melancholy pleasure, in suffering what you can scarcely conceive, for you do not know me. I am about to go out with a heavy heart, because my appearing this evening will stop any absurd story which the event of the day might give rise to. Do you think now I am cold and stern and artful ? Will even others think so ? Will your mother even—that mother to whom we must indeed sacrifice much, more, much more on my part than she shall ever know or imagine ? ' Promise not to love you ! ' Ah, Caroline, it is past promising. But I shall attribute all concessions to the proper motive, and never cease to feel all that you have witnessed, and more than can ever be known but to my heart—perhaps to yours.

" May God protect, forgive and bless you.

" Ever and even more than ever,

" Your most attached,

" BYRON."

" P.S. These taunts which have driven you to this, my dearest Caroline, were it not for your mother and the kindness of your connections, is there anything on earth or heaven that would have made me so happy as to have made you mine long ago ? And not less *now* than *then*, but more than ever at this time. You know I would with pleasure give up all here and all beyond the grave for you, and in refraining from this, must my motives be misunderstood ? I care not who knows this, what use is made of it—it is to *you* and to *you* only that they are *yourself* (*sic*). I was and am yours freely and most entirely to obey, to honour, love—and fly with you when, where and how you yourself *might* and *may* determine." [1]

By what mixed motives did Byron come to write such an open avowal ?

There is no doubt but that to have eloped with Caroline had never entered his mind, and would have filled him with horror. Was the letter then wholly false—probably not. The melodramatic situation had made him rather drunk— to be the hero of such an episode went to his head—what he wrote was literature and not life—in a literary sense it was true,

[1] *Byron's Letters and Journal*—Murray.

exactly the right letter for that occasion—and he was at the moment living in drama and not in life. He was grateful to Caroline for having placed him in such a situation and he felt so safe—utterly secure. For a moment there had been danger, but after this crisis she would plague him no more. He wrote the farewell of one of his own characters. He half convinced himself that they were both of them broken hearted.

To make her renunciation more secure he wanted it definitely acknowledged as her own decision—that would give her a rôle of antique virtue to play—and she would sustain it.

He had some pity for her pride, and the last thing he desired was that she should be made to feel a fool. There was more kindness and more safety in her being made to feel a heroine.

Alas, that Caroline could not read his mind. Had she accepted this letter as a final adieu the ending of their relationship might have had a certain dignity ; but she did not accept it as final, and her pathetic attempts to retain his affections were to end in disaster for both of them.

Meanwhile everyone was taking measures to get through the crisis as lightly as possible. Lady Melbourne had a scheme —it centred on Lord Byron. He must be married to some sensible girl, who would knock all the nonsense out of him. She looked about her, and her eye rested on her niece, Annabella Milbanke. *That* marriage, if it came off, would be a crushing blow to Caroline : to see someone so plain and dull become Byron's wife, to see a relation of her mother-in-law's married to him—and to have to meet him constantly—yes, Caroline would dislike that exceedingly. But if this scheme failed she must have an alternative, and he must be made to fall at once for someone else. It must be a lady of considerable position and talent—someone who would be a real rival to Caroline—Lord Byron must be paraded about publicly with his new love, and Caroline must know of it—must hear of it on all sides, and if that did not break her pride and bring her to believe that Lord Byron had never really cared for her— what would ? . . . Lady Melbourne looked around—her eyes set on " Aspasia " Lady Oxford—a brilliant, cruel, unscrupulous woman, of whom Broughton had written a few weeks before : " Lady Oxford, most uncommon in her talk, and licentious, uncommonly civil, made a push to get me into the Hampton Club." She was so exactly the opposite of Caroline that there could be little doubt that she would extinguish all the former's influence on Byron's mind.

Meanwhile Lady Bessborough also had a plan. Caroline must be got away from the Melbournes immediately—they were driving her mad. She and William must come to Roehampton and then perhaps go over to Ireland with them. It was so long since they had visited Bessborough. They should stay with Granville at Tixal on the way, and also with Hart at Lismore when they were in Ireland. The change would do them all good. William accepted joyfully. He too would be glad to be away from his family for a few weeks. He was disgusted with all this interference in a matter which concerned him and Caroline only. Everyone was delighted with the Irish plan except Caroline herself—she had the feeling that so long as Byron was in the same town as herself no one would treat her too badly, but she was terrified of being left alone, even with her family. If Lord Byron left London or she were removed she swore that she would run away again. She was in a highly nervous condition, not knowing what she wanted, and distracted about her mother. Lady Bessborough was still ill.

The doctors were made to say that Ireland would be the best cure for her—Caroline, terrified, announced that she was pregnant, and that the journey would be dangerous for her. If any proof is needed that she had never been Byron's mistress, it is supplied in this incident. When she told William that she was expecting a child he was overjoyed—he had wanted a second son—for he, more than any of the others, doubted whether Augustus were normal or not. He insisted that no risk should be taken and that a delay of ten days in the date of departure should be made.

Caroline wrote an abject letter to her father, fully acknowledging her part in bringing on her mother's illness, and promising to accept any conditions he might lay down if only he would not take her away from London within the next ten days.

The letter was backed up by an announcement to her

mother of her condition. But it seems that her appeal made little impression. Perhaps they didn't really believe that she was with child? When she wrote again, her request was reduced. Even five days' grace would be an inexpressible relief to her. She alludes rather humbly to the fact that few people (and certainly not Mrs. Petersen) were likely to believe her word of honour—but reiterated that in all faith she did believe herself to be pregnant.

But at last they did set out, and on the 12th of September they arrived at Tixal, where Harriet reported them to her sister Georgiana Morpeth.

" . . . My aunt looks stout and well, but poor Caroline most terribly the contrary. She is worn to the bone, as pale as death, and her eyes starting out of her head. She seems indeed in a sad way, alternately in tearing spirits and in tears. I hate her character, her feelings and herself when I am away from her, but she interests me when I am with her." [1]

Later she reported that " Caro had been excessively entertaining at supper," Lady Bessborough " gay and amiable," William had " laughed and eaten like a trooper "—only poor Lord Bessborough had proved very heavy in hand.

Lord Granville spoke about politics—and about the French invasion of Russia. He told them how, after the Battle of Salamanca, when the captured eagles were presented to Lady Wellington, she kissed them and, saying " They are mine," fainted away.

They were grateful to him for his stories, for it seemed to be weeks since they had any of them talked of anything but themselves. But to Lady Bessborough the visit was an uncomfortable affair.

No sooner had the Bessboroughs left London than Byron began to correspond with Lady Melbourne. On September the 10th he wrote from Cheltenham congratulating her on the fact that the sea now rolled between her and one of her torments. The felicitations were premature, as we know, for actually Caroline and her mother were only on their way to Tixal.

He made one extremely important statement to Lady Melbourne.

[1] *The Letters of Harriet Countess Granville.*

" Now (if you are sincere, as I sometimes almost dream),
you will not regret to hear that I wish this to end, and it shall
certainly not be renewed on my part." [1]

Nor were the concluding sentiments very gallant.

" It is true from early habit, one must make love mechani-
cally, as one swims ; I was once fond of both, but now I never
swim unless I tumble into the water, and don't make love till
I am almost obliged to. . . ."

The fact was that Byron only existed in relation to an audience—he had no existence *per se*, and where Caroline called
forth one attitude, Lady Melbourne called forth another, and
the one was as lacking in reality as the other.

Lady Melbourne was not long in answering Byron's letters
—and her answers were always such as to bring fuel to the
fire of their correspondence. Nor can she be wholly blamed
for this, for even Lady Bessborough was writing to her and
imploring her not to lose her hold of him.

Two days after the above letter Byron wrote again in an
effort to make the situation clearer. It was really delightful
to have such a good excuse to write pages about oneself daily
to such a remarkable woman, and one who did not suffer
fools gladly. But Byron was no fool—he knew exactly what
to say to Lady Melbourne—where to have a slighting cut at
Lady Bessborough, where to praise her own family.

In this letter of the 13th he confesses that Lady Bessborough's attitude in piquing him by telling him that Caroline's
attentions to him were given merely in order to make another
jealous, was more than half responsible for his behaviour in
the affair. Again he reiterates that he was never seriously in
love, and that before December he would succeed in curing
Caroline of all remains of affection for him.

And then he played his trump card.

" I was, am, and shall be, I fear, attached to another. . . .
The woman I mean is Miss Milbanke . . . I never saw a
woman whom I *esteemed* so much. But that chance is gone,
and there's an end."

How came Byron to make such an astonishing statement—
was it his response to the appropriate—to what people expected
of him—did he recognise the intention of Lady Melbourne's

[1] Lord Byron's Correspondence.

mind, and make it his own ? Did he only make the announcement because he felt he could do so in perfect safety, knowing Miss Milbanke to be already attached to a certain Mr. Eden ? Was it just a piece of flattery to Lady Melbourne ? If so, it was to cost him dear. From that moment their correspondence grew hectic. Lady Melbourne sent him Lady Bessborough's letters, Caroline's letters, even William's letter, and he in return sent her all his correspondence. The current of their intrigues grew more and more rapid. By September 15th Byron had decided that the only course for him was to take some step which would convert all Caroline's affection for him into hatred.

By the 18th he was playing to Lady Melbourne's weakest suit. " Miss M(ilbanke) I admire because she is a clever woman, an amiable woman, and of high blood, for I still have a few Norman and Scotch inherited prejudices on the last score, were I to marry."

Of high blood, yes, Byron recognised this . . . yet Georgiana and Lady Bessborough had patronised the Lambs. And now Caroline was William's wife—and Caroline was also being supplanted by one of Lady Melbourne's nearest relations in the affections of her lover. Fate was indeed ironical.

But Byron knew that too much cynicism in Lady Melbourne's eyes was not becoming. He explained carefully that though he had no desire to marry Caroline, though he believed that divorce and remarriage would ruin them both, yet if there were no other way out, he was ready to fulfil any obligations which his imprudent conduct had laid upon him.

" Wretched as it would render me, she should never know it ; the sentence once past, I could never restore that which she had lost, but all the reparation I could make should be made, and the cup drained to the very dregs by myself, so that its bitterness passed from her."

It was really quite affecting even to write such sentiments, and very pleasant when it was to someone who so perfectly appreciated their value.

It amused him too to realise that Lady Bessborough, thankful as she would be to see the end of the affair encompassed by any means, would actually never forgive Byron if he did not continue to adore her daughter.

Meanwhile to Caroline, Ireland was providing some diversion. It was very long since Lord Bessborough had visited his Irish tenants—the family were received with the greatest enthusiasm.

Lady Bessborough enjoyed it all, but her heart was heavy —Caroline was corresponding weekly with Byron. It seemed to her mother simply wanton.

The tone of the letter frightened him. He wrote rapidly to Lady Melbourne.

" If I marry, positively it must be in three weeks." On the other hand, on the subject of Annabella he had become a little flippant.

" Before I became candidate for the distinguished honour of nephewship to your Ladyship, it will be as well for us to know that your niece is not already disposed of to a better bidder ; if not, I should like it of all things, were it only for the pleasure of calling you ' Aunt.' " [1]

Lady Melbourne was a little alarmed. Byron was so anxious to marry, and she knew him to be so little attached to Miss Milbanke that he might very well marry someone of a totally different milieu—impulsively, and even before the Bessboroughs returned from Ireland. She started to prepare Annabella's mind for the startling declaration which was to be made to her. She tried to discover how far Caroline and Mrs. George Lamb had been right when they had told Byron of Annabella's attachment to Mr. Eden.

Miss Milbanke was not sympathetic to her aunt's description of Lord Byron's state of mind and heart. She wrote a careful analysis of the type of man she desired to marry. He was to have a strong sense of duty and strict moral principles, he was to be good tempered and well balanced. He was to treat his wife neither as a plaything nor as a mentor, but as a reasonable companion. Good looks, genius and passion were secondary considerations.

The description hardly fitted Byron, but Lady Melbourne was not to be so easily deflected, she persevered in her correspondence with both the parties concerned. It was bad luck for her that just at that moment Byron should have re-

[1] Lord Byron's Correspondence.

ceived a letter from Caroline full of the wildest reproaches, and that reading it through carefully he realised that Lady Melbourne had betrayed him by allowing Caroline to read one of his letters to her before the latter left for Ireland. He wrote sarcastically to Lady Melbourne.

The old woman was angry and afraid, but her answer was a masterpiece of careful handling.

" You are too suspicious after all I have said, it makes me half angry—in one of your last letters you hinted that perhaps I left your letter in the way on purpose. These are your ' wound-floats ' and show what those persons are to expect ' that lie within the mercy of your wit.' I cannot bear her having got that letter, whether she opened it or found it, 'tis all one, it will be long before I forgive it. . . . Once you told me you did not understand friendship. I told you I would teach it you, and so I will if you do not allow Caro to take you quite away. . . . I admire you extremely for your resolutions respecting her, but dear Lord Byron, you deceive yourself—you never will be able to keep to them. What ! pass your time in endeavouring to put her into a good humour and to satisfy her and to disguise from her that you are unhappy. Fine dreams indeed—the first is much beyond your power, and finding how ill you succeed, must inevitably prevent you from persisting in the latter.

" Do not however mistake me, I would not have you say a harsh word to her for the world, or anything that could be deemed insulting. . . . I do not mean to give any advice, you probably know much better than I do how to act. . . .

" I must, however, add that I think you attach too much blame to yourself—she is no novice and though I give her credit for being what one must believe every Heroine of Romance to be (except Mad. Cottin's), yet she knew enough to be on her guard, and cannot be looked upon as the victim of a designing man. All the world are very different in opinion. . . ." [1]

Then, after describing Caroline's recent letters to her, Lady Melbourne ended . . . " the result of all this seems to me that the best thing you can do is to marry, and that, in fact, you can get out of this scrape by no other means."

[1] Lord Byron's Correspondence with Lady Melbourne.

Byron could resist neither the flattery nor the argument.

At the same time Lady Melbourne had written bitingly to Caroline accusing her of having read deliberately the letter addressed to her mother-in-law. Caroline was angrier than she had ever been in her life. How like Lady Melbourne to have laid this trap for her.

" Once more I assure you upon my honour I never opened or intentionally read any letter of yours. I found a part of one on the floor (of my room in London—open) it was in a hand I used to receive myself—I made no secret of it—I I have committed no wrong. . . . I shall write no more, only entreating you not to write unkindly to my mother, who says instead of receiving delightful letters from you, she receives, at present, nothing but a few short guarded lines— and why ? Upon my soul, she is innocent and ignorant of this. . . . Oh that I had not been weak enough to return when Lord Byron brought me back. Thank you for the letters I received. I shall not reproach you for them—I deserve unkindness from you. I never have, I hope, I never have accused Lord Byron—he or you best know why he behaves ill to the woman he so lately professed to love . . . he may love who he pleases, I shall never reproach him—but he should not treat me with cruelty and contempt."

But Byron was working hard for the marriage with Miss Milbanke—he kept on reassuring Lady Melbourne that " Nothing but a speedy marriage could save him." For fortune he cared nothing. The only enquiry he hazarded was as to whether Miss Milbanke waltzed—a waltzing wife he could not stomach. Lady Melbourne was reassuring—if Annabella had ever waltzed, she should cease from waltzing immediately.

Then, said Lord Byron, if someone could convey to Miss Milbanke that he should like to propose if he were sure of being accepted—he should be very much obliged. Lady Melbourne was only too delighted to be charged with the embassage. But here she received her first check. Annabella was honoured and gratified, but " no " she would not marry Lord Byron.

And Lady Melbourne, who had overcome so many obstacles, recognised that here was serious female resistance to her wishes, which would take her a very long time to subdue. She wrote very humbly to Lord Byron of the failure of her

Viscountess Melbourne and her eldest son, Peniston Lamb

mission, and then, her first plan having failed, she tried to encompass the second solution—Lord Byron must sit at the feet of Lady Oxford.

Already the Bessboroughs were at Lismore—soon they would be home again, and when they were it was essential that Byron should be found in position.

Byron was relieved rather than unhappy at Miss Milbanke's refusal. He professed himself to have no desire whatsoever to marry except for the convenience of disposing of Caroline ; he said that after proposing to Annabella he had really felt some little remorse on her account, and that, after all, the mere fact of his having proposed to Miss Milbanke and having been refused by her would probably do him as much service with Caroline as though he had been actually married to Lady Melbourne's niece. Surely Caroline's pride would forbid the continuance of an attachment to one so fickle ?

In the letter he mentioned invitations to Lord Harrowby's and to Lord Oxford's—he was uncertain as to which he should accept. Perhaps Lady Melbourne was not unwilling to help him to a decision. Caroline was still writing to him, and the fact annoyed him. He wrote that he had a terrific project— to remain on good terms with Lady Cowper and Mrs. Lamb, and on the best terms with Lady Melbourne, and at the same time be quiet and cool as a mere common acquaintance with Caroline. But if he had to quarrel with one of the three he made repeated assurances that it should be with Caroline.

Then he added a significant sentence. " I mean (*entre nous*, my dear Machiavel) to play off Lady O(xford) against her, who would have no objections perchance. . . ."

Whilst plot and counterplot were being worked out in England, Caroline and her mother went to stay with the Duke of Devonshire at Lismore. They were anxious about Hart who was said to be flirting with Princess Charlotte . . . the story had got about, and Mr. Creevey was writing :

" Young P. and her father have had frequent rows of late, but one pretty serious one. He was angry at her flirting with the D. of Devonshire and suspected she was talking Politics."

Caroline had had the greatest hopes of Lismore—when she saw the ruined castle at a distance these hopes increased. She expected to be met by phantoms of the past. What was her disgust to find that the castle stood in the middle of the village, and that instead of mediæval ruins Hart led her into a modern apartment. She teased her cousin unmercifully about his Irish castle, and complained incessantly of the damp. After dinner, when all was dark, she opened the doors, allowing a large frog to enter the building—and insisting that he must be the rightful owner.

Accounts of such levity were utilised by Lady Melbourne to assure Byron that all Caroline's declarations of unhappiness were false, that in truth she was dancing and flirting and amusing herself to her heart's content.

Meanwhile, Lord Byron arrived at Eywood, and thought his hostess delightful. He was anxious that his visit to Lady Oxford should be reported in the *Morning Post*, and an account of it written to Lady Bessborough.

How increasingly thankful he was that he had not been accepted by Miss Milbanke ; even to Lady Melbourne he wrote : " all this is infinitely more to my taste than the ' A ' scheme." He also wrote himself to acquaint Caroline with his new attachment. She was disgusted and angry and replied impulsively, accusing him of double dealing and infidelity.

He was embarrassed, and Lady Oxford, to whom he showed the letter, was furious. Taking a piece of her own crested writing-paper, she made him write a reply under her dictation. It is said to have read as follows :

" November 9th, Eywood, Prestign.

" Lady Caroline,

" I am no longer your lover ; and since you oblige me to confess it, by this truly unfeminine persecution . . . learn, that I am attached to another, whose name it would, of course, be dishonourable to mention. I shall ever remember with gratitude the many instances I have received of the predilection you have shown in my favour. I shall ever continue your friend, if your Ladyship will so permit me to style myself ; and, as a first proof of my regard, I offer this advice, correct your vanity, which is ridiculous ; exert your absurd caprices upon others, and leave me in peace.

" Your most obedient servant,
" BYRON."

The shock of the receipt of that letter was such as to make Caroline seriously ill. In accounting for this it must be recollected that whilst Lord Byron had been proposing to Annabella Milbanke, making love to Lady Oxford, and abusing Caroline to his heart's content, he had also been writing her affectionate and soothing letters. All knowledge of his behaviour had been withheld from her by her mother, and the little she had learnt had been only by roundabout means, and not circumstantial. This letter came to her then without any preparation, and it almost unhinged her mind. She attributed the text to Lady Oxford, and her one desire was to return quickly to London and have an explanation from Byron himself.

The letter had reached her in Dublin. The next day the Bessboroughs sailed for England, and then Caroline committed the egregious folly of writing to Lady Oxford demanding explanations. This act decided that lady in her determination to prevent Byron having a meeting with Caroline. Lady Bessborough, who was really afraid for her daughter's sanity, begged him to give her an interview—even Lady Melbourne wavered—it might after all be the simplest way of ending this interminable affair, but Byron was obdurate. He stated that he had Lady Oxford's orders not to see her. Lady Melbourne, afraid that her own chains were being loosened, reproached him. He replied that he had done much for her— very much. He had been willing to marry Caroline if William would not take her back. He had obeyed Lady Melbourne " in my suit to the Princess of Parallelograms, my breach with my little *Mania*, and my subsequent acknowledgment of the *sovereignty* of *Armida*," more could not be expected of him ?

And yet, after all this, the 30th of November, which was the return of the Bessboroughs to London, saw also his arrival in the metropolis. Perhaps he thought that it would be as well to show Lady Oxford that she must exert herself if she meant to hold him.

An interminable correspondence with regard to the return of letters began. Caroline knew her own mind. She would return none of Byron's letters. Lady Bessborough implored him to be generous and give hers back—he consented, writing to Lady Melbourne : " This I will do on my return to you, and you only or Lady Bessborough, save and except the *boxful*—which I must, for certain reasons, burn in your presence, so pray have a good fire and fireguard on my next visit." [1] The trinkets, he explained, he could not return, having given them away before he went to stay with Lady Oxford. In the middle of December he returned to Eywood and Caroline went to Brocket, and arrived there she indulged in what was certainly a most curious proceeding. She built a large bonfire on the lawn, in which she placed all the trinkets ever given her by Lord Byron, and according to some, also an effigy of the poet—together with rouge, feathers, chains, rings and other symbols of the world. When a torch had been set to the whole, a page recited some verses written by Caroline herself —of which these are an excerpt :

> See here are locks and braids of coloured hair,
> Worn oft by me, to make the people stare ;
> Rouge, feathers, flowers, and all those tawdry things
> Besides those pictures, letters, chains, and rings—
> All made to lure the mind and please the eye,
> And fill the heart with pride and vanity—
> Burn, fire, burn ; these glittering toys destroy,
> While thus we hail the blaze with throats of joy.
> Burn, fire, burn, while wondering boys exclaim,
> And gold and trinkets glitter in the flame.
> Ah ! look not thus on me, so grave, so sad ;
> Shake not your heads, nor say the Lady's mad.
> Judge not of others, for there is but one
> To whom the heart and feelings can be known.
> Upon my youthful faults few censures cast,
> Look to the future—and forgive the past. . . .

Caroline enjoyed the melodrama vastly and Lady Melbourne enjoyed the account of it even more so. She wrote a description of it to Byron with *embellishments*. As for the poet, he concluded " that our friend is actually possessed by the foul fiend Flibbertigibbet, who presides over mopping and mowing." [1]

[1] Lord Byron's Correspondence.

1813

THE new year was inaugurated by a sort of guerrilla warfare between Caroline and Byron, in which there is no doubt as to who was the aggressor. The poet received a letter informing him that her ladyship's footmen now sported livery buttons bearing his family motto, amended to " *Ne crede* Byron "—he hardly believed in the reality of the joke, but he wrote a little anxiously on the subject to Lady Melbourne, knowing that she would view such a jest with even less sympathy than he did.

For a few days there was peace, and he began to make some arrangements concerning pictures. He asked Hobhouse to give Mrs. Mee a commission for a portrait of Lady Oxford, and he decided to send one of his own portraits, now stored at John Murray's, as a gift to that Lady. What was his indignation when he discovered that Mr. Murray had recently delivered the said portrait to Melbourne House, on the receipt of a letter in Byron's handwriting begging him to do so. This was more than flesh and blood could bear. " I am sure since the days of the Dove in the Ark, no animal has had such a time of it as I—no rest anywhere." [1]

He wrote directly to the miscreant, but Caroline replied blandly that she was perfectly ready to admit the forgery and the theft, and added that she had already " broken all but the sixth and the ninth commandments," and professed herself ready to break them too if Byron sought to obtain restitution. What was he to do—he was anxious, for everyone's sake, not to force a scene, but he was perfectly determined to obtain redress.

The situation was extremely harassing. One morning, as he was paying a business visit to Mr. Murray, a message was brought to the publisher requesting an interview for Lady

[1] Lord Byron's Correspondence.

Caroline on the following day. Byron was beside himself with anxiety. He had not given away the identity of the forger, and it was therefore impossible for him to implore Murray not to agree to a meeting.

For forty-eight hours he was horridly anxious as to what it might portend ; when he heard the result he laughed. Caroline had submitted a series of drawings with suggestion that they might be used as illustrations to his verses. He refused.

On the 22nd of February he had an interview with Lady Bessborough—she demanded the return of the remainder of Caroline's presents to him. This was embarrassing, for many of them were no longer in his possession. She was very anxious about her daughter's mental condition, and she begged Byron to see her. This was more embarrassing still, for Lady Oxford had absolutely forbidden him such an interview. If he acceded to the request he would only have another frantic woman on his hands. All he would promise was to continue to correspond with her, and to endeavour to have a soothing effect upon her. Any more ill-judged experiment can hardly be imagined.

In March a public scandal served to turn gossip into wider channels. The Prince of Wales's abortive efforts to dispose of his wife had come to a new flowering. Sir John and Lady Douglas had made a disposition to the effect that in 1802 the Princess of Wales had had an illegitimate child by Sir Sidney Smith.

For a moment " Prinny's " hopes were raised, but once again the evidence was disproved, and Caroline of Brunswick escaped her husband's vengeance.

Not so was Byron to escape from Caroline's anger. She was pestering him again for an interview. See her alone he would not, but he offered a meeting in the presence of Lady Oxford. Insult could go no further, thought the Ponsonbys, and even the Lambs were of the same opinion. To Byron it is probable that the suggestion was dictated by cowardice rather than a desire to anger Caroline. It must be recollected that Aspasia had once been one of Caroline's dearest friends, and that, strange as it may appear, during all the past months the two ladies had corresponded continually on the subject of Byron.

He was frankly afraid to meet her alone, and still more afraid of most witnesses. He would certainly prefer Lady Oxford to hear him abused and reproached than Lady Melbourne.

The suggestion was, however, refused, with contumely, but the correspondence about the return of Caroline's presents grew more and more feverish.

In particular there was a question of some ornament made out of the combined locks of Byron and Caroline. This had been destroyed; but he dared not say so. At last, to satisfy her he seized on an expedient that amused him immensely. The thought came to him when he realised that Lady Oxford and Caroline had hair of an almost identical colour and texture. He wrote to Lady Melbourne, delighted with his conceit.

" . . . The *double* hair amuses you—she will never discover the difference, and *of course*, *you* cannot know it, or tell it. It was a lucky coincidence of colour and shape for my purpose, and may never happen again, and surely is a very innocent revenge for some very scurvy treatment." [1]

At this moment his exasperation with Caroline knew no bounds.

" . . . to the latest hour of my life I shall hate that woman."

But even if Caroline herself desired to forget him, she could not do so. His name was on everyone's lips—a new poem of his, *Giaour*, had just been published and was having the greatest success. And then in the House of Lords, on the subject of Grattan's Catholic Emancipation Bill, he had made a really fine speech:

" Some persons have compared the Catholics to the beggar of *Gil Blas*: who made them beggars? Who are enriched with the spoils of their ancestors? And cannot you relieve the beggar when your fathers have made him such? If you are disposed to relieve him at all, cannot you do it without flinging your farthings in his face? . . . "

Brave words, and likely to appeal to Caroline, who had worshipped Fox, and married Lamb.

She was more than ever determined to get Byron back again, and for a moment Fate seemed to play into her hands. Lady

[1] Lord Byron's Correspondence.

Oxford was unwell, most inconveniently unwell, and Byron was bored and anxious, and packed her off to her husband to Cheltenham, once out of her clutches, the tone of his letters to Caroline was modified. On April 29th he wrote :

" . . . as I once hazarded everything for you, I will not now shrink from you. Perhaps I deserve punishment, if so, you are quite as proper a person to inflict it as any other. You say you will ' ruin me.' I thank you; but I have done that for myself already." [1]

Be that as it may, he did see Caroline—and alone. Of the interview we know little. Caroline, a rather unreliable authority for her own affairs, told Medwin that he wept and begged her pardon ; and Lady Bessborough we know, obliquely, stated that he had been seen on his knees in the middle of the room.

All that we know for certain is that William came back to find Caroline in tears, and was in a fury—accusing Byron of having insulted her. That young gentleman bewailed his fate loudly . . . " If I speak to her, he is insulted ; if I *don't* speak to her, she is insulted."

And he had more than Caroline's troubles on his hands. If Lady Oxford had been unwell when she left London, she had been extremely ill at Cheltenham. In some ways this was convenient, but Lord Oxford was not at all pleased. Byron had an unpleasant interview, but was tranquillised by Lord Oxford's determination to limit his revenge to setting sail with his lady for the continent. Byron was relieved and delighted. He was getting extremely bored with Aspasia.

On the 5th of July Lady Heathcote gave a great Ball. Now that Byron and Caroline had met in private he felt no necessity to refuse invitations to houses at which he might expect to meet her. In the crush before the first valse began, it so happened that Byron and Caroline were standing in the same group, with their hostess.

Lady Heathcote turned to Caroline. " Come, Lady Caroline, you must begin." Caroline answered in a low voice " Oh ! yes, I am in a merry humour." Then she whispered to Lord Byron : " I conclude that I may waltz now ? "

He was annoyed at the tone of her question, and replied

[1] Lord Byron's Correspondence.

sarcastically : " With everybody in turn—you always did it better than anyone. I shall have a pleasure in seeing you."

Caroline danced that valse in an agony of emotion : then she went into a small room to rest and recover as she felt ill. Supper was laid in this room. In a few moments Byron entered with Lady Rancliffe on his arm. Caroline took up a pair of scissors, she seized Byron's hand—he felt something sharp. " I mean to use this," she said. " Against me, I presume," he replied, and walked out with Lady Rancliffe.

Caroline's other hand held a wine-glass. In the agitation of the moment her grip tightened, and she broke it. Her hand was cut, and the blood began to flow over her gown. Lady Ossulston and several other ladies, who had followed Lady Rancliffe into the room, ran to her assistance. She was now in hysterics, and Lady Melbourne was called. It was long before they could quiet her, and get her to go home. The whole scene had taken place in the small dining-room, and most of the guests left the Ball unaware of it. But those who had witnessed it made the most of the tale. Some said that Caroline had tried to kill Byron with a glass dagger—others that she had tried to kill herself with a dinner knife—almost all were agreed that Lord Byron must have grossly insulted her to have been the cause of such a scene.

Byron himself went home at five o'clock with no knowledge of what had happened. He woke next morning to find himself the villain of a melodrama. Years afterwards, amongst his papers, the invitation to Lady Heathcote's Ball was found. Across the back of it was scribbled in his hand : " Ye dagger scene of indifferent memory."

He wrote at once to Lady Melbourne disclaiming all knowledge of the incident. " . . . had I been conscious of offending her I should have done everything to pacify or prevent her." [1] He could think of nothing in his conversation . . . "to produce cutting and maiming," nor did he know " where this cursed scarification " had taken place, nor when. He could not have left Lady Rancliffe when he met Caroline " to drown herself in wine and water or be suffocated in a jelly dish, without a spoon or a hand to help her."

On the whole Lady Melbourne, though she scolded him,

[1] Lord Byron's Correspondence.

was of the same opinion, and even Lady Bessborough felt uncomfortably that for the moment Byron's only crime was his existence. Thank God, he proposed to go to Sicily with his sister Augusta Leigh. The only factor which might make this plan fall through was Augusta's determination to take one or two of her children with her, and Lady Oxford had sickened Byron of everybody's children. After the Heath-cote Ball he went out of London and found other amusements in staying with the Websters, and in beginning a secret cor-respondence with Annabella Milbanke. There was much to amuse Lady Melbourne in the accounts of both adventures.

Meanwhile Annabella's letters filled him with astonish-ment. For any unmarried young woman to correspond with a man was sufficient to compromise her, yet here was the prudent Annabella not only writing to him, but taking her parents into the secret of their correspondence.

"What an odd situation and friendship is ours! Without one spark of love on either side." Lady Melbourne was not so sure of the truth in this statement, hope began to revive in her breast. She wrote to her niece, asking her again what kind of man she wished to marry. The answer was dis-couraging.

It was forwarded to Byron, who could make neither head nor tail of it. " . . . I shall say nothing because I do not understand it; though I daresay it is exactly what it ought to be."

Almost, Annabella made him think more kindly of Caroline. " See C ! If I should see C I hope not, though I am not sure a visit would be so disagreeable as it ought to be."

On October the 16th the most important event of the century took place. At Leipzig, in what was to be known as " the battle of the Nations," Napoleon was totally defeated and forced to retire to France. That in his retreat he managed to mop up the Bavarians was no reason to doubt that Leipzig was the beginning of the end. What this meant to England, which had been continuously at war for many years, and which had seen the whole map of Europe wiped out to make way for one gargantuan empire, what this meant to the disciples of Pitt and Nelson and Moore, can scarcely be realised to-day.

The black cloud, which had covered the sky since before

William and Caroline and Byron and their contemporaries could remember, was rent—a streak of light, livid indeed, but brilliant, had broken through to bring hope to England.

But to Byron, who saw life in drama, the disappearance of an empire was rather a matter of regret. He had come back to London in November. He frequented Holland House, where Lady Holland had no hesitation in loudly proclaiming her devotion to Napoleon and his fortunes.

She was at her old tricks again, making everyone as uncomfortable as she possibly could.

" Why does Lady Holland always have that damned screen between the whole room and the fire ? I, who bear cold no better than an antelope, and have never yet found a sun quite done to my taste, was absolutely petrified, and not even able to shiver. All the rest, too, looked as if they were just unpacked like salmon from an ice basket, and set down to table for that day only."

Caroline, touched by his softened attitude, voluntarily returned the stolen picture to Byron.

He was astonished and delighted, for he needed it now, not for Lady Oxford but for Lady Frances Webster. ". . . they have now, that is four, (the Mussalman's allotment), one picture a piece." Perhaps he attributed the restoration to the good offices of Lady Melbourne, for it is certain that at that moment she stood very high in his estimation. ". . . I have a letter from Lady Melbourne, the best friend I ever had in my life, and the cleverest of women." . . . " If she had been a few years younger what a fool she would have made of me, had she thought it worth her while, and I should have lost a valuable and most agreeable friend."

On December 2nd his *Bride of Abydos* was published, and was greeted with unusual enthusiasm.

Never had his reputation stood higher. One evening, when looking through some objects at Holland House, Lord Holland lit on a *thurible* ; he turned to the guests : " Here is some incense for you." Quick as a flash Campbell answered : " Carry it to Lord Byron, he is used to it."

1814

EARLY in the new year Byron took over Lord Althorp's apartment at the Albany the Albany had been Burlington House, belonging to Lady Holland and bought by the first Viscount Melbourne. It amused him to think of his friend Lady Melbourne inhabiting these rooms; he recalled how she and Lord Egremont had laid out the gardens, how Wheatley and Mrs. Damer had carried out the decorations, how Mortimer and Cipriani had ornamented the ceilings with the signs of the Zodiac, the four seasons, and morning, evening, noon and night, how Lawrence and Reynolds had painted the children there, how the Lamb boys had gone to Eton from there, and how finally it had served as one of Lady Melbourne's trump cards in her game for the supremacy in London society and royal favour. For had she not, just after she had perfected it, exchanged it with the Duke of York for his sombre but magnificent abode in Whitehall.

For the moment relations between Byron, the Lambs and the Bessboroughs were of a more or less pacific nature. They met at the Hollands and at the Lansdownes, and it looked as though a more normal era were opening out before them. Byron's desire was to marry. " A wife would be my salvation. I am sure the wives of my acquaintances have hitherto done me little good." [1] Perhaps Madame de Staël, disappointed of Hart, might not have been averse to having him for a son-in-law, but if so she was to be disappointed again.

On the 18th of March old Lady Spencer died. To Lady Bessborough it was a severe blow. She had a great affection and a great respect for her mother, and besides all this she was the last link with her own youth and with that brilliant circle which had formed round her sister. They were all dead now—Georgiana and Ca, Fox, the Bishop of Derry, Lady

[1] Lord Byron's Correspondence.

Bristol—the eighteenth was dead. She was left with her remote scholarly husband, with her brother who had been taken from them by Lavinia and forced into a different mould —with Granville, changed by Harriet into the nineteenth-century gentleman, a rôle which had always been possible to him. And now old Lady Spencer, whom Lady Stafford had loved and admired and recommended as a mentor to Granville, whom the raffish Bishop of Derry had respected— who had spent the many years of her widowhood in philan-thropic works—now she, who had always made a background of sense and order and seemliness for her daughter, had disappeared. No longer would Lady Bessborough be able to go down to Holywell and try what early hours and solitude and work could do to restore her shattered nerves.

Caroline, too, was sad. She had spent so much of her childhood with her grandmother; Lavinia's children, however, were not in any way distressed—Althorp wrote (later) of old Lady Spencer that she had " no natural talents or intelligence, but had taken great pains with herself." [1] To a later genera-tion it must seem as though he were rather drawing a portrait of Lavinia, the blue stocking, than of the simple, unpretentious old lady.

Whilst personal troubles overshadowed Roehampton and Brocket, public news was too good to allow of low spirits. On March the 31st Paris capitulated, and on April the 11th Napoleon surrendered. On the 20th of the same month the King of France entered London. The city was *en fête*. No one but Byron and Lady Holland ventured to deplore the fall of the Emperor.

Byron took his sorrows to Miss Milbanke, who replied rather frigidly with a voluminous correspondence on the liturgy. The young man was bored and perplexed. He felt ill and sent for a doctor—who frightened him considerably by taking more interest in his mental than in his physical symptoms. He wondered if he should be well advised to propose again to Miss Milbanke. Her refusal had piqued him.

. . . " If I were sure of myself (not of her) I would go on ; but I am not, and never can be, and what is still worse, I have no judgment, and less common sense than an infant. . . ." [2]

[1] *The Ponsonby Family.*   [2] Lord Byron's Correspondence.

And he assured Lady Melbourne that these were no empty words, but an expression of genuine conviction.

He was out of health and spirits; he published the *Corsair*, but the applause with which it was greeted failed to satisfy him. He wrote some impertinent verses on old Lord Carlisle, and every paper abused him and half London cut him—but, unabashed, he took up with the other half, and his reputation, already questioned, became notorious.

It was characteristic of Caroline that she chose such a moment to attempt a revival of their intimacy To the Albany she went, disguised as a page, and on arrival was told that his Lordship was out—undeterred she made her way to his apartment: so these were his rooms, these his possessions. Perhaps she studied the portraits of ladies adorning his chimney-piece—Lady Oxford was there, and others, but there was no portrait of herself. We know that she looked at his books, and across the fly-leaf of an open volume she scribbled: "Remember me," and then she made her way back to Melbourne House. When Byron returned he saw immediately, as he was meant to see, the open volume and the two words. To think that she had actually pursued him to his lair—that she had been alone in his rooms and probably sorted through all his belongings—he was indignant, and seizing a pencil he wrote beneath her lines:

> Remember thee—remember thee!
> Till Lethe quench life's burning streams
> Remorse and shame shall cling to thee,
> And haunt thee like a feverish dream.
> Remember thee! Ay, doubt it not,
> Thy husband too shall think of thee,
> By neither shalt thou be forgot.
> Thou false to him, thou fiend to me!

Caroline was for the moment unaware of the anger she had raised, and she came again—perhaps several times, certainly once that summer—and Byron, who could write (probably in all sincerity) to Lady Melbourne: "If there is one human being I do utterly detest and abhor it is she," was unable to resist her presence or her constancy. Few people enough were left who had an affection for him—not many who even tolerated him socially—soon there would be fewer still ; he knew that. Yet, with that morbid desire for self-revelation which was always so intrinsic a part of his character, he utilised this occasion to acquaint Caroline with the present direction of his affections—with his affairs past and actual. She listened in horrified interest. When she rose to go he pressed his lips to hers. " Poor Caro, if everyone hates me, you will, I see, never change—no, not even with ill usage."

She tore herself away from him : " Yes, I *am* changed, and I shall come here no more."

Perhaps for a second he wondered if he had said too much, been too explicit ; probably he brushed the scruple aside—Caroline would stick like a limpet whatever he might have said, he had heard her heroics before.

But this time he was wrong. Never were he and Caroline to be alone together again. And if her love for him were not, as she then supposed, dead, it was at least stunned so completely as to remain in eclipse for years, and to come ultimately to only a maimed and recollected existence.

An event of family importance, which took place during the year, was the marriage of Willie Ponsonby, Caroline's youngest brother, to Lady Barbara Ashley Cooper, the daughter of Lord Shaftesbury. The event was one of great rejoicing to Lady Bessborough. She and Caroline both had an especial affection for the delicate and affectionate William—they liked Lady Barbara, and the fact that she was a considerable heiress was reassuring to them. For the Bessboroughs were badly off, and Willie did not seem likely to become the type of person who acquires wealth.

Meanwhile, in Paris the map of Europe was being made over again—or rather it was being restored to what it had been in the days of Lady Bessborough's youth.

The Pope went back to Rome—Louis XVIII returned to Paris—Ferdinand made his way to Madrid—and, an innovation, William II was declared King of Holland and Belgium.

How pleasant it was to see a little variety again—not a vast block stretching from the North Sea to the Ægean, from the Bay of Biscay to the Danube. Such a polishing up of honoured crowns ; and dignity coming to fill the lives of old gentlemen who had made brave show with tawdry tinsel for a quarter of a century. Soon one would be able to travel once more on the continent—to do the grand tour—to become again cosmopolitan and civilised—the younger generation were singularly insular and limited—no wonder—unable as they had been to put their noses beyond Brighton pier. But before the scramble to the continent, which reminded Lady Bessborough sadly of that earlier interim of peace (?) :

There was an influx of foreigners to London.

The Emperor came, and the King of Prussia. On the 25th of June they were entertained at Petworth by Lord Egremont —that " shy and taciturn man of pleasure " who had been such a friend of Lady Melbourne, the great connoisseur and collector, who had encouraged Gainsborough and Flaxman, and whom Fox had always credited with a first-class brain.

The Melbournes were present at the fête—and they, too, had matter for congratulation, for Lord Melbourne had received an English peerage.

A few days later the members of Watier's Club [1] (to which Byron had recently been elected) gave a Masquerade at Burlington House to Wellington. Everyone went, and Caroline went too—and behaved very indecorously, according to Byron, who wrote sententiously to Lady Melbourne :

. . . " Not all I could say would prevent her from displaying her green pantaloons every now and then, though I scolded her like a grandfather." He himself was dressed as a monk.

Two months later, about September 20th, Lady Melbourne received a letter from Byron. She had received so many in the course of the last eighteen months that it must be supposed she opened it with little interest, anticipating the usual rigmarole of self-analysis. The first line read as follows : " Miss Milbanke has accepted me ; and her answer was accompanied by a very kind letter from your brother." So that was how it was all going to end—Byron and Annabella—Byron her nephew—the scheme which she had originated a year ago.

[1] Watier's Club : started by Louis Weltjie, the Prince of Wales's chef. The Prince had first known Weltjie as a gingerbread maker, selling his cakes in the street. Weltjie, after being royal chef for some years, sold the land on which Brighton Pavilion stands to his master. Weltje road, Chiswick, still recalls his name.

What can Lady Melbourne have felt when she knew that she had been successful ? When the plan had occurred to her, she had known less about her niece—and much less about Byron. The extent of the little doctrinaire's determination had been masked by conventionality—the extent of Byron's misdeeds had been unrevealed by mere acquaintanceship.

And then, besides these factors, the circumstances themselves had altered. Caroline had quietened down wonderfully since the spring—and, on the contrary, Byron's behaviour had passed beyond the pale of toleration.

Probably she would no longer have wished to instigate the match, but, at the same time, of the two principals and of the subsidiary characters involved in the drama, only one had a real place in her heart, and that was George Gordon—and in the tremendous gamble with fortune which the marriage would entail, he was the person who stood to gain something. Annabella was happy and respectable, she had much to lose—Byron was miserable and discredited, and he might re-establish himself and be happy. She had a weakness for him—he had such an appreciation and realisation of herself—and then he was amusing, and so few people amused her—and his genuine sincerity and frankness in their relationship touched her.

Perhaps with some such reflections she quieted her scruples and accepted the inevitable with a good grace. One word from her to her brother would have stopped the marriage— but she left it unspoken. And, after all, what she knew about Byron was from his own confidences to her ; and as has been said before, there were some things Lady Melbourne would not do.

Both she and Byron were exceedingly anxious lest Caroline should choose the occasion of the engagement for some outrageous exploit. But Lady Melbourne was ignorant of the scene at the Albany, and Byron had underestimated its importance. Caroline behaved with perfect propriety when she heard of the impending marriage—and it may be wondered whether Byron were not a little disappointed. At first it seemed as though his relationship with Annabella was to be all that could be desired, but in November, when he went to stay at Seaham, doubts began to arise in his mind.

He disliked his future mother-in-law extremely—and he

found Annabella " the most silent woman I ever encountered," and this was not to his taste. " I like them to talk, because then they think less. . . . Much cogitation will not be in my favour."

Finally he wrote despondingly :

" I can't yet tell whether we are to be happy or not. I have every disposition to do her all possible justice, but I fear she won't govern me, and if she don't, it will not do at all."

Annabella herself was nervous. " . . . I hear of nothing but ' feeling ' from morning till night, except from Sir Ralph, with whom I go on to admiration." Annabella had made scenes ; he had believed her to be incapable of so much animation.

Caroline was at Brocket with William. Lady Bessborough and her husband had started off on a continental tour ; it was long since she had been in France. Many memories came back to her—memories even of her childhood and Queen Marie Antoinette.

How long, long ago that seemed now, and how few of those parties were left alive to recall them, and they were old—she was old and Bess was old. Indeed, it must seem that the Duchess Elizabeth looked very old now. For Lady Sarah, Lavinia's daughter, had written to her brother :

" Lord Erskine signalled himself by quoting at the Duchess of Devonshire, who sat opposite him, Milton's description of old age, with a most cruel exactness of memory.

" ' . . . But then thou must outlive
Thy youth, thy strength, thy beauty, which will change
To wither'd, weak and grey ; thy sensor then
Obtuse, all taste of pleasure must forgo.'

" The poor Duchess looked so exactly the picture of all this that the quotation was quite superfluous." [1]

Yes, they were all old now, new people had come to take their places, Sally Jersey with her singing and her dancing and her pet birds ; Lady Boringdon, who was clever and played with grace at billiards, and who was suspected of having written *Pride and Prejudice* and *Sense and Sensibility* [2]—and

[1] *The Letters of Sarah Lady Lyttelton.*
[2] *Recollections of a Long Life*—Hobhouse.

then that set of serious, critical, half-worldly, half-philanthropic young women: Harriet Granville, Emily Cowper, Sarah Lyttelton, and then her Caroline, and some lines of Pope may have come to her mind as they have to others in connexion with Lady Caroline.

> Strange graces still, and stranger flights she had,
> Was just not ugly, and was just not mad;
> Yet ne'er so sure of passion to create,
> As when she touched the brink of all we hate.

Lady Bessborough and the Duchess felt infinitely far removed from this new generation. They did not much desire to live in this new Europe—or rather this older Europe—which Castlereagh and Wellington had gone to Vienna to reanimate.

Byron's wedding was fixed for January 2nd. The Thames was frozen over, to the consternation of the excise officers and the delight of the gin-sellers.[1]

[1] *News from the Past.*

1815

ON the 2nd of January, 1815, in the drawing-room at Seaham, Byron was married to Annabella Milbanke. Scarcely anyone was present except Sir Ralph and Lady Milbanke and Hobhouse. Byron had a cold and complained of the hassocks which, he said, must have been filled with peach stones; for the rest, the ceremony was short enough and sufficiently private to please him.[1] One could scarcely be married with less fuss. Hobhouse had not seen the bride before. He was disappointed, for he found her " rather dowdy looking," wearing a " long and high dress though she had excellent feet and ankles." The lower part of her face he thought " bad," and the upper half " not handsome, though expressive." He augured very ill for the future and wrote that he felt as though he had buried a friend. In the afternoon the couple drove away—when Lady Byron was wished good fortune and happiness, she replied, " It will be my own fault if I am not happy." Lady Milbanke wept without remission and Sir Ralph was in high spirits at the accomplishment of the tremendous event. It was in general very much like other weddings.

The first letters which followed it gave rise to good hopes for the future.

George and Belle got on extremely well together. They were anxious to know what presents they were to receive from their relations; and they were startled and horrified to learn of a report that William and Caroline were about to separate. Byron wrote to Lady Melbourne to know whether or not it were " wicked scandal." Lady Melbourne replied immediately :

" It may or may not be ' wicked scandal,' but as far as I am informed—it is not true. They are in the country, to all

[1] *Recollections of a Long Life*—Hobhouse.

appearances like two turtle doves. There may now and then be a little sharpness introduced—but who knows that some part of the cooing of these same birds may not be scolding ? " [1] The Byrons were relieved. He was content, and wished no harm to anyone.

The spring sped along merrily. From the continent the Bessboroughs, the Morgans and others wrote letters of interest to the Lambs and the Granvilles. There were many interesting stories about Napoleon. Most of them centred round his personal care of the wounded, " his anxious visits to the field of battle, his feeling the pulse, and wiping the wounds and administering cordials with his own hands."

Now that he was safely in Elba, Byron and Lady Holland were no longer alone in their admiration of the Emperor.

By February the Bessboroughs were in Marseilles where Masséna did everything that was possible to make their winter agreeable. Lord Bessborough was suffering from gout and unable to do much, so the theatres and parties fell to Lady Bessborough's sole lot. Some years ago she would have enjoyed them, but she was too old now to derive much pleasure from these diversions, if Georgiana had been there to share them . . . if Granville had still relied on her letters . . . then it might have been different. But now, she could not write to him frequently on mere personal matters—if only she had some great and important piece of news to convey to him which might make her letters valuable to him once more. On the 3rd of March she heard a strange report. It was only whispered in lobbies and ante-rooms, it was so wild and improbable that she scarcely dared to write.

It was to the effect that Napoleon had escaped from Elba, had actually landed in France with a handful of men, was now, this very night, only a few miles away at Fréjus. She hardly believed it, yet she wrote it to Granville—if it should be true—she would not be denied the privilege of being the first to impart the news.

There followed days of intense excitement—the confirmation of Napoleon's landing—the report of the loyalty of Antibes —the uncertainty of the Emperor's exact whereabouts, the rush to enlist, the march of troops—the enthusiasm that overlay

[1] *In Whig Society* (?).

the profound fear and disquiet which the Marseillais had at heart.

The civilians were rushing to enlist—the officers were, mostly, loyal to the King—but the troops were not to be depended upon. Masséna had sent some men he trusted to blow up the bridge over the Durance at Sisteron, but before the work had been carried out, Napoleon had crossed unmolested. Who could fail to be anxious ? Lady Bessborough went to see the departure of the volunteers. People one knew, who had no connexion with the army, marching in the columns as private soldiers—their wives in tears. The peasants lamenting a new war in patient acceptance. The porters at the hotel disappearing—the waiters thinning out.

Had the troops been of the same mind as the populace, the issue would not have been in doubt, but they were getting more and more restive. It piqued the staff to be told of Napoleon's astonishment when he found the bridge at Sisteron intact.

The daily press printed a curious rumour. The Emperor was said to declare that he came back in an English frigate, accompanied by two English officers in uniform and with the consent of the English Government. Such monstrous inventions were really hard on unfortunate English visitors in France, who, if they were believed, might anticipate equally unpleasant treatment from both parties.

On the 17th March, the Duc d'Angoulême entered Marseilles and received an ovation. But shortly afterwards the situation began to alter for the worse so far as the royalist cause was concerned. The soldiers rallied in thousands round their old leader and Napoleon advanced triumphantly upon Paris. The Bessboroughs moved on to Nice in alarm, but hardly were they arrived there than wild rumours began to circulate. The commandant had embarked the heavy artillery and ordered what could not be carried away to be destroyed, The Italian inhabitants of the town lived in terror of being looted by a French army, and the English visitors were extremely uncomfortable when they saw their protectors retiring, fearing that the Niceois themselves might forestall the French in pillage and arson.

Genoa seemed to offer an hospitable asylum. But how was

it to be reached. The mountain passes were blocked by snow
—on the sea a contrary wind raged, and in his bed Lord Bessborough lay tortured by gout. Lady Bessborough had some
thoughts of imploring Masséna's protection, for he had now
passed over to the side of Napoleon—but when she recollected
that he had said so much to her, and so recently, in abuse of
Bonaparte that any recollection of her would probably only
spur him on to desire her muzzling by any means including
imprisonment. She wrote instead to the Duchess of Devonshire, appealing for her interest to procure them an English
man-of-war on to which Lord Bessborough might be embarked.

The appeal was not in vain. The frigate came, they were
all embarked and carried to safety. At Genoa amongst other
people they found the Princess of Wales.

Lady Bessborough first saw her at a ball and failed to recognise her—she was short, fat and elderly, with a very red face,
rat's-tail eyebrows and a black wig on which rested a wreath
of red roses. She was unsuitably dressed in a débutante's
white frock, and was accompanied by a small English boy of
dubious origin.

Her delight at meeting English visitors was not reciprocated.

Here, for two months, the Bessboroughs lived a round of
enforced provincial gaiety, their minds bewildered by Bonaparte's meteoric course, their hearts heavy with the knowledge
that Frederick and many cousins and friends were with the
Allied armies.

In England it was as though the country, aroused three
months ago from an interminable nightmare, had fallen asleep
again and renewed it. This well-remembered pall of dread
and agitation seemed to weigh more heavily upon the mind
after those hundred days of respite. Once again no one knew
what each day might bring forth, what death might not be
reported, what disaster forthcoming. Yet beneath the turmoil
and the strain of nations, particular lives numbered small
events. Byron wrote to Lady Melbourne that Belle was
expecting a child. This was cause of satisfaction and it looked
as though, after all, the marriage might turn out well.

So pleased indeed was Byron that, when they returned to
London, he asked Caroline to visit them. She went; probably hoping to find them alone, but was met by Lady Mel-

bourne, Lady Noel and Byron's sister, Mrs. Leigh, in addition
to Annabella—the last-named treated her coldly. After a few
minutes Byron joined them. He had probably arranged the
meeting with a view to its being a formal recognition of the
good terms on which they hoped henceforth to live. He did
his best to be kind and to lighten the situation, but Caroline
thought him very nervous. She herself was hardly able to
speak. It was the last time she ever saw him.

In the following month Harriet Leveson-Gower gave birth
to a son. To Granville it was an event of great joy. He
wanted to ask his brother-in-law, Lord Morpeth, to be godfather to the child, but the scale of christening presents was
still very considerable. Harriet wrote dubiously to Georgiana
on the subject :

" . . . the penalty attached makes me feel shy about it.
If you are as poor as we are, the amassing of such a sum
would be impracticable. Do not, therefore, show him this,
if some prosperity has not befallen your finances." [1]

By the beginning of June the news of the war became so
grave that all private anxiety seemed to be suspended. It
was known that the Duke of Wellington with some 80,000
men and Bonaparte with some 100,000 were both on the soil
of Flanders sparring for an entry.

The fate of Europe lay in the impending battle. Many
English people had gone over to Brussels to be near the army.
From the great Duchess of Richmond to the small Mr. Creevey,
each and all were anxious to be near the scene of the battle.

The events which followed have been too often described
to require repetition. They were dramatic in the extreme.
The ball at the Duchess of Richmond's—the sudden arrival
of an estafette for Wellington, the Duke's request to the
daughter of the house for a map, his pointing out the spot
where the battle would take place, the rush of all the officers
back to their regiments.

Followed the deadly silence—the complete absence of news
—then the distant sound of cannon, then silence again, and
once more the sound of cannon. Then the arrival of the
first wounded with no news, save that of their own section,
of the battle. Then more wounded, with frightful accounts

[1] *The Letters of Harriet Countess Granville.*

of the number of killed, then some retreating Dutch with a report that the battle was lost, that the French were at their heels. And every house preparing feverishly for the reception of the wounded, and finally some bolder spirits taking horses and carriages towards the scene of the battle in order to carry the injured back to safety.

And messengers sent back to England with wild rumours of a French victory and of countless dead, and old Rothschild incredulous, buying up the falling stocks on the panic-stricken Exchange. All these have been told in verse, in prose, and in picture, till they bear no more telling.

Frederick Ponsonby had not gone to the Duchess of Richmond's ball, he had dined with General Pack and slept on the road. On the morning of the 18th he had little anticipation of a battle till about ten o'clock when he heard artillery and saw a large enemy force in motion. Next he saw the Union Brigade, commanded by his cousin Sir William Ponsonby, charge with great effect, capturing two thousand prisoners and two eagles.

But he did not see what followed the manœuvre, for almost immediately after the charge of the Union Brigade he led his own regiment against a body of retreating French Infantry. Hardly had the mêlée started than a group of French Lancers came to the rescue of their compatriots. Taken thus by surprise and in the flank the Hussars suffered heavily.

Frederick received a severe cut on the face and both arms and as he tried to collect and withdraw his regiment, he got a blow on the head which knocked him unconscious from his horse. When he came to, he saw his men at the foot of the hill on which he was lying. He got to his feet and endeavoured to make his way back to them, but a lancer who came up behind him thrust his lance into his back with the words, " Coquin, tu n'es pas mort." The blade broke a rib and penetrated both lungs. His mouth filled with blood and he had difficulty in breathing, but he did not lose consciousness. He felt little doubt that his wounds were fatal.

A battalion of French Tirailleurs marched down the hill. The first man who passed took what he could find in Frederick's pocket. When an officer came by he gave him a drink of brandy, put a knapsack under his head and moved him into a position in which he was least likely to be injured should the cavalry pass over the ground. Then he left him, promising to send aid when the battle was over. Frederick did not imagine that by night he should be in need of any human assistance. He thanked the officer, little dreaming that he should meet him again years later in Paris. The Tirailleurs took up a position on the hillside and a soldier who fired over Frederick kept up a running conversation with him—according to his accounts he was killing a man at every shot. As the day wore on, it was evident that the Allies were advancing. The young Tirailleur said good-bye to Frederick. "Adieu, mon ami, nous allons nous retirer!" The retreat of the French was followed by a charge by a squadron of Prussian cavalry.

Frederick was kicked on the head and bruised all over. Night fell and the cold air revived him. He was plundered again, this time by our allies, the Prussians. The French had told him that the Duke of Wellington was killed and that several English regiments had surrendered. Later in the night an English soldier came and had a look at him, and agreed to stay with him till help could be found. Water was even more necessary to Frederick than any assistance, but it was impossible to obtain a drop. When there was some light the soldier saw a dragoon—he beckoned to him and they tried to place Frederick on his horse but failed—the man then went off to fetch a wagon and never returned. After eighteen hours Ponsonby was rescued by an officer of his regiment who had come with a canteen of water and a conveyance.

He was taken to the inn at Waterloo which had been the Duke's headquarters, and there for a week he lay between life and death—unable to be moved into Brussels.

On the field of battle Wellington surveyed the carnage sadly —he needed to reappoint commanders to the brigades who had lost their leaders. As he named each man the reply came back—Dead—Wounded—Dead—Dead—till at last in despair he asked, "For God's sake tell me who is alive." The losses were appalling.

But in his travelling carriage, galloping as fast as sturdy horses could take him, Napoleon was being carried away from the army who had trusted in his star. The news of the victory travelled slowly outwards in widening circles. It was the 25th of June before it reached Genoa.

And then it came in a terribly garbled guise. There had been a colossal battle with proportionate losses—nothing was certain as to victory or defeat—only one thing was sure. Frederick Ponsonby had been dangerously wounded, and his condition was regarded as almost hopeless. To set the whole caravanserai in motion instantly was impossible, especially on account of Lord Bessborough's health, but Lady Bessborough and Willie started on the long journey for Brussels without an hour's delay. They travelled night and day. More news met them on the way. It seemed now more or less certain that the Duke of Wellington had obtained a great victory, but at every place at which they stopped to change their horses came news of more deaths. Frederick Howard, Morpeth's brother, had been killed and Sir William Ponsonby and many others.

When Lady Bessborough saw her son, she was horrified. It was impossible to understand how he had survived so many wounds.

But by the time she reached him he was out of danger—the convalescence would be very long, he might not regain the use of his arm but he was safe. Meanwhile, from England Caroline had also hurried out to be with Frederick.

Harriet slyly reported that he was in great dread of her "sisterly persecutions."

On the 23rd of July Lady Bessborough, reading her paper, saw Granville alluded to as Lord Granville of Stone. She caught her breath. So Granville had been made a peer and neither he nor Harriet had troubled to inform her. She was glad for his sake, because the probabilities were in favour of its preceding the offer of some diplomatic position, and this she knew that he desired. She wrote to congratulate him. It was August before Frederick could be moved back to England ; Lady Bessborough had gone ahead to make Roehampton ready for the invalid. Harriet reported him as looking thin but uncommonly well and happy.

Indeed almost everyone in England was happy, with the exception of Lady Holland, whom the Granvilles found "seated on the grass with Allen and a plate of Baba, very cross and absurd about Bonaparte, ' poor dear man ' as she calls him." [1]

She had sent him books to amuse him on his journey to St. Helena and was loud in her condemnation of the Allies' severity.

The complete collapse of the Empire seemed hardly credible.

William Lamb saw the officer who had been to see Napoleon at Malmaison and endeavoured to persuade him to join the Army on the Loire in order to make one more effort. This man told William that the Emperor had replied,

" C'est trop tard, tout est dit—La France est divisée, et ne sais plus ce qu'elle veut. Les Français ne sont rien s'ils ne sont pas triomphants. . . . Je n'avais vue autre moyen qu'une guerre victorieuse,—si j'avais réussi ils se seraient tous réunis autour de moi." [2]

It was a clear vision of the situation, and it explained Napoleon's desire to avoid the further shedding of blood to no purpose. The detached estimate seems to emphasise how little of a Frenchman Bonaparte felt himself to be. To the last he was a Corsican, governing an alien people, a people for whom it may even be that he had little sympathy. Once more the peacemaking had to begin all over again, but this time it was to Paris and not to Vienna that the monarchs and statesmen repaired. And in their wake flocked all London society.

Houses were booked for the Duke of Devonshire, the Duke of Rutland, for the Castlereaghs, and the Kinnairds, the Shelleys and the Granthams, and a hundred more. At the Embassy the Stewarts entertained Schwarzenberg, Czernichef, Talleyrand, Pozzo di Borgo and Metternich. Presently came the Emperors of Russia and of Austria, and the King of Prussia to render thanks to Wellington and Blücher, and to see what Louis XVIII was willing to part with from amongst Napoleon's ill-gotten gains.

Undoubtedly the man who was of least account in all the hubbub was the King of France, and undoubtedly the heroic figure was that of the Duke. Duchesses and peeresses fought to obtain an invitation from him, sophisticated young dandies

---

[1] *The Letters of Harriet Countess Granville.*
[2] *Lord Melbourne's Papers*—Lloyd.

travelled to Paris to have a look at him, and of all their uninvited guests the French preferred him. They felt that he was their only protector against the barbarous Cossacks and the vindictive Prussians. Had he not stationed his own sentries on the bridges over the Seine, and given them orders to remain there whatever counter orders they might receive, when the Germans had declared their intention of blowing up the bridges?

Wellington was not unmoved by female adulation. Indeed he was unable to resist it, even though the public might find something comic in the sight of the three Allied Sovereigns and the great Duke being accompanied by Lady Shelley when they caracolled up and down the battalions at the great Russian review.

When Hart had decided to go to Paris he had not been long in persuading the Granvilles to accompany him. They " sight saw," they danced, they rode, they reviewed and they admired Talma, Mlle Georges and Mlle Mars. Hart bought up the whole town ; and Harriet bought a green silk petticoat for Lady Morpeth. Hot behind them, despite their protests, followed William and Caroline.

She was ill on the way south and had been treated by French apothecaries at every town through which they passed. When they reached Paris she sent for a doctor, but by a strange accident the Duke of Wellington was sent for instead ! [1] This filled the cousins with delight, for they had all maintained that Caroline had come out for the special purpose of setting her cap at the Duke.[2] Lady Granville described the Lambs with a vivid pen.

" Nothing is *agissant* but Caroline William in a purple riding habit, tormenting everybody, but I am convinced ready primed for an attack upon the Duke of Wellington, and I have no doubt that she will succeed, as no dose of flattery is too strong for him to swallow or her to administer. Poor William hides in one small room, while she assembles lovers and tradespeople in another. He looks worn to the bone. Whilst she was in Paris Caro received a letter from Byron. He seemed to be in the best of spirits and hoped she was as happy with the regiment as he was with his wife Belle."

[1] *The Letters of Harriet Countess Granville.*
[2] *Memoirs of Harriette Wilson,* by herself.

August was a brilliant month of pomp and gaiety ; the wounded of Waterloo were not yet cured, the dead hardly buried, but that uncertain terror which had over hung all their lives for nearly twenty years was annihilated. It was a triumph, not a sober victory hardly won. But by September all the galaxy of celebrated personages had dispersed to their homes and only the treaty-makers worked on at their task, which was not accomplished until November.

1816

THE peace-makers were so industrious that when the New Year came in the French commented gravely that the Allies had made so good a peace " qu'ils n'ont rien laissé à Désiré."

Byron had had a bad winter, he had been ill and irritable, so ill indeed and so irritable that there seems to be no doubt that Annabella believed him to be going off his head. Their finances were in a deplorable state, he talked of going abroad for some months in order to practise economy and then that Annabella and the child should spend that time at Seaham. But he was incapable of coming to any decision. At last the doctors advised Lady Byron to leave her husband and go to her parents. They believed that by this device Byron would soon be induced to exert himse'f enough to follow her. They also believed that a short separation would do good to the frayed nerves of both parties.

Taking an affectionate farewell of Byron, Annabella left, she made him promise that he would follow her in a few days, she expressed the greatest anxiety for his health and welfare. On her arrival at her destination she wrote him a playful letter signed " Pippin," desiring him to come down as soon as possible, and expressing her parents' desire to see him. Byron was still in bed in a state of lethargic misery ; he asked his sister, Augusta Leigh, to write to his wife for him. But although he felt sick and despondent his doctor saw marked signs of improvement in his condition, and made haste to communicate the good news to Annabella.

Her husband was neither going to die nor to go mad, soon he would be cured and with her again. What can these words have conveyed to the Princess of Parallelograms ? Did they open out unending vistas of unbearable misery ? Had she only sufficient courage to devote herself to a dying man, or had she no forgiveness for Byron if he were sane ? Had she only tolerated his presence believing him to be mad ? Faced with the possibility of decades of life lived with him, did she break down and tell her parents what Byron had told her of his life previous to his marriage ? What were the emotions that guided her no one will ever know, but, immediately after his doctor's favourable report, Byron received a communication from his father-in-law.

It acquainted him with the fact that Lady Byron would never return to his roof. The cause of this decision, it was, implied, would be evident to him, and its wisdom he must be forced to recognise. Byron was horrified and aghast. In addition he was bewildered. Annabella had never reproached him with anything, she had seemed devoted to him until the day of her departure. And, since his marriage, she really had not much to reproach him with. On one occasion he had been unfaithful, and on another, drunk. In both instances he had confessed his delinquency to her and been forgiven. He had hidden nothing from her. Since he had been ill it might be that he had amused himself by teasing her, but none of these things had been serious, and she had known of them. Of her he had always spoken with respect to everyone. She could find no fault with him on that score. He might have complained about the expense of marriage and about his financial situation. But against Belle he had never said one word, of that he was sure, for he had never " had a thought against her." As for his life previous to his marriage, why should that impinge upon the present ?

Annabella had heard much about him ; she had certainly known about Caroline, about Lady Oxford, about Lady Frances Webster. She had known about almost every person of significance in his life—almost. And half her desire to marry him had been for the very purpose of reforming him. Nothing new had happened. It was plain that his wife was acting under duress. He wrote her, imploring an explanation, demanding her return, dissociating her completely from the fatal letter. His communication was answered by Sir Ralph : " Lady Byron could not have any communication with him —he would know why."

Byron was distracted. He made every effort to send letters

by safe channels ; he attempted to see his wife privately ; he sent his friend Hobhouse to do his best in his interest. All was of no avail. Lady Byron said that she was acting of her own free will and without any compulsion, whilst Lady Byron's maid said that her ladyship wept from morning till night and was hysterical with grief.

Sir Ralph demanded a legal separation, but he refused to bring any charge against his son-in-law. The utmost secrecy had prevailed, but London began to gossip about Lady Byron's long absence at a time at which her husband was known to be ill. On February 5th Lady Melbourne wrote :

" There is a report about you so much believed in town that I think you should be informed of it. They say you and Annabella are parted and even state your authority upon which it is founded. In general, when reports are as false as I know this to be, I think the best way is to despise them. But really, this is so much believed, not withstanding my contradictions, that I think you ought to desire her to come to Town, or go to her yourself." [1]

Now if old Lady Melbourne had a genuinely disinterested affection for anyone outside her family, it was for Byron. She would have done much to preserve his marriage and to rehabilitate him in society. She had believed that his marriage to her niece would have this effect, and for this reason she had held her tongue and failed to communicate to Annabella certain facts which, eighteen months ago, she had been one of the only people to know about Byron. She realised that they would probably have prevented the marriage, but she did not dream that Annabella, hearing them long afterwards, would instantly leave her husband. And this was now what she feared had happened. She waited anxiously for Byron's answer. When it came it must have been a full account of the nature of the separation, for on the 14th she wrote again :

" If I omitted the other morning saying to you that if you wished to see me, or think I can be of any use, I will go to you at any time. I have received a letter from Lady Noel saying that it is not honourable to give information to any persons except those whom it is necessary to trust." [2]

She had recommended the marriage, she had urged it on,

[1] *In Whig Society.*   [2] Lord Byron's Correspondence.

and now she fully realised how completely ruined Byron would be if it broke down. She had gambled on Annabella, and Annabella had let her down. And now she accepted her full responsibilities. For weeks Byron's correspondence with the Milbankes continued.

He was ready to refuse a separation, ready to let them produce their charge in a court if they would. Hobhouse was indefatigable in the negotiations ; but the Milbankes were adamant ; neither Lady Byron nor the child should ever see or communicate with Byron again, and they knew what financial arrangements they desired made. Even to Hobhouse they would not hint at the cause of complaint.

From Byron's point of view this made the situation even worse, for he neither knew nor could find out just *what* Annabella knew about him and *what* she did not know. In his trouble Lady Melbourne and Hobhouse were not alone to stand by Byron. " Amongst those who have most warmly, most zealously supported you against every attack, William Lamb has been the foremost." And as for Caroline, she thought of what might perhaps have saved the situation had her impossible offer been accepted.

" . . . suppose people tell you anything is known that you think of consequence—deny it calmly and to all ; do not— do not fancy because every appearance is against you, that it is known. See your wife, and she cannot have the heart to betray you—if she had, she is a devil—and in mercy be calm." [1]

She then made a suggestion : Byron's friends understood that Annabella had found some paper which purported to give an account of certain episodes in Byron's past life. This anonymous document of uncertain content was what was supposed to lie at the basis of Lady Byron's decision. Since everyone knew of Caroline's infatuation for Byron—what then would be more naturally accepted than a corollary hatred for Annabella (it was indeed somewhat of a miracle that she did not hate Lady Byron) ? ; this being so Caroline suggested that she should admit to the authorship of the anonymous document. She would also confess to all the statements being pure inventions of jealousy and revenge.

[1] *Life of Lady Caroline Lamb*—Jenkins.

"Lord Byron, hear me and for God's sake pause before you rashly believe any report others may make. If letter or report or aught else has been malignantly placed in the hands of your wife to ruin you, I am ready to swear I did it, for the purpose of deceiving her. There is nothing, however base it may appear, that I would not do to save you and yours from this.

"O, Lord Byron, let one who has loved you with a devotion almost profane find favour so far as to incline you to hear her. Do not drive things to desperate extremes. Do not, even though you may have the power, use it ill."

It was a fantastic plan after her own heart. It was obviously impossible for Byron to accept her offer ; but it is a matter of interesting speculation as to whether it could not have succeeded in averting the disaster.

Common anxiety had even drawn Lady Melbourne and Caroline together.

"Could you know what your Aunt suffers, you would write or see her. God bless and preserve you."

But Byron, injured and suspicious, had no desire to see any-one. He was at last convinced that his wife really hated him —that being the case he withdrew his opposition to the separa-tion and ordered his lawyers to prepare the deed. The Milbankes began to haggle over the settlements. He made very generous concessions and prepared to leave England for ever. A few days before he was due to sail Caroline happened to be with Mr. Murray, who showed her some verses which Byron had given him to print. They were entitled :

FARE THEE WELL

Fare thee well ! and if for ever,
Still for ever, fare thee well !
Even though unforgiving, never
'Gainst thee shall my heart rebel. . . .

Caroline, so worldly wise for others, so hopelessly careless about herself, knew that if it were published it would create a scandal.—Lord Byron making poetic capital out of his grief —Lord Byron publishing his woes. She felt strongly that it would put the seal of duration upon his separation from his wife to whom many of his friends still hoped to see him reconciled.

She wrote advising him cautiously :

" You will draw ruin on your own head and hers if at this moment you show them. . . . believe me, who, though your *enemy*, though for ever alienated from you, though resolved never more while she lives to see or speak to or forgive, yet would perhaps die to save you."

But Byron was not in the habit of listening to advice, and when he had departed from his custom he could not see that it had done him much good, so he continued in his determination to publish the poem. He was now about to leave the country. Caroline received an invitation to go and see Lady Byron alone. She went in great apprehension, but hoping to do Byron some good. She was horrified at Annabella's appearance. She looked ill and exceedingly unhappy and, indeed, appeared to be broken-hearted.

Caroline did not like meeting the villains of her tragedies. Invariably she had painted them in the most sable shades and, inevitably, when she saw them, her impulsive heart and her keen critical sense made her feel for them. Annabella did not look at all like a devil, not even when she reproached Caroline with having known certain things about Byron at the time of their marriage, which, had they been told to Annabella, would have made her refuse to become his wife. We may have no doubt that Caroline lied to whatever extent it could, in her opinion, profit Byron.

She must too have tried to bring the discussion out of the past and into the present, for we hear of Lady Byron defending herself vehemently against the suggestion that she had deserted Byron. She stated categorically that, on the contrary, he had sent her away. Some one was lying. And, judging by Byron's evidently genuine grief and amazement, and symptoms even of shock, and Annabella's mien of quiet, determined depression, it seemed evident that it must be Lady Byron who was intentionally or unintentionally misrepresenting the truth.

How did she come to do this, and why ? Caroline could find no answer, and enquirers of later years have found a thousand different answers. One thing only is certain. Byron sailed on April 25th, 1816, never to see or hear again from his wife. Caroline longed to see him before he left, but she did not indulge herself.

If only Caroline had been equally well behaved in other directions, her marriage, despite the wishes of Emily Cowper and Frederick Lamb, might now have settled down to a quiet domesticity. But, alas, she seemed fated to be her own worst enemy, to bestrew her life with trivial incidents which she magnified till they had on society the effect of great events. Her pages had long been a feature of the staff of Melbourne House. In 1816 she had, amongst others, a mischievous youth who used to put squibs in the fire in order to irritate old Lord Melbourne. On several occasions Caroline had had to reprimand him, but despite warnings she was once more to find him engaged in preparing his trick. She was angry, and impulsively threw the hard playing ball she held in her hands at his head. The force of the impact cut him on the temple, and the boy screamed out, " Oh, my Lady, you have killed me." Caroline was horrified and dashed out to the porter's lodge to get assistance. As she entered it she shouted, " O, God, I have murdered the page." Her voice carried, some passers-by heard the exclamation. They had heard many odd things about Lady Caroline, but this was the worst.

First she had attacked Byron with a glass dagger, now she had killed her page. She ought evidently to be shut up. Inside the house the boy had his temple bathed. It proved to be only bruised and scratched, and he remained devoted to his mistress and in her service for many years to come. Caroline was thankful it had been no worse. The incident was over so far as the two principal actors were concerned, but outside the walls of Melbourne House it was only just beginning to take its effect. The gossip of the street corners reached the servants' hall ; from there it mounted to the dressing-room, and soon every drawing-room in London buzzed with the news of the fatality.

Emily and Frederick were known to detest their sister-in-law, there was no need to be careful in their presence ; everyone commiserated with them on William's unhappy fate, tied to his virago of a wife. The brother and sister were beside themselves with anger. What was the use of explaining away the incident when all London declared that Lady Caroline had been heard from the street proclaiming the fact that she had killed her page. Perhaps no one really believed that she had committed such an act. But how could they tolerate a woman who made herself the scandal of the town. William must be made to realise that nothing but a legal separation could save the situation, and separations were in fashion this year !

William sat amongst his books. He had begun an intensive study of the Patristic Fathers—he was very indolent, very gentle, very detached, as he listened to Emily's reproaches and Frederick's plans. It was certainly hard for them to have to be nearly allied to a person so wholly antipathetic to their tastes and standards. They told him that Caroline had ruined his career and his reputation, that she had poisoned the lives of their mother and father. They stated definitely and categorically that she was mad, that any doctor would tell him so. William felt the justice of one of their shafts. She did indeed bring ridicule and disrepute on their family, and that was hard indeed on his mother, who had given her life to the building up of the family fortunes, and who now, hating her daughter-in-law, as she undoubtedly did, yet took no part in the plans for her expulsion. For himself, William felt that since he was utterly disillusioned, since he cared nothing for a career or for ambition, since the whole of his life was a sham, it was not of much consequence to have sacrificed it to Caroline's happiness and peace of mind, such as they were.

As for his Caroline herself, she was evidently impossible, he knew it ; often she committed breaches of taste that made him shudder, but there it was—he loved her. It was beyond explanation, it was just a fact. He could tell Emily that she amused him, that her conversation fascinated him, but he could not adduce any reasons for the very simple statement that he did love her for herself, despite being alive to all her errors and frailties.

For some time he put up a brave resistance to the importunities of Emily. Caroline herself was quiet and filled with contrition, She kept to herself, and wisely did not plead her own cause. The fact that people believed her mad had come to her knowledge and had made a great impression upon her mind. Ultimately William was won over by Lady Cowper's arguments. After all, nothing public need be known.

Caroline would simply go down to Brocket and live there quietly, he would see her sometimes ; it would all be for the peace of mind of his family and for her own health. He acquainted her with his decision. She submitted and made no defence. He knew that she was deeply hurt and that she still loved him.

The family assembled at Melbourne House : Lord Melbourne, Lady Melbourne, Emily, Frederick and George. The lawyers arrived and William entered. Everyone was there except Caroline. She had accepted the situation, she was ready to sign any document which William desired her to sign. She had done him much harm and she owed him that act of obedience. She herself was not present at the interview, and after a few minutes a question arose with regard to Augustus which required her decision. William said he should go upstairs to her apartment, where she was waiting to know that her fate had been sealed, and learn her wishes.

What were her feelings as she sat there, expecting to hear her lawyer's footstep as he brought her the deed to sign. What were her feelings when she did hear footsteps and the door opened to admit William. Downstairs they waited — Lord Melbourne, Lady Melbourne, Emily, Frederick, George, and the legal gentlemen. At first they discussed the advantages likely to arise from the act which was being drawn up, then they fell silent ; William was very long in returning. Minutes passed, a quarter of an hour, half an hour, three-quarters of an hour. Caroline must be raising objections, she must be making a scene. Poor William, well, it would be the last scene he would have to endure from her as long as he lived.

But an unconscionable time had elapsed since he had left them. The lawyers were getting fractious. Perhaps if the sitting adjourned to Caroline's room they might cut short her tantrums and rescue William. Slowly, like a procession, they made their way up the narrow winding stairs and along the dark passages till they came to the door of Caroline's salon. It was closed. No sound as of angry words came from within. They paused. Then at last someone of them opened the door gently. In a large armchair sat William Lamb with Caroline on his knees—she was feeding him with thin bread and butter.

The legal gentlemen rolled up their papers, Frederick and

Emily inveighed against the wanton folly of their beloved William, and Lord and Lady Melbourne felt relieved that anything so drastic, so unpleasantly final, should have been avoided.

Once again Caroline had saved herself from the consequences of her indiscretions, but the strain had told on her. Whilst all these long documents were being drawn up against her, whilst she was deprived of William's presence, knowing that all the time his mind was being poisoned against her, whilst all this was going on, she had needed work to distract her mind, and she had found work for herself. Indeed the servants said that her ladyship had sat up late into the night burning the midnight oil, engaged in covering page after page with her scrawling writing. Actually, in the space of a month, she had performed the remarkable feat of writing a three-volume novel. The work contained her own life, as she saw it ; with embellishments.

The title was *Glenarvon*. The villain who gave his name to the book was Byron ; the hero, Lord Avondale, represented William Lamb bedecked with all the virtues, but on account of his free-thinking, working the ruin of his wife Calanthe (who naturally stood for Caroline herself). All the men and women of the Lambs' acquaintance were to be met with in its pages : Lady Granville (Sophia), Lady Oxford (Lady Mandeville), Sir Godfrey Webster (Buchannan), Luttrell (Filume), Allen (Hoiaouskim), and an excellent protrait of Lady Holland in the rôle of the Princess of Madagascar. A few characters were composite. Both the Duchess of Devonshire and Lady Bessborough went to produce Lady Margaret, and Lady Jersey and Lady Collier were united in Lady Augusta.

It has been the habit of critics to describe *Glenarvon* as unreadable, yet in the midst of its fantastic and exaggerated story two virtues emerge clearly. Caroline could delineate character with a shrewd insight into human nature, and her taste and education contributed to an easy and sometimes charming style.

Glenarvon was her apologia—nor was it wholly biassed ; she had a critical sense and a keen interest in the characters of her world. Life interested her sometimes even more than her own justification. Caroline wrote down all that had happened, all she had observed, and then decorated it with ornament and imagery ; but the foundation rested on facts, and she even printed Byron's letter written to her under Lady Oxford's dictation with a mere change of name to disguise its origin. When she had finished the book she felt that she had produced a work of general interest, not indeed a creative work, but all the same, something which, portraying the inevitable, the implacable reaction of one nature upon another and of circumstances upon all, had in it the elements of real life and of real tragedy.

But now that she and William were reconciled to each other the point of the publication of *Glenarvon* no longer existed. It had been meant to provide an enquiry into the circumstances leading up to the severance of their marriage, and now that all was well, she had only to tear it up.

But Caroline had worked on it for a month, and she could not bear to destroy it, instead she revised it. The parts about Lady Melbourne she eliminated, the end she changed. Then she decided to send for a copyist. It was essential to preserve the greatest secrecy and to this end Caroline made use of the most curious subterfuge.

The copyist had never seen Lady Caroline. Caroline therefore arrayed her governess, Miss Welch, in her own clothes, placed her at a harp and endowed her for the evening with her own personality, while she herself dressed as a boy of fourteen, christened herself William Ormonde, and sat at a table covered with manuscripts. The copyist entered, the pseudo Lady Caroline received him and explained that she had sent for him in order to obtain a copy of a work written by the boy Ormonde. The copyist took away the text and promised to return in a week. When he came back, he found the pseudo Lady Caroline alone. She had a sad tale to tell. William Ormonde had been taken ill and had died, but they must continue his work. Now that the poor boy was dead it was more than ever necessary to preserve his book from oblivion.

What the copyist thought concerning this singular tragedy we are not told, but at any rate he was not slow in finishing his task.

Caroline now had a manuscript in a state in which she could

send it to a publisher at any time. Still she hesitated. Then occurred one of those not infrequent scenes which seemed to pursue her. The cause of it is unknown, but the participants were William and Caroline, Lord Melbourne and Lady Bessborough.

Caroline considered that she was being persecuted and her mother insulted.

That night she sent the manuscript to Colburn. The publisher decided to produce it in three volumes, with a cover representing Love contemplating a burning heart, and below the motto " *L'on a trop chéri.*" Caroline was delighted, but enjoined the greatest secrecy. Not one soul knew of the existence of the book excepting Miss Welch, Caroline, Colburn and the copyist, until the day of its publication, when it appears to have been sent, on Caroline's instructions, to most of those who had contributed to its subject matter. William first heard of it from one of his friends—he rushed home to learn the truth and tax Caroline with the production.

For once in his life he was very angry. " Caroline," he said, " I have stood your friend till now, I even think you ill-used, but if it is true this novel is published, and, as they say, against us all, then I will have nothing more to say to you."

Caroline admitted the authorship, William was furious, but when he read the book there is no doubt that his attitude altered. " However sorely it may have tried his sense of humour to see every virtue attributed to himself," there seems no doubt that he was touched at her portrayal of him ; and the other sketches interested him too—perhaps he thought some fair, others generous.

It was terrible to have published such a document—the very thought of it made him shudder. But against that side, perhaps, he weighed the constant persecution to which Caroline had been subject—Emily's criticism and undisguised hatred, George's loudly voiced contention that she was mad, Frederick's determination to make her release William from the tie of marriage, and then perhaps he thought, too, with a little annoyance, of his mother's support of Byron. It had galled him. Perhaps she deserved some slight retribution— he had always regretted her attitude towards Lady Bessborough. And it may be that William was not too ill pleased that his family should see their conduct described in black and white. He had had to suffer from them almost as much as Caroline herself, and possibly *Glenarvon* first made him realise many things which he had vaguely felt but now analysed; made him see more clearly the connexion between cause and effect.

Had Caroline written *Glenarvon* solely for her husband's perusal the work might have justified itself. He took his stand firmly. " I will stand by you or fall with you." Caroline was overjoyed.

. . . " He sees and feels, deeply feels, the unpleasant situation it is for him, but he loves me enough to stand firm as a rock, and to despise such as come forward to ruin one who never hurt them."

But if William were generous, he had come off well in *Glenarvon*—others had not been so kindly treated. George Lamb wrote indignantly demanding a separation. Lord Melbourne declared that he would not live in the same house with his daughter-in-law. Lady Holland was furious with Caroline and Lady Jersey cut her; even Lady Bessborough, though pleading extenuating circumstances, confessed to Hobhouse that she had rather Caroline had died than that she had lived to write it.

Harriet Granville felt too disgusted with her cousin to wish to see her ever again.

But now that William had decided to stand by her, Caroline felt it her duty to go out with him and face the world. The very bitterness of the attacks against her and the rudeness to which she had to submit were powerful factors in attaching her husband more closely to her cause.

What she suffered becomes apparent when we read the letter she wrote to Lord Granville, who perhaps for old sake's sake—since the book must have been as distasteful to him as to Harriet—went up to her at a ball and spoke to her. She professed her overwhelming gratitude for his civility—her genuine affection for her cousins, and she went on to beg him not to judge her too hardly—not to believe in the common gossip about her, but rather to suppose in charity that where her husband, supposedly the injured party, could forgive her, others need not be more severe. Finally she represented to him the necessity in all self-respect for her appearing in public—a proceeding which had evidently been much criticised. The case she made out for herself seemed convincing, had she gone into retirement the injury to William would have been greater. The effort to carry the situation bravely was a debt to him. But we suspect that she paid it at a not excessive cost to herself !

Caroline was sincerely devoted to her cousins, who whatever their good intentions always ended by detesting her.

Harriet indeed overcame her dislike to the extent of visiting Caroline, but the meeting was not a success. She wrote acidly to Hart, who seemed still devoted to his cousin :

" I went yesterday to Whitehall, followed the page and Lady Asgill through the dark and winding passages and staircases. I was received with rapturous joy, embraces, and tremendous spirits. I expected she would have put on an appearance of something, but to do her justice she only displayed a total want of shame and consummate impudence, which, whatever they may be in themselves, are at least better or rather less disgusting than pretending or acting a more interesting part. I was dragged to the unresisting William, and dismissed with a repetition of embassades (*sic*) and professions. I looked, as I felt, stupefied. And this is the guilty, broken-hearted Calanthe who could only expiate her crimes with her death. I mean my visit to be annual." [1]

What were Hart's reactions to these sisterly shafts ? Was he amused to see the Victorianisation of Harriet ? For her, penitents should wear a badge of office ; Magdalenes might be forgiven, but they must keep to their remorseful rôle. He understood Caroline better than anyone, for he and she and William, too, were psychologically of the eighteenth century.

Gradually, the repercussions of *Glenarvon* died away, till Madame de Staël, meeting Byron in some salon, could ask him whether the portrait of Glenarvon was his ? And he could reply, cynically, " If it is my portrait, it cannot be good, for I did not sit long enough."

This year, as though to give one further twist to her emotions, Lady Bessborough received an urgent message to go to see

[1] *The Letters of Harriet Countess Granville.*

Sheridan. The messenger said that he was dying and that he demanded to see her.

For some years he had been bankrupt, living miserably on the donations of his old friends and Lady Bessborough had been amongst the subscribers.

This she had given for the sake of old times, but she had seldom seen him and never voluntarily.

Now as she climbed up the mean and dirty staircase to the squalid little room where Hecca and a few friends were sitting by the dying man, she was filled with horror at the full circle of his life. He had been born obscure, penniless, with few friends—he had achieved great wealth and social success, political fame almost, and now, at the end, he was once more unknown to the gay world, poor, and it seemed as though all his adult life had been only a dream.

When she saw him she knew that he had only a few hours to live ; he registered in her mind only as a suffering human being—the days of their friendship and the days of his persecution were wasted away. But when Sheridan saw her, he saw only the woman who had slighted the utmost powers of his devotion. With his last strength he turned to her and said in a meaning tone that even after his death he should haunt her. Lady Bessborough reproached him bitterly with his lifelong persecution of her.

But Sheridan only answered stubbornly that he did not intend to be forgotten. Realising that her presence was only an irritation to the dying man and an agony to Hecca, she left. Why was life so contrary ? There was she who had had a real friendship for Sheridan, and Hecca who had adored him, and Chéri himself who had *adored* her, and *liked* his second wife, and had wrecked his life in an endeavour to transform their rôles. When she learnt of his death she felt nervous for some nights, but no untoward apparition came to frighten her. She thought with regret of the brilliant, feckless young man who had stuffed his windows with bank-notes to prevent them rattling ; who had left his great speech on Warren Hastings at Deepdene and been obliged to speak extempore, who had " refused to hide his head in a Coronet " and who had insisted on paying large liabilities for which he was not responsible, whilst small debts remained undischarged till the bailiffs had become so much members of the family that they were pressed into handing round the ices. Such charm, and so much talent had finished very sordidly. Hecca lived on for some time, scolding and complaining.

Meanwhile in public matters the year had been one of rejoicing. The income tax had again been abolished and Princess Charlotte had been married in May to Prince Leopold. Her parents' unpopularity had in her early years diminished the interest taken in the Princess. What could be expected of the progeny of the Prince Regent and Caroline of Brunswick ? Then tales began to be noised abroad of the wretchedness of her situation. How she was bullied and humiliated by her jealous and disappointed father, how she was prevented from seeing her mother. Then came the story of her running away, of her summoning her Uncle Sussex, and of how she had been persuaded by him to return under false promises from her father, after which escapade she had been confined as a prisoner and deprived of all her ladies, who had been replaced by friends of her father.

For the first time the country at large began to realise Princess Charlotte, and the first thing they knew about her was that she was high spirited and courageous, and that it seemed that she disliked her father as much as most of the populace did. From that moment her place in the public heart was assured. In society she played little rôle. Her father had not allowed her to appear in public. Everyone was sorry for her, but rumour had it that she was coarse and rough, like her mother.

Then all at once came the question of marriage. Since Princess Charlotte had never " come out " it was with undisguised surprise that England learnt that the Prince Regent was contemplating marrying his daughter to the Prince of Orange.

At first it seemed as though Princess Charlotte would welcome any means of escape from her imprisonment, then it was learnt that she had changed her mind and absolutely refused to marry the Prince of Orange. She had no intention, so she stated, of taking up her residence abroad, and it was evidently impossible for the ruler of the Netherlands to live in England. Everyone applauded her. It became evident that she was intelligent as well as brave. As the only child of

Richard Brinsley Sheridan

the heir-apparent, her duty was to live in the country which she might one day rule.

People said that her father was furious, that he had long been jealous of her popularity with the mob, and had hoped by means of this marriage to induce the people to forget her. Be that as it may, he had to bow before his daughter's unalterable decision. It was evidently no use providing another foreign ruler, a prince without a territory must be sought out, one who would be ready to establish himself in England.

And so, in 1816, there arrived in London Prince Leopold of Saxe-Coburg-Saalfeld, third son of the reigning prince of that name. He was accompanied by Baron Stockmar. The young prince was handsome, he was serious, he was extremely intelligent ; Princess Charlotte had no reason to disobey her father's wishes on this occasion, for she fell in love with Prince Leopold. Everyone was delighted. The marriage promised well both privately and publicly. The Princess was affectionate and good hearted, the young man was wise and patient beyond his years ; there seemed, therefore, a good chance that he would mould his wife into a very strong and dignified woman, who would make an excellent queen whenever she was called to fill the throne.

The marriage took place in the late spring. It was a matter of rejoicing, and to none more truly so than to the bride and bridegroom. After the wedding they went to live at Claremont and settled down to a life of quiet happiness in which they were scrupulously careful not to flaunt their popularity in the faces of their unpopular relations.

In September the Cowpers went abroad, and Caroline had a relief from their constant criticism. Emily sent her mother a dress of *épinglé* velvet from Paris ; she said she had meant it as a present, but " I know, my dearest Mamma, that you would not like me to get into debt." [1]

And if people like the Cowpers were beginning to feel the pinch, the condition of England as a whole was deplorable. Now that the fever of the war had subsided the body of the nation began to realise its wasted and aching condition. Unrest was general, and the situation was summed up in a handbill :

[1] *In Whig Society.*

" Present state of Great Britain : four million people on the point of starvation, four million with a bare subsistence, one and a half million in straitened circumstances, one half million in dazzling luxury." [1]

The year ended with a monster meeting of protest at Spa Fields.

[1] *News from the Past.*

1817

IN spite of discontent and distress the Prince Regent chose
the opening of Parliament in January 1817, as an appropriate occasion to declare his opinion " that the British Constitution was *perfect*," and it was " with surprise and grief "
that he had heard it criticised by his subjects. On his return
to Carlton House he was attacked by a hostile mob, who,
besides shouting abuse at him, succeeded in breaking one
of the windows of the state coach. There was much excitement in Royal circles, much discussion and criticism; but
at Claremont not a word was heard.

Perhaps Princess Charlotte felt with her cousin, Princess
Sophia of Gloucester, " we *may* think, we *must* think, we *do*
think, but we need not speak." Her life was of the quietest,
a walk in the grounds with Leopold, the superintendance of
some charities, and evenings spent in the new and absorbing
pastime called " drizzling,"—whereby Princess and peers,
duchesses and countesses succeeded, after many hours of labour,
in extracting a few grains of gold from old lace or old trimming.

By the 25th of March it was known that Princess Charlotte
was definitely with child. It was a relief to feel that the succession would be secured, and that another life would stand
between Charlotte's wicked uncles and the throne. People
thought of the Duke of York, the Bishop of Osnabrück, but
unfortunately that thought immediately suggested the vision
of Mrs. Clarke and the sale of commissions, of military disasters
and unpleasant enquiries. There was no doubt that as he had
grown older he had become more genial and philanthropic
and developed Whig sympathies; no doubt too that his wife,
who had brought two innovations to " Oatlands " in the shape
of week-end parties and Christmas-trees, was a pleasant,
respectable woman—still the Yorks hardly seemed suited to
represent Great Britain.

Then they thought of the Duke of Clarence : he had been a friend of Nelson and a good sailor, but how about Mrs. Jordan and her countless progeny ?   Had not poor Mr. Cobbett been outraged one night when he dined with the Duke when an army of Fitz-Clarences had been ushered in to the strains of Haydn's *Creation* ?

Next fancy rested upon the Duke of Kent.   Something of a Jacobin it was whispered?—("after his death he was to appear to the spiritualist Owen at a séance, and report the pleasing intelligence that there were no titles in Heaven").   A great martinet (one of the survivors of his regiment remarked fifty years afterwards, " The Duke of Kent, yes, I remember him well.   He was a very bad man.   He would not let us drink ").   Something of an eccentric—had he not begged leave of parliament to dispose of his estate by lottery ?

And after the Duke of Kent came Ernest, Duke of Cumberland, so hated even by his own family that when a clergyman reading out the commandments in front of the Duke of Cambridge came to the words, " Thou shalt do no murder," Adolphus remarked loudly, " I don't, I leave that to my brother Ernest."

And as for Cambridge and Sussex—the former, despite his Whig principles, his respectable though morganatic marriages and his championship of his niece, never enjoyed any popularity, whilst the latter, who was to spend almost twenty-five years in Hanover, was only known to Englishmen by the doubtful notoriety gained by having urged the Prince of Wales to marry Caroline.

Indeed none of the brothers seemed suited to represent nineteenth-century England, and the people looked gratefully towards Princess Charlotte and wished her well.

In the spring the Granvilles went to Paris.   There they found Madame de Staël dying, and Madame Récamier still beautiful.

Wellington arrived in June.   He talked a lot about Caroline and said that she amused him to the greatest degree, " especially her accidents."

Harriet did not care for these praises of her cousin and she prided herself on obtaining an equal success with the Duke by the opposite method of frigid hauteur.   Neither did she care very much for the accounts which Lord Gower brought them on his return from Rome of the Duchess Elizabeth. She was now established in Italy, and busily engaged in superintending new excavations. She was reverting to type now that the pressure of financial and social oppression were over. Taking to her father's ways with more than his sanity. Looking back on her early life she felt that despite the struggle, or because of it, she had done well for herself. To her son she wrote a description of her vicissitudes :

" I was without guide, a wife and no husband, a mother and no children ; travelling for my health which was impaired by sorrow, and by myself alone to steer through every peril that surrounds a young woman so situated : books, the arts, and a wish to be loved and approved ; an enthusiastic friendship for these my friends ; a proud determination to be my letter of recommendation, these with perhaps manners that pleased, realised my projects and gained me friends wherever I have been." [1]

All that had been some twenty or twenty-five years ago, and now she was in Rome and " digging *à qui mieux mieux*," with Souza and Cardinal Consalvi. " Bringing up great curiosities," " adored by all the artists," whom she protected, as her father had done, employed constantly, and " paid magnificently." So that even the innkeepers all along the road enquired of any passing English, " Connaissez vous cette noble Dame ? " And soon a medal was to be struck in her honour.

But sometimes Rome got hot and dusty and she longed. for " five quiet months at dear Chatsworth," and she communicated her thoughts to her stepson, who alone amongst the Cavendishes really appreciated her.

Harriet heard of the proposal and became alarmed. She wrote gravely to Hart :

" Do you correspond with the Duchess, and have you carefully avoided pressing her to be much with you, or giving her any hold of that kind upon you ? My fears are on your part the difficulty of ever saying to her, ' No, you shall not,' . . . harshness does not belong to your nature."

But Hart was busy making a zoo at Chiswick, and the arrival of his elephants and kangaroos were of much greater concern to him than the desires of his stepmother, or the fears of his sister.

[1] *The Two Duchesses.*   [2] *Letters of Harriet Countess Granville.*

The year wore on quietly. The Bessboroughs were at Roehampton, the Lambs at Brocket, Byron abroad and Annabella in retirement. After the terrible storms of 1816 an infinite calm seemed to have descended upon them. The month of November was looked forward to with pleasurable excitement.

On November 2nd an article in *The Observer* stated that : " Few domestic events have excited a more lively, and, at this moment, a more impatient interest than the expected accouchement of her Royal Highness the Princess Charlotte." But the initiated were anxious. Almost the same day Lady Granville wrote :

" We are all much interested for poor Princess Charlotte. I fear it is bad. Lord Gower writes word there is a difference of opinion. They are uncertain whether she has twins and whether she will have strength to go through the labour." [1]

At Claremont all were anxious. The Princess's general health was bad. Sir Richard Croft, the Royal accoucheur, was present and other doctors ; as well as Stockmar, the Prince's physician. The foreigner was uneasy, the English doctors were timid, all was not well, but they dared try no other expedient than bleeding their patient. Stockmar thought her very weak, and doubted if she would survive the ordeal. Leopold was distracted by his friend's doubts and implored him to intervene. Stockmar made suggestions, but he was a foreigner, she was the only child of the Prince of Wales, and he could do no more.

When the labour came on it was frightful. In vain the doctors administered brandy until the Princess protested she would have no more. At 9 p.m. on November 5th she was delivered of a still-born boy. She had borne the agony with great self-control and patience, but four and a half hours afterwards she collapsed and died. Everyone was horrified. And Lady Hawkesbury (now Lady Liverpool, the wife of the Prime Minister), who had been so eloquent about the deaths of Nelson and Pitt, must be quoted ; for eleven years she had not blunted her pen or diminished her appreciation of the macabre.

[1] *The Letters of Harriet Countess Granville.*

" November 7th,
Walmer Castle.

" The shock was really almost too much for me, and I
felt afraid I was going to add to poor dear Lord Liverpool's
painful feelings. He set off for London last night. I never
saw him more overwhelmed, this is a blow indeed, a dreadful
one in *every* way. But He who ordered it can make the chastise-
ment a salutary one, and I trust He *will* do so, and that we
shall have humility, and see the full extent of the unsteadiness
of all worldly happiness and greatness.

" Prince Leopold has a very pious mind, thank God for it !
The Regent received the tidings with feelings and resignation.
On first hearing the very worst from Lord Bathurst he struck
his forehead with both hands in silent agony, and then bowed
his head (still in silence). He then held out his hand to Lord
Bathurst, and calling his brother the Duke of York to him he
threw himself into his arms. How thankful He must now feel
that He allowed her to marry according to her choice, and that
latterly he and she were on the very best terms.

" He entreated the Duke of York to go to Claremont with
every sort of kind offer to his poor son-in-law. Poor, poor
Claremont ! What excesses of happiness and of misery had
it not witnessed ! My dear sister, I can write no more, when
I think of all she said to me the last few times I saw her, of
her hopes, her happiness, of their real domestic comfort, of
their regular charity, good example, what have we but blind,
humble submission to support us ? Addio, Addio." [1]

The calamity was taking on overwhelming proportions in
the public mind. On November 9th *The Observer* remarks :

" We continue to live most grievously afflicted : numbers
of females have been troubled with hysterics and other fits
since the first intelligence was communicated to them of the
death of the Princess." [2]

Considerate friends wrote accounts of the funeral to those
who were absent :

". . . The crowd, bustle, struggle for places, etc., and all
the military in the Church took off very much from the
solemnity of the ceremony, and that parts of it were even

---

[1] *The Letters of the First Lady Wharncliffe.*
[2] *News from the Past.*

ludicrous. Poor dear Prince Leopold sat at the head of the coffin, apparently in an agony of grief, covering his face with his hands, and *now* and *then* relieving his feelings by a flood of tears. . . .

" *P.S.* Of course you will immediately know that Princess Charlotte is the cause of black wax, they say it would be wrong to seal with red." [1]

The Royal Dukes began to take second thoughts on the subject of marriage. Society dismissed the probability of the Regent's attempting to obtain a divorce, and people said it was a great shame that the Queen had not troubled to be with her grand-daughter at Claremont, and that she was an unnatural old woman.

[1] *The Letters of Sarah Lady Lyttelton.*

1818

THE mourning for Princess Charlotte was as universal as it was sincere. It was expressed in the most diverse ways, witness the Black Ball which took place at Haverford-west in January 1818, at which the rooms were hung with crêpe, lit by black wax candles ornamented with cypress leaves and ornamented by " three transparent ones with the names of the lamented Princess Charlotte inscribed upon them."

In February Caroline was worried by a most disagreeable occurrence.

The press was full of a rumour that the young Duke of Devonshire was no Cavendish at all, but a changeling. To have her beloved Hart teased was bad enough, but to be told that her *own Glenarvon* went far to confirm the rumour was worse. There was some reference in it to " Lady Margaret's " having changed a child and this was taken to refer to an act of the late Duchess of Devonshire. Caroline was vigorous in her denials and extremely penitent for the harm she had unwittingly caused.

She was extremely concerned about her cousin's health. One night she appeared at the opera with a beautifully embroidered sac on her arm. " What have you there ? " asked Lady Bessborough, to which Caroline replied, " Well, dear Mamma, it is a piece of very curious rhubarb, quite like a bon-bon. I brought it to recommend it to Hartington. It will do him all the good in the world, Mamma, he is looking so ill." [1]

That the peace offering was accepted may not be doubted, for Hart bore Caroline no grudge for the scandal and remained her devoted friend. Emily Cowper was less charitable in her comments. " One cannot," she wrote, " pity her for any annoyance that comes to her through that infernal book, as

[1] *Book of the Boudoir*—Lady Morgan.

it is so richly deserved." But all the same Lady Cowper, who had fought so bitterly against her sister-in-law, was at this moment engaged in doing her a good turn. The subject was a matter of no less grave importance than Caroline's admission to the sacred precincts of Almack's.

This early nineteenth-century night club was run by a committee of lady patronesses, including Lady Jersey and Emily Cowper, and without their consent no one could enter its portals. The obtaining of tickets was, therefore, a matter of intense rivalry and jealousy.

> Hence the petitions and addresses,
> So humble to the Patronesses,
> The messages and notes, by dozens,
> From their Welsh Aunts twentieth cousins,
> Who hope to get their daughters in
> By proving they are *Founders Kin.*
>
> LUTTRELL.[1]

Since the publication of *Glenarvon* Caroline had been deprived of her membership. But now, as Emily Cowper wrote :

" She has been quieter lately, as her only object is to push herself on in the world, which is, I assure you, very uphill work, though William gives her all the help he can, and now as he *will* stick to her I think it better to give her any lift I can, for her disgrace only falls, more or less, on him. I have, therefore, fought a battle for her and put her name down to Almack's Balls in spite of Lady Jersey's teeth. Let people do as they like in their own *private* society, but I think it hard to exclude a person from a ball where six hundred people go if they really are received everywhere." [2]

Did Emily Cowper find some little satisfaction in using her influence to make society accept Lady Bessborough's daughter ? That is as may be, but in any case she had her own very genuine anxieties at the time. Lady Melbourne was ill, and whatever may have been Emily's sentiments for her friends or acquaintances, her devotion to her family cannot be questioned. In February she wrote : " Mamma, I think, continues

---

[1] *London in Regency and Early Victorian Times*—Batsford.
[2] *In Whig Society*—Mabell Countess of Airlie.

getting a little better, but slowly, and I am afraid will not be well till there is a change of weather, which I rather hope from the sun to-day, is beginning."

Alas, she was too optimistic. No change of weather brought any aid to Lady Melbourne, and on the 16th of April she died. To William, her loss was a catastrophe. He had disappointed her in every way, in his career, in his marriage, in his intellectual attainments. But she understood him, and she was absolutely devoted to him. Worldly, violent, unscrupulous, as she had been in many ways, her love for her second son was great and she never gave him bad advice. She had kept him out of many scrapes, and despite her dislike of her daughter-in-law she had been of late a factor rather for the solidity of his marriage than for its dissolution. She had begged him to take his politics seriously, she had implored him to lay a foundation for the great career to which she believed him destined, and, it is a strange irony that the date of his beginning to work perseveringly coincides almost exactly with the death of the one person who really cared for his honour.

With what feelings did Lady Bessborough learn of the disappearance of her enemy ? Such an old rivalry, going back as it did almost to her girlhood, would leave a sense of something missing ; and then Lady Melbourne, hard as she had been to Caroline, had known how to control her, and how to bully old Lord Melbourne and William, and it *had* been her intention that her son's marriage should last. So even her opponents regretted Lady Melbourne. There were very few left now of the old Devonshire House set. " Prinny " remained, and Bess, and Lady Salisbury and Lady Bessborough —that was all.

Byron, from Italy, wrote letters of real sorrow. " The time is past in which I could feel for the dead, or I should feel for the death of Lady Melbourne, the best and kindest and ablest female I ever knew, old or young." [1] That he could write this, despite the failure of his marriage, of which she had been the promoter, argues that the young man realised how sincere she had been in their curious friendship.

In May the public were interested by the Duke of Kent's journey to Germany for the purpose of marrying Prince

[1] Lord Byron's Correspondence.

323

Leopold's sister. He was very near to the throne, and his choice was a popular one.

Caroline and William had retired to Brocket for the period of their mourning. Lady Morgan's letters from Paris to Caroline and to her friends gave them mild amusement. The price of clothes was a source of incessant correspondence : Paris was proved to be very dear. " To have a plain dress made up cost a guinea and a half in France and, whereas, to buy a little muslin gown in London cost only ten shillings, in Paris it cost forty shillings. On the other hand four pairs of satin shoes could be bought in Paris for fifteen shillings which did not seem excessive, and there were some " tricoté " silk scarves which the French wore round the head in two bows, which were really very elegant."

Then Lady Morgan wished to know whether her friends were " in love with the warm bath, a practice now becoming fashionable." And she told them in horrified confidence that when she had mentioned to a French lady that her sister was about to increase her already immense family, the woman had replied : " Pourquoi fait-elle ce vilain métier la ? Des femmes comme il faut, never have more than two or three, at most."

In return for all this gossip there was little to say of London. Berlioz's *Faust* had been given and considered very poor ; but it was on this occasion that the sole lustre of the house was for the first time lit with gas. And this phenomenon was said to be " beyond all description and well worth going any distance to see."

There was a *bon mot* of the Miss Berrys " that no friendship could cross the North of Oxford Street," and news of two changes of address. " The Charlevilles exchanged their *maisonette* in Berkeley Square for Queensberry House," and the Stuart Wortleys bought what is now Crewe House, in Curzon Street, for £12,000.

In June 1818 the country was in the throes of a General Election. Lord Liverpool's Government having voted £1,000,000 for the erection of new churches, and £400,000 to the Spanish Government in compensation for the abolition of their slave trade, having proposed annuities of £6,000 per annum to the Duke of Kent and to his brothers the Dukes of

Clarence and Cambridge (who had decided to follow his example and marry German Princesses), feeling that it had done so much for religion and humanity, dissolved itself on the 10th of June.

The result of the General Election was not in doubt. It was bound to be a Tory victory, and only the extent of the victory was in question. The principal interest centred as usual round the Westminster Election, where this time Sir Francis Burdett, supported by Sir Samuel Romilly, stood for universal suffrage, annual parliaments and voting by ballot.

George Lamb was one of their opponents. The scene at the hustings, " partook," according to the *Morning Chronicle*, " of that Saturnalian licence, which on all occasions, distinguishes our popular elections." [1]

When the new parliament assembled, it was seen that the Whigs had gained thirty seats. But this success was sadly marred by the suicide of Sir Samuel Romilly in November of the same year.

His death, the death of the Queen, the general poverty and unrest in the country, gave a depressing colour to the end of the year. Harriet Granville echoed its tone when she wrote to her sister.

" I dined at Cavendish Square (with the Bessboroughs) yesterday. It was rather a mournful ceremony, ' *les convives* ' were all *tristes*, the room looked funereal, and Rover howled and whined without intermission." [2]

A dinner the day before at Mr. Canning's was somewhat more *lugubre*.

And Lady Caroline loudly complained.

" I see no end to the mourning (for Princess Charlotte) and really believe we shall end by wearing it of an *evening* as long as the Prince Regent. I hear everybody goes still in black gloves to the Pavilion." [3]

---

[1] *News from the Past.*
[2] *The Letters of Harriet Countess Granville.*
[3] *The Letters of the First Lady Wharncliffe.*

1819

THE elections had brought Caroline a friend of a new description. In her desire to be of use to her brother-in-law George, she had written to Mr. Godwin, the unitarian philosopher, requesting his support. The letter was a purely formal one : " Lady Caroline Lamb presents her compliments to Mr. Godwin, and fears his politics will incline him to refuse her request of his interest for Mr. George Lamb. She hopes, however, it will not offend if she solicits." [1] It did not offend. Mr. Godwin was one of those philosophers who consider that admiration, bed and board is but a natural tribute to their intellect. He had no intention of supporting George Lamb, but his refusal was one which was calculated to please Caroline and stimulate her interest.

" MY DEAR MADAM,

" You have mistaken me. Mr. George Lamb has my sincere good wishes. My creed is a short one.

" I am in principle a Republican, but in practice a Whig. But I am a philosopher, that is, a person desirous to become wise, and I aim at that object by reading, writing and a little conversation. But I do not mix in the business of the world and I am too old to alter my course, even at the flattering invitation of Lady Caroline Lamb."

Two factors in the letter went straight to Caroline's heart— " I am a person desirous to become wise " . . . that fact he stated—" I am a person desirous to talk about myself." This he implied.

Caroline, not unnaturally, felt attracted towards a character whose traits so nearly resembled her own. Alas, she forgot, as she was always to forget, that two people desiring to talk about themselves rarely remain friends. She invited Godwin

[1] *William Godwin and his Companions.*

to Brocket. Perhaps he could help her and also help Augustus.

For once the relations-in-law had nothing to criticise. The father of Mary Shelley, who, thirty-five years before in proposing to Harriet Lee, had written " it is more, much more the image of what you might be, and are fitted to be, that charms me than the contemplation of what you are," and who went on to explain that in the event of her accepting him " he would employ his day in . . . the refined . . . expression of mutual attachment,"—was no Byron. Though it was true that he showed the greatest aversion for the bonds of marriage, he was the friend of Charles Lamb, who called him " a good natured heathen, with an abominable nose," and the owner of a book-shop (under the name of Edward Baldwin.)

He might be somewhat of a bore—and somewhat of a sponge —but no scandal was likely to arise from Caroline's friendship with him. And if she had pleasure in seeing him, she had still more pleasure in corresponding with him. She wrote detailed and often vividly accurate descriptions of herself.

" . . . yet do not fancy that I am here in rude health, walking about and being notable and bountiful. I am like the wreck of a little boat, for I never come up to the sublime and the beautiful,—merely a little, gay, merry boat, which perhaps stranded itself at Vauxhall or London Bridge ; or wounded without killing itself as a butterfly does in a tallow candle. There is nothing marked sentimental or interesting in my career. All I know is that I was happy, well, rich, and surrounded by friends. I have now one faithful, kind friend in William Lamb, two more in my father and brother, but health, spirits, all else are gone,—gone how ? O, assuredly not by the visitation of God, but slowly, gradually, by my own fault." [1]

Her health was undermined, but, though about this time she wrote " The loss of what one adores affects the mind and heart," she had not yet lost her sense of humour, for on another occasion she wrote to Godwin :

" I value my exalted relations for what they dare to do and have done, and I fear nobody except the Devil, who certainly has all along been very particular in his attentions to me, and has sent me as many trials as ' Job.' "

[1] Godwin Correspondence.

In January Emily Cowper gave a most successful Childs' Ball at Panshanger. It irked Caroline to feel that she and William must live in a shameful retirement, whilst her sister-in-law cut a figure in the world. Augustus was tall and handsome, she tried to persuade herself that he was like any other boy of twelve. She concealed his attacks which were extremely frequent, and assured everyone that he was now completely cured.

Having attended Emily's Ball she determined to show the family that William had no cause to be ashamed of his wife and son. In a fit of pique she sat down and wrote out hundreds of invitations for a date only three days ahead.[1] The roads were blocked with snow; there would be no moon on the night of the Ball—everyone refused. Caroline could never admit defeat—she promptly put the party off to the following night. Only six people came besides the Cowpers, and Emily's account of the affair is steeped in gall. " Cherubina had been out-doing herself in absurdity . . . six hundred people had been expected, musicians had been sent for from London, the extravagance was reckless, and William was fretted to death and liable to fly into a passion at any moment ; but, notwithstanding all this, he let her have her way."

Poor William had cause enough for frayed nerves. His political career seemed at a standstill, his finances were in an inextricable muddle, and though Caroline wrote a long treatise on how to economise in the running of the stables at Brocket, she rose from her escritoire to plan a party like the recent fiasco, which was not only ruinous but also ridiculous, and then Augustus, to whom he was very much attached, showed—he knew it without doubt—no sign of improvement. The boy was not actually imbecile but, as Torrens says, there was " rather a constant promise of a maturity which was watched with unceasing anxiety, but never came." [2] And then in addition, there were his recurrent fits.

Two years before, in 1817, William had asked the physician, Sir Gilbert Blair, to recommend a tutor for Augustus, who should at the same time be a doctor. Robert Lee offered his services and was accepted. William told him with what

[1] *The Letters of Lady Palmerston.*
[2] *Life of Lord Melbourne*—Torrens.

seems a touch of irony that the Greek and Latin classics were to be the chief subjects of study. And so from 1817 onwards Dr. Lee formed a part of the Lambs' establishment. A discreet young man, with indifferent powers of memory, he kept a surprisingly uninteresting diary recording the conversations which he heard at the dinner-table : How " Lady C. thought it would be an improvement if ladies lived in different houses from their husbands and only simply called on them." [1] How Mr. Sheridan remarked that it would be delightful " to have cards left on one by one's husband—that before the Revolution this was the case in France—the house was divided completely. How Mr. Lamb said that it was because it was so bad it was all swept away. How Mr. Lamb also said that there would be no doubt it was advisable to marry, but that those who are not rich ought not to marry at all," as " people confined to one room, like pigeons in a basket, must fight."

Rarely did he chronicle an expression of opinion regarding people, but he did report that when Caroline mentioned to William that her sister-in-law, Lavinia Spencer, was going abroad, Lamb remarked, " May she go, and the devil go with her ; she is a cold, hard person."

Already Hart was in Rome, and Willie Ponsonby, and Lord and Lady Bessborough, besides the Duchess of Devonshire. In the cold spring of 1819 only Parliament and lack of funds kept William and Caroline from joining them.

After Bess's archæological enthusiasm and the Ponsonbys' appreciative letters, Aunt Lavinia's epistles struck a surprising note. From the first town in Italy she wrote :

" You are already apprized of our having passed the Simplon. . . . Oh may I never see rock, torrent, cascade, or snow-topped mountain again. . . ." [2] Nor was Milan considered any compensation for the hardship endured. " I went out yesterday to see the Duomo, York Minster is worth a hundred such." By the time she reached Rome her temper was evidently not of the sweetest. " That witch of Endor, the Duchess of Devon, has been doing mischief of another kind to what she has been doing all her life, by pretending to dig for the good of the public in the Forum. She, of course,

[1] *Diary of Doctor Robert Lee.*
[2] *Letters of Sarah Lady Lyttelton.*

has found nothing, but has brought up a quantity of dirt and old horrors, and will not be at the expense of carrying it away and filling it in, so that she has defaced every place where she has poked. She is the laughing stock of all Rome with her pretensions to Maecenas-ship." And later she wrote from Naples in equal displeasure :

" Oh England ! England ! dear, clean, delicate, virtuous England, catch me out of you when once I get to you ! Lord S. is, thank God, gone to kill pigs with the King to-day ! "

If the letter-bag provided amusement for the inhabitants of Brocket, the newspapers recorded events of greater interest. One day Caroline read :

" May 24, 1819, at Kensington Palace, H.R.H. the Duchess of Kent, of a daughter. Present the Arch Bishop of Canterbury, the Duke of Sussex, the Duke of Wellington, the Bishop of London, Mr. Canning, and Mr. Vansittart." [1]

So the old King had a grandchild and the unappreciated Cumberland was once again further from the succession. But the universal pleasure at this news was soon forgotten in a series of tragic events. Poverty and the spread of new ideas of reform had made the country restive. The election had stimulated the elements of discontent, and though the members were returned, meetings continued all over the country.

In August, at St. Peter's Fields in Manchester, 80,000 workmen and their families gathered together, armed with sticks, and wearing caps of liberty, to demand the abolition of the corn laws, universal suffrage, annual parliaments, and voting by ballot. The meeting was known to have been prepared from some time. It had not been forbidden, its conduct was perfectly orderly ; but suddenly, amongst the demonstrators, there appeared a regiment of yeomanry, and in another moment the cavalry were ordered to charge.[2] Three or four hundred people were injured, several were trampled to death in the panic which ensued, and three were cut down with sabres. The meeting was dispersed, and the indignation in the country was general. Meetings of protest were called. But the Government approved, the Prince Regent approved, and

[1] *News from the Past.*
[2] For account of Peterloo see Lady Wharncliffe.

Lord FitzWilliam, who had attended a meeting in York, was dismissed from his Lord Lieutenancy. William Lamb disapproved exceedingly, but now that the flood gates of disaffection had been loosed he realised that strong measures were needed to stand up to the consequences.

And so when Lord Liverpool brought in the Six Acts which were to preserve the country from insurrection, and which provided "against the training of persons in the use of arms and the practice of military evolutions," which made the laws against seditious libels more secure, and which were designed "to prevent delay in the administration of justice in cases of misdemeanour," Lamb voted for the Government and against his own party, thereby losing much prestige with the Whigs. Already he was developing that independence of party which was to be attributed by his enemies to opportunism, to cynicism, to anything but the simple fact that he always acted in accordance with his own judgment. As Torrens says of him :

"He had no exclusive faith in religion, or politics, or law. He could argue eloquently, lucidly, willingly, for Anglicanism as against the Curia, the Kirk or the Tabernacle ; but nobody could convince him that there was not a deal of good in all these, and that kindly honourable and learned men might not honestly consider their pretensions superior. He would banter alternately Tories and Radicals for opposite faults . . . but he would not forget his inherent weaknesses and often infirmities, or be mesmerised into that delusion that patriotism and wisdom were of the Whigs alone. And the bitter experiences of his private life had sown tares in the field of his affections, till at length he had made up his mind there was nothing for it but to let them grow together with the harvest." [1]

In later life he was to say that no man could hope to be anything until he had discovered that he was a fool. And the year 1819 seems to mark the full flood of the tide of disillusionment. The breaking down period of his life was over. He had nothing left to lose in hopes or illusions, and faced with this total destruction of his conceptions of life he seems, with the vote on the Six Acts, to have said " Yes " to existence,

[1] *Life of Lord Melbourne*—Torrens.

to have made an affirmation, as though in his mind the time had come to see what he could piece together out of the wreck of existence and belief.

Old Lady Melbourne had taught her children to be worldly. But William, though he might " roll and snore," " loll and swear," was no cynic ; he felt now that he had no great panacea, no quick Heaven on Earth to offer to his compatriots ; he might do them some little service in righting the wrongs of individual cases, in dealing with the circumstances of life and not with its philosophy. And thus he laid the foundation of that great career for which his mother had looked with such unchanging certainty, little thinking on what a field of ruin it would be raised.

By Christmas the King was known to be very ill. Lady Bessborough and the Duchess must have reflected on the irony of a fate which had robbed the heir-apparent of a throne, when he might perhaps have filled it with credit and which seemed now to offer it to him at a moment in which he was least capable of fulfilling its duties.

1 8 2 0

ON the 30th of January, 1820, England was startled by the death of George III. Startled because the sixty years of his reign stretched back into a period which very few could remember; only venerable octogenarians had any recollection of an England under another monarch, and despite the long years of his illness and incapacity he was regretted.

We have no letter from Lady Liverpool on the death of her " dear and valuable " King, but her sister, Lady Erne, gives us a faint reflection of what must have been her sentiments in :

" It is quite soothing to me, dearest Caroline, to find you feeling so much like myself about our dear and excellent king. England will not seem England without him. He was exactly the right character for us, and long will it be, I fear, before England holds such another." [1]

The newspapers endorsed her views; and George III was everywhere extolled to the detriment of his eldest son; even in the realm of the arts his taste was declared superior : " His Majesty's chief amusement, it is known, was music, and that of the highest character for grandeur and sublimity of composition, by which he not only gratified a well trained ear, but exalted his devotional feelings : but he had little relish for the meretricious bravuras of the Italian stage, and less for the fantastic and bewitching movements of the ballet. Had the voluptuous waltz been introduced at his Court, the royal frown would constantly have forbidden its repetition ; its German origin could not have saved it," wrote *The Observer*.

The situation in regard to the succession became suddenly, unexpectedly critical, for on the day of his father's death the Prince Regent was so seriously ill that he had to be bled to

[1] *The Letters of the First Lady Wharncliffe*.

the extent of two and twenty ounces ; and it looked as though the Duke of York's conviction that he was destined to the throne was about to be justified. Lady Liverpool, in whom we must, alas, infer an equal attachment to any royalty, wrote gravely : " The King has rallied, yet we rejoice in trembling." But it is to be feared that more people trembled than rejoiced at the news. George IV was exceedingly unpopular at the time of his accession, and the situation with regard to his wife caused some alarm.

Immediately after the news of the King's death, *The Morning Chronicle* published a letter written by her on the 31st of December. It ran as follows :

" I have been much alarmed about a rumour relating to our ever beloved and lamented King's health ; if, in the event of anything happening to our beloved monarch, I put my only trust in the generosity of the great nation to protect me from the hands of my enemies." [1]

If the construction was a little peculiar, the intention was evident. The Queen Consort intended to claim her rights, and most of the press and all " the mob " supported her.

On the 31st of January *The Observer* had printed the following paragraph :

" By the death of His Majesty George the Third, the late Princess of Wales becomes Queen Consort, instanter, and that without the ceremonial of a coronation. . . . As Queen Consort, her Majesty will immediately demand (if not previously offered it) a suitable establishment from Parliament."

When the new King had recovered from his illness he viewed the pronouncements of his wife and of the press with extreme disgust. He was still anxious to divorce Caroline and absolutely determined that she should never have her rights as Queen Consort. He approached Lord Liverpool on the subject. This statesman and all his Cabinet were of opinion that it would be extremely unwise to force an issue. They advocated a generous offer of funds provided Caroline would reside abroad. Only if she were to land in England were they prepared to consider the Sovereign's personal grievances.

But in February an event took place which carried public

[1] Quoted *News from the Past.*

attention away from the sordid details of royal matrimonial difficulties. It was no less than the discovery of a plot to blow up the entire Cabinet and various other personages who were to attend a government dinner at Lord Harrowby's House in Grosvenor Square. When this unpleasant undertaking had been accomplished, it was intended to send up a rocket which was to be a signal for the mob to rise and attack the Bank, whilst another section was to storm the gaols and release the prisoners. This at least was the story which the Government spy, Allen, brought to Lord Liverpool. The members of the dinner-party were informed, but were vowed to the greatest secrecy.

All the preparations went on in Grosvenor Square for a brilliant reception, but when the evening came, the guests who had assembled at Fife House never left it ; and early in the evening a party of police made their way to Cato Street, Edgware, where, in a loft above a stable, it was said that the conspirators had established their head-quarters. Surprised in their retreat, the plotters offered resistance. One constable was killed and several more were injured, but Arthur Thistlewood, the head of the gang, was arrested, together with a number of his accomplices.

A wave of anxiety swept over the country. It was only a few days since England had learnt of the assassination of the Duc de Berri, as he entered the Paris Opera House ; and now this terrorist plot in London, though abortive, seemed to echo it. Lady Harrowby was Granville's sister, Granville himself would have been at the dinner. Harriet and Lady Bessborough shuddered at the thought, and Lady Liverpool, whose husband was to have been the principal victim of the plot, could find no words vehement enough to describe her emotions. But her sister, the Duchess Elizabeth, wrote from Rome to their sister, Lady Erne, voicing the general feeling of oppression.

" It is too true what you say, that one must learn to bear with the loss of all feeling of security. We were scarcely recovering from the feeling of horror which the Duc de Berri's assassination had given us, when this newspaper from England really threw us into consternation. . . . Dear Sister, I hope you will stay a little in Town, these are such anxious times, and if one is alone every circumstance is magnified, and grows more appalling. Stay in Town, it will do you all good. Louisa, Lord Liverpool and yourself." [1]

For some weeks the tread of life was sobered, but by the month of May the measure had grown gay once more. And ladies were able to think of lighter matters

" The great event which at present occupies the public mind is the abolition of hoops, announced in Tuesday's *Gazette*, preparatory to the Drawing Room fixed for the 15th of next month at Buckingham House. I fear we shall regret them, despite their unbecoming appearance. They had the effect of leaving a little room among the Drawingroom crowds."

Despite such an innovation, when Harriet Granville met Lady Cowper she found her " thin, pale, nervous and bored." But if the introduction of hoops and the discovery of treason could not dissipate Em's boredom, an event was soon to take place which put her and all the other ladies of England into a frenzy of excitement. On the 9th of June she wrote: " The Queen has given us all a fillup. Some are sorry, some glad, but all on tip-toe to know the result." [2] For this event was nothing less than the arrival of the Queen Consort in England. *The Times* greeted her in a sympathetic vein:

" Her Majesty has before engaged the public attention, has before challenged a public scrutiny, and has before retained her position in life. But then she had the virtuous King of England, George the Third, for her protector : she had her child living, the heir to the royal crown of these dominions, she had Mr. Perceval for her defender, an acute, sincere and pious man." [3]

The Government were placed in an extremely disagreeable position. Lord Liverpool had promised to act if the lady set foot in England, and now George IV was demanding the fulfilment of this promise. Meanwhile, Caroline was being received with enthusiasm by " the mob " and with sympathy by half the country. The Government placed Brandenburg House at Hammersmith at her disposal, and Lord Thanet obtained for her a house in South Audley Street. Lord

[1] *The Letters of the First Lady Wharncliffe.*
[2] *The Letters of Lady Palmerston.*
[3] *News from the Past.*

Thanet's support meant Lord Cowper's support, for the latter had become the devoted admirer of this powerful and eccentric old nobleman and followed him in all his enthusiasms, and by this means Lady Cowper was to find herself, much to her disgust, in a Queenite household.

On the 6th of June the King insisted that the House of Lords should hold an enquiry into the Queen's conduct and endeavour to establish a cause of divorce. The peers were unwilling to push things to such lengths. Wellington and Castlereagh for the King, Brougham and Denman for the Queen, met and endeavoured to find a compromise. Then Mr. Wilberforce tried his hand at the business and bore an offer to the Queen : it was suggested that Caroline should go away, and that she should receive £50,000 per annum and all royal honours for so doing. In return, she must submit to having her name left out of the Liturgy. The Queen was contemptuous of such an arrangement, and so, on July the 8th, despite many forebodings of failure, the Bill of Pains and Penalties, which was designed to deprive Caroline of her title and dissolve her marriage, was introduced into the Upper Chamber.

Everyone was sorry that things should have come to such a pass, except the two protagonists themselves. They appear to have been delighted at the prospect of revenge, and each was so sure of their success that neither played their part so as to increase their popularity. Whilst Caroline drove through the streets in an open carriage, sporting pink roses in her hair, a large black wig, and heavy black eyebrows, and accompanied by her chief supporter, Alderman Wood, and that dubious child, Billy Austin, the King refused to show himself at all and sulked in his cottage at Windsor, with no other amusements than ejecting trespassers and listening with anxiety for the approach of Lady Conyngham's carriage.

The whole nation was now involved in what was fundamentally a private quarrel ; but since the rivals were public personages, people had a right to pick sides, and the equipages which drove up to Brandenburg House were watched with avid curiosity. Lord Thanet called and, as was to be expected, Lord Cowper, Lords FitzWilliam, Essex and Darnley followed in their wake. The Duke of Gloucester came for the sake of old friendship, so he said, and Prince Leopold came, as was perhaps only civil—to see his mother-in-law.

But most frequent of all visitors was Lady Jersey, and perhaps alone amongst the Queen's supporters, she believed Caroline to be innocent. For the most part, moderate opinion was more or less unanimous, and drew into its camp such diverse characters as Lady Bessborough, Lady Cowper, Harriet Granville, the Duchess Elizabeth. It held that the whole trial was a monstrous mistake, that the Queen was undoubtedly guilty, but that, whether proof could or could not be obtained on the matter, she had certainly been so much sinned against that any action could only result in the pot calling the kettle black, and that the one thing to be prayed for was courtesy and restraint from all sides, and some means of diverting the House from a definite declaration.

A few Kingites there were, as well as Queenites, but these were for the most part those whom affection or political ties bound to Lord Liverpool ; the unhappy *promoter* of the Bill. They were, of course, headed by Lady Erne, and Louise Liverpool. Caroline, who a few years past would have liked nothing better than to have taken a leading part in the fray, was saved, perhaps by ill-health, or it may have been by age and wisdom, from any active part in the controversy. And the family were in a greater anxiety about Caro-George who, having been long ago much in love with Lord Brougham, could not but feel strong sympathies with his client, and was with difficulty restrained from visiting Her Majesty.

The Queen was fortunate in her two legal advisers. Denman was extremely sound, he was universally respected, and his apparently sincere conviction of her innocence did much for her cause. Brougham, on the other hand, was brilliant and able to cope with the most cunning attacks of her enemies. No one believed that he had the smallest doubt as to Caroline's guilt, but it was impossible to disconcert him, and almost equally impossible to hate this fantastic personage who, whilst venerable peers spent unhappy Sundays in endeavouring to formulate replies to his questions, was himself engaged in playing leapfrog with Duncannon's children at Roehampton. His high spirits were never to desert him, and many years after, when an anxious monarch sent for the Lord Chancellor, on urgent business, there was not a little consternation because Brougham, away on a country visit, was discovered engaged in playing hunt the thimble with the Grand Seal of England, to the prodigious delight of his host's small daughter.

The Government sent over to the continent for a shipload of witnesses to be brought against the Queen. These were, for the most part, Italian servants of dubious probity, and their appearance and evidence was a decided blow to the King's cause. The populace were extremely angry, and peeresses saw their husbands go off to the House of Lords with anxiety. The Duke of Wellington was hissed and almost torn from his horse; and Lord Fitzroy Somerset shared his fate. Houses in the neighbourhood were barricaded, and everyone was anxious for fear that the Guards were not to be depended upon.

Lady Bessborough's enjoyment of the excitement was more virile than that of the younger generation. The danger in which they believed themselves to be stimulated her. Not since the days of the Gordon riots had the houses of London been barricaded, and that was forty years ago now. But still, the veterans of the eighteenth century delighted in commotion and danger, whilst the next generation consoled themselves with the knowledge that so long as the military did not side with the mob the situation was really not so dangerous as its outward manifestation suggested. One and all they were distressed at the mean spirit which forbade the Queen to enter the House of Lords by the Royal entrance. Harriet Granville judged rightly that such an insult would do damage, and she used her influence to induce her husband, Morley and Hart to get up when the Queen entered the House. In return for these kind offices she had the pleasure of hearing that Hart had been cheered all the way from London to Chiswick and back by the mob. Meanwhile, on the Queen's exit and entrance, a charming incident occurred. Caroline was seen driving with Billy Austin and the believers in her innocence shouted loudly: " God bless you and your mother. Three cheers for the Queen's son." As Lady Cowper exclaimed, it was like living in Bedlam, and all were mad upon some point—whether it was Lady Holland on the subject of

Napoleon, or the mob on the subject of Billy Austin, or Lady
Jersey on the subject of the Queen.[1]

Sally was indeed beside herself when it appeared as though
the evidence of the Courier Bergami would tell against the
Queen. " Lady Jersey, her face all drawn into strong lines,
looks fifteen years older. She talks on sadly about the Queen
and cries real tears all the time she is talking. Her Majesty
is not so low ; she roars with laughter." [1] Indeed, if she
considered the actions of her supporters, the Queen had much
cause for laughter.

Petitions and addresses to Her Majesty were engineered
with more enthusiasm than skill.

All through the hot month of August the investigation
went on, and Hart's villa at Chiswick proved a Paradise for
the weary.[1] Even Emily Cowper approved : " The Duke of
Devonshire lives very magnificently at Chiswick, the garden
is so well kept up and in such high order and the elephant
such a nice plaything." And Harriet echoed her praises.
" Hart is improving Chiswick, opening and airing it ; a few
kangaroos who, if affronted, will rip up anyone as soon as look
at him ; elks, emus, and other pretty sportive death-dealers,
playing about near it." [2]

Sometimes in the evening George Lamb and William
Ponsonby, accompanied by some adventurous ladies, would
row down the river past Brandenburg House and peep at
Caroline, sitting out on the lawn with Alderman Wood and a
dozen people at her feet, or else they would sit under the
cedars, discussing the Duchess of Kent, who was raving about
her baby, whom she declared to be " L'image du feu roi—le roi
Georges in petticoats," or they turned to laugh over the new
fashionable colour, which was called in Paris, " Chagrin de la
Reine d'Angleterre," and was said to be pink ; or to sigh over
the recent death of the Duchess of York. She had been the
most attractive of the Royal Duchesses, and her establishment
at Oatlands, with its week-end parties, and its Christmas
festivities, would be missed. Willie Ponsonby would tell
how on

" Christmas day the great dining-room was converted into

[1] *The Letters of Harriet Countess Granville.*
[2] *The Letters of Lady Palmerston.*

a German fair, and booths were erected round the sides, stored with various commodities ; in the centre was placed a tree or *mat de cocagne*, the branches of which were garnished with oranges, cakes and gingerbread. How on one table at the end of the room, were displayed all the presents which the guests had brought from Town to lay at the feet of Her Royal Highness ; on the other were placed those which Her Royal Highness presented to them for keepsakes." [1]

And someone would quote from her last whimsical letter to Lord Lauderdale.

" MON CHER LORD L.,
Je fais mes paquets, je m'en vais incessamment. Soyez toujours persuadée de l'amitié que je vous porte.

Votre affectionnée amie,

F.

The 8th day of September saw the close of the examination of the witnesses in the Queen's trial and it was then decided to leave out the divorce clause from the Bill. This gave a most comical look to the proceedings.

It was tantamount to saying that however bad the Queen was, the King was worse, since under no circumstances could he be allowed to divorce his wife.

The enquiry still went on ; the object was now to leave Caroline his wife, but no Queen ; it was a poor compromise. Though the enquiry continued, the tension was relieved and people began to be able to think of other things.

Emily Cowper went with her father to visit Augustus, who was staying with Dr. Lee at Miss Webster's cottage at Brompton. For years Caroline had tried the patience of her friends and relations, by lengthy accounts of her son's health, and enquiries as to any possible cure for his disease. But lately she had assured them that he was immensely better—indeed that he was cured.

Perhaps Godwin had suggested that she was doing harm by exaggerating the boy's condition. Emily was suspicious of her sister-in-law's assurances and William's affirmations, she wanted to see for herself. Caroline discouraged the visit, well knowing its intention, but she could not prevent it. Lady

[1] *Memoirs of Colonel Gronow.*

Cowper was not surprised to find that the boy's improvement came only from keeping him on a very low diet and the frequent application of leeches. As she had anticipated, no real cure had been effected.

It may be that, having no boy herself, she grudged her sister-in-law her son, such as he was. And not only did she grudge her Augustus, but still more acutely—faced with her own servant problems—did she grudge Caroline certain excellent old retainers at Brocket. More especially the butler Hagard and the housekeeper Dawson, who were servants of inestimable value even for those days. Why they cared to stay on with Caroline, she could not imagine.

No action of Caroline's could find approval with Emily. The former was now beginning to suffer from the disease which was to cause her death, but her natural high spirits, her feverish activities and her courage concealed the symptoms from those who surrounded her. Having parted with Dr. Lee, who was now with Augustus at Brompton, she engaged for herself, and on his recommendation, a certain Dr. Walker. Emily's comments on the subject were scathing. She believed that Caroline was more interested than she should be in the Scotch doctor, and she could not understand her brother's apparent good humour.

William looked on with a cynical smile at his sister's indignation. He knew the truth, and he made allowances for Emily. In many ways she was having a trying summer. Her mother-in-law, old Lady Cowper, believed to be dying, had startled them all by marrying a young apothecary who had attended her in Florence. It was very mortifying, and then old Lord Melbourne was getting extremely difficult and she had often to complain : " I wish Papa did not ride me quite so hard, that I had some diversion in my favour. Only think he is just now gone (at 11 o'clock) and he has been with me *sans cesser* ever since the morning at one.

" He came to Minny's dinner, went out with me, danced with me and would not go home to dress for dinner, but preferred being *en bottes*. It's like the Old Man in Sinbad. Moreover he professed that he hated London and sighed for Brighton. How people change ! Although he never exceeds Tierney's prescription and only drinks one glass of laeger, he manages *somehow or other to be drunkish*. I suppose it must be the fog that makes him so." [1]

If it may fairly be said that Lady Cowper, when out of a job, occupied herself in hating Caroline, it may also be stated that Caroline, when out of a job, occupied herself in exclusive self-analysis, the results of which she poured out upon some chosen recipient. For the moment it was Godwin who had to hear of all her difficulties. Her general complaint was, " I have nothing to do—I mean of necessity." It was repeated in many phrases :

" I am tormented with a superabundance of activity and have so little to do, that I want you to tell me how to get on. It were very well if one died at the end of a tragic scene, after playing a desperate part, but if one lives, and instead of growing wiser, one remains the same victim of every folly and passion, without the excuse of youth and inexperience, what then ? " [2]

No one could have had a better understanding of Caroline's deficiencies than she had herself. Even their insignificance she recognised. " I am like a boat in a calm, in an unknown, and to me unsought for sea, without compass to guide. . . .

" Now this is probably the case with millions, but that does not alter the matter ; whilst the fly exists, it seeks to save itself."

There is in these expressions of failure something sad— brilliantly gifted, endowed with courage and generosity, possessed of a just, critical and fearless judgment, possessed too of good intentions enough to make a saint, and a knowledge of herself and of the world sufficient to make a Lieven—why did Caroline fail at every stage of her life to touch reality— why did she succeed as the years went by in driving from her every human being who had loved her ? The answer is perhaps to be found partly in her astonishing and immature egoism, partly in the want of mental balance, derived perhaps from a physical cause, and to which this immaturity may have been due.

In October wives crowded back to London to join their hard-worked husbands.

" Here we are, the linen loaded, the streets full, horses

[1] *The Letters of Lady Palmerston.*
[2] *William Godwin and his Contemporaries.*

dying on the road, the Greenman all in a bustle, the pick-pockets all on the alert, cutting off all the trunks of the unwary. At all the turnpikes, coming along, they said ' Mind your trunks.' " [1]

At the second reading of the Bill the majority was only twenty-eight in its favour. And on the third reading on 6th November this majority was reduced to nine. Lord Liverpool accepted the division as a sign of defeat and the Bill was dropped. The general opinion was voiced in doggerel ;

> Gracious Queen, we thee implore,
> Go away and sin no more.
> Should that effort be too great,
> Go away—at any rate.[2]

Individuals reacted according to their nature. Of the King it was reported by Lady Erne that he was " in a dreadfully nervous state, so much so that they thought of sending for the Archbishop of Canterbury to calm his mind." When he had somewhat recovered, he shut himself up and refused to see anybody, and insisted on having new keys made to all the gates, to keep the neighbours from having access to the Park and *alentours* at Windsor. There were those who feared that he was going the way of his father.

The Queen, on the other hand, drove in state to a thanksgiving service at St. Paul's, an action which was considered to be in deplorable taste. But, on the whole, everyone was relieved. All the populace wore laurel leaves stuck in their caps and white cockades ; some churches even flew white flags.

And though Lady Erne loyally wished that it might rain plentifully and extinguish the fireworks and illuminations, and generally damp the ardour of the demonstrators and cool their heads, the general impression was one of satisfaction.

---

[1] *William Godwin and his Contemporaries.*
[2] *The Letters of the First Lady Wharncliffe.*

1 8 2 1

BEFORE the beginning of the New Year the Queen had ceased to figure in general conversation. The trial had lasted so long, every possible aspect of the case had been sifted and worried, every shred of evidence had been investigated; the whole matter had become boring, and after the slight increase of interest at the conclusion of the trial, the subject slid into oblivion.

By February the King felt it safe to come out of his retreat at Windsor, and he even went so far as to put in an appearance at the opera. His arrival was the occasion for a great demonstration of loyalty. The few cries of "Where's your wife, Georgie?" were drowned in the general cheering, and many people thought that the King had in this visit performed the first wise act since the accession. The tension in England was relieved, and once more a general exodus to the continent began to take place. Amongst those to leave England were Lord and Lady Bessborough. They made Paris their first stopping-place. Caroline saw them go with a heavy heart. When her mother was absent from England she felt less able to cope with the enmity of the Lambs. But she expected them back in six months, or at the worst in the autumn. The merciful future hid from her the fact that she was never to see her mother again.

In May came the news of Napoleon's death. Lady Holland mourned, and the papers were respectful. "We cannot conclude this article without recommending his faithful followers to the generosity of the British Government, and we hope that such honours will be paid to his remains as will prove to posterity that regard alone for the repose of the world imposed upon this country the policy of detaining him a captive," wrote the *Gentleman's Magazine*.[1]

[1] Quoted *News from the Past*.

From Paris Lady Bessborough wrote highly indignant at the small amount of interest which the event seemed to arouse amongst the French. Indeed, Lady Holland seemed to be alone in mourning the fallen Emperor.

In London preparations were going on for the Coronation, which was to take place in June. Many foreigners came over the Channel. Venerable peers, whom even the Queen's trial had not drawn to London, were seen on the road in cumbersome travelling carriages. Chinese bridges ornamented the water in Green Park; a display of fireworks was arranged for the amusement of the mob.

In May died Lady Liverpool. She was younger than the Duchess Elizabeth, much younger than Lady Erne, but she had been for some time in failing health. She who had derived so much interest from the deaths of her acquaintances, made certain arrangements concerning her own burial which led people unacquainted with her passion for the macabre, to believe that her last illness had touched her faculties.

" For," wrote one lady, " poor Lord Liverpool is nearly dead. She left it in her will that between her death and burial no one was to touch her but himself, and when he had placed her in the coffin, he nearly fainted. Now, as she was such a really good woman, I can only imagine that her disease went to her brain."

It was a shock for old Lady Erne, living on quietly at Hampton Court, and it decided the Duchess Elizabeth to come back from Rome to comfort her family.

Of all the three sisters, her life, after its many troubles and mistakes, was now the happiest. With her father's gusto for life and his appreciation of the arts she enjoyed every moment of her time in Rome.

There were old people in the town who remembered her father. The Bishop of Derry—he had been rich and powerful, he had entertained and employed half the artists and craftsmen of Rome, and what a fête they had had when he had succeeded to his peerage, and now here was his daughter, rich too and powerful, and as liberal a patroness of the arts. Had not a medal ever been struck in her honour ! When Bess looked at the profile of the dignified Roman matron engraved on the plaque, did she think back to those days when a post as governess to the Duke of Devonshire's illegitimate daughter had seemed to be a Heaven-sent deliverance from destitution ? But no, she had little time to think of herself. She was arranging to meet Lady Bessborough in Switzerland, and then to go home and see her bereaved family.

In Paris Lady Bessborough also began to make her plans for going to Switzerland. Willie's boy was ill, and the mountain air might do him good, and her presence might enable her daughter-in-law to go to London for the Coronation. Yet, with a vague premonition of evil, she hated to turn her back on England and to advance farther into the continent.

And now in London the great day of the Coronation had dawned, and happy ticket-holders rose at four o'clock in the morning and started off for the Abbey. The drive from St. George's Hospital to the Abbey occupied about four hours, and then came the long wait inside the church. Opinions varied as to the effect of the scene. Some pronounced the King's attitude to have been the acme of grace, others had observed a great many *œillades* between the monarch and Lady Conyngham, and reported that George had had frequently to call for brandy. Most people were of opinion that the Royal brothers, waddling in their tight, plain uniforms, were a deplorable spectacle. Leopold's appearance was the rallying-point of all praise, and the Archbishop's lengthy sermon of all disapproval. During the proceedings the Queen drove up to the Abbey and endeavoured to gain admission. She was refused entrance by the guard. Public opinion supported her affirmation of her right to be present, but the fact that she got out of her carriage and was more or less engaged in a brawl at the door of the church, alienated sympathy. As her supporter, Lord Thanet, said : " The spoiling the Coronation was very good, but the manner of doing it, very ill."

At the subsequent banquet the magnificence was so great that it was felt with satisfaction that foreign visitors must have been impressed. The foreigners in their turn electrified London by the glories of Prince Esterhazy's ball and the Duke of Gramont's fête.

Bess had arrived in time for the end of this trail of gaiety

She had become cosmopolitan in her tastes, and spoke with horror of various English habits. Used as she was to the conversation of the most brilliant men in Rome, she was filled with indignation when she was forced to withdraw from the dinner-table just before the Duke of Wellington began to tell his best stories, " according to your terrible custom here, we were gone, which I lamented over, and had to talk with Mrs. Boothby on ruffs and caps." [1]

She now became a prey to that malady which sometimes attacks elderly English ladies who spend any considerable period in the Holy City. She was *plus catholique que le Pape*, but furthermore when she stayed with Hart or with the Granvilles, her hosts were concerned to know where to hang the enormous portrait of Cardinal Consalvi which went everywhere with her in her carriage.

Early in August, when the King had started on his triumphal journey to Ireland, news came that Queen Caroline was very ill. From the first, there was little hope of her recovery, and she herself was aware of her condition. " I am going to die, Mr. Brougham, but it does not signify," and on the 17th of August she was dead. " The Queen is now, for the first time, at rest from persecution and annoyance," [2] wrote *The Traveller*.

Everyone hoped that the King would put off his tour and pay some sign of respect to his wife's remains, but it took time for the news to reach him, and when he heard it he decided that it was too late to cancel the preparations made for his reception in Dublin.

Orders were given that the mourning and the sum voted for the expenses was to be the same as that ordered for the death of Queen Charlotte, but as Caroline had desired in her will to be buried in Brunswick, the sum sufficient to carry the official mourners to Windsor proved beggarly when it was applied to a continental journey, and furthermore, no arrangements were made for the return journey of those who took part in the *cortège*. These oversights caused a feeling of deep resentment, and the funeral procession was disgraced by several riots and demonstrations. The whole business was

[1] *The Two Duchesses.*
[2] *News from the Past.*

348

managed with a want of dignity and want of feeling that were most distasteful to the public.

Lady Bessborough had missed the Duchess in Switzerland ; she regretted it.

There was so much that they had in common, so much that they had now, almost alone, in common. Willie's boy seemed to be getting worse ; she would be thankful when his mother returned from England. She felt nervous and anxious and a little homesick.

Barbara Ponsonby returned to them after attending the Coronation. She was alarmed at her little boy's appearance and decided that it would be best to try what the climate of Italy would do for him. Lord Bessborough was agreeable. Willie took it for granted that his mother would come too. They were miserable and anxious, and she had so much more hold on life, she was so much more competent than they. So she travelled still farther from England with a heavy heart. The belief that she should never see England again grew upon her.

Some instinct told her that now she could write to Granville more freely, more as she used to write, that what she wrote now could have no consequences. The distressing scenes she lived in as the boy's illness grew worse seemed to sensitise her perceptions and her memories. She was nearer now to Granville than she had been for many years, more aware of Georgiana than ever she had been since her death, and to this heightened awareness was added a great peace. She felt curiously remote from all bitterness, and as she seemed to grow nearer to those she had loved she seemed to grow correspondingly farther and farther from those she had disliked ; indeed, their figures receded from her consciousness till they had shrunk to a scale which rendered hatred impossible.

In Turin the boy had seemed to rally a little. They moved on to Parma, where the symptoms grew rapidly worse. The child had recurrent convulsions. Snatching a moment's privacy she wrote to Granville to tell him of their hopelessness and of the kindness of the Empress Marie Louise, who had sent her two doctors to consult with theirs. . . .

As she wrote she heard them calling for her and she left the letter as it was. The three days and nights which followed

349

were too agitated for her to have any opportunity of finishing her letter, so she sent it as it stood without signature . . . she wanted to feel in communication with Granville even though what she wrote was hardly worth the frank.

On the 5th of November the child died. Lady Bessborough had been up night and day for a fortnight, she was exhausted, and she had a threatening of dysentery. Willie and Barbara were anxious to get away from Parma as soon as the funeral was over. She encouraged the plan and made no reference to her own indisposition. In Florence they would all feel better and happier. And so on the 6th, immediately after the funeral, they set out on their journey.

They had to cross the Apennines and the November cold was intense. She had had some fever when she started and the cold brought on a chill. On the second day, Wednesday, she was taken ill with violent pains. The party stopped at a small inn ; it was a wretched place, cold and uncomfortable. They got out the medicine chest and she took various medicines which seemed likely to relieve the pain, but they produced no effect.

It was now apparent to them that she was dangerously ill. At all costs Willie determined to move her ; there might be a risk in the journey, but what was it compared with the horrors of an illness in this wretched tumbled-down hovel, miles from any doctor or from any human assistance. He begged her to allow him to have a bed made up in her travelling carriage. She consented, since he thought it was for the best, and since the attendance of a doctor would give him comfort, but she doubted whether she could bear the jolting of the carriage over the rough roads ; and of one thing she was perfectly certain, it would be useless. She would die, whatever they did, and this was the meaning of the curious sensation which she had become aware of during the last months. She knew now what it had been : the loosening of all the ties which held her life to this world. She was going to die and, as it happened, she who had cared so much for life, at the approach of death cared for it no more.

On Thursday they started again, and all through the day and through the following night they rattled along, and, somehow, she survived. At six o'clock on Friday morning they were in Florence. And here she was able to be as comfortable as warm rooms and good doctors could make her. Almost at once she responded. Willie thought her much improved, but her own opinion and that of the doctors agreed —there was no hope.

She passed a bad night, but Saturday again brought relief; yet in the evening she was worse again, and even Willie realised now that she was dying. From the first moment of her illness he had never left her. She knew that she could not endure the pain much longer, and she was glad of it. She would have liked to see Caroline again, to have spoken to William about her, to have seen Bess, who would now become the sole repository of so many memories; to have said good-bye to Frederick who would miss her, and to Duncannon; to have had a last meeting with Granville to whom the great red box of his letters would so soon be dispatched. Yet, in these last moments she sent him no message. What was there left to say which he did not know? Perhaps *there* lay the tragedy of their relationship. And yet this very fact of having no message to send him was a lesson to him if he could sense it. The greatest lesson she had ever given him.

She had seen many deaths, her mother's peaceful end, Sheridan's dying (which had been terrible), and Georgiana's death—most terrible of all. She had a belief that physical pain, bravely borne, could atone for past sins, and she accepted her own pain, consciously, to this intention. No agony could last for ever, and in the end came peace.

On Sunday morning, the 11th of November, she died. Willie wrote a short note to Granville. It had the formality of very great grief.

The letter travelled slowly to England. What were Granville's feelings when he read it? Was he glad to know that all that bound him to the past was gone from this world, or did some vision of his youth, vivid with its forgotten emotions, touch him, or did he only feel that at sixty, Lady Bessborough had lived her life?

Caroline, in moments of happiness so ungovernable, was calm in grief. The loss was too great, the heartache too real for any embellishments. Her thought was for her father. How would he be able to bear the breaking of this long habit and way of life ? He was ill and old, she determined to send out Dr. Lee to bring him home. Bess was kind, she owed much to Lady Bessborough, and though temperamentally unalike, she could appreciate personalities far removed from her own.

She promised Caroline to let Lee travel out with her to Florence, and she said that she would see for herself what state of health Lord Bessborough was in.[1]

By the end of the year Willie was back in London. Harriet went to see him in Cavendish Square, and was moved by the gravity of his grief, but Caroline she could not like even at this moment, too much lay between them.

At the end of the year all the family gathered at Derby, and Lavinia's son-in-law, the Hon. W. H. Lyttelton, wrote to Frederick Spencer :

" The melancholy and tedious affair of poor Lady Bessborough's funeral is but just over. You have heard she was brought all the way from Italy to be buried at her own request next her sister, in the Cavendish vault at Derby. It would have been wiser and kinder not to have made any such request, and the moral I draw from it is that sentiment is neither good feeling nor sound principle." [2]

[1] *Diary of Dr. Robert Lee.*
[2] *The Letters of the First Lady Wharncliffe.*

1822

TO two people, Lady Bessborough's death was to mark a turning-point in life : to Caroline it meant a loss of advice and support which could only end in disaster. Devoted friends she still had in her father, in William Ponsonby, in Hart, and in William Lamb ; but how were four charming, weak men to combat the jealousy and enmity of women such as Emily Cowper and her relations ? And Caroline herself was wholly incapable of defence ; devoid of feminine deceit and of masculine ruthlessness, she was not long destined to resist the attack.

To Harriet Granville, on the other hand, Lady Bessborough's death brought a greater relief than she at first knew. She had never hated her aunt, in certain respects she admired her, in other respects condemned. Yet, though she was not wholly conscious of it, the very *fact* of Lady Bessborough's existence lay heavily upon her ; recalling as it must those long years, almost the half span of human life, during which Granville and Lady Bessborough had been for each other that which it is hardly possible for any human being to be except once in a life-time—it had all ended years ago, ended even before Harriet's marriage—yet the recollection of it was bitter ; bitter that the thing should ever have been, bitter that such a thing should crumble ; whichever way she looked at it, it gave Harriet a pang, and those constant letters had been weekly reminders of what at any rate one of the parties concerned still suffered.

The result of their arrival had been to throw Harriet into herself, and she, who was by nature so spontaneous, had carefully to guard her words and her emotions. The pressure had distilled a certain bitterness. Now that it was removed she expanded, she became wholly herself. By nature tolerant and warm-hearted, all the bitterness and all the hard, critical attitude which she had adopted was cast aside, and her warm sympathies and generous understanding soon found excuses even for her cousin Caroline Lamb.

When she had been to see William Ponsonby at Cavendish Square it had been too soon after her aunt's death for her to know what a release this event was to be to her, and this visit was the last occasion upon which she spoke with evident dislike of Caroline. During the years that followed she did many kind things for her, and alluded to her often with understanding and sympathy.

In February Dr. Lee started off to join the Duchess Elizabeth in Paris. Caroline was now overwhelmed with grief, irritable and fantastic.

William Ponsonby came often to Brocket. Lamb liked him and they sat long into the night discussing every subject from gossip to the Patristic Fathers. One night the talk was upon the richest men in England. They agreed that Hart came first in wealth, then Grosvenor, and then Mr. Portman.

A few months later they were expecting the return of Lord Bessborough. Caroline took Augustus to meet them at Rochester the day after they landed. The reunion was a sad one, and as Dr. Lee comments : " At first there was a good deal of feeling on all sides. . . ." He looked with interest at his charge, Augustus, and noted in his journal : " The boy has grown much, particularly in the extremities, but his head is small, and there is a lamentable appearance of vacancy in his look. His attacks are the same although Sir A. Carlisle promises great things from animal diet, etc." The boy was quiet and affectionate, Caroline and William were both devoted to him, but any hope of his ever being normal had had to be given up.

The country was becoming more prosperous, the new machinery at Manchester and Glasgow was bringing wealth into the country. " The woollen manufactures of the fine valley of Stroud in Gloucestershire are equally busy, and hard pressed to produce their broadcloths, blue, black, and scarlet, from twenty-five shillings to thirty-five shillings a yard, for China, Hindustan, Mexico, Peru, Chile, and other places. These are no longer taken to London by weekly waggons but by daily plying vans." [1]

[1] Quoted *News from the Past.*

New wealth brought new luxuries. Oranges were selling for one shilling and two shillings each. The Granvilles stayed at the Pavilion at Brighton, and thought the King " scudding into dinner with Lieven on one arm and the Marchioness on the other " more slim and active than ever before. Emily Cowper, hard and blasée, had suddenly grown to take an interest (which seemed to bear the same stamp as the interest she took in all that pertained to the Lamb blood) in a young man of the ginger whiskers who worked in the War Office—one Lord Palmerston.

England seemed after much rocking even since Waterloo to have come to a position of equilibrium. There was really little to talk about except the Greeks. It was said that Lord Byron was determined to help them against the Turks. The Duchess Elizabeth wrote from Rome that he was collecting money and arms and surgeons for their assistance. Caroline heard the rumour with emotion. They had talked much of Greece together. Then, on a windless day, fell what seemed to the beholders indeed to be a great bough, but proved to posterity to be a mighty oak. Lord Londonderry committed suicide. Lord Palmerston's letter to Emily Cowper describes the event.

" On Saturday his mind became affected and during that day and Sunday he laboured under strong delusions. . . . Lady Londonderry watched by his bedside all Sunday night, Dr. Bankhead sleeping in an adjoining room. This morning at seven o'clock Lady Londonderry called Dr. Bankhead, saying that Lord Londonderry wished to speak to him. While she was out of the room Lord Londonderry had risen from his bed and gone into his dressing-room. Dr. Bankhead on entering found him standing in the dressing-room with his back towards the door and his head looking up to the ceiling, and Lord Londonderry exclaimed, ' It is all over ! Catch me in your arms.' He immediately fell and instantly expired, holding in his hand a small penknife with which he had put an end to his existence. The knife belonged to a pocket book and had been overlooked ; it is probable that if he could have been got through a day or two longer the disorder might have been mastered."

The general opinion was that if Bankhead had put blisters on his feet, if it had done no other good, it would have prevented such a catastrophe by making it impossible for the Foreign Secretary to rise from his bed. The Tories were horrified, and even the Whigs wondered who could replace him. From Rome the Duchess Elizabeth wrote, " When such a man can come to such a death, one is fearful of what events may not yet have in store for us. . . . The horror of such an event is almost beyond the grief of it." He was buried in the Abbey to the angry shouts of a hostile crowd.

To the empty Foreign Office went George Canning, the disciple of Pitt, the friend of Granville, of Hart, and of William Lamb, the clever, unlucky Mr. Canning, now a disappointed middle-aged man. With this appointment, the lives of Granville and of Lamb were to be altered, but the change did not come immediately. The only incident of the autumn was the announcement of Lord Liverpool's decision to marry again. It was only just over a year since Louisa's death. " I am sure that we all feel alike about it, and most sincerely do I wish him happy," wrote the Duchess. But she and Lady Erne, who had looked after him during the last year with great devotion, were a little hurt. Of course everyone said that his choice of Louisa's best friend was very touching, still, he might have waited a little longer before announcing his engagement.

1823

THE year 1823 was a peculiarly quiet one. Life, public and private, sailed on an even keel. Small talk centred round Mr. MacAdam's plan for converting the paved streets of London into roadways, and his experiments on Westminster Bridge and St. James's Square ; on the issue of licences by the Lords of the Treasury for fifty cabriolets to ply at the hackney coach-stands ; on the invention of roller skates.

More serious talk dealt with Monroe, the American President's pronouncement of selfish isolation, and on Lord Byron's arrival at Naples carrying arms, provisions and medicines for the Greeks.

Gossip described how the Duke of Wellington, staying with the Granvilles at Colinstead, had peppered his host's face to the extent of nine small wounds, which caused much pain though no serious injury. How Harriet had invited the Duke of York, and how he had told Lady Jersey, " No, Ma'am, I will not go there. Lady Granville is very clever, people say, far too clever for me, Ma'am."

In London, fog prevailed with strange consequences. " I do believe," wrote Emily Cowper, " there is something poisonous in the air of London at this season, but particularly this year. Everybody looks ill and complains, and the number of deaths is quite dreadful. The physicians themselves are astonished at it, and cannot think the reason. Some people say it is the *gass*, but I think this can hardly be. . . ."

To recuperate they all went to Brighton, and Harriet noted " the King all graciousness and nimbleness, the Marchioness twice as fat with *more* bracelets, the Duchess of Clarence in excellent taste, and Granville hawking and riding with the prima donna."

We have one picture of Caroline at this period. It is from the pen of an anonymous writer in Bentley's *Miscellany* who

met her at Miss Benger's in Doughty Street, and describes
her as " a gentle, lady-like, little woman, with slight remains
of comeliness, yet pleasing from the delicacy of her appearance
. . . there was nothing in her appearance of that passion
which breathes in every line of *Glenarvon* . . . all was lady-
like, correct, somewhat uninteresting—perhaps a little sad."

But if such was the faded impression she made upon this
unknown writer, the effect she produced upon her new friend
Bulwer Lytton was vastly different. He found her brilliant
and animated, and declared that " her manners, her thought
and her character shifted their colours like a chameleon."
More and more often the young man rode to Brocket, and
sometimes he found that a young Russell had arrived there
before him. These two boys were Caroline's last victims.

They enjoyed her extraordinary house parties. They were
amused and not indignant if a page wakened them at three
o'clock in the morning and informed them that Lady Caroline
was " playing the organ and begged the favour of their company." Quickly they would dress and hurry down, and then
sit silent on the stair till Caroline, bored with music, entertained them with extravagantly amusing conversation.

Bulwer Lytton was decidedly in love. He was jealous of
Russell and gave vent to scenes and reproaches. William
looked on, marvelling. He felt old enough to be Lytton's
grandfather and he was sorry for the boy, vexed that Caroline
should tease him. The young man was impressed by William's
attitude. " Lamb, by the by, was particularly kind to me ;
I think he saw my feelings. He is a singularly fine character
for a man of the world." William had no cause to be jealous.
What Byron had failed to accomplish was unlikely to take place
now. Caroline had, by a miracle, remained faithful to him then,
now the danger was over. She might be exasperating and preposterous, but fundamentally she was devoted to her husband.
She enjoyed his society, she admired and respected him, and the
very fact that always he eluded her, always he was detached and
self-sufficing, held her resentful and fascinated. Rows they
had, but always Caroline was the first to be reconciled, then
to be maddened by William's attitude " that nothing had taken
place," and that consequently no scene of forgiveness was
necessary. This year, whilst at Melbourne House, they had

one particularly violent quarrel. At the end of it, William, his nerves in pieces, ordered his horse and drove off to solitude at Brocket. An hour after his arrival he was startled by a sound of sobbing in his dressing-room, and opening the door he found Caroline in an agony of remorse, having had her horse saddled and galloped down to Hertfordshire behind him. Her intentions and her understanding were so good, her love of him was so sincere, why was it that she was so impossible to live with. . . . The fact was that she only came into being amidst excitement and scenes, and when the natural supply of circumstance was lacking, she manufactured it as a back-cloth to herself.

It was very tiring. Yet, on the whole, 1823 was a year of quiet comfort and happiness.

1824

ALL eyes were turned towards Greece in the beginning of the New Year. The Duchess Elizabeth, who was nearest to the scene of action, kept all the family informed of current events. The expedition promised well; Byron had. given ten thousand pounds, besides arms, medicines and surgeons, and he had gone out there himself.

In February the Granvilles were appointed to The Hague. This first diplomatic appointment was the fruit of Canning's friendship.

Before they sailed, they were invited to stay at the Pavilion to take leave of the Monarch, and there they seemed to observe a breach between the King and the Marchioness. And they heard a little gossip about Emily Cowper and Lord Palmerston. Scandalmongers questioned how much she had taken her mother's advice to heart?

From Brighton the Granvilles returned to London and paid a last round of farewell visits. Everyone was there to bid them good-bye, except Hart. He was in Rome with his stepmother—nor were his sisters quite happy about him:

" I am alarmed," wrote Harriet, " at Hart's new amusement, for beyond that I have no fears, but it is *assez de son genre* to squiddle with a princess, and he was sure to be taken with all those little clap-trap of embroidered cushions, satin slippers, dressing gowns of cashmere, morsels of Petrarch, with which this one assails our nobility." [1]

But, if the Duke of Devonshire were in any danger, his ideas were soon diverted. Early in March the Duchess Elizabeth caught cold, and after a few days a high fever set in and the doctors diagnosed congestion of the lungs; this turned to pneumonia, and in a week she was dead. Hart

[1] *Letters of Harriet Countess Granville.*

wrote to Lady Erne's daughter that she should break the news to the old lady, now the only living daughter of the Bishop of Derry. " I grieve to have to inform you of the death of the poor Duchess, which took place here yesterday. I know the affection you felt for her, and how much shocked you will be at the event. I have not written to Lady Erne because I think the sad communication will better be made to her by you. The Duchess's illness was an inflammation of the lungs, for the last week she was in the greatest danger. She appeared to suffer very little pain, and constantly expressed her comfort and satisfaction with her attendants. Her whole conduct was remarkable for the fortitude, good sense and composure which she shewed, as well as the touching consideration for all around her. She knew her danger and made every arrangement, and charged me with affectionate remembrance to those she loved. She asked for a clergyman and had a most interesting conversation with him. . . . I am very anxious about poor Caroline."

And so Bess died, as perhaps she would have chosen, in the Imperial City which she, and her father before her, had loved so much, surrounded by weeping and devoted servants, with cardinals and bishops sending to enquire for her, with a crowd of artists and craftsmen calling at the porter's lodge to know how she was, with all the English visitors in a flutter, and her beloved Hart at her side promising to look after her children—those children whose presence might have disturbed even her equanimity.

It was a decent, dignified departure. But had Hart a little smile when he wrote that her conversation with the clergyman had been " most interesting " ? It was one of Bess's characteristics that to those who had most cause to hate her she had always proved irresistible and, what was most extraordinary, was that they felt for her not only affection but also respect. Her death overshadowed the Granvilles' arrival in The Hague. Harriet wrote that they were both much shocked—" she had so much enjoyment of life. It brings past times to one's mind and many nervous and indefinable feelings."

One and all they rallied round Caroline-George with affectionate concern. Hart was unremitting in his attentions to her, and Harriet wrote : " How happy you are in the power of being such a blessing to those about you ! G. tells me you have been such a comfort to her and everything to Mrs. Lamb." She was, as Lady Bessborough had been twelve years before, proud of this as of everything that did dear Hart credit. He was the richest man in England, he could have been the most powerful, he had greater possessions and estates than any other peer, he had good looks, and against all these only the handicap of his deafness. Yet his life seemed never to have a purpose. He rebuilt his mansions, he improved his estates, he looked after the affairs of his relations with unceasing care and generosity—he knew all the English statesmen and many of the leading European personalities, and sometimes at Devonshire House and Chiswick important reconciliations were effected, opponents met and in its friendly atmosphere came to an understanding ; he appreciated the stage, he appreciated the actresses. He was gay, he was charming, he was a *standby*—but it seemed as though, like Caro-George (albeit on the grand scale), he had no life of his own. Since his one bitter outcry when Caroline had married William Lamb he had taken no part in life, asked nothing of it.

At this moment the Lambs were at Brocket, and Caroline had just risen after some weeks in bed recovering from a riding accident. One June morning William met her with a grave face. " Caroline, behave properly, I know it will shock you. Lord Byron is dead." In Missolonghi, without friends or adequate medical assistance, Byron had died of fever, his campaign for the liberation of Greece only half begun. And now that he was dead nearly all those who had abused him united to praise him : even the *Edinburgh Review* wrote, " He set like the sun in his glory ; and his orb was greatest and highest at the last ; for his memory is now consecrated no less by freedom than by genius."

Caroline herself felt little at the moment. After that talk at the Albany, he had died for her, yet it was sad to think that his life had petered out drably, as their romance had petered out drably, to no accompaniment of trumpets or clashing bayonets, to no scenes of suicide or divorce. Sometimes had she dreamed of him lately, seen him fat and angry and hideous ? Had these been premonitions ? What, she wondered, were

Annabella's reflections ? Did she feel responsible for his wretched death, the close to his wretched exile ? Or was she thankful that Ada would never know her father—that, by the time the child grew up, Byron, the man, would be forgotten and only Byron, the poet, be remembered ?

The Lambs stayed on at Brocket. Caroline had yet another riding accident. She was low and ailing, but in the July she was on a horse again. One day she and her husband were taking a long ride together and William was some way in front, when, suddenly, he turned back and told her to go home immediately. She was surprised and, looking down the road, she saw some black *cortège* on the horizon. William hurried her back in silence and her questions remained unanswered till the next morning.[1] Then he told her that what he had seen approaching was Lord Byron's funeral car. What no bald statement of his death had been able to make her realise, this incident brought to her consciousness with the burning clarity of revelation.

Now, and for the first time, she knew and felt that she would never see Byron again, in this world. The shock came on top of two severe accidents ; she could not get over it. For weeks she wandered round or lay about, almost in a stupor. She seemed to have no more hold on life, no more desire to live. She was not suffering, she was simply annihilated. Conscious of her own eclipse, of the pall of depression and boredom that she spread about her, she tried to see whether brandy would help to dissipate the cloud and render her fit, at least, to entertain William's guests. But drink proved a complete failure. She abandoned it. However, it provided Emily Cowper with a new ground for disgust at her sister-in-law's conduct. Doctors came and went, they could find no remedy. Struck at once by her moral condition, they failed to recognise that there were present, in addition, the seeds of a fatal disease. They tried to distract her. They told her of the marvellous invention of a machine called a stethoscope, a wooden tube which enabled the physician to discover the progress of pulmonary diseases. She listened with attention. She was always interested in anything new ; but when they had gone back to London she drifted back into some dim,

[1] This story is of doubtful veracity.

363

haunted region. And thus the last year of the Lambs' married life wore itself out, bleakly.

For the Granvilles, on the contrary, a new life had only just begun. Tried out for a few months in The Hague, Canning now moved them to Paris, which was, as it proved to be, their home for many years. Harriet dreaded the entertaining for herself, but still she was unselfishly delighted at a post which was so exactly suited to Granville's temperament.

She found the society very artificial. She confessed that she believed that the Frenchwomen settled one day what they should say the next. She swore that she longed for Lent as much as the fashionables dreaded it. She was concerned at the immense number of dresses she had to buy, and at the extraordinary manner in which her head had to be dressed.

She told Georgiana how she had said of her appearance to her maid, " C'est affreux," and how the truthful Marie had answered gravely, " Oui, milady."

1825

THE year 1825 was a bad one for William Lamb. He lost his seat in parliament to the Radical Tom Duncombe; and the man of whom the Regent had said, " Sligo, mark my words, that man will some day or other be Prime Minister," now seemed destined to obscurity.

Duncombe had made many crude allusions to Lamb's private life, and these allusions were opportune ammunition for the batteries of Emily Cowper. Earlier in the year she had begun her supreme attack upon her brother's marriage. Now that Caroline was in general so subdued and absent, William resisted the enemy less well. In the past, when any crisis had arisen, Caroline had been so amusing and so delightful that anger had subsided in her presence. But now it was different. William's home life really was a wretched affair; and it might be, he thought, that Caroline was *not* quite normal. The plan of a separation had certain points to recommend it : he began to investigate its possibilities.

As to Caroline's views on an amicable separation, she wrote a letter which gives her opinion in no measured terms.

" Ask of those you think great scholars whether they weary of the word ' amicable ' separation, after twenty years of mutual attachment, resentment, forbearance, agreement to part, making it up again—But no, I will explain it.

" It is to idolise and flatter, to be entirely governed by a woman, who every day errs and is never restrained, never reproved while she is young, in health, and accounted clever —it is to retain her by protestations of kindness and love and when others wished to take her away. It is to laugh, show benignant humour, independent ideas, proud spirit, and when by her own fault she becomes miserable, ill, lonely, to find out all her errors—blaze them to the world and have strait waistcoats, physicians, with all the aristocracy of the country to say she had better go—go where ?

" Will you but tell me that, only do not, as Frederick Lamb and others would say—answer to the D——l.

" Let them go there if they like.

" I will not if I can help it."

To this she added a further comment. " They have broken my heart, but not my spirit, and if I will but sign a paper all my rich relations will protect me, and I shall, no doubt, go with an Almack's ticket to Heaven."

Much that she said was true, yet to resist the separation now that for the first time William, as well as his family, desired it was hardly possible. By the month of May three camps had been formed, and negotiations were already begun.

Emily Cowper, Frederick Lamb, and Lord Cowper were manœuvring William into position. Lord Brougham, William Ponsonby and the Duke of Devonshire supported Caroline with an equal energy. Duncannon and Frederick Ponsonby were inclined to sympathise with William whilst anxious to get the best possible terms for their sister, and the Granvilles were of much the same opinion.

Emily Cowper's letters bear at this period a charge of venom which should have been sufficient to negative their purpose. " Nothing can go better than our affairs here. For a moment William was foolish and used to go and see her and listen to her stories and laugh—then came quarrels, and she told William (Ponsonby) of his beating her, which was not true. He and our William quarrelled upon which he took the wise determination of seeing her no more.

" Lord Cowper has consented to be William's referee, and the Duke of Devonshire hers, and they are to consult Abercrombie and settle the terms. Duncannon and F. Ponsonby are quite fair, and Lord Brougham and William Ponsonby reckoned an ass and a jacknapes by everybody, and wrote William such an impertinent letter that the latter says he will have no communication with him, which letter was a great advantage to us, as it steadied our brother and put the others in the wrong. These are the things he says in his letter to him :

" That by this marriage William got a brilliant connection which his family wanted (was there ever such an ass ?). That he would never see his sister trampled on, by him, or his family (as if our forbearance were not proverbial but *tant mieux* for if he had been more reasonable William would have had more difficulty in throwing him over).

" I think the thing now settled, for she is anxious for an arrangement, finds all idea of putting it off impossible, and is desirous of avoiding publication. This is a favourable change and I take all the merit of it to myself, for in a quiet way I have bullied the bully.

" She threatened and raged for the first half hour about books and letters, and when she had done, I said in the quietest way : ' Well, I see all accommodation is impossible,' for this is exactly what was said to me last night. He said it was only trifling to make a private arrangement and he had now quite made up his mind to go into Court, that many disagreeable things might be said on both sides, but *that* in his opinion was quite a trifle compared with the advantage of having everything finally and completely settled, and so I went on, saying I was not quite of the same opinion, but that as she and William had both made up their minds there was no help for it. This produced a violent abusive letter to him next morning, which he did not understand till I explained it, and next morning came a letter to Lord Cowper begging him to speak to the Duke of Devonshire and saying how anxious she was for any settlement which would keep them out of Court, as there was no use in their appearing in Court like Mr. and Mrs. Bang, reviling each other, and so Lord Cowper is to meet the Duke and I hope all will be settled.

" I think the arrangement will be £2,500 now and £3,000 on Papa's death.

" A great deal more than she deserves, but I think it well worth while to get rid of her and to have the whole thing settled quietly, for of course on this arrangement she will be bound to publish nothing. The fact is that the books are still completely in her possession so that there is no fear of their coming out except in a moment of fury.

" She said we had all misrepresented her and told stories of her—but I am fully convinced that all that signified was her own doing. . . ." [1]

[1] *Lady Palmerston and her Times.*

367

him. It is a sad case. The boy is very strong and healthy but with the mind of a child and always in mischief." [1]

And Emily went on to imply that William had no realisation of his son's condition, and explained how she intended to take on the boy's treatment at a later date. Had Lady Bessborough been uncharitable when she had written that she disliked the Lamb connexion extremely, that she distrusted Emily and believed her to be false and malicious ?

In Paris Harriet Granville did all that she could for Caroline's comfort ; the latter was grateful and showed her gratitude by going out very little in society ; for this the Granvilles were thankful.

In England the reaction after the boom of the previous year was already beginning. In December the great banking house of Sir Peter Pole closed its doors, and seven other banks broke in quick succession. The financial situation was serious, and the industrial situation reacted to it. There was general poverty, and in the North and Midlands some rioting and some destruction of the machinery which had been the cause of over-production and unemployment.

[1] *Lady Palmerston and her Times.*

1826

WILLIAM was quite content to be out of parliament. Lord Liverpool's government coped conscientiously with the three-headed monster—corn, Catholics, and currency; but little important legislation was passed. In June there was a General Election, and Emily wrote captiously, "People think this new Parliament will be a curious one, such strange things have turned out. There are three stockbrokers in it, which was never the case before."

But she had other reasons for alarm, for before the spring was ended Caroline was in England again. On her return she felt, for the first time, the full measure of her freedom and her loneliness. She had described her arrival: "I am now with my maid at the Ship Tavern, Water Lane, having come over from Calais. I have no servants, pages, carriage, horses, nor fine rooms. . . . My situation in life is new and strange; I seem to be left to my own fate most completely, and to take my chance, rough or smooth, without the smallest interest being expressed in me."

The letter gives a sense of surprised immaturity which was characteristic. She had always been the centre of interest, of affection, of reproof, or hatred; and now that she was ignored, she felt bewildered. But her abandonment was not to last long. William Lamb heard of her arrival, and knowing that her own house was still let, he insisted that she should go to Brocket. And so Hagard and the other servants, who had wept at her departure, and never thought to see her again, welcomed her back in less than a year.

Emily Cowper was horrified. She thought it a "bad arrangement," except in regard to expense; she could not bring herself to tell Lord Melbourne of his daughter-in-law's return; she comments on the fact that William never mentioned Caroline to her, but that she knew that he sometimes rode down in the mornings to see her. William could never resist violence. He had submitted to Emily and Frederick's recriminations ; he had complied with their wishes, but now that he was relieved of their importunities he was determined to see as much or as little of his wife as he chose.

As for Caroline, she was thankful to be home again. She read, she rode, she sketched, and she looked forward to William's visits.

Whilst life went by so peacefully at Brocket, Harriet Granville, in the midst of the whirl of Parisian society, prepared to welcome Hart and Clifford. Their presence brought something real, and something of England and of Chiswick into her life.

When Hart left Paris it was to prepare for a longer journey. He had been appointed special Ambassador for the Coronation of the Emperor Nicholas, and by December he was in Moscow. His sisters were glad to see him playing a part in State affairs, and he filled his rôle with a magnificence which remained a by-word in Russia.

1827

BY 1827 a strange contentment seemed to have come to Caroline, and she described her life at this period with evident satisfaction :

" Happy, healthy, contented, quiet, I get up at half-past four, ride about with Hagard and see the harvestmen at work in the pretty, confined green country, read a few old books, see no one, hear from no one . . . this contrast to my sometime hurried life delights me. Besides, I am well, and that is a real blessing to oneself and one's companions."

A visitor with a flair for journalism asked her the state of her affections. Without hesitation she replied : " William Lamb first, my mother second, Lord Byron third, my boy fourth, my brother William fifth . . ." and lastly she named Russell. It seemed a fairly orderly list.

Augustus was with her. She seemed resigned to his condition, and his companionship was a pleasure to her. A great quietness seemed to encircle her. Such a peace and such a silence as had fallen on Lady Bessborough on her last voyage to Italy. Could it be that the wheels of life were running slowly and still more slowly ? Could it be that they would soon come to a standstill ? For the moment nothing suggested tragedy. It seems, on the contrary, as though the lull were a thing of stability which would endure endlessly. It seemed almost as though her life were suspended.

On the 5th of January the Duke of York died. He had been the most popular of the Royal brothers, and his death caused some genuine grief, not only to the King, whom he had always expected to succeed, but also to the nation at large. Since the death of his own duchess he had sat at the feet of the Duchess of Rutland, and when this lady also predeceased him, he had taken up his residence with the afflicted husband and died at his house.

Liverpool gave Wellington the vacant seat at the War Office, it was his last public act, for on February the 17th the Prime Minister had a stroke which, though it did not kill him, rendered it impossible for him to carry on his office. When the full extent of these implications was realised the excitement became intense.

" Well," wrote Creevey, " what is your real opinion as to who is to supply Liverpool's place ? I think somehow it must be Canning after all, and that then *he'll die of it. . . .*" It was a fatal prophecy. Canning was sent for and agreed to try to form a Ministry, and immediately Wellington, Eldon, Bathurst, and three other Ministers who were opposed to the Roman Catholic claims, resigned.

Undaunted, Canning opened negotiations with Lord Lansdowne, hoping for Whig support. These *pourparlers* broke down, but eventually a Ministry was formed, and one of Canning's first acts was to find William Lamb a safe seat (Newport) and to send him to Ireland as Chief Secretary. After being out of the saddle for nearly two years William was glad to be at work again, and he was glad to oblige Canning, whose *via media* made a strong appeal to him, and whom he knew to be abused alike by Whigs and Tories for his want of party spirit.

Nor was William the only one of the circle to receive the plums of office ; Lord Palmerston, to Emily Cowper's great delight, was moved from his subordinate post at the War Office to the Exchequer ; and about this appointment there was a curious anomaly, for eighteen years earlier Perceval had made Palmerston, then a mere boy, the same offer, but the discerning young man had sagely declined it, preferring to learn his work from the office-boy's rôle upwards. And now, after all these years, the same offer was repeated and he accepted it.

Caroline missed William's visits, but for his own sake she was glad that he was working again. Early in the year she had written : " To-morrow William Lamb says he will come . . . without wife or Parliament, or trouble of any kind, he ought now to have found in perfect quiet the true enjoyment he always pined for. Yet, if I mistake not, he is less happy then when plagued with these appendages."

Chiswick House

And now one of these appendages had been restored to him—and perhaps, one day . . .

Meanwhile, Canning was negotiating the Treaty of London, whereby the Great Powers were to ensure the completion of Lord Byron's conception of an independent Greece. Then in July the Prime Minister began to ail ; the kind and watchful Duke of Devonshire offered him Chiswick as his father had offered it to Fox. The country air would do him good, in a short time he would be fit for his duties again.

Like Fox, Canning accepted the offer with gratitude. Like Fox he went to the Palladian villa, like Fox he dragged about for a few days beneath its great cedars, and then, like Fox he died, in the best guest-room. And Mr. Creevey's prophecy was fulfilled. To his friends who had believed in him through all the disappointed and frustrated years of his life, and who had hoped great things from his eventual success, his death was a cruel and an ironical blow.

To the Granvilles, in particular, it was an overwhelming grief. Harriet wrote wretchedly : " It is a calamity of so fearful a nature, the loss so irreparable to his friends, to the world, it is impossible to look at its consequences or to define the happiness it destroys, the miseries it may entail, that one feels bewildered as well as grieved." What would happen to the Government no one could guess. Granville and William Lamb were prepared for immediate resignation. But eventually a reluctant cipher, in the shape of Lord Goderich, was thrust, despite his protestations, into Canning's shoes, and every man remained at his post.

But by the end of the year, the Prime Minister (" Snip Robinson," or " Goody Goderich," as he was irreverently called), who had never yet met parliament, decided that the ordeal would be unendurable, and it was known that he intended to resign, whilst he still held the record of being the only English Prime Minister who had never met the House.

1828

ON the 8th of January Lord Goderich resigned, and after a few days of uncertainty the Duke of Wellington accepted the Premiership. It was one thing for William to serve under Canning or his disciple; it was another to serve under the Duke, who was associated with " die-hard " views, so he came over to England to make his decision, and when he saw how the land lay he came to the conclusion that, caring more for facts than names," he should continue to hold his post under the Duke.

He went down to see Caroline, and was horrified at her appearance. She had alluded of late to ill-health and painful symptoms, but he was in no way prepared to find her in an almost dying condition. The doctors diagnosed dropsy. William arranged to prolong his leave, and Mrs. George Lamb went to stay at Brocket; William Ponsonby was also a constant visitor.

Caroline herself—whether aware of her condition or not they were uncertain—was quiet and gentle, and William reflected that if she had always been in such a mood their married life might have been an ideal one.

When he was away from Brocket she wrote to him, or if she were too weak to write herself she dictated a letter to her new physician, Dr. Goddard. The letters contained no complaints or recriminations; now, as always when she had something real to bear, she seemed to take a pride in exhibiting fortitude and dignity.

" I really feel better; the medicine agrees with me, and I have everything I can possibly want. Augustus has not been well, perhaps he leads too regular a life and does not take enough exercise and too much tea and bread and butter. Everybody I have seen makes great enquiries after you and after him. . . . I take my simple medicines, and as Dr. Goddard is writing for me, he will probably tell you what they are, (blue pills, squills, and sweet spirits of wine, an infusion of cascarilla bark). God bless you, my dearest William. I will write to you myself very soon. Do not forget to write a line to me. Everyone at Brocket is doing quite well."

She felt better, but there was no real improvement, and towards the middle of January the disease began to make rapid progress. William now seldom left the house. Then on the evening of Friday, January 26th, Caroline died, at the age of forty-three.

"Poor Caroline died on Friday evening. She went off without any pain and from complete exhaustion. Mrs. Lamb had hold of her hand at the time. She only fetched one sigh and was gone. Mrs. Lamb would hardly believe she was really dead, and only felt she was so, by the placid look her features assumed. William was not there at the time, but he had been with her a few hours before. He was hurt at the time, and rather low the next day, but is now just as usual and his mind filled with politicks. Augustus looked a little graver when he saw her and when he heard of her death, but nothing makes any impression on him." [1]

It was not to his own family but to Willie Ponsonby that Lamb opened his mind on the subject of his wife's death, and when the latter was questioned about his brother-in-law, he replied gravely that " William Lamb behaved as I always knew he would."

They had quarrelled at times and been rude to each other, but fundamentally Ponsonby knew that Lamb had always loved Caroline, and at this moment William Lamb was glad to feel his sympathy and approval. An obituary notice in *The Times* was variously attributed to Lamb and to Bulwer Lytton. Whoever wrote it had understood Caroline most completely, and the notice which appeared in the *Literary Gazette* and in another form in the *Annual Obituary and Biography* had much truth in it :

" Her character very early developed itself—wild and impatient of restraint, rapid in impulses, generous, and kind of heart—these were the first traits of her nature and they continued to the last." Then, after alluding to a three years'

[1] *Lady Palmerston and her Times.*

intimacy with Byron and remarking sagely that " the world is very lenient to the mistresses of poets " . . . " for their attachments . . . arise from imagination and not depravity " the Journal makes mention of her literary efforts and also cites the story of her meeting with Lord Byron's funeral adding : " She was taken home insensible : an illness of length and severity succeeded. Some of her medical attendants impute her fits, certainly of great incoherence and long continuance to partial insanity. At this supposition she was invariably and bitterly indignant." Finally, after touching on her separation from Lamb and her last illness and remarking that " her end at least was what the best of us might envy and the harshest of us approve," the *Literary Gazette* gives this description of her :

" In person Lady Caroline Lamb was small, slight, and in earlier life perfectly formed ; but her countenance had no other beauty than expression—that charm it possessed to a singular degree : her eyes were dark, but her hair and complexion fair ; her manners though eccentric, and apparently, not really affected, had a fascination which it is difficult for anyone who has never encountered their effect to conceive. Perhaps they were more attractive to those beneath her than to her equals ; for as their chief merit was their kindness and endearment, so their chief deficiency was a want of that quiet and composed dignity, which is the most orthodox requisite in the manners of what we term, par emphasis, society. . . . To the poor she was invariably charitable—she was wise : for them, she had consideration as well as generosity, and delicacy no less than relief. For her friends she had a ready and active love ; for her enemies no hatred ; never perhaps was there a human being who had less malevolence ; as all her errors hurt only herself, so against herself only were levelled her accusation and reproach. . . . Lady Caroline was indeed one of those persons who can be much wiser for others than for themselves. . . . Never was there a being with a better heart than the one whose character we have just sketched. . . . From what single misfortune or what single error did it ever preserve its possessor ? " asks the early Victorian journalist and adds : " The world does not want good hearts but regulated minds "—" Rightly cultivate the Head and the Heart will look after itself——"

And so, despite many good qualities, few people were left to regret Caroline. To William Lamb the sorrow which was sincere must have been qualified by some sense of deliverance, to her father it was mitigated by prolonged absence, to her son, by incapacity to realise his loss; to Bulwer Lytton and Russell by new interests. Only Willie Ponsonby and the Duke of Devonshire were made genuinely unhappy by her death.

Harriet Granville heard of the cousin's death through Willie Ponsonby. Of late years she had learnt to appreciate Caroline, but she regretted the waste of good material rather than the personal loss. " This account of her patience and resignation interests me very much, and makes me feel how much to education and subsequent events the errors of her life must be attributed."

Of her funeral the *Annual Biography and Obituary* writes : " On the morning of February 4th, Lady Caroline's remains were received in a hearse and six from the House in Pall-Mall, in which her Ladyship breathed her last, for the purpose of being conveyed to the cemetery belonging to Lord Melbourne's family at Hertford. Two mourning coaches and four, in which were Dr. Goddard, Dr. Hamilton, and two other gentlemen followed the hearse. The carriages of the Duke of Devonshire, Earl Spencer, Earl Carlisle, Earl Bessborough, Lord Melbourne, Viscount Duncannon, Mr. Wm. Ponsonby and Mr. Hunter, followed the funeral procession to a short distance out of Town. The Honourable William Lamb, husband of the deceased, and Mr. William Ponsonby, joined the procession at Belvoir, to attend the funeral, as chief mourners."

With Caroline's death the thread of our story breaks.

Old Lord Melbourne died a few months after Caroline. Augustus survived his mother eight years. William Lamb, now Lord Melbourne, evinced a touching devotion to his unfortunate son ; and Mrs. Norton tells us how she used often to see Lord Melbourne " drop whatever he was doing at the moment, in order to make sure that the boy was not being neglected by his attendants." Apparently healthy and happy it seemed as though Augustus might attain to the normal span of life, but in his twenty-ninth year he grew suddenly ill, and in spite of a short rally he died.

379

His father has left a vivid account of the scene : " Augustus was lying on a sofa near me ; he had been reading, and I thought he had dropped asleep. Suddenly he said to me in a quiet and reflective tone, ' I wish you would give me some franks that I may write and thank people who have been kind in their enquiries.' The pen dropped from my hand as if I had been struck, for the words and the manner were as clear and thoughtful as if no cloud had ever hung heavily over him. I cannot give any notion of what I felt, for I believed it to be, as it proved, the Summons they call the lightening before death. In a few hours he was gone."

Gone, with that irony which seemed to pursue William's life, at the moment in which he had first given his father a revelation of what their relationship could have been.

And with his death, the last link with Caroline was broken. He was not yet fifty, a parliamentary career was opening out before him ; two years later he was Home Secretary, six years later he was Prime Minister for the first time. Emily Cowper and the rest of his family urged him to marry, but he would not fall in with their plans. Was this due to the memory of Caroline, to the presence of Mrs. Norton, or to some vague belief that he was not made for the duties and responsibilities of married life ?

When Princess Victoria came to the throne he was still Prime Minister ; and now it became his task to fit the young Queen for her tremendous rôle. The part of counsellor, friend and almost that of father became him. He had seen so much of life, had known the exuberant figures of the eighteenth century, had seen the birth of the new age, had known personally obscurity and ridicule and defeat, and admiration and success ; and was left at fifty-eight with a discriminating sense of the values of life, and a knowledge of the Patristic Fathers, of the classics, and of English literature as great as was his knowledge of blue books and white papers.

Onto the crude enthusiasm and youthful intolerance of his charge he brought to bear all the sophistication of his dearly bought wisdom and tolerance. Life had aged him quickly ; by 1838 Lady Lyttelton could write of him as " Lord Melbourne (who begins to look picturesquely old) with the sword of State." But despite his disillusionment Lord Melbourne was never to despise the good things of life ; and the same writer remarks, with a kindliness which seems to show that she too was mellowing with age, " . . . I should think it would be hard to displace Lord Melbourne by any intrigue, constitutional or otherwise, while her present Majesty lives, unless he continues to displace himself by dint of *consommé*, and truffles, pears, ices, and anchovies, with which he does his best to revolutionise his stomach every day."

It was twenty-six years since he had stopped at Tixall on his way to Ireland, and Harriet Granville had noted that " William ate like a trooper." Lord Melbourne was a very different man from the young William Lamb, but his habits had remained the same.

The same year he was summoned to the death-bed of Lord Egremont. The meeting stirred many memories. The old man spoke to him of life with a philosophy which accorded well with his own views. His memory went back into the mid-eighteenth century, and he mused questioningly on the varied moods of nearly a century. Four times he had seen the wheel turn from a simple life to luxury and vice, then from vice to religion ; then from religion to the excesses of the Regency ; and now back to order and seemliness once more. William was moved by the last hours of this brilliant and fantastic personage with whom he had so much, how much, in common ?

He might so easily have been another Lord Egremont, another charming and discriminating dilettante ; but now it seemed as though the circumstances of life had forced achievement upon him. He was tutor to the most powerful child in Europe, and he had been Prime Minister for five years

But 1840 saw the accomplishment of that which no intrigue could accomplish. In this year the Queen married her cousin, Prince Albert of Saxe-Coburg-Gotha. This marriage was very near to Melbourne's heart, but bore the seeds of his own displacement. For Prince Albert was a true child of the nineteenth century, precise, self-confident, intolerant, sure of his own capacity to mould circumstances ; and very soon his influence predominated over the Queen. He believed in statistics, in railways, in the Crystal Palace, and before his energetic materialism Melbourne gave way.

In 1841 he gave up the Seals of Office to Sir Robert Peel,

a Victorian of the best description, and went to live at Brocket where his brother Frederick, now retired from diplomacy and married to an Austrian wife, came to look after him. Lady Lyttelton's augury concerning the bad effects of rich diet were verified, for he suffered from two paralytic strokes. Sarah Lyttelton wrote again rather sententiously : " He is said to be much better ; but with his unwholesome diet and great increase of size lately, I should not wondre if his time were but short. He is extremely happy. . . . Alas, if he had a real home fifty years ago and a good example before him, one should be looking at his approaching end with happier feelings. But then those allowances will be made in mercy. I can't help feeling that I shall (if I survive him) wear my cousin's mourning with much sincerity, for the strange, inconsistent, but amiable man." [1]

Sometimes Emily came to see him. Lord Cowper had died some years before, and in the year of the Queen's marriage she had married the jaunty Lord Palmerston, who was bidding fair to make his mark in politics. This marriage to a man she had loved for many years drew the best traits of love and unselfishness from her strong but circumscribed affections. William had resented her excursions into his life, but he never doubted her sincere affection for himself ; her visits were a pleasure, bringing with them as they did the stir and excitement of Westminster.

When he was alone at Brocket he would be wheeled into the picture gallery, and there tell the servant to pause before the picture of his mother. What a remarkable woman she had been, what a realist ! How well she had done for her difficult family. How little doubt there was that if she had lived his own marriage would have held. How proud she would have been of his years of office !

Then slowly he was rolled back into the drawing-room to receive the many visitors who came to enquire for him. Mrs. Norton was very kind, despite the terrible scrape he had got her into ; but he confided to one of his friends that " Caro was the only woman he had ever really loved."

It was a tedious business waiting for death, but William treated the matter with his invariably tolerant courtesy. The

[1] *Letters of Sarah Lady Lyttelton.*

end came on November 24th, 1848. For twenty years he had .been a widower. When the Queen heard that Lord Melbourne was dead she was sad, but the Prince Consort would not approve of undue grieving which impaired one's efficiency ; and after all he had lived a long and honourable life, so perhaps all was for the best.

Of the rest of Caroline's family and connexions little need be said : her father lived on amongst his prints and bibelots until 1843. A little bewildered by the disappearance of all the brilliant women who had dominated his youth, he drifted, like a ghost, from Roehampton to London and from London to the continent, making as he went detailed but increasingly shaky pencil drawings of the places he visited, until at last he faded away entirely, unobtrusive in death as he had been in life.

" Poor pregnant " Maria Duncannon had predeceased him, leaving thirteen children, and having had the satisfaction of seeing her daughter Augusta married to Lord Kerry, in her bedroom, on the day before her death. Duncannon, who now succeeded to the title, held it for only four years and died whilst filling the office of Viceroy of Ireland in 1847.

Frederick had died ten years earlier from the delayed results of the wounds he had received at Waterloo. His widow, Lady Emily, lived on, however, until 1877, and on each anniversary of the battle of Waterloo, a detachment of the 12th Lancers waited on her with a bouquet to commemorate her husband's gallant conduct and miraculous escape on the occasion of the battle. So, by a strange irony, twenty years after Caroline's death, the kind, but ineffectual and delicate Willie, the " Benjamin " of the family, was the sole survivor.

Moreover, his mild parliamentary career, which had seemed unlikely to bring him into any prominence, was to win him a peerage. He lived on until 1855. His marriage to Lady Barbara Ashley Cooper had brought him considerable wealth, and as Lord de Mauley he was an important landowner, the proprietor of both Hatherop Castle, Gloucestershire, and Canford in Hampshire. But if Caroline's generation were not as a rule long lived, at the time of her death, and for several years afterwards, there were two survivors of the early days of Devonshire House.

One was quiet little Lady Erne, the daughter of the portentous Bishop, and sister to the Duchess Elizabeth. She lived on discreetly at Hampton Court until 1835, devoted to her many grandchildren and deeply interested in all that concerned their lives ; and the other was old Lady Salisbury, who met a terrible end in 1835, when she was burnt to death at Hatfield House. In commenting on the event Thomson, in *Queens of Society*, writes · " Nothing but the jewels in which she had decked herself for dinner were found to mark out as hers the poor skeleton recognised. A worldly life closed by an awful end."

But Apollo Raikes of an earlier generation comments more charitably. . . .

" There has perished old Lady Salisbury, whom I have known all my life as one of the leaders of ' ton ' in the fashionable world. She was a Hill, a sister of the late and Aunt to the present Marquess of Downshire. . . . She was one of the beauties of her day and famed for her equestrian exploits. Till a late period in her life she constantly hunted with the Hatfield Hounds in a sky-blue riding habit with a black velvet collar, and a jockey cap, the uniform of the Hunt, riding as hard and clearing the fences with as much ardour as any sportsman in the field. She was the last remnant of what may be called the old school in England, and of that particular clique composed of the Duchess of Devonshire, the Duchess of Rutland, Ladies Sefton, Cowper and Melbourne, etc., who for so many years gave the ' ton ' to society in London.

" . . . She scrupulously adhered to the state of former days ; she always went to Court in a Sedan chair with splendid liveries, she drove out in a low phæton with four black ponies in the park, and at night her carriage was known by the flambeaux of the footmen."

George IV had died in 1830, after some years of curious isolation at Windsor. Sitting by himself amongst his thousand souvenirs, the fans, the gloves, the handkerchiefs, the faded flowers that recalled occasions of past gaiety, he seemed fearful of breaking the dream by any contact with reality. He would send for his old suits and finger them questioningly, and only Lady Conyngham continued to penetrate into this hinterland of memories.

He feared to meet his people, and they in consequence

began to lose interest in him. When he lay dead, the Duke of Wellington, alone in the room, regarded him thoughtfully. His reign had known great events, but he had had no part in them ; his life had been a drab sequel to so much promise. Suddenly the Duke's eye lit on a locket which hung round the King's neck. He turned it over. It held a miniature of Mrs. Fitzherbert, and the kind-hearted old man determined that she should be informed of the fact. She had written to the King a few days before he died, but had of course received no answer.

She lived on quietly at Brighton, and the new King, the late Duke of Clarence, was very kind to her. He might not make a distinguished monarch ; he might spit out of the windows of the Royal coach till the angry Cockney crowd cried out, " George the Fourth wouldn't have done that," but he was kind-hearted and conscientious and respectable ; and he did all he could for Maria. Mrs. Creevey talked to her of her life being written ; " she said she supposed it would be sometime or other, but with a thousand lies ; but she would be dead and it would not signify. I urged her to write it herself, but she said it would break her heart." She died the year that Queen Victoria came to the throne, and perhaps this was as well, for the Court of the Prince Consort might have been embarrassed to know how to treat her.

And now it remains only to speak of the Cavendishes. Hart continued to improve his great estates, to comfort and counsel his sisters in all their difficulties, and to scandalise his acquaintances by that freakish vein which had manifested itself in the purchase of kangaroos and elephants for the enlivenment of Chiswick. He was very lonely now, out of sympathy with the Victorian generation. Attacked by one paralytic stroke, he recovered, learnt to write with his left hand, was charming and whimsical as ever, but succumbed to a second stroke in 1858. Considerate in death as he had been in life, he left Chiswick to his two sisters. Both were now widows. After many years at the Paris Embassy, years which had been filled with self-sacrifice on the part of Harriet, who detested entertaining, and wanted nothing but a small country place in England and the sole company of her " dear angel "—Lord Granville had died, leaving his wife broken-hearted.

She was glad to go to Chiswick and to meet Georgiana; but Lady Carlisle only lived to enjoy the legacy for eight months. And so Lady Granville had to spend the last four years alone.

Chiswick's bitter-sweet memories: the walls which had echoed to the laughter of Georgiana Devonshire, and of Lady Bessborough: to the periods of Fox and Sheridan: to the outbursts of Lady Melbourne: to the voice of dear Granville, and of Canning: the rooms which had known Hart and Georgiana Carlisle, Caro-William, and Caro-George—those saloons which had sheltered so many French refugees, and had been the scene of so many political reconciliations, now heard and held only the click of an old lady's knitting-needles, the scratch of a hesitant pen.

A few years passed, and even these small sounds ceased. . . . The generation of the Devonshire House set was dead.

More time passed and Chiswick was to resound to the complaints of the sick and the tread of nurses. . . . The nineteenth century was full in its course.

The turn of a century: in London the brown wall of Devonshire House was demolished, the stately façade of which George III had complained that it looked down "contemptuously on the Queen's House," was destroyed. At Chiswick the Palladian villa was emptied of all its human inhabitants, to stand dreary and dilapidated. A few curious visitors steal along its deserted paths, a few tired people rest beneath its ageing cedars.

Chiswick is open to the public. . . . The Devonshire House set has been dead so long that its setting has been relegated to the impersonality of a museum.

INDEX TO BIBLIOGRAPHY

Annual Biography and Obituary, 1829.
Airlie, Mabell Countess of : *Lady Palmerston and her Times.*
    Hodder & Stoughton.
—— *In Whig Society.* Hodder & Stoughton.
Bellamy : *An Apology.* J. Bell.
Beresford : *Life in the Eighteenth Century.* Routledge.
—— *Life in Regency and Early Victorian Times.* Batsford.
Berry, Miss : *Journal and Correspondence* (ed. Lewis). Longmans.
Black, Clementina : *The Linleys of Bath.*
Buckingham, Earl of : *Courts and Cabinets.* Hurst & Blackett
    (now Hutchinson).
Burke : *Thoughts on the French Revolution.*
Burney, Fanny : *Diary of.*
Bury, Charlotte Lady : *Memoirs.* Colburn (now Macmillan).
Byron : Correspondence with Lady Melbourne. Murray.
—— *Letters and Journals.* Murray.
Childe-Pemberton, W. S. : *Life of the Earl Bishop of Derry.* Hurst
    & Blackett.
Colchester, Lord : *Diary and Correspondence.* Murray.
Christie : *The Transition from Aristocracy.*
Creevey : *Papers.* Murray.
—— *Life and Times of.* Murray.
Devonshire, Georgiana Duchess of : *The Sylph.*
Doran : *A Lady of the Last Century.* Macmillan (late R. Bentley).
Creston, Dormer : *The Regent and his Daughter.* Butterworth.
Dunkerley : *Life of Lord Melbourne.* Sampson Low.
Fitzgerald, Percy F. : *The Family of George III.* Tinsley.
ffrench, Yvonne : *News from the Past.* Gollancz.
Foster, Vere : *The Two Duchesses.* Blackie.
Fulford, Roger : *The Royal Dukes.* Duckworth.
Godwin : *William and his Companions.* H. S. King.
Granville, Castalia Countess : *The Private Correspondence of Lord
    Granville.* Leveson-Gower. Murray.
Granville, Harriet Countess : *Letters* (ed. F. Leveson-Gower).
    Longman & Green.
Greville : *Diaries.* Longmans.
Gronow : *Memoirs.* Smith, Elder & Co.
Guedalla : *Life of Lord Palmerston.* Benn.

Hall, E. C. : *Memories of the Great Men and Women of the Age.*

Hammond : *Life of C. J. Fox.* Methuen.

Hamilton, Lady Anne : *Secret History of the Court of England.* Eveleigh Nash.

Haslip, Joan : *Life of Lady Hester Stanhope.* Cobden Sanderson.

Hobhouse : *Recollections of a Long Life.* Murray.

—— *Life of C. J. Fox.* Constable

Holland, E. V., Lady : *Diary.* Longmans.

Holland, Elizabeth Vassall, Lady : *Spanish Journal.* Longmans.

Holland, Lord : *Further Memories of the Whig Party.* Murray.

Holland, 4th Lord : *Memoirs.*

Jenkins : *Life of Lady C. Lamb.* Gollancz.

Jerningham : *Papers.* Macmillan (late R. Bentley).

Lee, Robert, Dr. : *Diary.* Hurst & Blackett.

Lennox : *Letter Bag of Lady Sarah.* Countess of Ilchester.

Literary Gazette, 1828

Lyttelton, Sarah Lady : *Letters* (ed. Hon. Mrs. H. Wyndham). Murray.

Macquoid, Percy : *The Age of Satinwood.* Lawrence.

Malmesbury, Earl of : *Diary.* Macmillan (late R. Bentley).

Markham, Violet : *Paxton and the Bachelor Duke.*

Marriott : *England after Waterloo.* Methuen.

—— *Queen Victoria and her Ministers.* Murray.

Maurois : *Byron.* Lane.

Morgan, Sidney Owenson, Lady : *Book of the Boudoir.* Colburn (now Macmillan).

—— *Passages from my Autobiography.* W. H. Allen.

Octogenarian, An : *Sheridan and his Times.* Hope.

Ponsonby, Sir J. : *The Ponsonby Family.* The Medici Society.

Rae : *Life of Sheridan.* Macmillan (late R. Bentley).

Raikes : *Journal.* Longmans.

Redcliffe, Lord Stratford de : *Memoirs.*

Redding, Cyrus : *Fifty Years' Recollections.*

Rogers, Samuel : *Table Talk.* H. A. Rogers.

Ros de, Georgiana Lady : *Memoirs.* Murray.

Sandars, Lloyd : *Lord Melbourne's Papers.* Longmans.

Sergeant : *George IV, Prince and Regent.* Hutchinson.

Shelley, Frances, Lady : *Diary.* Murray.

Sitwell, Edith : *Bath.* Faber.

Sitwell, Osbert : *Brighton.* Faber.

Stanhope, Lady Hester : *Memoirs*, as related by herself to her physician Dr. Meryon. Colburn (now Macmillan).

Strachey, Lytton : *Queen Victoria.*

Torrens : *Life of Lord Melbourne.* Macmillan.

Trotter : *Life of C. J. Fox.* Phillips.

Wharncliffe, 1st Lady : *Letters.* Heinemann.

Wharton, G. and P. : *The Queens of Society.*

Wilkins : *George IV and Mrs. Fitzherbert.* Longmans.
Willson, Beckles : *The Paris Embassy 1800–1914.* Unwin.
Wilson, Harriette : *Memoirs.* Nash.
Wraxall : *Memoirs.* R. Bentley (now Macmillan).

INDEX

DATE DUE

261-2500			Printed in USA